The Rush to German Unity

The Rush to
GERMAN
UNITY

Konrad H. Jarausch

New York   Oxford
OXFORD UNIVERSITY PRESS
1994

Oxford University Press

Oxford   New York   Toronto
Delhi   Bombay   Calcutta   Madras   Karachi
Kuala Lumpur   Singapore   Hong Kong   Tokyo
Nairobi   Dar es Salaam   Cape Town
Melbourne   Auckland   Madrid

and associated companies in
Berlin   Ibadan

Library of Congress Cataloging-in-Publication Data
Jarausch, Konrad Hugo.
The rush to German unity /
Konrad H. Jarausch.
p.   cm.
Includes bibliographical references and index.
ISBN 0-19-507275-8 — ISBN 0-19-508577-9 (pbk.)
1. German reunification question (1949–1990)
2. Germany (East)—Politics and government—1989–1990.
3. Germany (East)—Social conditions.
4. Opposition (Political science)—Germany (East)
5. Germany—History—Unification, 1990.
I. Title.   DD290.25.J37   1994
943.087—dc20   93-625

2 4 6 8 9 7 5 3 1

Printed in the United States of America
on acid-free paper

Preface

"Can you help get me out?" a young East German implored on a gray summer day in 1964. Walking across the ruined center of my birthplace Magdeburg, we were talking about the imprisonment of citizens of the German Democratic Republic (GDR) by the Berlin Wall. His anguished request caught me off guard and made me, someone who had become a fortunate outsider, angry at my own impotence. Twenty years later, I sat in a drab apartment in Potsdam with a dissident couple, once again discussing Socialist Unity Party (SED) repression and German division. Although these former track stars resented the Communist bureaucracy, they were determined to stay and transform the country from within. Their choice of opposition over escape indicated a growing legitimacy of the unloved regime.

Such encounters kept me going back, if only to express my sympathy. I came to the GDR with a double perspective: Raised in West Germany, I was pursuing my academic career in the United States. Though crossing the Berlin border at Friedrichstrasse was always unpleasant, the people on the Eastern side seemed more unpretentious and genuine than their sophisticated but blasé Western cousins. The other German state fascinated me precisely because of its improbable contradictions: The grayness punctuated by red banners, the economic backwardness, and the lack of freedom were appalling. But echos of Weimar radicalism also revealed an alternate vision, committed to antifascism, social justice, and peace.

My scholarly interest in the GDR grew almost inadvertently. When gathering material for monographs on World War I, Imperial German students, and Third Reich professionals, I worked in the central state archives in Potsdam and Merseburg for extended periods of time. Though I found much of the formulaic Marxist-Leninist scholarship tiresome, I enjoyed personal debates with East German colleagues. To further dialogue, I chaired the joint U.S.–GDR subcommission on history, sponsored by the International Research and Exchange Board. Out of our bilateral conferences on National Socialism in 1987 and 1989 grew a greater understanding of the problems of GDR historiography. Since I am not trained as an East German specialist, I will approach the subject primarily from the larger perspective of German history. Recently, I have become more concerned with cultural influences, which are leading me from quantitative studies towards a social history of experience.

The unforeseen upheaval of 1989–1990 thrust the topic of German unification upon me. On the continent, a torrent of polemics poured forth from partisan interests seeking to direct and document the civic movement in the GDR. In the United States, German reunification dominated television screens and newspaper headlines, producing a plethora of contradictory commentary. In December 1989, I chipped off my own piece of the Wall, and during the following summers tried to sort out conflicting claims by researching and interviewing in Berlin, Leipzig, and Bonn. To present key texts, Volker Gransow and I edited a volume of documents on German unification, called *Die deutsche Vereinigung. Dokumente zu Bürgerbewegung, Annäherung und Beitritt* (Cologne, 1991). I also organized a symposium on the transformation of historical scholarship in the GDR during December 1990, published in *Zwischen Parteilichkeit und Professionalität. Bilanz der DDR-Geschichtswissenschaft* (Berlin, 1991). Because surprisingly little German material has made its way across the Atlantic, initial English language accounts are incomplete and not always reliable. The present book therefore recounts the dramatic story and reflects upon its meaning for the participants and the rest of us.

A contemporary history, written so close to the events, is especially indebted to the help of others. It rests on discussions with dozens of colleagues on both sides of the Atlantic, including Werner Bramke, Georg G. Iggers, Jürgen John, Burkhart Koch, Jürgen Kocka, Anna Maria Kuppe, Christiane Lemke, Karl-Ulrich Mayer, Lutz Marz, and Gero Neugebauer. Foundations like the International Research and Exchange Board, and the Lurcy Charitable Trust funded the research expenses. Archives and libraries, most notably of the Leipziger Volkszeitung, the Bundespresseamt, the GDR Institute of the Free University of Berlin, the Gesamtdeutsches Institut, the East Berlin Stadtbibliothek and the Hoover Institution also supported the work. Important organizations, such as the Neues Forum, Demokratie Jetzt, the Umweltbibliothek and parties like the East-CDU allowed access to their holdings. Crucial actors, including Wolfgang Baumann, Hans Büchler, Gregor Gysi, Lothar de Maizière, Markus Meckel, Hans-Joachim Meyer, Walter Romberg, Wolfgang Thierse, and Klaus Wolfram, granted informative interviews. The Sektion Geschichte der Universität Leipzig aided local study through a guest professorship in the summer of 1991. The Center for Advanced Studies in Behavioral Sciences at Stanford University provided the leisure for writing during 1991–1992. Finally, the Forschungsschwerpunkt für Zeithistorische Studien in Potsdam facilitated the revisions in the summer of 1992.

Since this book is the product of the civic courage of thousands of East Germans, I want to dedicate it to their love of freedom. No doubt, unification has brought with it a host of material and psychological problems. But it also offers a greater chance for working out a better future. May the Germans and their neighbors seize upon it!

Chapel Hill, N.C.   K. H. J.
April 1993

Contents

Tables

Abbreviations

ABM	Arbeitsbeschaffungsmassnahmen
ADN	Allgemeiner Deutscher Nachrichtendienst
AAZ	*Augsburger Allgemeine Zeitung*
AfNS	Amt für nationale Sicherheit (see MfS)
APZG	*Aus Politik und Zeitgeschichte*
ARD	Arbeitsgemeinschaft der öffentlich-rechtlichen Rundfunkanstalten
BfdiP	*Blätter für deutsche und internationale Politik*
BPA Dok	Bundespresseamt Dokumentation
BRD	Bundesrepublik Deutschland (see FRG)
BR	*Bonner Rundschau*
BZ	*Berliner Zeitung*
CDU	Christlich Demokratische Union
CEH	*Central European History*
CSCE	Conference for Security and Cooperation in Europe
CSU	Christlich Soziale Union
DA	Demokratischer Aufbruch
DA	*Deutschland Archiv*
DBD	Demokratische Bauernpartei Deutschlands
DDR	Deutsche Demokratische Republik (see GDR)
DKP	Deutsche Kommunistische Partei (FRG)
DJ	Demokratie Jetzt

DPA	Deutsche Presseagentur
DSt	*Deutsche Studien*
DSU	Deutsche Soziale Union
EA	*Europa-Archiv*
FAZ	*Frankfurter Allgemeine Zeitung*
FDGB	Freier Deutscher Gewerkschaftsbund
FDJ	Freie Demokratische Jugend
FDP	Freie Demokratische Partei
FT	*Flensburger Tageblatt*
FR	*Frankfurter Rundschau*
FRG	Federal Republic of Germany (also BRD)
GA	*Generalanzeiger* (Bonn)
GDR	German Democratic Republic (also DDR)
GMH	*Gewerkschaftliche Monatshefte*
GPS	*German Politics and Society*
GSR	*German Studies Review*
HA	*Hannoversche Allgemeine*
HAbl	*Hamburger Abendblatt*
HB	*Handelsblatt*
IFM	Initiative für Frieden und Menschenrechte
KPD	Kommunistische Partei Deutschlands
KSA	*Kölner Stadt-Anzeiger*
KZSS	*Kölner Zeitschrift für Soziologie und Sozialpsychologie*
LDPD	Liberal-Demokratische Partei Deutschlands
LVZ	*Leipziger Volkszeitung*
MfS	Ministerium für Staatssicherheit
MM	*Münchener Merkur*
MP	*Morgenpost* (Berlin)
NCDDR	*Neue Chronik DDR*
ND	*Neues Deutschland*
NDPD	National-Demokratische Partei Deutschlands (GDR)

NF	Neues Forum
NP	*Neue Presse*
NPD	National-Demokratische Partei (FRG)
NRZ	*Neue Ruhr Zeitung*
NYT	*New York Times*
NZ	*Neue Zeit*
NZZ	*Neue Züricher Zeitung*
OZ	*Osnabrücker Zeitung*
PDS	Partei des Demokratischen Sozialismus
Reps	Republikaner
RM	*Rheinischer Merkur*
RP	*Rheinische Post*
Sbl	*Sontagsblatt*
SDP	Sozialdemokratische Partei (GDR)
SDZ	*Süddeutsche Zeitung*
SED	Sozialistische Einheitspartei Deutschlands
SPD	Sozialdemokratische Partei Deutschlands (FRG)
Stasi	Staatssicherheit (see MfS)
StZ	*Stuttgarter Zeitung*
taz	*die tageszeitung*
TS	*Tagesspiegel*
UFV	Unabhängiger Frauenverband
VL	Vereinigte Linke
WamS	*Welt am Sonntag*
WAZ	*Westdeutsche Allgemeine Zeitung*
WP	*Washington Post*
WR	*Westfälische Rundschau*
WW	*Wirtschaftswoche*
ZdF	Zweites deutsches Fernsehen
ZfP	*Zeitschrift für Parlamentsfragen*
ZK	Zentralkommittee der SED

Germany after reunification. (Map courtesy of the German Information Center, New York)

The Rush to German Unity

Introduction

The German Upheaval

The opening of the Berlin Wall on November 9, 1989, was a complete surprise. During an evening press conference, Günter Schabowski, secretary of the Socialist Unity Party (SED) of Berlin, read the draft of a new travel law: "Applications for private trips abroad may be submitted without further preconditions. . . . Permission will be granted immediately."[1] Since this news was not meant to be released until the following day, journalists, without prior briefing, were stunned and confused. Only at the last minute had the Central Committee included free personal movement in the bill that intended to liberalize emigration. The SED leaders hardly realized what they had just set in motion.

The ruling Marxist party justified the Wall as "antifascist protection" against Western revanchism. In early 1989, Erich Honecker, the East German SED chief, still predicted that it would stand another hundred years, as long as it was required. But most GDR citizens did not feel threatened by the West and resented this curtailment of their freedom to travel. To ease the pressure of protests, the Krenz government gambled that granting the wish for free movement would stabilize its embattled rule. Since many members of the GDR elite had been able to go to the West, they fundamentally underestimated public hunger for lifting the restraints. With its most popular decision, the Communist regime inadvertently paved the way not only for its own demise, but for the collapse of East Germany as a separate state.[2]

Penned in for twenty-eight years, the people of East Berlin rushed to the Wall. They did not wait for television commentators to analyze the announcement; they wanted to test the regulations themselves. As the restless crowds grew bigger and bigger, border guards frantically requested orders from headquarters. In an effort to avoid another Chinese Tienanmen Square massacre, the new GDR leader Egon Krenz decided against using force in hopes of bolstering his popularity.[3] At first the

3

guards tried to stamp visas onto identity cards, but around midnight they gave up: people and cars crossed the frontier in an ever-swelling stream. A few daring souls even scaled the barrier at the Brandenburg Gate and danced with joy. Long separated by the East–West conflict from above, Berliners began to unite spontaneously from below.

The opening of the Wall removed the central symbol of the Cold War. The death strip of concrete, barbed wire, and minefields separating the former capital had become infamous. Desperate attempts to cross it had cost about four hundred lives. Unwilling to risk a third world war to prevent its construction, American presidents from John Fitzgerald Kennedy to Ronald Reagan instead had used it as photo opportunity to speak out against communist repression. Espionage novelists such as John Le Carré memorialized it and creative spirits painted colorful grafitti on it to overcome the ugly barrier with art. Constant reference to *die Mauer* had made it a universal metaphor.[4] By opening the border to the mass exodus, the SED initiated an upheaval that would ultimately overturn the postwar order in Central Europe.

The Present as Past

The resulting unification of the Germanies came rather unexpectedly. None of the Eastern experts had foreseen the collapse of the GDR or predicted its timing, speed, or consequences. In mid-1989 British historian Michael Howard still predicted that East Germany would never be swallowed by the West. When the long stalemate ended, the rapidity and the extent of unification confounded the commentators. Within one year two competing states with different systems of government, opposing military alliances, contradictory economic systems, incompatible social structures, and conflicting ideologies merged into one. Despite repeated crises, the process continued to accelerate and at times threatened to escape control.[5]

The participants themselves perceived unification as an historic change. During the events, Chancellor Helmut Kohl of the Federal Republic of Germany (FRG) and GDR Premier Lothar de Maizière wrapped themselves in the mantle of history. The vigorous debate about the form of unity constantly invoked historical precedents. Commentators argued that the merger of the East into the West cleaned up the territorial debris of World War II. The collapse of the GDR helped overcome the division of Europe and meant the end of the Cold War on the continent. The 1989–1990 caesura was so deep that many Germans have started dating their own lives with reference to it. The causes, course, and consequences of unification present an exciting challenge to historical understanding.[6]

Because of its rapidity, German unity has been overreported and underanalyzed. Caught up in the excitement, journalists created a spotty record, overexposing some incidents and leaving others unreported.[7] To discredit the SED regime, dissidents published documents from secret police files. Fallen leaders tried to cash in on curiosity by spilling secrets in exposé memoirs. Postnational intellectuals polemicized against unification and fueled popular myths like the GDR "sellout" to capitalism.[8] Such highly emotional commentary only offers fragments of interpretation.

Scholarly analysis never quite managed to catch up with the unending news. Historians argued about the nature of the Eastern "revolution" and the legitimacy of a German national state.[9] Social scientists focused on the economic collapse of communism, the post-totalitarian transition, and the East–West rapprochement.[10] More astute observers celebrated the rebirth of "authentic language," the recovery of a civil society, and the return of liberal democracy.[11] Since most instant analyses concentrated on single issues, they have failed to provide a comprehensive picture of the events.

Transforming a polemical present into a placid past has triggered a contest for public memory. Even as the events unfolded, participants generated narratives in order to lay claim to their place in history. Rival politicians and officials tried to shape the record in press releases and interviews. Instant videos, quick picture books, and early chronicles also attempted to organize the confused happenings according to certain points of view. To a literary observer, this posturing seemed "somewhat post-modern." The actors tried "to make history" and knew at the same time that they would "land inside a museum within a week."[12]

After reunion, the many different recollections coalesced into two rival discourses. To mobilize public support, government pronouncements created a heroic tale of liberation and unification. The official version celebrated the overthrow of post–Stalinist repression and applauded the Eastern choice of Western democracy. Disappointed intellectuals offered a catastrophic counternarrative in order to create an opposition identity. Their alternative tale deplored the failure of the revolution and denounced the ravages of capitalist restoration. The competition among these contradictory discourses polarized the collective memory of events.[13]

How can a historian approach such a contemporary controversy? Lack of access to government secrets renders a person-centered narrative premature. Instead, the abundance of slogans, speeches, and interviews suggests reconstructing the process as a discursive struggle. The wealth of material on citizens' movements inspires a social evocation of popular aspirations. The flood of official print points toward a political analysis of government decisions. The outpouring of criticism makes a cultural exploration of intellectual reservations promising. The torrent of statements on détente encourages a diplomatic study on the international ramifications. The assymetry of information and the logic of events favor a layered approach to the interplay of popular hopes and intellectual fears with the political and diplomatic decisions that created the new Germany.[14]

The unlikely heroes of the upheaval are the people of the GDR. Once docile East Germans suddenly spoke out and took control of their lives. In the confusing spectacle, they formed a colorful parade of harried refugees, earnest protesters, socialist reformers, ordinary workers, novice parliamentarians, and new entrepreneurs. For a brief moment, each group held the spotlight on center stage, only to be eclipsed again. The East German rising was helped and encouraged by Western relatives, journalists, and businessmen, After initial hesitation, Bonn ministers, bureaucrats, and journalists took the lead. By welcoming unification, the Kohl cabinet not only encouraged Eastern hopes, but also convinced the Western public of its inevitability.[15]

Intellectuals played a more paradoxical part. Initially they took pride in the fact that their criticism helped overthrow the Honecker regime. But eventually they were disappointed that their warnings of the consequences of unity fell on deaf ears. Caught by surprise, German neighbors were equally overwhelmed. Countries like France, Poland, and the Soviet Union, which had repeatedly suffered the brunt of German military fury, were reluctant to allow the restoration of a unified state. But internal and external skeptics found that they could do little to stop the people of the German Democratic Republic from pressing ahead.[16]

The surprising upheaval poses many unresolved questions. Commentators do not even agree on what to call it. Was it merely a policy "reversal" (*Wende*), an "implosion" of the regime, or a popular "revolution"? The sequence of events is equally contested. Who made such decisions as the rejection of force during the Leipzig demonstration on October 9, 1989? The character of the process is also controversial. Was it a democratic liberation by the people of the GDR or an authoritarian takeover by Western capitalists? The deeper causes of the confusing developments remain similarly obscure. Did the ineptitude of the Communist leadership or the courageous protests of the dissidents bring down the post-Stalinist GDR?[17]

The transformation from democratic awakening into national unification resists interpretation. The civic movement and return to capitalism fit into the general East European pattern. But Germany's transition from communism was different, since nationalism did not destroy a state but revived a country thought to be defunct. The perplexing process developed in three stages, beginning with the East German rising, continuing with the national turn, and ending in the merger of the GDR and the FRG.[18] The unexpected beginning and outcome raise a double question: What roused East German citizens out of their apathy and made them overthrow their repressive regime? And why did this silent majority turn away from reforming socialism and opt for unification with the West?

The surprises of unification demand a multifocal as well as multivocal history. Since the information sources are uneven and the processes unpredictable, it is especially important first to reconstruct the course of major events. Before undertaking theoretical flights, one must be firmly grounded in the empirical evidence. Yet poststructuralist critics caution against naively constructing a "master narrative" on unity. The unexpected transition from revolution to unification contains too many tensions to yield a single plot. The focus of action constantly shifted among Leipzig, Berlin, and Bonn as well as among Germany, the Soviet Union, and the United States. The driving force moved from socioeconomic complaints to cultural concerns and to political demands. The temporal focus of debate alternated between a problematic past, a frustrating present, and an imagined future.[19] This cacophony of clashing voices should not be reduced to artificial harmony.

Understanding German unification requires going beyond the simplifications of celebration or catastrophe. Pictures dramatized by the media can serve as a starting point for exploring the background of a problem. Then careful reconstruction will help clarify the sequence of internal and external developments and concluding reflections will help interpret their significance. The incompleteness of the record renders any early account tentative, since additional evidence is likely to amplify or correct details. But if it asks the right questions, even a first reading can clarify the outline of events and help structure the subsequent debate.[20]

Lines of Division

The partition of Germany began with Hitler's collapse. The utter defeat of the *Wehrmacht*—the vaunted German war machine—left the Third Reich prostrate in May of 1945. Though unanimous on extirpating "militarism and Nazism," wartime conferences could not agree on what to do with the vanquished enemy beyond transferring sovereignty to an Allied Control Council. To facilitate occupation, the London Protocol of September 1944 and Potsdam Agreement of August 1945 split Greater Germany into four zones, assigned East Prussia to Russia, put the areas east of the Oder-Neisse line under Polish administration, returned the Sudetenland to Czechoslovakia, and restored Austria. The Potsdam agreement stipulated that "for the time being no central German government shall be established," but essential administrative departments were to be set up and the economy treated as a whole.[21]

Even without a formal decision on division, the zonal structure fractured German unity. In their respective territories, the occupiers rebuilt bureaucracy, education, and the economy in their own mold. While West Germans were exposed to liberal capitalism, central Germans came under the spell of Soviet communism. Over twelve million refugees were expelled from their homes in the lost territories of the East. The legacy of total defeat was military occupation and four-power control. But liberation from Nazi dictatorship also created a chance to make a fresh start.[22]

The Cold War turned de facto separation into de jure division. Though not responsible for its outbreak, Germany was both a battleground and a participant in the East–West struggle. With the common enemy defeated and joint tasks like de-Nazification behind them, the dissimilar Allies fell to quarreling about such spoils as reparations. Clashing ideologies of democratic capitalism and socialist planning prevented cooperation in economic rebuilding through the Marshall Plan. With the consolidation of the western zones, temporary occupation lines hardened into the impenetrable Iron Curtain. Successive crises such as the currency reform, the Berlin Blockade, and the Korean War sharpened confrontation in Central Europe.[23]

The East–West conflict prevented the restoration of a reduced but united Germany. Each side viewed its share as a strategic buffer zone that would enable it to conquer the rest. In the fall of 1949 the estranged victors sponsored the establishment of hostile client states, called the Federal Republic in the West and the German Democratic Republic in the East. While the "economic miracle" gradually made the former more independent, the latter largely remained "a Soviet homunculus." As negative mirror images the German regimes focused upon one another and embodied the contending ideologies of anticommunism and antifascism. In divided Germany the global conflict also turned into a "cold civil war."[24]

Reunification attempts inevitably failed. To cushion division, politicians as well as occupiers tirelessly promised an eventual return to unity. But the victors feared the resurgence of German power and were in no hurry to let go of their conquest. Afraid of losing their privileges, the leaders of the successor states similarly dragged their feet. Their clashing ideologies inspired incompatible strategies. The West was forever calling for "free elections," confident that capitalist democracy would win, but the East demanded a confederation of the two states that would preserve its own "socialist achievements" by law.[25]

The discrepancy between rhetoric and interest created endless posturing in four-power negotiations. When the West beckoned with economic aid, the East replied with military neutralization. Beyond diplomatic confrontation, both regimes sought to destabilize each other domestically. According to the "Hallstein doctrine," Bonn refused to recognize the GDR regime as not popularly elected and sought to isolate it internationally. As representative of the progressive proletariat, the East financed opposition to rearmament and sent thousands of spies. At the same time, both successor states also joined mutually hostile alliances such as NATO and the Warsaw Pact and competing economic blocs such as the EC and COMECON. While many older people vainly hoped for a miracle, younger Germans grew bored with the reunification quest.[26]

The building of the Wall cemented the division. Begun on August 13, 1961 under Honecker's personal command, the closing of the GDR frontier was an admission of economic weakness. Since 3,429,042 registered refugees had fled East Germany after 1945, *die Mauer* was a desperate attempt to stop the population drain to the West. With Soviet backing and Warsaw Pact approval, the politburo decided to "erect a barrier against the activities of West German revanchists and militarists." Though it claimed to keep subversion out, tight control, "usual at the border of every sovereign state," was actually intended to hold the citizenry in. The SED justified the step as prerequisite for building socialism and maintaining peace.[27]

Though it triggered a firestorm of criticism, the barrier eventually had a stabilizing effect. By cutting off communication, the Wall tore countless families apart. The sealing of the border also sundered the remaining institutions such as the joint Olympic team. But its solidity also suggested that the SED state was here to stay and that East and West Germans had better live with it. After a painful struggle, Protestant bishops abandoned their national organization and developed a new perspective as "church within socialism." In 1968 GDR participation in the suppression of Czechoslovak democratization once more demonstrated Ulbricht's determination to crush all challenges. Those who believed in the Marxist ideal were shocked to learn that the Socialist Unity Party (SED) only meant to preserve its rule.[28]

During the 1970s détente, West Germany tried a different *Ostpolitik*. Since overthrowing the regime seemed futile, Willy Brandt realized that communication with the East could only be maintained by dropping confrontation. His social-liberal coalition switched to conciliation and signed a series of nonaggression treaties with its Eastern neighbors. To mitigate the effects of the division, foreign policy planner Egon Bahr of the West German Social Democratic Party (SPD) suggested fostering "change through rapprochement" with a "policy of small steps." Its first fruit was the 1971 Berlin agreement that aimed at "practical improvements of the situation." The four powers reaffirmed Western transit rights in exchange for tacit acceptance of GDR control over East Berlin.[29]

The second step was the 1972 Basic Treaty between East and West Germany. This agreement sought to establish "normal good neighborly relations" between the two successor states. In exchange for de facto recognition, the East made concessions in "humanitarian questions" such as travel rights for older citizens. Cooperation culminated in the Helsinki Accords of 1975, which ratified existing borders but established new standards for human rights. While optimists hoped that acceptance would reduce division, realists supported the treaties as the beginning of a modus vivendi between two separate states. Even if it initially stabilized the regime, conciliation in the long run undermined the hold of the SED.[30]

In the 1980s the Germanies settled into a curious mixture of ideological hostility and practical cooperation. Though the SED insisted on sharp distancing from Bonn and expanded the secret police (*Stasi*), East Berlin needed Western help. While the Christian Democratic Union (CDU) clung to anticommunism, it continued to pursue a pragmatic *Ostpolitik* after returning to power in 1982. FRG credits were a meeting ground, since they kept the East afloat and provided opportunities for Western business. Another shared interest was disarmament, because neither side wanted to become a nuclear battlefield. Eased travel regulations and in-creased cultural contacts as well as city partnerships restored some human ties.[31]

Close cooperation could not overcome the hostility of the estranged brothers. Highly publicized state visits of Helmut Schmidt and Erich Honecker signalled growing normalization, but while Bonn sought to improve relations in order to strengthen national unity, East Berlin cele-brated each token of recognition as proof of sovereignty. Honecker baldly claimed that East and West could unite as little as fire and water. Progres-sive Westerners accepted the existence of two states within one nation as the foundation of peace. Ignoring the GDR opposition, the Social Demo-crats sought to foster liberalization by entering into dialogue with the SED and producing a joint paper on European security. Aware of "a community of responsibility," the successor states groped towards a spe-cial relationship between unity and independence.[32]

By 1989 international pressure for changing the European division grew. Inaugurated by President Gorbachev, Soviet perestroika stirred re-formist hopes throughout the Eastern Bloc. When Moscow refrained from intervening, open opposition challenged the Communist regimes espe-cially in Poland and Hungary. Everywhere the planned economies were beginning to stall.[33] In the GDR the gerontocratic SED leadership refused to follow the Russian lead. The ideological spokesman Kurt Hager sneered that Berlin did not need to change its wallpaper just because its neighbors were remodeling. But beneath the immobile surface, the East German people grew increasingly restive. Encouraged by Eastern Eu-ropean examples, a civic movement gathered in the shadow of the Pro-testant church, ready to challenge Stasi repression and demand open de-bate.[34]

In spite of such tremors, the postwar order seemed unshakable. In the FRG, conservatives began to speculate that Soviet acceptance of self-determination might provide a chance for German reunion. But liberal opinion agitated to strike the reunification mandate from the West Ger-man constitution of 1949, called the Basic Law.[35] In the international arena, Soviet–American relations slowly warmed toward real détente. When visiting Bonn that summer, Gorbachev was touched by the warm reception that bordered on "Gorbi-mania." During his own subsequent trip, George Bush called for the Wall to be razed as a sign of good will. While its foundations had begun to erode, the fortified Iron Curtain con-tinued to look immutable. Forty years of conflict and cooperation had only postponed the solution of the German problem.[36]

The Breach in the Wall

Since the opening of the Wall came as a surprise, it produced initial euphoria. For three days Berlin virtually ground to a halt, as hundreds of thousands of East Germans flocked to see, touch, and buy a piece of the forbidden West. The mood was giddy. A spontaneous *Volksfest*, a people's celebration, erupted in the scarred former capital. Excited Westerners met the wide-eyed Easterners with cheers, handing them glasses of champagne. Border guards received flowers that helped to replace forbidding frowns with friendly smiles. Strangers hugged and kissed. Into the early morning hours cars crowded the glittering Kurfürstendamm, honking their horns. Hardly anyone downtown really slept. It was as if the city had to make up in one night for everything it had missed for years.[37]

The next morning there were long queues in front of Western banks. Easterners crowded to pick up the 100 DM (Deutsche Mark) of "welcome money" for each individual. All too soon the hard currency was spent on a teddy bear, a pound of coffee, or a quick beer. West German politicians joined the throngs, and Mayor Momper celebrated the reconnecting of the divided city. Chancellor Kohl abruptly flew back from a state visit to Poland, only to be met by jeers from leftist crowds. Former chancellor and mayor of Berlin Willy Brandt hit the right note when he intoned: "What belongs together can now once again grow together." Even the international press got caught up in the excitement; the *New York Times* announced the opening of the border in a massive double headline.[38] CNN images of dancing, happy people flew around the world. Not in decades had the Germans been able to bask in such a wave of sympathy.

The gigantic Wall party produced a severe hangover. The millions who crossed the border left a mess of discarded bottles, fast food wrappers, and other debris. With the opening of dozens of new transit points, traffic in Berlin and other frontier regions broke down. In many factories production virtually ground to a halt when their personnel failed to show up. Foul fumes spewing from antiquated Eastern cars aggravated pollution in the West. Long lines in shops gave rise to cruel jokes about poor country cousins. During subsequent weeks, people began to sense that their lives were to change dramatically. The initial excitement yielded to second thoughts.[39]

In the GDR, the Krenz government was like the sorcerer's apprentice: the SED vainly tried to control the popular passions it had unleashed. Leading dissidents like Bärbel Bohley worried that people would be blinded by the glitter of the West and give up on reforming their own state. In the FRG, the Kohl government wondered whether to dampen or encourage Eastern hopes for change. While conservatives welcomed the upheaval as a chance to restore unity, the left warned against the return of nationalism. Germany's neighbors also worried about the breakdown of their diplomatic serenity. Russian, French, and American leaders remembered the blood spilled during two world wars and pondered the implications of the change. Though the breach in the Wall allowed Easterners to travel, GDR reluctance, FRG hesitation, and international concern left unclear what its consequences would be.[40]

The German upheaval triggered a flood of emotions. "Nobody can escape it," the novelist Cees Noteboom noted, "and nobody knows what will happen." Especially Easterners who had suffered from the division began to hope for reunification, no matter what problems it might cause. Western cold warriors delighted in the defeat of the communist enemy and the triumph of capitalism. But intellectuals fretted over the crumbling of their Marxist faith and the resurgence of nationalism. Foreign editorials warned against German military might, invoking memories of the world wars. Among former victims the trauma of the Holocaust left deep-rooted fears of ethnic and racial prejudice. European businessmen were concerned about economic hegemony, the domination of the continent by a powerful German currency. Even decades of peaceful cooperation and domestic stability had not been able to eradicate these deep-seated historical fears.[41]

During such an earthquake, no bystander can be entirely unaffected. Strong feelings are inevitable but need not block understanding, if they are confronted consciously. Before passing judgment, one should at least inform oneself about the actual events. After all, who has *not* been wrong regarding some important aspect of German unity? Capitalist triumphalism about "winning the cold war" is as misplaced as Leftist dejection about the loss of a utopian dream.[42] Understanding such dramatic changes with so little temporal distance requires an unusual mixture of critical awareness and human compassion. Only time will tell whether the return of German unity will be a blessing or a curse.

I

THE PEOPLE RISE

1

Running Away

A hole in the Iron Curtain started the mass exodus. When Hungarian soldiers cut the barbed wire fence on May 2, 1989, desperate East Germans began to cross the Austrian frontier. Those who were turned back or were less daring crowded into West German embassies in Budapest, Prague, and East Berlin. Though the GDR protested against "crude interference in [its] sovereign affairs," Bonn welcomed the refugees from poverty and repression: "When they come to us, we accept them as Germans. We will not throw them out by force."[1] Sure of a warm reception, more and more East Germans sought to leave without permission, since they had given up any hope for change.

In mid-August 661 refugees rushed across the Austro-Hungarian frontier. When overcrowding closed the embassies, desperate East Germans fled during a peace picnic sponsored by the pan-European Union. Others were stopped and one was shot by a Hungarian border guard. With several thousand thronging around the FRG legation in Budapest, the Red Cross set up tent camps for those unwilling to go back in spite of their government's frantic efforts to retrieve them. Though leery of accepting too many migrants, Chancellor Helmut Kohl urged Hungarian leaders to open the border. But East German foreign minister Oskar Fischer threatened them with dire consequences. Caught in the diplomatic crossfire, Budapest wanted the Germans to resolve the issue themselves. In the makeshift camps crowded with six thousand refugees, impatience grew.[2]

The Hungarian cabinet faced a difficult dilemma. Bloc solidarity and a travel agreement with the GDR mandated the return of all refugees to East Berlin. But assisting in such a "barbaric, antihuman cause" would reduce chances for Western aid. Since the East Germans refused to let their citizens go, Hungarian Foreign Minister Guyla Horn worked out a one-time release of over one hundred with Red Cross documents. When refugee numbers continued to swell, Horn became convinced that a more "radical solution" was necessary to allow all East Germans to leave. Gambling on Russian neutrality, the Hungarians chose Western "human rights" over Eastern control in order to advance their own democratic reforms. In spite of furious objections from East Berlin, Budapest rejected the role of policeman and dared to break ranks with its Warsaw Pact ally.[3]

At midnight on September 10 customs agents raised the border gates. After weeks of nervous waiting, the would-be émigrés were overjoyed: "It's like Christmas," a young worker said, hugging his teary-eyed girlfriend in a blaze of television lights. A thousand little GDR cars and one hundred and twenty-six buses rushed to the border. Instead of arresting fugitives, Hungarian soldiers smilingly waved them on. A reddish-brown Lada, crammed with four adults and one child, was the first to cross: "I can't believe that it actually worked," the stunned driver said. With blaring horns, the Trabis and Wartburgs just kept coming. Champagne mingled with tears at a bar just across the border. "I have dreamed of [flight] since I was a child," a young teacher exclaimed. "But I never thought it would come like this. We planned for weeks, but even when we left East Germany, I never believed we would be here." Some swam across rivers to get from Czechoslovakia into Hungary. Others drove up from vacations in Bulgaria or Rumania. Still more took the train to freedom.[4]

In West Germany, the convoys were welcomed with cheers, bananas, beer, and pretzels. After crossing Austria in a few hours, the tired and anxious refugees arrived in the Bavarian town of Passau. Friendly speeches, media cameras, and free balloons created a carnival atmosphere. Flashing victory signs, the alternately sad and elated Easterners could not comprehend that they had exchanged the Germany of their nightmares for the Germany of their dreams. As a symbolic gesture, many scraped "DR" from their "DDR" national plates to leave just the West German "D". Others drank "a little drop to German harmony." In the first twenty-four hours more than eight thousand celebrated their escape toward the West. This was the biggest East German exodus since the building of the Wall.[5]

The mass flight disturbed the tranquil accommodation to German division. East Berlin accused Hungary of violating its treaty obligations "under the cover of night and fog," a damning reference to Nazi methods. But Gorbachev refused to intervene. The Soviet news agency Tass only warned Bonn against encroaching on GDR "sovereignty and independence."[6] FRG Foreign Minister Genscher vowed he would never forget Budapest's "humanitarian decision." In Western capitals, however, the touching reunion set off alarms over the specter of unification. "As thousands of East Germans seeking freedom streamed across the Hungarian border," the *New York Times* correspondent Craig Whitney commented, "the 'German question,' the dream, or fear, of German reunification also came alive with them."[7] Though international leaders believed the issue had been permanently shelved, the unexpected mass flight from the GDR reopened the question of German unity.

Pressure to Escape

The stampede to the West was more than a popular revolt against East German travel restrictions. The SED had penned its population in by force, fearing that many people would vote with their feet for the Federal Republic. Bonn invited such defections by defining citizenship to include any "refugee or expellee of German stock" who came from within the 1937 borders. This broad construction was intended to allow the repatriation of ethnic Germans who were uprooted during and after World War II. Originally East Germany agreed that "there is only one German citizenship." But during the 1970s East Berlin sought to establish a socialist nationality by claiming that its people belonged to a separate state. To underscore its independence, the GDR thereafter treated West Germans as foreigners.[8]

The West nonetheless continued to welcome Eastern refugees as fellow countrymen. The Federal Republic refused to recognize GDR citizenship so as to maintain a common sense of nationality. To the penniless migrants, this legal stance conveyed many practical advantages. Bonn not only provided special resettlement aid but also offered all the social benefits of its wealthy welfare state. Even if they had worked and paid in the East, retired people could claim the higher pensions of the West! No wonder that 3.454 million registered refugees fled to the capitalist FRG between 1950 and 1961, ten times more than went to the GDR to join "real existing Socialism."[9]

East–West travel was a sensitive gauge of German division. Confrontations dried up movement, while cooperation increased the flow (see Table 1). Initially, the Wall stopped the manpower loss, reducing migration to twenty thousand in 1962. But the restriction of movement caused a prison mentality that inspired incessant attempts to escape. In the 1970s, harsh restrictions and brighter economic prospects cut the outflow virtually in half. Increasing self-assurance and human rights pressure opened the door wider during the 1980s. With more official permits, fewer people had to flee through other countries or across the Wall. East Berlin also freed over one thousand jailed citizens annually for payment of about 100,000 DM per head. But the problem remained intractable. When Erich Honecker tried to get rid of the discontented by releasing 34,982 in 1984, twice that many immediately applied to leave.[10]

TABLE 1. East German Refugees, 1961–1988

	Total	Official Permits	Flight through Other Countries	Direct Escapes	Ransomed by FRG
1962–1970	229,652	146,129	56,970	21,105	5,448
1971–1979	131,176	85,434	27,576	7,816	10,350
1980–1988	203,619	150,918	36,152	2,672	13,872
Total (+1961)	616,066	382,481	163,815	40,100	29,670

Formal emigration was so arduous as to deter application. The 1988 GDR travel law "allowed permanent departures for humanitarian reasons," such as reuniting families or letting pensioners go west. But permits could be denied on broad grounds of protecting "national security"; "public order or other government interests"; and "citizens' rights, principles of socialist morality and social needs." Based on human rights principles established by the Conference on Security and Cooperation in Europe (CSCE), a GDR citizen could "request" permission to apply. Afraid of losing their manpower, the authorities exerted much pressure to reconsider and only accepted a fraction of these petitions. The few who persisted and qualified could file an application, stating acceptable reasons. Then they had to wait for a response, often for years.[11]

Even under the best of circumstances this procedure was demeaning. Fulfilling mysterious regulations and their arbitrary interpretations required countless visits to the local police and other offices. Filing for emigration often meant the loss of one's passport and de facto confiscation of real estate, bank accounts, and other personal property. While the case was pending, would-be émigrés were reassigned to onerous tasks such as scrubbing toilets or simply fired from their jobs. Friends and acquaintances would break off social contact out of fear of being associated with subversives. During the interminable transition, some sought shelter in the church while others turned to public protest in order to be jailed, hoping to be freed more quickly by Western ransom. Stigmatizing emigration as expulsion traumatized refugees and left them with a burning hatred of communism.[12]

Personal travel was similarly circumscribed. Aside from Poland, which was quarantined to prevent contagion from solidarnosc, private trips to socialist nations needed no special justification. But only retirees could visit up to thirty days in the West—as long as someone else paid their expenses there. Young and working-age people might leave merely for "pressing family matters" such as birthdays, weddings, or funerals.[13] During the late 1970s, about forty thousand Easterners were annually allowed to travel to Western relatives. The number of retiree trips slowly rose from around 1.3 to 1.6 million. A decade later, rules had relaxed further. By 1988 approximately 2.7 million GDR citizens visited West Germany, about one half under retirement age.[14]

Professional trips were strictly rationed as well. Many Communists, some bloc party members and a few nonparty experts were designated as "travel cadres." These specialists could go freely abroad, if their institutions came up with convertible currency. This status was a real prize, since it granted access to international debates and Western consumer goods. It required professional nomination and entailed a security check on whether one had Western relatives or voiced criticism. Besides leaving behind families as hostages, travelers had to report foreign contacts to their superiors or the Stasi. No wonder the cooped-up majority resented those exceptional athletes, artists, or party members who could move freely. In the GDR, fear of losing the population transformed travel from a basic right into a coveted privilege.[15]

Growing restlessness during the late 1980s stemmed from rising expectations, fueled by Soviet perestroika. The reform climate propagated by Russian president Gorbachev increased both illegal flights and official permissions. Compared to the changes in Poland or Hungary, the stubborn immobility of the SED became so galling "that even GDR citizens realized they had had enough." Many people gave up on their country, believing it was "dead or about to die." While Protestant clergy counselled parishioners to stay, courageous pastors like Rainer Eppelmann showed sympathy for the plight of people trying to leave. In the shadow of the church, émigrés founded short-lived human rights support groups. Dissidents, however, refused to cooperate with them since they feared that agitation for emigration would detract from efforts to reform the GDR.[16]

In response, the SED opened a small safety valve to keep the pressure under control. In 1988 the regime raised emigration to 29,033, and in the first half of 1989 it allowed 38,917 citizens to leave, about one-third of those who had applied. At the same time, illegal flights rose to 5,202, and another 1,002 were prosecuted for trying to escape. By "increasing the travel possibilities to the West," Honecker sought to obtain more docile subjects.[17] Since further plans to ease regulations were never announced, the small cracks only raised hopes for opening the door wider. Another 133,000 filed applications to leave.

In the spring of 1989, ominous signs multiplied. When four people fled into the FRG embassy in Berlin, Erich Honecker once again refused to tear down the Wall. Though the regime officially disavowed any "orders to shoot," GDR border guards continued to fire on fleeing refugees. In February a twenty-year-old waiter, Chris Gueffroy, was killed trying to cross the Wall, and in March another young man died while seeking to escape by balloon. More cautious East Germans sought asylum in Western missions, much to the embarrassment of diplomats. Though attempted flight was punished by imprisonment, embassy refugees usually obtained release because of the attendant publicity. Yet others turned south and tested the less fortified borders of Czechoslovakia or Hungary. In June alone about 12,500 East Germans arrived in West Germany, 2,000 of whom had crossed illegally. With no concessions from the SED and the escape routes known, a growing number of GDR citizens waited for the right moment to run.[18]

During the summer of 1989 the pent-up desire for free movement burst all bounds. Each evening's vicarious emigration via FRG television turned into real flight. The media vision of Western "travel freedom, higher standard of living, free speech, and pluralism" proved irresistible. When news of successful border crossings in Hungary spread like wildfire, this fantasy suddenly turned into a practical alternative. Sensible people who had hitherto considered the risks too great were swept away by the news images of a hero's welcome in the West. Convinced that "nothing is going to change here," they finally saw a way to turn secret wishes into reality. Vacationing in Hungary allowed them to hedge their bet. Should the government clamp down, they could return as dutiful citizens; should the border open, they could easily escape.[19]

When hundreds fled, panic set in among the rest. "With everyone who went before me, fear grew that I would no longer make it out in time," recalled a young disk jockey. "China also played a role" as example of potential repression. Should they not take advantage of an opportunity which might never return? Among the more than two hundred thousand GDR vacationers in Hungary and neighboring countries a kind of hysteria developed. The unique chance triggered a collective response that pulled even many who had not intended to leave into the westward rush. No official warnings, no thoughts of difficulties ahead would stop them now.[20]

Mass Exodus

The mass flight caught Western politicians by surprise. The Bonn establishment vacillated between trying to preserve its improving relations with East Berlin and responding to humanitarian concerns. Considered part of domestic politics, inter-German relations were handled directly in the chancellor's office. But Helmut Kohl's attempts to contact Erich Honecker personally to defuse the confrontation and find a lasting solution produced no results. Contacts between FRG State Secretary Walter Priesnitz and GDR attorney Wolfgang Vogel that had proven valuable in earlier crises remained ineffectual. Hardly any embassy refugees were willing to return home with assurances that they would be allowed to leave later.[21]

When the GDR proved unresponsive, attention shifted to the Hungarian government. During a secret visit to Bonn, Minister President Nemeth and Foreign Minister Horn indicated that they would follow the UN refugee convention and the free movement provision of the CSCE Charter. Although Horn personally warned GDR Foreign Minister Oskar Fischer, the SED leaders proved unable to act without Honecker, who had recently undergone gallbladder surgery. The leaders, counting on Eastern bloc solidarity, refused to resolve the refugee deadlock. During early September, the West German government began to prepare a tent camp for five thousand refugees in Bavaria. Encouraged by assurances of economic good will, Hungarian reformers overcame the resistance of their own Stalinists in league with the SED and resolved to open the frontiers. Because of East Berlin's isolation, Budapest's new thinking, and Bonn's patient insistence on human rights, the crisis was temporarily resolved.[22]

The SED failed to develop a workable strategy to stem the migration tide. Initially, the party tried to ignore the exodus and deter embassy refugees by failing to release them to the West. With Honecker sidelined, the leadership hesitated to deal with the popular flight. On August 29, an

alarmed politburo for the first time discussed the mass flight. Not wanting
to confront the real causes, the aging leaders preferred to blame fresh
attacks of the Western enemy. Isolated by Soviet reforms, Günter Mittag
counselled holding the line: "We must present our positions offensively."
Instead of engaging the reasons for dissatisfaction, the SED leaders sought
"to close the Hungarian hole" and postponed real debate. Through this
lack of action, the regime missed its last chance to stop the exodus. The
communist daily *Neues Deutschland* blamed the Western "media circus,"
and regional newspapers polemicized against the "boundless hate-
mongering of the FRG."[23]

When its citizens kept running away, the GDR government tried to
take countermeasures. As a warning to the FRG, the SED cancelled the
visit of an SPD delegation to Bonn. The secret police attempted to prevent
"the abuse of travel to or through the Hungarian People's Republic." The
official press launched a concerted campaign with fake letters to the editor,
claiming "the GDR is my home." Accusing the West of trading in human
beings, East Berlin resorted to an old propaganda trick: "I have witnessed
how FRG-citizens are 'made,'" said an express-train cook who claimed
that Western secret services had kidnapped him to force him to defect.[24]
Since such lurid propaganda usually turned out to be fabricated, East
Germans ignored the official warnings. By the end of September, some
thirty thousand escapees had crossed the Hungarian frontier.

When travel to Budapest was cut off, refugees occupied the West
German embassies in Prague and Warsaw. Since they could reach the
Czech capital without visas, hundreds of East Germans scaled the legation
fence within full view of guards who failed to stop them. Embarrassing
pictures of more than two thousand men, women, and children jammed
into a muddy compound and sharing four toilets flashed around the
world. Now the Czech and Polish governments were also caught between
humanitarian impulses and fear of GDR retribution. When the Prague
party claimed that the crisis was destabilizing its own power and Moscow
failed to support him, Erich Honecker had little choice but to agree to
another "one-time" gesture. Intent on having nothing spoil his fortieth
anniversary of the GDR's founding, the SED leader sought to regain
control through another concession that signaled growing weakness instead.[25]

In secret negotiations at the United Nations, a compromise was hammered out. With Soviet Foreign Minister Shevardnadze's blessing, Oskar
Fischer and FRG Foreign Minister Genscher agreed: "In an effort to end
the untenable situation . . . in Prague and Warsaw, the East German Government has arranged to expel to West Germany the East Germans illegally staying in these embassies by train through East German territory."
Routing refugees through the GDR legalized the emigration, and calling it
"expulsion" was an attempt to take the sting out of the mass desertion.
Hans-Dietrich Genscher flew to Prague on September 30 and announced
the breakthrough from the embassy balcony: "This was the most moving

hour in my political career." In the Bavarian border town of Hof, cheering West Germans met the freedom trains carrying 6,300 GDR refugees with open arms and mounds of gifts.[26]

The new escape route only intensified the pressure. On Honecker's personal orders, the Communist press refused to shed any tears for the emigrants, since "they eliminated themselves" from the socialist community. But within twenty-four hours, thousands of new refugees streamed into the West German embassy in Prague. GDR representatives protested these "repeated violations of international law" and demanded that the occupiers be "ejected" from the West German legation. When Bonn refused, GDR representative Neubauer and Minister Seiters in the chancellor's office worked out a new compromise, allowing the newcomers to leave in consideration of the "condition of the children."[27]

On October 3, the trap once again snapped shut. SED leaders suspended travel without visas to Czechoslovakia until West Germany agreed to stop accepting refugees. By requiring visas and pulling a couple of thousand citizens out of trains bound for Prague, East Germany virtually closed the borders to its one remaining ally. Feeling "imprisoned" in a "bankrupt" state, hundreds of youths blocked the tracks and tried to jump onto the refugee trains on their way to the West. In Dresden about ten thousand angry protesters confronted the secret police with cobblestones against watercannons in a pitched battle that damaged the main train station. After the lines had been cleared, another 7,600 refugees from Prague and more than 600 from Warsaw reached the West. Defiantly, Minister Erich Mielke ordered the Stasi "to prevent public provocative-demonstrative actions and to stop illegal departures from the GDR." But the unprecedented disturbances suggested that popular aspirations were becoming more difficult to contain.[28]

By mid-October, demands for free travel began to undermine the stability of the post-Stalinist system. Churches and opposition groups dared to criticize the policies that made "many thousands leave their home, our country," especially among the young. Changing its tune, the communist press now claimed that "socialism needs everyone" and promised to search for the reasons of the exodus within the GDR. But after years of defamation such sympathetic noises were not enough.[29] With the fall vacation, the refugee stream resumed and another 1,700 émigrés poured into the Warsaw embassy. After popular pressure forced Honecker's fall in mid-October, the GDR cabinet instructed the minister of the interior to prepare a travel law "immediately." A week later, the new party leader Egon Krenz publicly promised that every citizen would receive a passport and a visa in the revised bill.

As a sign of good will the government reinstated free access to Czechoslovakia on November 1. At the same time a propaganda campaign against Western secret service interrogations was initiated to discourage potential escapees. When an additional 4,500 refugees crowded into the Prague embassy by November 3, GDR authorities agreed to allow emigrants "to leave Czech territory directly to the FRG by showing a personal identity card." Encouraged by this breakthrough, forty thousand more citizens fled within the next five days. Because West German services were overtaxed, Chancellor Kohl appealed to the East German population to stay in their country. The flight of hundreds of thousands to the West could not be a solution to the German question: "We want them to lead their lives and find their happiness in their own traditional home."[30]

In the long run, only a complete lifting of travel barriers could calm the refugee hysteria. Since one-time concessions followed by new limits had only inflamed the population, the new East German leadership understood that it had to gamble on greater liberality in order to remove this grievance. During the mass demonstration of November 4 at the Berlin Alexanderplatz, placards prominently featured calls for "travel without ifs, ands, or buts." The long awaited draft law of November 6 promised the right to go abroad for thirty days as well as to emigrate, and the streamlining of the travel authorization process. At the same time it contained broad grounds for denying applications and limited the amount of hard currency that could be taken out of the country to 15 DM. Outraged, hundreds of thousands demonstrated in Leipzig and other cities, demanding complete freedom. Even the docile TV, the rubber-stamp parliament, and the pliant party youth criticized the bill.[31]

This pressure ultimately forced the SED to abandon decades of restriction. The main thrust of the revised draft, announced on the evening of November 9, was directed toward easing the rules for "permanent exit." Visas would be granted quickly, without previous requirements, and citizens would be able leave via all border crossing points. Ironically, this astounding concession went utterly unnoticed in the euphoria over the permission for short-term travel, which toppled the Wall. The removal of legal and physical barriers only highlighted the political and economic disparity between East and West. Novelist Christa Wolf's dramatic appeal to stay in order to promote reforms fell on deaf ears. Even after the Wall crumbled, about two thousand GDR migrants continued to register in the Federal Republic every day. With their most liberal act, the SED leaders hastened their own fall from power.[32]

The reasons for the exodus were deep rooted. According to a devastating Stasi analysis, "the great majority of [refugees] resent problems and deficiencies of social development, especially in the personal sphere and living conditions." Most important was "dissatisfaction with the supply of consumer products" and the lack of a thousand little necessities. People expressed much "irritation about inadequate service" in shops or restaurants. Equally widespread were complaints about "deficits in medical care and treatment." Many citizens disliked "travel restrictions within the GDR and abroad." Unsatisfactory working conditions and production problems also aroused unfavorable comment. "Inadequate [or] inconsistent implementation of performance principles" compounded "discontent with the progress of pay and salaries." There was much "anger about the bureaucratic behavior of managers and state officials." Finally, "the media policy of the GDR [generated] misunderstanding" because of what was perceived as a cavalier attitude toward the truth.[33]

Opinion surveys confirm the widespread disenchantment. Between 1982 and 1987 discontent had dropped from 38 percent to 17 percent. But two years later 68 percent of East Germans believed that things were getting worse. To Western interviewers, refugees stressed the "lack of freedom of speech" (74 percent) and "travel restrictions" (74 percent) as their leading motives. Also important were the inability to control one's own life (72 percent), unfavorable prospects for the future (69 percent), and political repression (65 percent). But the lower living standard (56 percent) and inadequate working conditions reinforced political frustration and eroded loyalty. Most were so alienated from the GDR as to be impervious to last-minute appeals.[34]

The mass flight also proved unstoppable because the refugees were some of the most energetic GDR citizens. During 1989, some 343,854 people (more than 2 percent of the population) left East Germany. They came disproportionately from East Berlin; the smaller cities in the south of the GDR; and the ecologically devastated industrial regions around Dresden, Chemnitz, and Leipzig. The émigrés were younger than the national average, including especially the vigorous eighteen-to-forty-year olds (56.5 percent compared with 34.1 percent for the rest). Since there were more males and singles among those who left than in the population as a whole, these people were more ready to take risks.[35]

Unlike the stereotyped marginal misfits portrayed in SED propaganda, virtually all refugees had been employed in steady jobs. Though most worked in industry, trade and commerce, health care, construction, and transportation were particularly overrepresented. Moreover, two-thirds were skilled, while around one-sixth had completed college and occupied a position of authority (such as doctors or teachers). The departure of well-trained cadres hit service sectors like medical care particularly hard, creating disastrous bottlenecks. Though many emigrants were already better off than the average citizen, they moved in order to improve their prospects, which they felt had reached a dead end in the East. In spite of SED propaganda denunciations, these were capable and hard-working people who uprooted their lives for the greater potential rewards of the West.[36]

In the fall of 1989 the trickle of individual flight turned into a torrent of mass migration. In four cycles the initial rupture led to increased repression, renewed pressure, and ultimate release. The removal of barbed wire on the Hungarian frontier triggered the first wavelet in August but prompted stern warnings from East Berlin. The official border opening in September loosed a wider stream but also precipitated new travel restrictions. The Prague embassy deal in October released another wave but the GDR increasingly isolated itself in the Communist bloc. Finally, the abandoning of exit requirements in November opened the floodgates, but the new travel law tried to channel the tide. Though the government saw each concession as a final attempt to regain control, the population responded as if it were the last opportunity to get out. Even for citizens who wanted to return, demands for emigration became inextricably linked to the desire for free personal movement. In the end, every opening only increased the surge.[37]

The East German exodus of 1989 differed markedly from earlier migrations. The mass flight from the GDR was more spontaneous and rapid than many religious, economic, or political population movements. The interdiction of travel through the Wall made the situation especially explosive. The thought that refugees were only going to "Germany" and not to a "foreign country" made it easier for them to leave. The depth of dissatisfaction with the regime motivated especially energetic and educated people to flee. The disparities between East and West were so large that neither partial concessions nor the complete opening of the border could stop the flow. Hence the exodus was a curious blend between domestic labor movement and international search for political asylum.[38]

Consequences of Flight

For the emigrants an array of welfare state measures cushioned the shock of arriving in the West. The FRG had developed a formal processing procedure, based on its experience with earlier refugees, ethnic migrants, and asylum seekers. Newcomers spent the first days in crowded reception camps in Giessen or Berlin-Marienfelde so as to receive proper documentation for subsequent entitlements. Welcome money of 150 DM per adult helped immigrants over the letdown that often followed the euphoria of escape. Then came counselling about support possibilities, reinforced by a pamphlet describing various programs. Personal contacts or individual flexibility facilitated further decisions about future residence and kind of work. After a physical examination, new arrivals proceeded to their eventual destination, where they lived for several months in transitional shelters until they found a permanent home and a job.[39]

GDR refugees received special priority in housing assignments. Supplemental funding as well as furniture and moving credits of between 3,000 and 10,000 DM helped the new start. All educational diplomas and degrees were recognized, and students were offered scholarships to resume training. Prior East German contributions to health insurance, unemployment, and social security were treated as if they had been paid into West German funds. Finally, political detainees received tax breaks, special credits, and other benefits. Private citizens and charity organizations also extended a helping hand.[40] These generous provisions speeded integration into a different social system for the new citizens. Nevertheless in 1989 the flood of migrants strained this well-conceived but bureaucratic procedure beyond capacity.

For many refugees, the transition was difficult. Since few had been in the West before, most newcomers found the move like "jumping into cold water." Virtually all hoped for a higher living standard than in the East, but many worried about finding a place to live or suspected they would need additional training for jobs. These mixed expectations were borne out by their actual experience. Though most Easterners found their Western cousins helpful, many complained about arrogant treatment by bureaucrats. Within two to three months most had secured a job, but two-fifths had to accept work below their professional qualifications. Initially, refugees found it hard to cope with the pace, competitiveness, and achievement orientation of their new colleagues. Getting decent housing in the overcrowded market also turned out to be complicated, although most located suitable quarters eventually. Many bought electronic gadgets and expensive furniture to document their new wealth.[41]

In spite of aid, the move to the West required a painful adjustment. For children, the future seemed bright, because West Germany offered more possibilities for advanced training. But adults sometimes found it difficult to establish personal contacts and make new friends. A few people with exaggerated dreams of "the golden West" or with too little initiative failed to adapt. But most hard-working refugees soon felt integrated and did not rue their decision. Hardly anyone intended to return to the East, even if conditions there improved. While about one half of the emigrants professed no political allegiance, one-quarter leaned to the center right (Christian Democratic Union and Christian Social Union), twice the number that identified with the Left. To heal the rupture with their home, these Eastern refugees overwhelmingly supported unification.[42]

West Germans reacted to the stream of newcomers with a mixture of sympathy and anxiety. Touched by the human drama of escape, most hosts cordially welcomed the fresh refugees. Since the exodus seemed to re-enact some FRG founding myths, memory of earlier flight and compassion mingled with interest in obtaining skilled laborers. Between 1984 and 1989, surveys showed that willingness to help increased from three-fifths to three-quarters, while fears of job competition and spies were cut in half. From August to October general approval of the influx rose from one-third to well over one-half, and criticism declined correspondingly. In thousands of small individual acts, friends and strangers helped with gifts of clothes and furniture as well as with money and advice.[43]

When migrants continued to pour in, long-standing concerns about a housing shortage and lack of jobs surfaced. Since they blended in more easily, GDR refugees ranked above ethnic Germans from Eastern Europe, some of whom scarcely spoke the language, and asylum seekers from the Third World, who were visually and culturally alien. But the arrival of more than eight hundred thousand foreigners fed an ugly envy, especially among the poorer people, who felt most directly threatened. Almost two-fifths of West Germans resented extensive government subsidies to the new arrivals that they could not obtain for themselves.[44] A new kind of "prosperity chauvinism" led to antiforeign violence and vandalism. In a curious rejection of national solidarity, the far right Republikaner party played on such fears to attract protest votes. But churches and intellectuals urged tolerance, and the government launched a public relations campaign to increase acceptance.[45]

Instead of examining the issues, the West German media reinforced the emotional impact of the exodus. Almost daily, newspapers printed touching stories of the mass flight with little analysis of its long-range consequences. Influential magazines, such as *Spiegel* and *Stern*, ran interviews with leading politicians as well as photo essays on the intolerable conditions in the embassies. Gripping TV pictures of escapes from the GDR provided diversion for the slack time of late summer and carried the excitement into the fall. Stage-managed broadcasts announced important breakthroughs: Hungarian Foreign Minister Guyla Horn disclosed his decision to open the frontier during the evening news. Many GDR citizens interpreted such newscasts as encouragement to flee, since the risks seemed low and the welcome promised to be warm.[46]

Westerners got caught up in the human drama vicariously. Ordinary West Germans rediscovered feelings of collective solidarity that had long been submerged by the quest for individual prosperity. In other countries as well, newspaper articles, magazine pieces and television soundbytes triggered a surge of compassion, since the aspiration of free personal movement was universal. Eastern journalists and pastors castigated this media blitz as "war reporting." But their critical attempts to reflect on the implications of a GDR collapse were drowned out in the general euphoria. By appealing to human sympathy, the media spectacle brought new movement into the hardened fronts of the cold war.[47]

After initial hesitation, Helmut Kohl recognized the refugee crisis as an historic opportunity. In his seventh year in office, the chancellor was powerful but unloved. Born in the Rhenish village of Oggersheim, he was a Christian-Democratic career politician. After a successful state governorship in Rhineland-Palatinate, he toppled the tired Social Democratic/Free Democratic coalition government in 1982. Inaugurating a conservative turn, Kohl restored prosperity and twice gained re-election by substantial margins. Though ungainly in appearance and homespun in rhetoric, he possessed an unfailing instinct for popular sentiment. In his own party, the CDU, he quickly eliminated potential rivals like Heiner Geissler and he ran the coalition with the FDP with an iron hand. His dislike of public speaking and his embarrassing faux-pas like the Bitburg affair constantly provoked intellectuals. The SPD accused him of weathering storms rather than solving problems. But as an historian, he combined deep patriotism with European sympathy.[48]

Vice-Chancellor Hans-Dietrich Genscher had a better press. Coming from the Eastern city of Halle, he was a trained lawyer. As leader of the small Free Democratic Party (FDP), he became foreign minister in the social-liberal coalition during 1974. When Helmut Schmidt faltered eight years later, Genscher led the FDP into a coalition with the CDU. With his sadly wrinkled face, the tall FDP politician excelled in finding common ground. Although initially considered devious, he became respected as a negotiator and cornerstone of European stability. A strong supporter of *Ostpolitik*, he was one of the first to recognize the potential of Soviet perestroika. Washington skeptics who denounced "Genscherism" were soon forced to follow the same conciliating course toward Moscow. Though Kohl and Genscher often irritated each other, the CDU/FDP government depended upon their cooperation for its parliamentary majority. Both of them were old enough to remember the carnage of World War II, and felt a sense of national responsibility.[49]

The unforeseen exodus created material and political challenges for the Kohl-Genscher cabinet. The arrival of tens of thousands of refugees forced emergency measures and ran up costs that overtaxed local resources. Diplomatic confrontations over exit permissions from Hungary and Czechoslovakia endangered the successful *Ostpolitik* of "small steps." Though the political elite agreed on the constitutional mandate to help the Eastern newcomers, the major parties reacted with different emphases. Deputy SPD Chairman Horst Ehmke attacked the government for having encouraged flight through its policy of welcoming refugees. A Berlin spokesperson of the Greens, the environmental party, even called for a closing of the Western border to the East. But liberal leaders like Count Otto von Lambsdorff favored keeping the door open and reforming the GDR.[50]

In the Bundestag debate on September 5, Chancellor Kohl underscored the moral duty to help the refugees. Since the exodus demonstrated the popular preference for the social market economy and parliamentary democracy, he attacked the Social Democrats for cozying up to the SED. In responding to the exodus, the CDU could fall back upon decades of national solidarity rhetoric. But the SPD wavered between Johannes Rau's welcoming the migrants and Oskar Lafontaine's playing to social envy aroused by the strains of integrating the Eastern masses. Though mayors increasingly complained about overburdened town services, the government refused to abandon its policy of welcoming refugees. Only when housing shortages grew worse did Bonn begin to discourage further migrants and to emphasize reform in the GDR as the preferable alternative.[51]

The "reunification from below" was grist on the rightist mill. Appealing to conservative voters and former refugees, the CDU ritually claimed that "the German question remains legally and politically open." An entire Ministry for All-German Affairs sought to overcome division by anti-communist propaganda. Nevertheless, the chancellor worked to improve relations with the GDR and looked for "a free and united Germany in a free and united Europe" in the distant future.[52] In the FDP, national-liberal traditions combined with demands for human rights and hopes for the introduction of a market economy. Deterred by the revanchism of refugee politicians, only a few Western writers like Martin Walser or exiled GDR critics like Freya Klier tried to keep hope for unity alive.[53] Since "reunification within the FRG" would not solve the German problem, the Right had to transform its patriotic rhetoric into practical policy.[54]

The East German exodus posed a greater challenge to the assumptions of the Left. As the party of *Ostpolitik*, the SPD was strongly committed to the existence of two separate German states. Willy Brandt had even denounced reunification as "the basic lie" of the Federal Republic. The socialist leadership had sought to foster reforms through a closer dialogue with the SED and issued a joint declaration that demarcated commonalities as well as differences.[55] Preoccupied with Third World problems, the Greens abhorred all national sentiment. Much to the dismay of the Right, Hessian moderate Joschka Fischer suggested "striking the reunification mandate from the preamble of the Federal constitution."[56] Torn between sympathies for human rights and socialist utopias, intellectuals tried to reconcile these contradictions by supporting GDR reforms.

During September 1989 the refugee drama reawakened the national issue after decades of dormancy. Initially confusion reigned in all ideological camps. Conservative circles, led by the CDU Bundestag chairman Alfred Dregger, considered the mass flight "an indication of . . . the unity of the German nation" and demanded a more active unification policy. Concerned about international fears, the chancellor's office preferred instead to stress human rights as a method of achieving the same end. In the Christian Social Union (CSU), Bavarian Minister President Max Streibl suggested increased pragmatism, but Finance Minister Theo Waigel still referred to the boundaries of 1937. The FDP wavered between developing inter-German trade with the SED and overcoming European divisions within the Helsinki framework.[57]

The SPD had even more difficulty in arriving at a unified response. While Egon Bahr, the architect of détente, counselled "not dreaming about unity but developing commonalities," ex-chancellor Helmut Schmidt warned against a renunciation of unity. Provocatively, party council chairman Norbert Gansel demanded reversing the "change-through-closeness" course so as to promote "reform through distance" from the SED. When elder statesman Willy Brandt rediscovered his national heart, the party leadership was hard pressed to find a self-determination formula open enough to accommodate Oskar Lafontaine's European vision as well.[58] Only the Greens had no questions about opposing the restoration of a national state. With these discussions in the parties, the media, and among intellectuals, the unification issue suddenly took on new life.[59]

Among neighboring countries the reopening of the German question aroused more unease than sympathy. Soviet leaders resolved the dilemma by encouraging GDR reform so as to preserve their ally. The refugees had to be let go, but Bonn should keep its hands off the GDR. In the spirit of his "European house," Gorbachev could not very well deny self-determination. But Russian spokesmen warned against "destabilizing the situation in Europe" by expanding NATO to the East.[60] The French similarly admitted the principle while hoping to postpone the practice. President François Mitterrand understood that "reunification is a goal for all Germans," but cautioned against precipitating a "birth by forceps." London was also loath to increase German power and to give up any spoils of its hard-won victory in World War II.[61]

Other nations proved more understanding. The American government supported German hopes to a surprising extent. U.S. ambassador to Bonn Vernon Walters expressed his sympathy quite candidly. Commentator Henry Kissinger considered the unification discussion "inescapable" as long as it did not lead to neutralization. In a telling interview, President Bush refused to share European fears about a united Germany, as he believed Bonn's commitment to the West to be unshakable. Summing up the general ambivalence, he only warned against forcing the issue.[62] Bronislaw Geremek of Polish Solidarity argued that "Germany should be reunified," provided that it "does not constitute a danger for another country." For the European Community, Jacques Delors also professed not to be shocked as long as German unity reinforced the integration process.[63]

Undeterred by foreign concerns, German politics "lost its speechlessness" on unity during the fall of 1989. The 1973 Supreme Court order "to keep the claim to reunification alive at home and to advocate it tenaciously abroad" only left room for disagreement on appropriate methods for reaching this goal.[64] Even if Rightists like Franz Schönhuber appealed to envy, most politicians supported the reception of refugees, arguing rather about how to cope with the growing social strains. Instead of trumpeting reunification rhetoric, the majority preferred to advocate GDR reform and self-determination, but remained confused on whether to maintain ties to the SED or to support the opposition. Except for a small nationalist minority, the political elite was sincere about embedding unification in European integration. The only dispute was about the relative priority of the two aims.[65]

As a result of renewed debate, public attitudes shifted dramatically. By mid-September four-fifths of West Germans in a television survey considered reunification desirable, and over one-quarter called it possible in the near future. By mid-October almost nine out of ten polled by the *Bunte Illustrierte* supported unity and almost half believed that there was now a realistic opportunity to achieve it. Coupled with the continuing flight from the East, this growing groundswell in the West restored unity as a practical goal of politics: "The chance for reunification has never been as great as now," according to CDU spokesman Karl-Heinz Hornhues. "The less we talk about it, the bigger it is."[66]

Unity from Below

The slow liberalization of the Eastern bloc offered an unprecedented opportunity for fleeing the GDR. When Gorbachev's perestroika restrained

Soviet tanks, the Iron Curtain rusted through in Hungary and Czechoslovakia. Though East Germans had few contacts with Poland, Solidarity
showed how citizens could challenge a communist regime. The SED government, leaderless during Honecker's long illness, could not decide on a
clear policy. Its oscillation between continued prohibition of emigration
and partial loosening of travel rules provided both a motive and a chance
for escape. Mixing humanitarian concern with national self-interest, Western attempts to open the closed door aided flight. Bonn paid little attention to the problem of integrating an enormous number of newcomers. In
the climate of détente, solidarities based on military confrontation gave
way to aspirations for human rights.[67]

Since GDR citizens had no real voice, they could only vote with their
feet. Many frustrations pushed East Germans to leave. Some moved out of
material concerns such as lack of housing, thwarted career prospects, a
dearth of consumer goods, and inability to travel. But a number of political motives, such as lack of free speech, the dim outlook for the future, and
Stasi repression played a role. The pull of the glamorous West was also
powerful. Television series and reports of older relatives returning from
visits created an exaggerated image of the good life in the Federal Republic. Instant citizenship and effective integration measures promised to ease
the transition. Ultimately, the mass flight developed out of tens of thousands of individual decisions. Hope of success and fear of being left behind created a self-reinforcing dynamic that proved unstoppable. To the
West Berlin sociologist Fritz Haug the exodus seemed a mixture "of psy-
chosis and plebiscite."[68]

The mass flight initiated the downward spiral that led to the eventual
collapse of the GDR. The physical consequences were serious. The unre-
mitting manpower drain robbed the GDR of the equivalent of the workforce of one medium-sized company per day. Bottlenecks developed, especially in medical services and other businesses requiring particular skills.
The psychological results were even more debilitating. The departure of
many of the best and brightest demoralized the remainder and engendered
a pervasive loss of self-confidence. Dutiful citizens began to ponder
whether it made any sense to stay behind. The political repercussions
were most disastrous. "The wall was basically a metaphor for a system
that could exist only if it closed itself off," Günter Schabowski reflected.
"A society that can keep its citizens from leaving the country merely by
use of force disqualifies itself."[69]

The exodus galvanized the timid opposition to speak out more boldly.
The quasi-revolutionary situation produced by the refugee crisis encouraged dissenters to form organizations to challenge the SED. According to
secret service reports, the mass flight also made a broader public receptive
to the civil critique of the GDR. By running away, East German citizens forced the showdown between Erich Honecker's old guard and the
younger proponents of reform in the politburo. The paternalist language
of the draft travel law of November 6 also contributed to the lack of
credibility of Egon Krenz's new policy.[70] The desperate opening of the

Wall failed to stop the continuing emigration, since freeing personal travel exposed the enormous disparity between East and West. Because the crisis eventually engulfed all areas of private and public life, the exodus was the chief trigger for the implosion of the GDR.

The refugee stream posed the question of German unity with fresh urgency. For decades West German politicians had been able to call for "reunification," sure that the eventuality remained remote. With similar hypocrisy, Western leaders were able to support such dreams, confident that their check could never be cashed. The unexpected human hemorrhage of the GDR exposed this charade and called the international division of the country into question. The unabating exodus rekindled old fears of German power among leftist critics and neighbors, such as Polish Communists. For conservative Germans and some sympathetic outsiders the drama awakened fresh hopes. Helmut Kohl began to talk cautiously about "a new chance for the reunification of our fatherland."[71]

Somewhat unexpectedly, the German question returned to the forefront of domestic and international debate. While some commentators left established positions, others clung all the more resolutely to old verities. The American columnist William Pfaff argued for the continued independence of a noncommunist "Prussian-Saxon state," whereas an influential British journalist warned against the rise of a "fourth Reich."[72] In East Berlin, the senescent leadership opposed travel concessions because it rightly saw them as a prelude to unification. In Bonn, Foreign Minister Genscher rejected unilateral national solutions and called for overcoming division through European integration: "Bringing Western and Eastern Europe together also means a rapprochement between the Germans."[73] Though the path was still unclear, the people's flight began the rush to German unity.

2

Protesting for Freedom

The democratic awakening began in the streets of Leipzig. Choking air, fouled water, and crumbling buildings plagued Saxon citizens and aroused resentment against East Berlin. On September 4, 1989, youthful peace protesters emerged from the sanctuary of the Nikolaikirche, shouting "We want to leave." The secret police tore banners that demanded "an open country with free people" out of their hands, a picture captured by Western journalists who were attending the trade fair. Not intimidated, the restless groups grew larger during the peace service on the following Monday. Claiming that the "illegal assembly . . . disturb[ed] public order and safety," the police proceeded more brutally and detained about one hundred demonstrators.[1]

Repression only bred further dissent. On September 18 protesters marched silently with candles in their hands, forming and reforming fluidly so as to offer no clear target to the security forces. About five thousand demonstrators ignored warnings in the press and assembled on September 25. In contrast to those who wanted to get out, they chanted "We are staying here!" Prodded by nightstick-wielding police, they circled the center city ring with shouts of "Gorbi, Gorbi" and called for the legalization of opposition groups. Time and again protesters broke through cordons, inviting those in uniform to "come and join us." Curious spectators merged with the milling throng and the crowd gradually lost its fear.[2] Encouraged by growing support, this courageous minority reclaimed its right to free speech, singing "We shall overcome."

The SED met this unexpected challenge from the streets with increased force. On September 26, Stasi chief Mielke suggested pressing the church to cease the vigils and using "punitive and legal measures" against provocateurs. In letters to the editor and resolutions from workers' collectives, state-controlled newspapers tried to incite public "indignation against the disturbance of our peace by antisocialist forces." Undeterred,

twenty thousand citizens assembled nonviolently on October 2 in Leipzig
to appeal for reforms. Some policemen, secret service agents, and army
reservists began to doubt that the demonstrators were "rowdies and devi-
ants." But other officers redoubled their determination to take surveillance
photos, use their clubs, and let their dogs attack. Tension grew when
militia leader Günter Lutz urged the readers of the *Leipziger Volkszeitung*
"to cease tolerating treason."[3]

On October 7, the confrontation became more violent. During the
celebration of the GDR's fortieth anniversary, security forces no longer
held back against taunting youths. Mercilessly, they beat peaceful demonstrators and turned water cannons on the crowd. Shocked East Germans,
who had seen such scenes only on Western television, met the repression
with shouts of "Nazis." Two hundred and ten protesters were arrested,
searched, harassed. Needing ever more force to clear the streets, the SED
began to lose control. Without clear instructions, Leipzig leaders did not
know what to do. Traditional means of intimidation were failing to contain a popular anger that fed on police brutality. The very size, anonym-
ity, and peacefulness of the crowds were their best defense. The next
Monday demonstration would either bring "a breakthrough or civil war."[4]

On October 9, the crisis came to a head. Since four hundred SED
members had been ordered to attend, the Nikolaikirche service was so
packed that neighboring churches had to be opened. In spite of Stasi
threats, the vigil proceeded. The fearful congregation was resolute and
defiant. To avoid bloodshed, Bishop Hempel warned, "Force does not
solve any problems." Prompted by the mobilization of the security apparatus, frightening rumors swirled among the seventy thousand people
outside: Schools closed early in expectation of violence; officers were
carrying weapons and had orders to shoot; hospitals were stocking up on
blood plasma; armored vehicles with reinforcements were moving downtown.[5]

Suddenly loudspeakers blared an announcement, repeated on the radio: "Our common concern and responsibility have brought us together
today. . . . We all need a free exchange of opinions about the development
of socialism in our country." Cabaretist Bernd-Lutz Lange, Gewandhaus
orchestra conductor Kurt Masur, pastor Peter Zimmermann, and three
SED district secretaries urged open discussion: "We ask you earnestly for
prudence so that a peaceful dialogue will become possible." This joint
appeal broke the spell of violence. Chanting "no new China," the demonstrators shouted "We are the people!" Miraculously, the massive armed
force yielded to calls for restraint and let the marchers proceed. The civic
courage of Leipzig citizens prevailed because the Neues Forum, the leading opposition group, counselled peace, while the police, unsure of instructions and discipline, hesitated to use force. Whatever its ultimate
cause, the October 9 compact opened the streets to peaceful protest and
freed public debate.[6]

Sources of Dissent

Protest had always faced special difficulties in the GDR. As in all Soviet bloc countries, the Communist party enjoyed dictatorial control over public life. Roughly every fifth adult belonged to the SED, which had enrolled 2.3 million members. Though other parties of the "democratic bloc" retained nominal independence, they could not pursue policies of their own. The SED ruthlessly suppressed intermediary associations, permitting only its own mass organizations to claim public space. From nursery school on, Marxist political education sought to eliminate individualism and create a "socialist personality." Additional constraints made it even harder to establish an organized opposition than in other Eastern European states. The stationing of more than 380,000 Soviet troops in the GDR was a none-too-subtle reminder that Moscow could intervene as it had in 1953 against the workers' uprising.[7]

The existence of West Germany both helped and hindered criticism. Western media provided alternative views as well as an outlet for dissenters. But the threat of capitalist influence also spawned special vigilance. Unwelcome opponents could simply be deported to the Federal Republic, depriving the opposition of potential leadership. Real discussion could take place only within the SED, leaving the politburo to set the boundaries of accepted discourse. Whenever criticism became too threatening, unruly intellectuals like Wolf Biermann or reform Marxists like Rudolf Bahro were expelled. Ordinary citizens withdrew into private "niches," cultivating their dachas and gardens. Most East Germans developed a dual consciousness, using politically correct speech in public and voicing personal doubts only to friends.[8]

The biggest obstacle to opposition was the secret police. With 109,000 members and up to 300,000 part-time informers, the dreaded Stasi employed about one of every twenty-five adults. As "sword and shield of the party," it did the political dirty work of the SED. Though under "party control," the German Cheka had great latitude of action. To suppress dissent it initially relied on brute force, imprisonment without charges, and police harassment. Since civil rights existed only on paper, the Stasi moved in an extralegal realm, based on administrative decree. The uncertainty about whom one could trust created an immobilizing fear. Surveillance of telephone calls, international mail, and popular restaurants was commonplace. Only conspiratorial excesses and military inflexibility sometimes limited the grasp of the "listen and grab company."[9]

During the 1980s, the Stasi gradually shifted from physical intimidation to psychological manipulation. It penetrated dissident circles so effectively that every fourth member seemed to be in its pay. Subversion allowed sowing dissension within critics' ranks so as to immobilize the opposition. The Stasi could mobilize the state for "preventive countermeasures" or rally "progressive opinion" in mass organizations and the media.

The secret police also used positive incentives for cooperation. Officers supervised their informers with almost loving solicitude. As the only ones who could get things done, Mielke's men saw themselves as the problem solvers of the GDR. This smothering blanket of state security criminalized dissent and punished nonconformists by damaging their careers. But anyone willing to risk these consequences could break with the regime.[10]

The only institution with some degree of freedom was the united Protestant church. Catholics were less visible because of smaller numbers (one million) and withdrawal from public life. Since Lutheran pastors clung to nationalist anticommunism, the SED vigorously promoted atheism during the postwar years. Though the evangelical community lost many nominal members, the remaining eight million became more cohesive. From the late 1960s on, a new group of leftist clergymen sought to reach an accommodation with the state. Flexibly called "church within socialism," their *modus vivendi* promised loyalty to the GDR in return for a degree of public acceptance. During the 1980s younger theologians turned to social action and worked to democratize socialism. Afraid of religious integrity, the Stasi worked especially hard to infiltrate the church.[11]

Protestantism retained some autonomy, since it pursued spiritual rather than temporal ends. Church buildings served as a quasi-public forum, with doors open to strangers and yet closed to the police. Those who were persecuted by the party and desperate to escape sought the shelter of the altar for consolation and encouragement. Other critical spirits who were not always that devout flocked to the church to discuss pressing issues with open-minded clergymen. These cries for help, although repeatedly straining relations with the SED, prodded some daring pastors to develop an independent point of view. Reluctantly, a Protestant activism emerged that rejected flight but sought to improve life within the GDR. By criticizing "the principle of isolation" from the West and calling for an open dialogue, the church retained moral authority. Addressing public concerns theologically in the "conciliar process" dampened and facilitated criticism at the same time.[12]

At first, dissent crystallized around the issue of peace. New Testament teaching against war inspired Protestant clergymen to get involved. Since it used pacifist slogans against NATO, communism invited criticism on identical grounds. In the early 1980s the Western debate about intermediate-range missiles spilled over into Eastern media and triggered discussions within the church. To allay the fear of nuclear war articulated in the "Berlin appeal," concerned pastors and laymen deplored official hypocrisy and urged the SED to contribute to disarmament. Following the biblical call to beat "swords into plowshares," young people began to form peace circles. From 1983 on Protestants sponsored annual "peace seminars," which drew clergy and laymen from all over East Germany. Individual churches like the Nikolaikirche started prayer vigils that gradually assumed an important role. While the ecclesiastical hierarchy favored cooperation, radical parishioners sought confrontation with the state.[13]

Caught between its pacifist rhetoric and militarist practice, the SED reacted nervously. Religious attacks on mandatory military indoctrination turned schools into battle grounds. When pacifists rejected the draft, the church's sheltering of resisters became another bone of contention. Eventually, Stasi repression of peace activities transformed dissent into a question of civil rights. Stepping out of the shadow of the church, an opposition group coalesced in 1985 as "Initiative for Peace and Human Rights" (IFM). Intellectuals like Bärbel Bohley, Ulrike Poppe, or Wolfgang Templin wanted to search for their own answers, independent of institutional concerns. Issuing its own newsletter *Grenzfall*, the small and fragmented IFM developed a secular critique of the GDR in private debates and public protests. In 1987 peace activists succeeded in getting approval for an Olof Palme peace march, which brought the antiwar message to a wider public.[14]

Another focus of protest was the environment. Though ecological data were kept secret, much of the East German air had become so unbreathable, the water so undrinkable and the soil so toxic that the disaster could no longer be covered up. Scriptural injunctions about stewardship of the earth motivated the church to take an interest. The rhetoric of the Western Greens and the international environmental movement also spilled across the frontier. In 1983–1984 informal circles began to debate ecological issues, later energized by the Chernobyl nuclear accident. By 1986 activists at the Berlin Zionskirche founded an "environmental library" to collect and disseminate information on the gravity of the problem. Barely tolerated by the hierarchy, this *Umweltbibliothek* published a defiant newsletter that violated state law. To silence the opposition, the Stasi raided the library in November 1987 and locked up its leaders. During a Rosa Luxemburg demonstration in January, other dissidents like Bärbel Bohley were arrested and expelled to the West.[15]

Growing environmental concern would not be suppressed. Another group, called " Ark," formed to address "clean air, dying trees, water and the groundwater table, garbage disposal, and urban ecology." This "green-ecological network" pursued projects and coordinated activities through its underground newsletter. Local groups sponsored tree plantings, river marches, ecology days, and public seminars and sent open letters to the authorities. The most daring coup was the production of a video film on lignite strip mining and chemical pollution that was broadcast on West Berlin TV as "Bitter News from Bitterfeld." The SED resented environmental criticism because it contradicted claims about the good socialist life. The public responded to ecological appeals, because they touched on local concerns.[16]

In May 1989, election fraud turned issue-oriented protest into political opposition. The SED leaders intended the local balloting as a ringing affirmation of their antiperestroika course. But dissidents, frustrated by the lack of reform, exposed the charade of staged acclamation and sought to regain real choice. Aware that "the public mood had deteriorated considerably," members of "so-called religious grass-roots groups and applicants for emigration" sent observers to 131 Berlin polling stations. In an election party at St. Elisabeth's Church, regime opponents tabulated their reports in front of West German correspondents. The official 99.9 percent approval of the SED candidates suppressed between 10 and 15 percent abstentions and no votes, especially in university and church districts.[17]

Outraged, underground critics charged election falsification. More than one hundred scattered protests throughout the GDR demanded the liberalization of domestic policy. Instead of being discouraged by mass arrests in Leipzig, opponents publicly denounced the polling procedures and "protest[ed] against the validity of the election" to national and local authorities. The Stasi responded by pressing church officials and harassing individuals and even advised local mayors how to deny the illegality of the balloting. But massive force could not stop monthly demonstrations against "election fraud" or "the burial of democracy." From its reports the opposition documented election violations in a brochure, called *Wahlfall 89*, which persuaded some church leaders to join the protests. Government denials reinforced the "well-organized and coordinated action of hostile, oppositional forces." The blatancy of the fraud threatened SED power by exposing the hollowness of its democracy.[18]

By the summer of 1989, a small but determined opposition had emerged in East Germany. Encouraged by Western journalists and leftists, critics formed loose networks "aimed at weakening, subverting, and destabilizing" the SED regime. According to Stasi estimates, 150 grass-roots groups coalesced under church protection: 35 promoted peace, 39 dealt with ecology, 23 touched on both, 39 addressed Third World issues, 10 focused on human rights, and a few discussed feminism and draft resistance. With a leadership core of some 60, about 600 dissidents could call upon about 2,500 protesters. Most activists were between twenty-five and forty years old and preferred "alternative" lifestyles. As intellectuals, they worked in white-collar jobs in cities like Berlin, Leipzig, Chemnitz, Halle, and Dresden. They communicated through personal contacts and used primitive technologies, such as mimeograph machines.[19]

Dissidents worked systematically on "the creation and legalization of an internal opposition." Their goals revolved around a democratic socialism, disarmament, human rights, and a healthy environment, but failed to address economic stagnation. By directing public attention to political issues such as the Chinese student massacre, the informal groups formulated a devastating critique of "real existing Socialism." Somewhat restrained by the Helsinki Accords, the Stasi retaliated with elaborate "countermeasures to destroy" criticism through "progressive forces," media pressure, police sanctions, and prohibition of foreign contacts. Since Mielke believed "we still have things under control," the SED failed to placate such reform hopes with concessions. The party's refusal to tolerate a loyal opposition left its critics no choice but to overthrow the entire regime. The same repression that had guaranteed conformity before now made protest all the more explosive.[20]

The Civic Movement

During the fall of 1989, the failure of the SED to reform triggered a rash of new groups and political programs for change. Years of debates in Protestant peace and human rights seminars and months of preparatory discussions culminated on August 26 in a proposal for the founding of a "Social-democratic Party in the GDR." Independent of the Western SPD, Protestant pastors Martin Gutzeit, Markus Meckel, and Arndt Noack and the historian Ibrahim Böhme emphatically demanded political reform: "Things cannot go on like this. Many wait for *something* to change. But that is not enough! We want to do our share." Arguing that the necessary democratization of the GDR required the breaking of the SED power monopoly, the signers appealed for "an open intellectual debate about the condition of our country and its future path." Their goal was *"an ecologically oriented social democracy,"* based on human rights and the protection of the environment. In contrast to SED dictatorship, this return to parliamentary democracy implied the rule of law, regional autonomy, a social market economy, liberalization of business structures, and free trade unions—in short, the Swedish model.[21]

The FRG press hailed the emergence of a political opposition in the GDR. Though Western SPD leaders were loath to give up their SED contacts, they expressed sympathy for the revival of democratic socialism and supported the upstart's application for membership in the Socialist International. But the SED reacted nervously to the threat to its unity, because it feared the break-up of the shotgun marriage of the SPD with the KPD, which had created the Socialist Unity Party in 1946. Because Ibrahim Böhme, the secretary of the new party, was a Stasi informant, the initiative made little headway initially. But on October 7 the Social Democratic Party of the GDR (SDP) was formally founded in Schwante with a passionate if confusing speech by Markus Meckel. In the first weeks more than a thousand people joined.[22]

A more radical attempt at socialist renewal was the founding of the United Left (*Vereinigte Linke*, VL). During early September restless SED members and trade unionists met secretly in Böhlen to "create a left socialist alternative in the spirit of socialist democracy and freedom." Trying to recapture revolutionary "council democracy," the United Left formed a "coalition of reason" in order to spearhead a "fundamental rebirth" of GDR society. Its revitalized Marxism included socialized property, self-determination of producers, social security, political democracy, and ecological transformation of industry. Though directed toward work-

ers' soviets, this was a program of intellectuals that helped stimulate discussion within the SED. But conspiratorial methods, aversion to formal
organization, and popular disenchantment with socialism severely limited
the VL's influence on the emerging opposition.[23]

The rise of a broad civic movement called *Neues Forum* (NF) had more
immediate impact. On September 9, 1989 six doctors, four physicists,
three clergymen, three students, and fourteen other intellectuals from all
over East Germany threw off their "political apathy" and founded the
New Forum. In a courageous book on "the tutelary state," the lawyer Rolf
Henrich had deplored "the failure of real existing socialism" to allow free
speech. Other critics such as the painter Bärbel Bohley, physicist Sebastian Pflugbeil, molecular biologist Jens Reich, construction specialist
Rainer Schult, and pastor Jochen Tschiche agreed that "communication is
apparently blocked in our country." Appealing for an "awakening 89,"
they called for "a *democratic dialogue* about the rule of law, the economy,
and the culture. We have to think and talk publicly *with each other and in the
whole country* about these questions." To get people to discuss vital problems and find a common course of reform, "we are forming *a political
platform* for the whole GDR."[24]

The New Forum attracted much attention. It vocalized the common
need for debate without dictating the outcome. The initiators tested the
GDR constitution by registering with the authorities on September 19.
Communist newspapers derided the initiative as a "treasonous platform"
or "fifth column." The ministry of the interior rejected the application on
the grounds that "there is no social need for the association." By collecting
twenty-five thousand signatures within the first month, mounting public
protests, and involving the authorities in debates, the New Forum made
permission to organize into a test case of human rights. When writers and
rock musicians enthusiastically endorsed the call for dialogue, civic opposition spread like wildfire throughout the GDR. Western leftists and intellectuals encouraged the movement with frequent contacts. But other Eastern dissidents found its program too vague, and created their own
groups.[25]

On September 12, another cluster of dissidents emerged to demand
"Democracy Now!" The Berlin physicist Hans-Jürgen Fischbeck, the
historian Ulrike Poppe, pastor Wolfgang Ullmann, and film director Konrad Weiss urged people to get "involved in our own problems." To implement traditional values with new methods, they called for an end to "state
socialism" and a "peaceful democratic renewal." Inspired by Soviet perestroika, they advocated "an alliance of all reformers," including Chris-
tians and critical Marxists. To give direction to public debate, this new
group *Demokratie Jetzt* (DJ) presented coherent "theses for a democratic
transformation of the GDR."[26]

The Democracy Now program sought to develop socialism in the
direction of freedom. The GDR should move "from authoritarianism to

democracy" by granting the human rights of free speech, assembly, and travel and by lifting control over media, education, unions, and other organizations. The "bureaucratic command economy" ought to be replaced by a free market with social safeguards. Finally, the "exploitation and degradation of the environment" had to be eliminated. This somewhat tentative catalogue not only listed the shortcomings of the East German system with devastating frankness, it also summarized endless discussions about the renewal of human rights in peace circles. Less popular than the broad New Forum, the ideologically cohesive brain-trust of DJ hoped to run its own candidates in elections and began to issue a broadsheet in October.[27]

The "Democratic Awakening" (*Demokratischer Aufbruch* or DA) launched a more moderate appeal for renewal two days later. The Protestant clergymen Friedrich Schorlemmer, Rainer Eppelmann, Probst Heino Falcke, Bishop Gottfried Forck, and church lawyer Wolfgang Schnur sought to counteract the splintering of the opposition by creating a common organization. Their September 14 flyer proposed "a socialist society on a democratic basis," including human rights to speech and travel, educational and penal reforms, and the ending of SED dominance. At the same time the DA demanded an ecologically sensitive economic policy, based on competition and a freer market with real prices as well as independent trade unions. Considering "present political structures" and mere discussion insufficient, this group sought to become involved in "political action."[28]

Due to its Protestant origins, the DA projected a more conservative image than the secular initiatives. In spite of professions of "social solidarity," the secret police considered it "reactionary." Though the chairman Schnur was an informer and the Stasi tried to prevent the meeting, the DA managed to constitute itself formally on October 1. When other groups refused to follow its lead "toward the common goal of an open, independent, democratic society," it gradually became more traditionalist than the rest. Because of its close religious ties, however, Democratic Awakening could use the machinery of the Protestant church and received a disproportionate share of media attention in the West.[29]

The political ferment also inspired an autonomous feminist movement. The East German constitution formally guaranteed complete sexual equality, and social policy established free day care for four-fifths of all mothers. More than nine out of ten women held jobs out of economic necessity. Informally, however, patriarchal attitudes lingered and practical obstacles proved discouraging. Because shopping and cleaning were more time-consuming than in the West, women suffered more from dual pressures of jobs and home. Because the official Democratic Women's League failed to address problems like unequal pay, women discussed inequality in church, university, and literary circles. When the civic movement did not respond to feminist concerns, a "violet offensive" formed on September 26 "to combat the inequality of the sexes in society." By raising consciousness and advocating reforms, these feminists sought to break with sexism in work, reproduction, government, law, and education.[30]

In early November, feminist scholars at Berlin's Humboldt University also spoke out. This circle was indignant that "women's interests do not yet play any role in the present dialogue." To create a critical awareness of "the real position of women," they demanded fundamental changes from the SED, such as quotas, attention to women's problems, a reorganization of the League, a legislative committee, sponsorship of clubs and media, male sharing of responsibilities, and improvement of services. When the government was slow to take up these questions and the Communist organization proved inflexible, a diverse group of feminists founded an Independent Women's Association (UFV) in early December. In a rousing keynote speech, Ina Merkel warned male reformers that gender problems were central to achieving democracy: "Without women, you cannot create a state to be proud of."[31]

Ironically, the last group to formalize was the Greens. Initially, ecological concerns were expressed through grassroots newsletters and networks. Since all opposition groups featured environmental protection in their programs, it did not seem necessary to create a new organization. Only when ecological issues appeared to get lost in the general upheaval did activists gather on November 5 to found a Green party. "The healing of our destroyed environment has central importance for the renewal of our society." The meeting called for a radical break with proponents of permanent economic growth and competition that threatened the survival of the planet.[32]

The Greens made the environment a higher priority than other groups. Their program demanded a "thorough ecological rebuilding of our country in sharp opposition to destructive, wasteful growth and Stalinist treatment of people, the economy, and the environment." Glaring examples of abuse were the disaster areas of Leipzig, Bitterfeld, Halle, Dresden, Chemnitz, and Cottbus. Rejecting consumer capitalism, the Greens warned that "the senseless, shortsighted desire to catch up materially" would create a Western-style "cut-throat society" in the East. Appealing for grassroots activism across borders, the ecologists promoted "a green renewal." Though some concerned persons responded, the civic movement as a whole focused on political change. After years of deprivation, most East Germans remained intent on procuring better consumer goods.[33]

Split into competing groups, the civic movement remained fragmented. Bureaucratic repression, Stasi infiltration, and expulsion of critics kept a single leader from emerging. The informality of illegal networks did not allow personal rivalries, regional conflicts, and programmatic differences to be reconciled. Dissidents followed a moral approach to politics that precluded compromise. Ideological divisions along religious, secular, and political lines kept the rising ferment from finding a single voice. Even if the "multiplicity of initiatives" proved a strength, the democratic awakening frittered away much energy in internal strife.[34]

In religious circles, the leading spokesman was Rainer Eppelmann. Short and bearded, this former mason was a charismatic pastor at the Berlin Samariterkirche. Responsive to the problems of youth, he became an early pacifist who constantly stretched the boundaries of dissent. Eppelmann was an irritant for the church hierarchy as well as the state.[35] Among intellectuals, the painter Bärbel Bohley was most prominent. Small and fragile, she was "the mother of the revolution." Pushing for artistic freedom and women's rights, she cofounded the Initiative for Peace and Human Rights (IFM). Bohley possessed great personal courage and did not mind saying unpopular things. Although both leaders were harassed and imprisoned by the Stasi, they did not get along. To topple the SED, Eppelmann advocated forming a party while Bohley remained wedded to the dream of a grassroots movement.[36]

The diverse opposition, nevertheless, sought a basis for "common political action." On October 4 the Social Democrats, IFM, Democratic Awakening, Democracy Now, New Forum, and the pacifists met to issue a joint declaration, which stated: "We are united in our will to transform state and society democratically." Leading dissenters like Ibrahim Böhme, Rainer Eppelmann, Sebastian Pflugbeil, and Wolfgang Ullmann insisted on human rights according to CSCE standards and on the release of imprisoned protesters. More dangerous for the SED was their demand for "minimal conditions for democratic elections" such as choice, secrecy, freedom, and UN control. Promising cooperation, they called upon "all GDR citizens to work with us in the democratic renewal." Read by Eppelmann to two thousand people in the Berlin Erlöserkirche, this joint declaration was an open challenge to the communist power monopoly.[37]

Despite vague references to a common nationality, the civic movement rejected reunification. "In my opinion the GDR could and should exist as an independent entity in Europe. We are a socialist country and ought to continue to be that," Jens Reich of the New Forum explained in early October to the BBC. "Of course reforms and changes are necessary, but I can't see German reunification on the agenda—I don't believe it is realistic and that we actually want it." Time and again, the opposition affirmed the need for an independent identity. Dissidents were reluctant to endorse unity because they feared Stasi reprisals such as expulsion to the West.[38]

A deeper reason for opposing reunification was the hope for an alternative to capitalism. The writer Rainer Schedlinski, another informer, argued: "In the GDR I see a chance that the experiment of socialism or a planned economy might still work, if it is legitimated democratically." According to church leader Manfred Stolpe, another consideration was the rejection of war: "The main thrust of history is today not a greater Germany, but the common effort to secure peace in Europe and the whole world." Finally, many joined the artist Bärbel Bohley in resenting the tutelage of the rich West: "We want to find our own way." All groups shared the hope that GDR renewal might de-emphasize the border and make it eventually disappear. Such opposition scruples disappointed popular reunification hopes. Signs of a persisting sense of East German identity also offered the SED the hope of recapturing the dissidents' allegiance through reform.[39]

By early October 1989, the opposition initiatives had produced a growing civic movement for reform. Gradually dissenters left the sanctuary of the Protestant church and became a public voice. Including only a few workers, this *Bürgerbewegung* drew primarily from professionals in science and technology, medicine, and teaching as well as artists who were informed enough to develop an independent point of view. Led by thirty-five to forty-five year-olds, dissent resonated "among youths and increasingly also among students of all subjects" who were impatient with the shabbiness and duplicity of their lives. In 1975 during Honecker's early rule, only 14 percent of the young rejected Marxism. But a decade later, the share of critics among youths had grown to 46 percent and by October 1989 as many as 62 percent broke with communist ideology![40]

An authentic product of the GDR, the opposition developed from within socialism. Its program was informed by Protestant aversion to politics and sought to recover the humanistic essence of Marxism. Bitter experience of Stalinist abuses inspired demands for participatory democracy that would restore bourgeois civil rights. Fear of nuclear war also motivated pacifist appeals for détente. Horror stories of capitalist exploitation generated calls for social solidarity and ecological renewal. Debasement of culture as propaganda led to insistence on intellectual freedom. In spite of some Western contacts, the opposition was not a fifth column but an indigenous protest, directed at the renewal of the GDR. Starting with a few hundred activists, the *Bürgerbewegung* grew so quickly in the fall of 1989 that it began to threaten SED rule.[41]

Patterns of Protest

The formation of political groups increased the size of the demonstrations. The mass exodus spurred critics of the regime to call for reforms in order to make East Germany a better place to live. Motivated by the same fundamental discontent as flight, the protests steadily increased from a few hundred to hundreds of thousands of participants. Western television coverage enabled acts of symbolic defiance to reach a wider audience, spreading unrest. Police brutality also generated outrage, and arrests provided a renewed reason for protest. With each successful march, more people dared to participate, since growing numbers decreased the individual risk. At the same time, the Stasi fretted over losing control.[42]

During the fortieth anniversary of the GDR on October 7, tension came to a head. A peaceful crowd of seven thousand demonstrated against election fraud in Berlin while similar protests erupted in Leipzig, Dresden, Chemnitz, Halle, Erfurt, and Potsdam. Not wanting the celebration tarnished, General Mielke reacted with massive force. Civilians in leather coats and uniformed police clubbed, pushed, and grabbed about a thousand demonstrators, herding them into waiting trucks. After a bumpy ride through dark streets, those arrested were dumped in jails. Many were beaten and mercilessly interrogated about imagined treasonous conspiracies. They were kept standing for hours, denied food, water, and sleep and could use the bathroom only with a guard. After signing incriminating confessions, first-time dissidents were usually warned and let go after a day or two. Repeat protesters were fined and presumptive ringleaders remained jailed, cut off from legal recourse or friends. Instead of cowing the crowds, this brutal repression only spurred them on.[43]

The threat of bloodshed only intensified the commitment to nonviolence. Exceptional courage on both sides eventually led to the renunciation of force. In the spirit of religious pacifism, demonstrators practiced civil disobedience and rejected provocations by secret agents who tried to supply a pretext for Stasi reprisals. Compared to the uniformed might of the state, the weak protesters had nothing but the integrity of their cause. Since the authorities risked their careers, they had more difficulty deciding in favor of restraint. Even Communists were appalled by the repression in China, which contradicted their professed humanism. President Gorbachev had made it abundantly clear that the Red Army would not put down domestic unrest as it had in 1953. Honecker's rigid rejection of perestroika frustrated many SED intellectuals who were ready to try some reforms. The unresolved succession crisis prevented any clear signal from East Berlin, allowing local leaders unusual latitude.[44]

The first break in the confrontation came in Dresden. The former Saxon capital was still reeling from police actions against refugees trying to flee on freedom trains. Disturbed by more than 1,300 arrests, Mayor Wolfgang Berghofer met with a committee of twenty citizens on the morning of October 9 to initiate a peaceful dialogue. The second rupture in the cycle of violence took place in Leipzig later that same day in the negotiations between three prominent intellectuals and three district secretaries. After this local agreement had prevented mass carnage, Egon Krenz decided to hold the Stasi in check, preferring to combat dissent politically. The final step was the unprecedented ADN wire service report about the demonstration of 110,000 Leipzigers on October 16. It broke the official silence and signalled toleration of dissent to the entire GDR.[45]

Through mass marches the SED sought control of the streets to symbolize its dominance over public space. The SED loved parades to prove its popularity by prepared applause. Official marches were carefully staged by the party and the Stasi, with participants ordered to appear long in advance. It was a dubious honor for a factory or a school to be deputized, since it meant endless waiting, walking, and waving of prefabricated banners. On the reviewing stand the party bigwigs received the programmed acclamations of their subjects and the precise number of people lining the streets was predetermined! Misled by the cheers of massive May day or Free Democratic Youth (FDJ) parades, Erich Honecker believed that such command performances expressed genuine popular support.[46]

The demonstrations of the civic movement were quite different. Made known by word of mouth, called by crudely printed flyers, or announced in church, the marches formed spontaneously. There were no clear leaders or followers; onlookers melted into the ranks and marchers dropped out when they had enough. Protesters placed candles before the hated Stasi headquarters and kept rowdies from using force. Collective chanting called for political reforms, new leaders, and free travel. Hand-made placards bore scrawled slogans: "Now or never—freedom and democracy." By the end of October leading dissidents as well as reform Communists began to address the crowds. Once overcome, pervasive fear turned into a euphoric hope. The joyful solidarity of strangers gave many who had never dared express their opinion the courage to speak out. Repeated week after week, the protests fed on themselves. As a manifestation of rising unrest, the mass marches became a heady lesson in direct democracy.[47]

Posters and chants carried an unmistakable message. With legalization, choruses grew more assertive and banners reflected the shifting public mood. On October 9, seventy thousand citizens of Leipzig begged earnestly, "No violence," calling "Gorbi, Gorbi!" and "We are no rowdies—we are the people!" A week later, 110,000 demonstrators were ready to shout their demands: "We want reforms!" and "Allow the New Forum!" Occasional signs called for "Freedom of the press" and "Free travel for all." On October 23, the 225,000 gathered in the Saxon city carried "a forest of banners and placards" with such demands as "Let the people lead" or "The cart is stuck in the mud, the old drivers must go!" New-found freedom inspired acerbic wit: "Stay in the country and fight daily," one poster varied the proverbial injunction to work fairly. Another alluded to Krenz's wolfish teeth: "When Egon speaks of reforms, remember the three little pigs." A banner captured the democratic spirit: "As we demonstrate today, so we shall live tomorrow."[48]

On October 30, the crowd swelled to 350,000 in spite of police obstruction. Growing freedom made the chants more daring and the posters more biting. Protesters demanded free elections and proclaimed "The Wall must go!" as well as "The rule of law is the best state security." A lonely placard also quoted the forbidden verse of the GDR anthem: "Germany, united fatherland." In response to the restrictive draft of a travel law, 450,000 attacked the party's failure to provide foreign currency on November 6: "Thirty days and no cash, Egon you are trash." More generally, the people intoned: "SED, its hurts to see." Though angry shouts of "Lazy dogs" and "Henchmen" were directed against the secret police, the protesters refrained from force. While thousands called for the fall of the Wall, a new chorus began to sweep the crowd: "Germany, fatherland; Germany, fatherland."[49]

TABLE 2. Estimated GDR Protest Size, 1989 (in thousands)

Week	September 25	2	9	October 16	23	30	November 6
Leipzig	6.5	20	70	110	225	350	450
Berlin			7	3	36	500	55
Other		11	60	77	414	309	550+
Total	6.5	31	137	190	675	1,159	1,055+

From the "heroic" city of Leipzig demonstrations swiftly spread throughout the GDR. Though the SED desperately tried to head off unrest by promising reform, frustrated citizens insisted on taking to the streets. By the third weekend of October, protests spilled from leading cities such as Chemnitz, Dresden, Erfurt, Magdeburg, or Rostock into smaller towns like Altenburg, Gera, Jena, Neubrandenburg, Plauen, and Weimar (see Table 2).[50] In spite of shorter days and rainy weather, participation exploded from a few thousand to more than one million between late September and early November. The protests grew inexorably once they articulated the deep dissatisfaction with the post-Stalinist regime.[51]

Ever wider circles of society participated in the demonstrations. The first hundreds recruited themselves from the youthful subculture that had been experimenting with alternative life-styles. The next thousands derived from circles of intellectuals and white collar employees who supported human rights. The following tens of thousands consisted of older, traditional skilled laborers and younger workers who wanted to get better consumer goods. The final hundreds of thousands were a cross-section of the previously apolitical population, which sought to seize the chance for fundamental reforms.[52] Eventually the movement grew so irresistible that it engulfed large segments of the party, the bureaucracy, and the secret police. In the demonstrations, an administratively suppressed society constituted itself as active citizenry.

Street protests triggered a frenzy of dialogue. Instead of calming criticism, the SED's willingness to discuss changes encouraged people to speak up at home and at work. On October twelve students at the Berlin Humboldt University demanded political and academic freedom. Three days later a scholarly panel at Leipzig focused on SED mistakes such as the manipulation of information. "We want to talk about everything," district secretary Roland Wötzel said, promising he would work for reforms such as travel freedom. Artists, writers, and actors passed resolutions in favor of human rights and performed texts that celebrated free speech. Intent on controlling dissent through debate, party leaders tried to discipline unruly members; but docile papers suddenly printed unaccustomed reports of controversial disputes.[53]

Still officially proscribed, opposition groups boldly demanded "a democratic dialogue." The New Forum strove to use the urgent problems as a lever for toppling the post-Stalinist system. A three-hour debate in the Leipzig Gewandhaus on October 22 touched on many issues, ranging from political freedom to educational reform. Academic seminars, party circles, mass organizations, and other groups vented the thousand little frustrations of daily life and more fundamental questions like civic rights. The walls of many buildings were plastered with flyers, declarations, and announcements. On October 29, pent-up "resentment against long impotence" erupted, in caustic speeches against the city government. Even in factories, formerly silent workers began to speak out, calling for the resignation of union bosses. In a raucous assembly at Buna, SED secretaries were booed by fed up "proletarians" who suddenly knew: "We have the power!"[54]

Impatient intellectuals sought to push public dialogue toward concrete results. On October 28 the Deutsche Theater in Berlin celebrated the rehabilitation of Walter Janka, a victim of Stalinism purged in 1957. That same evening three thousand people crammed into the Erlöserkirche to protest against "the sleep of reason" and to discuss the brutal repression of the October 7 demonstration. Dissident writers, including Volker Braun, Christoph Hein, Helga Königsdorf, Stefan Hermlin, Heiner Müller, and Christa Wolf, gathered to dispel "the night-birds of fear, mistrust, depression, and despair." Thoughtfully, poetically, or satirically, these literary stars professed solidarity with the democratic awakening. Remembering the suppression of the Prague Spring of 1968, they distrusted the sincerity of the post-Honecker leadership, demanding instead freedom of speech and information and free elections.[55]

Frantic SED efforts to placate opposition by offering changes were too transparent a ploy to fool its intellectual critics. Wary citizens "question peacefully in the street and patiently in discussion, so that they can do more than believe and hope in the future. They want to control, no longer just trust, they want to choose and that presupposes choice." Not content with a paper constitution, the author Günter de Bruyn called for "not merely a formal but a real division of power." Others demanded thorough reforms in order to restore credibility. For the sake of socialism with a human face, these writers demanded a more fundamental renewal than the politicians were willing to concede. As a small positive sign, the SED pulled the plug on the anticapitalist propaganda of Eduard von Schnitzler's infamous "black channel" on East German television.[56]

On November 4 the protests climaxed at the Alexanderplatz in Berlin. When prominent actors and entertainers called for free speech and assembly, between five hundred thousand and one million people responded. Permitted reluctantly, the biggest demonstration in GDR history was peaceful, festive, and orderly, thanks to a security partnership with the police. In the immense forest of banners, popular wit coined new slogans, such as "Asterix into the Politburo" or "DDR = Direct Democratic Reforms!" Mixing biting chansons with stirring oratory, the speakers included fourteen theater people, six writers, three clergymen, two students and one New Forum member along with five SED and LDPD politicians. Expressing gratitude to the illegal demonstrators for initiating the public dialogue, lawyer Gregor Gysi proposed the strengthening of human rights. To restore public trust, prominent artists demanded an independent investigation of police brutality.[57]

This demonstration inaugurated a "revolutionary renewal." When former Stasi chief Markus Wolf and Berlin SED secretary Günter Schabowski tried to defend the Stasi or the party, they were mercilessly booed. In contrast, demands for legalizing the New Forum and calls for the resignation of the government earned ringing applause. "It is as if someone had opened a window after all the years of intellectual, economic, and political stagnation," writer Stefan Heym commented. "In the last week we have overcome our speechlessness and have begun learning how to walk tall." Novelist Christa Wolf suggested ironically: "What if there were socialism and no one left?!" To overcome distrust, journalists demanded free media, artists called for independent unions, and students urged academic freedom. Summing up the crowd's feelings, writer Christoph Hein urged the creation of a democratic socialism "which does not make a travesty of this word."[58]

Millions of spectators participated vicariously in the demonstrations via television. The East German state network reported the entire Berlin protest live and formerly staid newscasts of the *Aktuelle Kamera* suddenly became fascinating events. The new openness of GDR media coverage led to a flood of critical exposés that tried to address problems long denied. Though Western journalists were still shadowed by Stasi operatives, their broadcasts grew less circumspect and began to capture the rising excitement. Reporters who had considered the GDR beat a form of banishment raced to Berlin in search of the story of the decade. While West German newspapers had already begun to note demonstrations in mid-September, it took the foreign press until the second week of October to switch attention from the exodus to the protests.[59]

Media pictures and commentaries reversed established clichés. East Germans who were formerly cowed suddenly marched in the streets with visible pride. Previously mute masses were now finding a voice in chants and on banners. Potentially violent crowds were proceeding silently, in self-imposed order, holding candles in their hands. Even foreign skeptics who had considered the Honecker system the most solid in the Communist bloc began to realize that something dramatic was happening. The nonviolent methods borrowed from the U.S. civil rights movement and the goals of achieving human rights created instant sympathy for the *Bürgerbewegung* abroad. Before most Germans had sorted out their own feelings, perceptive commentators in other countries interpreted the rise of dissent as a prelude to inevitable unification. Abroad, amazement therefore mingled with an undercurrent of growing concern.[60]

Eastern unrest forced Bonn's politicians to devise a proper response.

News reports supported the democratic awakening but criticized its organizational disarray and programmatic confusion. Since the civic movement did not fit the FRG political spectrum, Western parties had difficulty finding suitable GDR counterparts. In initial contacts with various
reform groups, experienced professionals often patronized East German
amateurs and used them for their own ends.[61] Except for the left wing of
the SPD, which hoped for reforms within the SED, politicians in Bonn
shed few tears about the travails of Erich Honecker's regime. Nonetheless,
foreign policy analysts worried about a deterioration of relations with the
GDR, business circles loathed the instability that threatened, and peace
groups feared for the future of détente. While refugee functionaries and
anticommunists welcomed unrest as a chance for unity, leftist spokesmen
warned against nationalist interference and advocated internal changes in
the GDR.[62]

President Richard von Weizsäcker tried to resolve these contradictions
through a reform dialogue. He suggested talking with dissidents *and* the
SED so as to make the division obsolete. While the SPD vacillated, Helmut Kohl offered East Berlin incentives for change: "If the GDR leadership begins fundamental political and economic reforms, then the FRG
government under my leadership is ready to support this new course
through comprehensive and far-reaching cooperation." In his state of the
nation address on November 8, the chancellor praised the courage of
protesters and called for "free self-determination of all Germans." Balancing refugee solidarity with help for reforms, Kohl cautiously tried to
advance unity by increasing GDR freedom while at the same time accepting greater European responsibility.[63]

Toward a Civil Society

The recovery of personal self-respect propelled the democratic awakening
and broke the spell of SED repression. In the fall of 1989, the tension
between public conformity and suppressed private feeling suddenly
snapped as citizens experienced a new resolve: "We are staying here," they
said; "We want reforms." The shared elation of the marches, banners, and
chants empowered the powerless and inspired the vision of a genuine
democratic community. "Isn't it fantastic how people throw off their fear
and lift their heads these days! It was clear to me that things could no
longer go on as before," a young mathematician confided to his pastor in
mid-October. Though the economy was failing, he "would never have
thought that things would happen so fast. This borders on a miracle."
Successful protest brought democratic assertiveness: "The most important
thing is that we are not content with little concessions, but extend reforms
to all areas so as to break open and renew the whole system."[64]

Where did normal citizens find the courage to revolt? In contrast to
the Leninist model of revolution, unrest did not stem from class struggles

but from rising expectations. Instead of a cadre party, the driving force was a loose network of dissidents. The decision to act was based more on moral feeling than on rational calculation. Even if every march reduced the risk, the threat of reprisals loomed large until October 9. Ultimately, the awakening was a psychological explosion which tried to regain individual self-respect. The tension between private criticism and public conformity had become so unbearable as to drive people onto the streets. The solidarity of the like-minded broke through solitude and created a new sense of community. The catharsis of protest purged the atmosphere of long-time repression by the SED.[65]

Above all, the *Bürgerbewegung* sought the restoration of "civil society." To shed total state control, opposition programs demanded the creation of a quasi-political public space for free speech and association. Demonstrators called for the actual observance of those civil rights that existed on paper but had been sacrificed to Marxist egalitarianism in practice. Only the rule of law could curb the secret police and guarantee the free intercourse that was the foundation of all civic life. Gaining autonomy for churches, universities, and other social institutions required the abolition of the communist dictatorship, written into the constitution as "the leading role" of the party. Having learned from bitter experience, dissenters insisted on the classic division of power between legislative, executive, and judicial branches. With truly free elections, the opposition could hope to overthrow the SED government and install a reform cabinet.[66]

The struggle for civil society also aimed at direct democracy. The agenda of the civic movement was not simply an attempt to restore nineteenth-century liberal freedoms. The experience of demonstrations and discussions suggested a new twentieth century form of grassroots participation, more responsive to popular wishes than parliamentary procedures or bureaucratic decisions. Instead of returning to political parties, the reformers preferred a loose citizens' movement, consisting of networks and directed at solving practical problems. Their rejection of the inefficiency of a planned economy and interest in introducing market mechanisms were limited by a strong sense of social solidarity and ecological responsibility. Determined to regain human rights, the civic movement simultaneously sought to reinterpret and expand them.[67]

The rise of the *Bürgerbewegung* had revolutionary consequences. The eruption of demonstrations and formation of opposition groups created a broad but splintered opposition. When protest participation jumped into the tens of thousands in early October, "many progressive forces, especially members of the SED, believed the socialist political and social order of the GDR in serious danger." According to the Stasi, the leadership, recalling the uprising of 1953, feared that growing popular distrust "threatens great social shocks which the party might no longer be able to control." Since force would produce incalculable bloodshed, party leaders decided "to solve all problems with political means." Though intended as a means of safeguarding SED hegemony, the tactic of open "political

debate and dialogue with all social groups" allowed criticism of the regime's repressive structure and self-destructive policies to become public.[68]

The civic challenge accelerated the changes unleashed by the exodus.
In the GDR, the growth of an opposition compelled the SED to abandon
its old leadership and to compete in an unprecedented struggle for power.
In the Soviet Union, Mikhail Gorbachev was delighted that the GDR was
at last falling into line and hoped that reform would more effectively
stabilize the regime. In neighboring Eastern countries, dissidents felt encouraged in their own efforts for change. The surprised West Germans
welcomed the protest, hoping that internal change would improve life in
the East and lessen the division between the two Germanies. In other
Western countries, the GDR unrest evoked much sympathy coupled with
concern about the stability of the European order. To awed participants
and spectators alike, the democratic awakening suggested a popular rising
of elemental force. After the heady days of October neither Germany nor
Europe would ever be the same.[69]

3

Overthrowing
Post-Stalinist Rule

The fortieth anniversary of the GDR failed to stabilize the tottering regime. Though the people hoped for a signal of change, the SED staged elaborate celebrations to demonstrate the superiority of Communism. On October 3, veterans of the antifascist resistance gathered to demonstrate the historical legitimacy of the East German state. Three days later Erich Honecker regaled four thousand dignitaries, seventy foreign delegations, and a national TV audience with accounts of economic triumphs such as the production of a mega-chip. In response to the mass exodus, he denounced the "boundless slander campaign against the GDR." When one hundred thousand members of the party youth FDJ marched with torches to affirm their undying loyalty, the crowd shouted "Gorbi, Gorbi" to express its disappointment with the immobility of the old guard.[1]

After the customary military parade on October 7, Mikhail Gorbachev tried to explain the logic of perestroika. But a rigid Honecker wanted only to be complimented on his life's work. The Soviet visitor spoke frankly to the SED politburo about the need for courageous changes: "If we fall behind, life will punish us immediately." When hostile protesters spoiled the official reception by demanding real reforms, the police brutally beat them down. In many East German eyes and in copious foreign media comments, the staged celebrations only demonstrated the weakness of the regime. Russian calls for action signaled a lack of international respect, and mass arrests illustrated a growing loss of domestic support. Even some SED politicians began to realize that "Honecker must go."[2]

After the celebrations, pragmatic Communists finally challenged the post-Stalinist leadership from the inside. Mass exodus, popular demonstrations, and Gorbachev's visit encouraged criticism. But the party's prohibition of factions, the rebels' political isolation, and General Secretary Honecker's presumed popularity held doubts in check. On October 8, the heir apparent Egon Krenz overcame his scruples and presented a reform platform to central committee members Wolfgang Herger, Siegfried Lorenz, and Günter Schabowski. When Honecker angrily rejected this attack, Krenz insisted: "Erich, it is not directed at you, but I am concerned about our country." Two days later, the politburo debated a FDJ report about the deteriorating mood of the young, as well as the Krenz critique. Though some leaders failed to comprehend the full implications of this confrontation, all agreed with Stasi chief Mielke that "the situation is extraordinarily grave."[3]

Craftily, Honecker defended his power. His lieutenants Günter Mittag and Joachim Herrmann joined Krenz and Schabowski in redrafting the final version of the policy declaration. Their confusing text, published on October 12 in *Neues Deutschland*, mixed old propaganda with new expressions of concern, such as "socialism needs everyone." Western observers considered it a hopeful sign, but dissidents like Bärbel Bohley remained unimpressed. On the following day the district secretaries Hans Modrow, Hannes Chemnitzer, and Günther Jahn also criticized the SED leadership, and ideologue Kurt Hager publicly signaled flexibility. On October 13, however, Honecker gained a reprieve by obtaining the approval of the bloc parties for a modest course correction. Though Western papers predicted his imminent fall, the GDR media pretended that all was well.[4]

The struggle between the old guard and the successor generation swiftly came to a head. Without established procedures for change, the transfer of power required a palace coup. After compelling Honecker to renounce force against protesters, Krenz persuaded the titular government head Willi Stoph to take the initiative in demanding the general secretary's removal. Then he consulted with union boss Harry Tisch and Berlin district chief Schabowski on strategy. Long dissatisfied with the lack of leadership, Stasi head Mielke supported the change. Relieved when the Leipzig protests stayed peaceful, Honecker remained unaware of the plot.[5]

The decisive session of the politburo on October 17 opened with a bombshell. As an additional item to the agenda, Willi Stoph introduced "the removal of Erich Honecker and the election of Egon Krenz as general secretary." Stunned and hurt, Honecker listened to his trusted associates explain the need for new leadership: "Such a decision has long been overdue." Even a quick switch of sides could not rescue his henchmen Mittag and Herrmann. In a face-saving gesture, the official explanation listed declining health as the reason for Honecker's retirement. The following day the district secretaries unanimously approved the change. On Honecker's recommendation the larger Central Committee endorsed Egon Krenz's appointment as general secretary, chair of the council of state, and head of the defense committee. While the deposed leader thought himself a victim of "a grand conspiracy," his successor took the helm, eager to steer a more flexible course.[6] Would Krenz be only a "transition figure," as derisively predicted by the Western press? Or would he become, as he himself hoped, a German Gorbachev?[7]

The Hardliners' Fall

To dissidents "Stalinism" became a veritable code word for the East German system. Party apologists claimed that they had overthrown the few old men who were responsible for the evil, so as to preserve socialism. But opponents argued that the entire regime was oppressive and needed to be transformed.[8] Such polemics confuse the historical with the structural meaning of the term. In particular, Stalinism refers to Josef Stalin's regime of terror, which promoted Soviet collectivization and industrialization during the 1930s. In spite of achievements, it was marked by the arbitrary rule of a single leader, the ludicrous cult of his personality, and the rampant power of the secret police. More generally, Stalinism suggests a crude form of communist control. It connotes party dominance through an apparatus, justified as dictatorship of the proletariat.

Under Honecker, the regime lost its original harshness and softened into "post-Stalinism." Because of its location on the frontline of the cold war, the GDR did not dare break openly with its Stalinist legacy. In a limited "de-Stalinization" the SED leaders turned from primitive police-state methods to more subtle measures of control such as economic incentives and media manipulation. But even after the elimination of irrational aspects of repression, many problematic features of Josef Stalin's legacy lived on. The regime abandoned neither the primacy of the party, the principle of democratic centralism, the dominance of the nomenclatura, nor the information monopoly of the government. In effect, the Stalinist brutality of the early years gradually gave way to a post-Stalinist bureaucracy.[9] How did this "administrative Socialism" actually work?

The government of the GDR functioned like an elaborate holding company of the SED. Written into the 1968 constitution, the leading role of "the Marxist-Leninist party" became in practice the dictatorship of one man. By dominating the Communist party, the general secretary ran both state and society. Two dozen close advisors were gathered in the politburo, which made all crucial decisions. Setting the agenda and presiding at meetings, the general secretary dominated its proceedings and shared power only as he saw fit. About two hundred delegates formed the party Central Committee, which had to approve major policies. But it served as a sounding board rather than as a source of initiative. Below them, the secretaries of the fifteen districts from the Baltic to the Erzgebirge implemented policy and reported back to the politburo. Their subordinates wrestled with day-to-day problems and tried to keep the system going.[10]

In contrast to the party, the official government had little authority. The chairman of the council of ministers was the titular head of state. The

prime minister supervised a cabinet that could do nothing without approval of the corresponding Central Committee (ZK) sections. The parliament, called *Volkskammer*, rarely met and only to rubber stamp party
decisions. As a postwar remnant, Christian (CDU), liberal (LDPD), nationalist (NDPD), and peasants' (DBD) parties were allowed to survive to
mobilize middle-class constituencies. But they were allied in the "democratic bloc," controlled by the SED. Mass organizations such as the trade
union (FDGB), party youth (FDJ), and women's league (DFD) functioned
as transmitters of party orders rather than as representatives of their membership. Democratic centralism maximized top-down control and mini-
mized feedback from below.[11]

Communist ideology was the conceptual glue that held the disparate
pieces together. To its partisans it possessed obvious advantages.
Marxism-Leninism provided a scientific interpretation of the past that
explained the problems of the present. By drawing on the humanistic
values of the Western heritage, it suggested an appealing future of justice
and equality. Moreover, it prescribed methods of class struggle that inspired a righteous crusade of progressives against reactionary forces.
Though some East German intellectuals tried to develop Marxism into a
critical perspective, most GDR politicians used the Leninist tradition
dogmatically. Ideological debate revolved around how to apply the time-
less truths of the Red classics to the current situation. Since democratic or
anarchist alternatives within socialism were prohibited, Marxism-
Leninism became the sole language of politics.[12]

Dogmatism became a chief weakness of SED rule. To the elite, called
"nomenclatura," the doctrinal foundation gave an enormous self-confidence.
It divided the world clearly into friends and foes while providing an
altruistic rationale for the rulers' privileges. For many intellectuals who
resented the crudeness of party propaganda, the underlying ethos nonetheless remained attractive. They could voice criticism only by invoking
different shadings of the sacred texts. Among the masses, ceaseless "ML"
indoctrination produced an apathetic retreat into the niches of private life.
Dogmatism also blocked perception of certain problems that should not
exist, since Marxism-Leninism did not allow for them. While pragmatists
tried to deal with reality, the fog of ideology often covered current difficulties like a suffocating blanket.[13]

Bureaucratized dogma left little room for frank debate. The "Wandlitz
syndrome" (living in a walled-in forest compound outside of the capital)
cut the leadership off from the daily cares of the ordinary people. Its
coveted privileges of chauffeured cars and Western shopping subtly cor-
rupted judgment, since these luxuries were contingent on Honecker's
benevolence. The secrecy of Stasi reports allowed Mielke to manipulate
information, rendering it impervious to challenge because there could be
no independent corroboration. The injunctions of party discipline and
sanctions against deviant leaders inhibited free discussion even in the

inner circle. In Honecker's closed system, debate functioned as a ritual of assent rather than as a source of critical information or alternative views.[14]

Public discourse was carefully orchestrated, with all spontaneity removed to avoid embarrassing surprises. Stasi surveillance drove criticism underground to prepolitical areas of personal trust among friends at work, fellow believers at church, or relatives at home. Slip-ups in information control were damaging. The joint SPD-SED peace paper of 1987 did not just transmit politburo views but also presented reformist arguments that triggered much unintended debate in local party cells. When the leadership confused the bearer of ill tidings with his negative message, reporting grew ever less truthful. The rather unreliable economic statistics are a case in point, since they documented plans rather than performance. In the late 1980s, East German leaders largely lived in a make-believe world, unaware of either actual economic conditions or mounting popular discontent. The immobility of the SED stemmed not only from its post-Stalinist politics but also from its aged leaders' loss of touch with reality.[15]

For eighteen years hardliner Erich Honecker ruled the GDR with an iron hand. Born in 1912 into a communist miner's family in the Saar Basin, he was apprenticed as a roofer. After agitation training in Moscow, he fought the Nazis until the Gestapo caught him in 1935 and incarcerated him for a decade. Honecker claimed to have survived the Third Reich penitentiary by faith in Marx and strength of character: "I was quite self-reliant." After Soviet liberation, he made his way to Berlin, worked for the SED, and founded its party youth organization, the FDJ. In contrast to skeptical intellectuals, the self-educated Honecker was a true believer for whom ideology was revealed truth, indispensable for building a better society.[16]

After toppling the aging Walter Ulbricht with Soviet help in 1971, Honecker surprised with his flexibility. In contrast to his authoritarian predecessor, he allowed rock music, Western television reception, more foreign travel, and cultural experimentation. By proclaiming "the unity of social and economic policy," he concluded a social contract with the population, offering increased prosperity in exchange for political conformity. Like Stalin, he built his power on personnel decisions, creating a loyal clientele by making all higher appointments himself. With the compulsively secretive Mielke, he directed the Stasi octopus that stretched its tentacles everywhere. With the pliant Herrmann, he dictated the media line, spread daily through instructions from Berlin. Only in the economic realm did he admit ignorance and rely on the cynical Mittag to force production into line with his political goals. The "smoldering disagreement" between pro-Moscow security hardliners and pro-Western economic specialists stalemated the politburo. This Byzantine structure produced a kind of "socialist absolutism."[17]

Soviet perestroika and Eastern European ferment worked as a delayed solvent within the GDR. Once resisted as a compulsory subject, the

Russian language grew genuinely popular as a conduit to the exciting debates in Moscow. When the East German economy stalled, nationalist disdain for Polish chaos gave way to interest in the emerging freedoms among neighboring countries. As loyal critics, prominent writers like Christa Wolf pushed to expand the boundaries of legitimate discourse. In a much-discussed play, Christoph Hein satirized the politburo's immobility by portraying a loss of faith in the Holy Grail by the knights of the round table.[18] Leading SED intellectuals like the historian Jürgen Kuczynski, former spymaster Markus Wolf, and the jurist Jens-Uwe Heuer began to advocate democratic socialism in print.[19] Within and without the party, unofficial debate eroded orthodoxy.

Gorbachev's rising star caused Honecker's popularity to fade. During the paranoid Brezhnev years, the East German leader had gained much popular support by advocating disarmament and easing German-German relations. When the Soviet Union began to liberalize, the lack of change in the GDR was particularly galling to the intellectuals and the people at large. Since he personally disliked the flamboyant Gorbachev, Honecker held out against perestroika, determined to wait for Moscow's return to Stalinism. Long resented by other Warsaw Pact nations for its superior economic performance, East Germany became isolated in a quickly evolving Eastern Bloc. Internal critics attacked party dictatorship, complained about inadequate supplies, deplored travel restrictions and denounced the lack of free speech. In November 1988, Honecker's prohibition of Soviet anti-Stalinist films and the German edition of the magazine *Sputnik* incensed 180,000 subscribers and triggered eight hundred protest petitions from SED faithful. While eleven thousand party members resigned in 1988, another twenty-three thousand were expelled![20]

In the end, Honecker became the victim of his own dictatorial success. Official acclaim as well as his isolation gave him a false sense of security and led him to underestimate the breach in the Iron Curtain, public disaffection with the regime, and the deterioration of the economy. Honecker's unwillingness to share power left the country leaderless during the decisive months in the early fall, and gave the politburo a chance to analyze the crisis on its own. But when he returned from surgery, Honecker was preoccupied with the coming anniversary, and failed to see the SED's vaunted unity fracture under pressure from below. "We have to go our own way," he insisted to a confidante. "We cannot permit what is happening [in Russia]. We must deal with the few crackpots which are concerning us now."[21]

Younger politburo members rebelled and opportunists switched sides. Since they were not part of the original builders' generation, Egon Krenz and Berlin district chief Schabowski opted for a more flexible course. Dissatisfied district leaders like Modrow and former Stasi mastermind Wolf advocated an open dialogue with opposition forces. At the universities, reform Marxists discussed the outlines of a more attractive socialist democracy. Without instructions from above, apparatchiks became disoriented. Party members grew scared and irritated, unsure how to respond to the criticism hurled against them in offices and factories. When Honecker insisted on celebrating the founding of the GDR without confronting the exodus, the demonstrations, or economic stagnation, his political credit was used up. To save the system through more popular policies, the successor cohort finally mustered the courage to overthrow the hated gerontocracy.[22]

The Pragmatists' Failure

Honecker's successor Egon Krenz was himself a product of the GDR system. Born in 1937 into a Mecklenburg servant's family, he went to school during the postwar reconstruction and was caught up in the enthusiasm of building a better socialist world. Trained as a teacher and dabbling in journalism, he joined the party youth group in 1953 and quickly advanced because of his engaging smile, uncommon devotion, and organizational talent. After volunteering for military service, Krenz studied for three years in Moscow to become a member of the nomenclatura. In 1974, Honecker picked him as chairman of the state youth organization (FDJ) to help secure the loyalty of the young to the SED. Even if he sometimes resented his role as "professional young man," Krenz did his job so well that in 1983 he became a full member of the politburo in charge of legal, security, and youth issues.[23]

Eastern hints and Western headlines treated Krenz as "crown prince" designate. In this ceremonial role, he participated in the party decisions and represented the GDR on travels abroad. But his lack of real power proved frustrating and led to rumors of alcoholism. As a way out of this personal predicament, Soviet perestroika seemed attractive, since it promised party-sponsored reform without loss of control. The public had little confidence in Krenz, however, believing he had authorized election fraud, supported Chinese repression, and ordered force against demonstrators. "They could hardly have found anyone worse," a Leipzig mail carrier fumed. Because of their distrust of the new leader, demonstrators tried to rhyme: "Egon Krenz, we aren't your fans!"[24]

On October 18 Krenz announced a drastic change of course. In a programmatic speech to a national TV audience, he attempted to wrap himself in Gorbachev's mantle. Candidly, he admitted economic problems such as "irregularity in production," lack of technological innovation, and "inefficiency in exporting." Though he saw no need for the New Forum, he welcomed "a sincere domestic dialogue" with critical citizens. Rejecting talk of reunification, he insisted that "socialism on German soil is not up for grabs." Concretely, Krenz set four priorities. To cease living beyond its means, the GDR had to salvage its economy with fresh investments. To regain the dissidents' loyalty, it had to improve "socialist human rights." To respond to popular wishes, it had to liberalize travel rules. To capture rising civic energy, it had to initiate a novel dialogue. By confronting "the seriousness of the situation," Krenz sought to seize "the great chance" to establish a more credible socialism.[25]

This curious performance managed to alienate almost everyone. With his dark suit, striped tie, and enormous teeth, Egon Krenz looked more like a used car salesman than a statesman whom one could trust. Reading virtually the same text on television as to the ZK was a public relations blunder. What smacked of sedition to party old-timers seemed unnecessarily tepid to young dissidents. The new leader also undermined his credibility by using stale SED vocabulary to sell his fresh goals. Though his speech indicated greater realism than Honecker's celebratory rhetoric, it failed to sketch a compelling new vision. Krenz spoke more of rectifying glaring abuses than of attractive vistas for the future. Since the old guard had stifled debate on genuine alternatives, its successors had no conceptual basis upon which to outline new programs.[26]

The key metaphor of change, the "turn" (*Wende*), did not go far enough. As Christa Wolf noted perceptively, it merely implied a different tack while sailing to the same goal. In the party, traditional "concrete heads" were terrified and reform Marxists dejected. Only pragmatists or apparatchiks embraced the new secretary. Distrusting the same old faces, the public labeled them "wrynecks" (*Wendehälse*), strange birds who could turn their necks completely around. The opposition was most disappointed of all. Even if it welcomed the different tone, the New Forum distrusted "push-button glasnost" without guarantees that it would not be reversed. Though delighted by Honecker's fall, Western leaders like Chancellor Kohl called for substantive political reforms. While foreign editorials treated Krenz as a stage villain, commentators who knew him personally asked that the new man be given a chance.[27]

In consolidating his power, Egon Krenz made symbolic gestures that suggested political liberalization. To break the momentum of the exodus, he immediately ordered the preparation of a new travel law. To dampen the demonstrations, he faced dissatisfied workers in a Berlin factory, promising "to tackle all those problems together." As a signal of responsiveness to church critics, he met with Protestant bishop Werner Leich. Journalists continued to demand media freedom, however, and artists called for "legally safeguarding dialogue" with all opponents. Trying to restore trust, Krenz made the Berlin police justify its use of force against protesters and initiate a thorough investigation of the numerous complaints. When angry citizens charged that the new course was a trap, Berlin party chief Schabowski swore that "the party, the ZK, and General Secretary Krenz are serious" in their commitment to change.[28]

To cement formal authority, the Volkskammer elected Krenz as head of state on October 24. The new leader claimed to be delighted with an unprecedented fifty-two negative votes. But Democracy Now distrusted his "dialogue between clashing ideas and opinions," and held him responsible for the crisis. When lawyers demanded human rights, Schabowski informally met with the New Forum to show that discussions with the opposition had begun. As a reward for embracing perestroika in the GDR, Soviet President Gorbachev invited the new leader to Moscow. To neutralize Bonn's unification pressure, Krenz talked with Chancellor Kohl by phone about improving inter-German relations. From the beginning, the successors were caught between rising popular expectations and their limited ability to make concessions.[29]

In subsequent weeks the gap between reform promises and actual performance widened. On October 27, the government declared an amnesty for border violations and desertion from the Republic. But skeptics pointed out that the restoration of travel to Czechoslovakia fell short of establishing the human right of free movement. Members of the bloc parties within the government coalition began to throw off their accustomed servility. The chairman of the liberal LDPD, Manfred Gerlach, called for more democracy and the legalization of the New Forum. Critics within the Christian CDU demanded "reforms and renewal" with real elections, rule of law, and freedom of religion. At about the same time Democracy Now suggested a referendum on the leading role of the SED. Party members grew increasingly confused over how to respond.[30]

Through limited concessions Krenz sought to dampen popular unrest. In "Sunday discussions" in Berlin, more than twenty-two thousand aroused citizens complained to district party chief Schabowski and Mayor Erhard Krack about political immobility, police brutality, elite privileges, election fraud, media manipulation, suppression of dissent, and dozens of other irritants. On October 31 planning chief Gerhard Schürer shocked the politburo by disclosing the full extent of economic deterioration "which [threatened] the solvency of the GDR." Only fundamental reforms coupled with outside help could avoid a decline of the standard of living by 25–30 percent. Through his Moscow visit on November 1 Egon Krenz sought Soviet support and hoped to make his policy of renewal "irreversible." But in his press conference on the same day, he again rejected opening the Wall, moving toward reunification, or giving up the SED leadership claim. Since the party wanted to contain debate within its own ranks, it continued to be driven by events and never succeeded in capturing the lead in reform.[31]

During the first days of November the leadership crisis deepened. Since old faces were proving incapable of pursuing new policies, the trade unions toppled Tisch, several districts threw out their secretaries, and the bloc parties CDU and NDPD forced out their heads. On November 3, Egon Krenz announced on television the removal of old-timers Hermann Axen, Kurt Hager, Erich Mielke, Erich Mückenberger, and Alfred Neumann from the politburo. To show the sincerity of the new beginning, he sketched the outlines of a SED action program that called for political reform, truthful information, human rights, economic restructuring, and renewal of education. Unimpressed by promises that had been broken before, the opposition called for free elections and freedom of speech.[32]

Three days after the Alexanderplatz demonstration, the old Willi Stoph cabinet resigned. In factories and homes there was spontaneous jubilation. Berlin marchers shouted "all power to the people and not to the SED." The tenth session of the Central Committee on the following day ratified the resignation of the politburo and reduced its size. Since the party ranks blamed the old guard, the ZK elected less tainted figures such as Hans Modrow, Wolfgang Herger, and Gerhard Schürer instead. Pushed forward by the "mood of rebellion," Egon Krenz scathingly denounced the Stalinist leadership for fueling the "political crisis." An unprecedented demonstration of ten thousand party activists meanwhile intoned, "socialism means change without relapse." As proof of good faith, the new government legally recognized the New Forum.[33]

On November 9, the new leadership gambled on opening the Wall. Approved by Gorbachev, the easing of travel restrictions was a desparate bid to regain credibility. Because the security forces were overwhelmed by the refugees, the Ministry of the Interior proposed the breach in the border and the ZK ratified the change without discussing its far-reaching effect. Though the people were overjoyed, this long-awaited concession failed to stabilize SED rule. The politburo hardly imagined that 5.2 million Easterners would visit their Western cousins within the first four days! Instead of stopping the flight, the removal of the barrier redoubled emigration. Refugees ignored intellectuals' warnings of the false glitter of consumerism. Though many faced initial unemployment, migrants left in higher numbers than ever before (see Table 3).[34]

After the euphoria subsided, Krenz began to lose hope that he could master the crisis. When the general secretary explained the SED action program to 150,000 Berliners on November 10, its once daring slogans already sounded obsolete. Free elections, the rule of law, media freedom, economic reform, realistic planning, artistic liberty, support for research, and better education only aimed at those practices already followed in the richer West. Trying to outflank the opposition, SED leaders proposed a

TABLE 3. GDR Exodus 1989–1990 (in thousands)

| | *1989* | | | | | |
	July	*Aug.*	*Sep.*	*Oct.*	*Nov.*	*Dec.*
Eastern Refugees	11.7	21.0	33.3	57.0	133.4	43.2
Unemployed Newcomers	25.9	31.9	45.3	61.7	119.9	129

| | *1990* | | | | | |
	Jan.	*Feb.*	*March*	*Apr.*	*May*	*June*
Eastern Refugees	73.7	63.9	46.2	24.6	19.2	10.7
Unemployed Newcomers	132	140	132	114	100	90.4

new direction that was at once too radical for many party members and too timid for the population at large. According to numerous reports, local leaders and members felt betrayed. "The comrades' trust in the party erodes day by day."[35]

For the first time in decades, the Volkskammer met on November 13 to make real decisions. A national television audience avidly followed its debates. Revolts in the docile bloc parties made the outcome unpredictable. CDU members ousted the corrupt Wolfgang Götting and picked Protestant lawyer Lothar de Maizière as chairman, since he seemed untainted by collaboration. But parliament disappointingly elected orthodox peasant leader Günter Maleuda over the liberal Gerlach as its chair. Alarmed by disclosures of an enormous state debt, the deputies also chose Dresden district chief Hans Modrow as prime minister, since he was the only SED leader with enough integrity to be credible. Normal citizens viewed the rapid changes with mixed emotions. According to surveys some were satisfied with Krenz's half-measures, but most hoped for more far-reaching reform: though 93 percent wanted truly free elections, 87 percent vowed to stay in the GDR.[36]

Hans Modrow's appointment as prime minister temporarily stabilized the GDR government. Both Eastern citizens and Western media considered him the most hopeful leader of the successor generation. He had an unassuming personal style, and his commitment to perestroika had led to a severe reprimand during February 1989. In contrast to an almost total lack of faith in Krenz (whose approval rating was less than 10 percent), more than two-fifths of East Germans found the Dresden district secretary sympathetic. Modrow's new cabinet, presented on November 17, was smaller (twenty-eight instead of forty-four members). New faces, such as economics minister Christa Luft and minister of religious affairs de Maizière, outnumbered old figures like foreign minister Oskar Fischer and defense minister Theodor Hoffmann. The gradual emancipation of the bloc parties made the cabinet more genuinely a coalition. The government included only sixteen SED members in addition to twelve ministers from other parties.[37]

In announcing his program, Modrow also found a convincing tone. Stasi chief Mielke pathetically protested his dismissal, saying, "but I do love you all." In contrast, the new prime minister asked for "an advance in trust," promised to "lead the GDR economy out of its crisis" and vowed to continue democratization. In contrast to Krenz's vague promises, Modrow detailed precise political reforms, economic initiatives, educational changes, ecological improvement, and administrative liberalization. Although he rejected reunification speculation, Modrow seemed nonetheless interested in strengthening "cooperative coexistence" between the German states and in establishing links to the European Community. Speaking for the civic movement, Konrad Weiss welcomed the new prime minister as a "reform politician," only demanding more citizen control and speedy elections. When Modrow insisted on a separation of party and state, power began to shift from the SED back to the official government.[38]

The emergence of a competent cabinet hastened the erosion of the SED. The Stalinist legacy divided the party over personnel, power, and privilege. Feeling cheated by the expulsion of discredited leaders like Honecker and Mittag, older comrades wanted to redouble the struggle against "the danger of counterrevolution." Younger members, applauding the rehabilitation of dissidents like Walter Janka, demanded democratization and looked to unknown reformers like Gregor Gysi. The replacement of hundreds of district leaders and lesser functionaries created confusion about the proper response to opposition demands. Decades of frustration drove two hundred thousand members, mostly workers, to turn in their party books by the end of November. Reformers threw off discipline and began to organize and demonstrate in the streets. This grassroots pressure finally forced the party to schedule an extraordinary Congress capable of replacing the entire leadership.[39]

Shocking disclosures of police brutality and corruption undermined public trust. Volkskammer hearings on the repression of protests revealed an unexpected degree of state violence. Moving testimony of victims documented the use of excessive force and discredited official claims of correctness.[40] The liberated media also exposed the glaring "misuse of office." Television reports showed the luxurious government compound in Wandlitz, known as "Volvograd" because of its expensive Swedish cars and hard currency shopping. Not a day went by without sensational revelations about lavish vacation homes, or extensive hunting preserves. Minor by Western standards, these transgressions were unpardonable in Eastern eyes because they violated the party's claim to moral superiority. Not even television specials on Krenz's modest lifestyle, debates with Berlin workers, or interviews with foreign correspondents could repair the damage.[41]

On December 3, Egon Krenz finally gave up. The mysterious disappearance of foreign-currency czar Alexander Schalck-Golodkowski brought pressure for the removal of the general secretary to a head. When district secretaries called for the dissolution of the politburo and Central Committee, both bodies resigned in order to help the SED survive. Three days later Krenz reluctantly followed a cabinet demand and also stepped down as chairman of the council of ministers. The reasons for his failure in little more than forty days were both personal and structural. As an individual leader Krenz hesitated too long in breaking with the old guard and acting on his doubts. He used too many "good old cadre phrases" in promoting the *Wende* to be believed. Popular distrust ran too deep. Intent on tactical corrections, he proposed no novel vision that might have inspired party reformers, dissidents, or the masses.[42]

In structural terms Krenz foundered on the legacy of post-Stalinism. Since they could gain power only through conspiracy, the successors were utterly unprepared for democratic politics and for uncensored reporting by the media. Years of bureaucratic repression had produced such elemental revulsion that trust could not be restored with cosmetic concessions. Somehow the public sensed that Krenz wanted to abandon Stalinist abuses merely so that he could continue Leninist policies. Since the people were unwilling to settle for the appearance of freedom when they might have its substance, the secretary remained a "transition figure," always coming too late. Though he toppled the repressive Honecker, helped avoid bloodshed against the demonstrators, and permitted the opening of the Wall, Krenz could never quite do enough. The long blockage of reform not only undermined the ancient hardliners but also discredited their successors, the younger pragmatists.[43]

Unification Plans

The overthrow of post-Stalinism fundamentally transformed relations between the German states. In spite of humanitarian concessions and a common interest in disarmament, the Honecker government had been hostile to the Federal Republic, since it felt threatened by the larger and wealthier West. The less defensive successors were more willing to expand contacts. In his maiden speech Krenz had proposed "closer long-term relations between the GDR and FRG" in order to stabilize economic, ecological, political, cultural, and humanitarian ties. To counter unification speculation, the press printed loyalty declarations praising East German social achievements. Opposition figures expressed similar sentiments, rejecting Western tutelage in the search for their own path to reform.[44]

The new government was slow to establish contact with Bonn, as it was preoccupied with internal problems. When Krenz hinted that "a realistic cooperation of equal partners will make truly practical solutions possible," visiting FDP spokesman Wolfgang Mischnick promised economic help for further reforms. On October 27, the new leader discussed the continuation of useful contacts on the telephone with Chancellor Kohl. On the one hand, Krenz declared the question of German unification to be dead during his Moscow press conference: "There is nothing to be reunited." Merging incompatible systems such as socialism and capitalism would only threaten European stability. On the other hand, he proposed the formation of common military, economic, travel, and media commissions to the Central Committee. Krenz tried to resolve the dilemma of popular hopes and party fears by stressing GDR sovereignty *and* intensifying contacts with the West.[45]

The unforeseen consequences of the Wall opening forced a fundamental rethinking of the future of the two Germanies. A torrent of almost nine million people poured across the frontier in the first week. Virtually all returned home to the East. Most "only want[ed] to see how it looks on the other side," buy some bananas or appliances in the well-stocked stores, and meet long-lost relatives. To cope with the throngs, additional trains were put into service and ever more border crossing points added. Freeing travel proved the sincerity of reform, but the warm welcome of Eastern cousins in the West reawakened dormant hopes for unity. Overwhelmed by FRG affluence, the poet Thomas Rosenlöcher noted ironically: "The GDR's only chance is to be swallowed up by this country." Though pollsters disputed its level of intensity, all surveys agreed that East German support for unification grew noticeably during the last weeks of November.[46]

The GDR government responded by preparing a "treaty community." "To prevent radicalization," Krenz and Kohl talked more concretely about intensifying cooperation. At the same time Prime Minister Modrow sought to shore up international support for GDR independence by reaffirming to the BBC that "the existence of two German states [is] the basis for stability in Europe." East German leaders tried to strengthen Western skeptics who talked, like Berlin Mayor Walter Momper, about "days of reunion, not of reunification." But Modrow also understood the need for a positive goal of his own: "We propose to underpin the community of responsibility between both German states by a treaty community that goes far beyond" existing agreements. Reversing decades of SED separatism, his bold plan opened the door to closer association of the two German states within the European house. In formalizing cooperation, this concept of *Vertragsgemeinschaft* was designed to safeguard GDR independence by creating stronger national ties to the West.[47]

In Bonn, the fall of the Wall stimulated discussion of reunification as well. The mood of the chancellery "fluctuated between hope and fear: hope that this was the end of the SED regime and fear that it could trigger a mass flight into the FRG." Overwhelmed by events, Helmut Kohl was reassured when President Gorbachev emphasized "a peaceful transition" in the GDR during a phone call. On November 16 an excited Bundestag debated the implications of "self-determination." While Christian Democrats, Liberals, and Social Democratic moderates hoped for unity, left Socialists and Greens advocated renewal of an independent GDR. Counselling restraint, Chancellor Kohl made material help conditional on Eastern reform, confident that freedom would lead to unity.[48]

The media amplified the unification debate. Conservative commentators declared unity "inevitable," liberal journalists like Rudolf Augstein endorsed it, and some leftist columnists began to reconsider their stance.[49] Only intellectuals like the novelist Günter Grass rejected "the reunification slogan" in order not to frighten German neighbors by talk of restoring a national state. This animated discussion strengthened public sentiment in favor of unity. On November 20, 70 percent of West Germans endorsed unification while a mere 15 percent remained opposed. For the first time in years, a slim majority thought union might actually happen within the next decade.[50]

Unification rhetoric made East Berlin nervous. Prime Minister Modrow refused to go beyond proposing a treaty community and Egon Krenz argued that "the border opening is no reunification." On November 26, thirty-one writers (including Christa Wolf), reform Marxists (such as Wolfgang Berghofer), church figures (like Günter Krusche), and opposition leaders (among them Ulrike Poppe) drafted an appeal "for our country." Celebrating their self-liberation from Stalinism, the signers saw a simple choice: "Either we can insist on GDR independence" and try to "develop a society of solidarity, offering peace, social justice, individual liberty, free movement, and ecological conservation" *or* "we must suffer . . . a sell-out of our material and moral values and have the GDR eventually taken over by the Federal Republic" through economic might.[51]

This manifesto for "a socialist alternative to the FRG" became a rallying cry for East German identity. Presented two days later by the writer Stefan Heym at a press conference, the appeal mobilized supporters of socialist reform. Within two weeks two hundred thousand people signed this invocation of "antifascist and humanist ideals." The renewal of socialism offered party reformers and regime critics a platform for cooperation. The initiative was only tarnished when Egon Krenz affixed his signature to the text. The clarion call reverberated across the border and inspired thirty-three FRG leftist intellectuals to draft a parallel appeal for GDR independence as antidote to nationalist currents in the West.[52]

On November 28 Helmut Kohl surprised the Bundestag with a "Ten-Point Plan for German Unity." The chancellor had been under considerable pressure to assert his leadership. But the German question contained grave dangers of stirring up foreign resentment, Eastern rebellion, and Western backlash. When Nikolai Portugalov indicated on November 21 that the Soviets were "thinking . . . even about the quasi-unthinkable," foreign policy advisor Horst Teltschik pressed the chancellor to "assume the lead of the movement" toward unity. Sure of Washington's support, Kohl's collaborators sought to minimize foreign criticism by proposing "a stepwise process" of unification "in cooperation with the GDR" and "embedded internationally." Though based on numerous prior consultations, the ten-point program was not even cleared with the coalition partner FDP for fear of leaks. The chancellor gambled on not informing his allies, since he worried that prior consultation would amend his ideas out of existence. After long hesitation, the CDU leader decided to run an enormous risk in order to seize an historic opportunity.[53]

Kohl's plan combined pragmatism with vision in suggesting stages on the way to unity. Complimenting the East German people, EC neighbors, President Gorbachev, the Hungarians, and Czechs, he restated previous positions in the initial points. First, the chancellor announced immediate medical assistance and offered "the necessary foreign currency" for travel, if the GDR chipped in. Second, he promised to continue practical cooperation, strengthening ecological, postal, and railroad connections with the East. Third, Bonn was prepared to offer additional help, as long as the reforms became "irreversible." Kohl supported dissident demands for free

elections, breaking the SED monopoly, and conversion to a market economy: "We do not want to stabilize untenable conditions." But these "factual preconditions" would make help effective. Fourth, Kohl endorsed Modrow's "treaty community" and suggested building on common institutions
such as the existing bilateral commissions.[54]

The proposal's broader goals were more controversial. In his fifth
point, the chancellor declared himself "ready to go a decisive step further"
by developing "confederative structures" between the Germanies "in order to create a federation, that is a federal order." Studiously vague, this
notion implied "new forms of institutional cooperation" such as a joint
government committee, shared topical commissions, and a common parliamentary body. "Nobody knows today how a reunited Germany will
look in the end. But I am certain that unity will come if the German
people want it." Sixth, Kohl referred to Gorbachev's concept of "a common European house" and promised that inter-German relations would
"remain embedded in the general European process." Essentially, Kohl
sought to combine "a warm patriotic heart and a cool European head."[55]

The plan went to great lengths to place German aspirations within a
framework of international cooperation. As seventh point, the chancellor,
therefore, committed himself to strengthening European integration and
suggested GDR association with the European Community. Eighth, Kohl
vowed to maintain CSCE momentum by developing new institutions for
security cooperation in Europe. Ninth, he emphatically endorsed further
disarmament on the continent. Tenth, he concluded: "With this comprehensive policy we are working for a situation of peace in Europe, in which
the German people can regain their unity in free self-determination."
Postponing thorny issues like security arrangements, Kohl attempted to fit
unification into a "European architecture." His proposal tried to balance
Eastern hopes for decisive action with Western fears of an upheaval. The
Ten-Point Plan did not specify a fixed timetable but attempted to suggest
"a political direction, leading into the future."[56]

Kohl's coup drew a disproportionate response. The plan's moderating
intent was generally obscured by its surprise effect. There was reason
enough to be startled, since the proposal initiated a "paradigm change
from pragmatic acceptance of division to an operative pursuit of political
unification." In the West, the Bundestag reacted with near unanimity.
Predictably, CDU/CSU parliamentarians hailed the initiative as an "historical contribution." Though miffed by being excluded, FDP leader
Hans-Dietrich Genscher had to approve a plan that contained many of his
own ideas. Reluctantly he admitted, "Helmut that was a great speech!"
Moderate socialists like Karsten Voigt and Hans-Jochen Vogel were delighted and joined the national consensus, commenting: "The chancellor
has taken a great step toward us" by adopting the SPD's gradualist approach.[57]

The Left alone spoiled the harmony. Oskar Lafontaine feared for his
political profile, soon broke ranks, and refused to sign a common declaration. Radical socialists rebuked Kohl for failing to accept the Polish fron-

tier. The Greens were even more critical, insisting that the East Germans had an "unhampered right to determine their own path" which might lead elsewhere.[58] Public opinion, however, welcomed this "vision that brings us closer to unity." Conservative, moderate, and some leftist papers supported "confederation" as a suitable compromise. Skeptics found little fault with the substance but belittled it as a campaign ploy to steal the thunder from the right. Only when the international outcry grew loud did some commentators have second thoughts.[59]

In the GDR reactions were somewhat mixed. Pleased "that my offer of a treaty community has been accepted," Prime Minister Modrow suggested building such a common foundation before speculating about the future. Less flexibly, Krenz made negotiations dependent upon recognizing "the existence of two independent, sovereign German states." The official media were ambivalent, warning of reunification "irritations," but admitting constructive elements of cooperation. The bourgeois bloc parties responded positively to the Ten-Point Plan. For the CDU, Lothar de Maizière welcomed the confederation proposal as "an interesting concept that combines important elements of our own ideas." NDPD leader Günter Hartmann claimed to have invented the notion in the first place.[60]

In early December GDR opinion swung towards unity. Many intellectuals recognized that some form of unification was inevitable but were, like the exiled writer Günter Kunert, uneasy about the return of a greater Germany. In search of a reform identity, leftist New Forum and SDP leaders rejected the plan as an "evident takeover of the GDR." Moderate church or opposition figures considered the initial points constructive, promising further scrutiny. More important than formal statements was the growing echo among the demonstrators in the streets. By late November almost half the protesters were shouting "Germany, united fatherland;" ever fewer waved GDR flags or remained undecided. SED partisans began to fear that Kohl's "strategy has a chance to succeed."[61]

The specter of unification created much apprehension abroad. The Soviet Union deplored Kohl's attempt to dictate conditions to East Berlin, worried about the security of existing frontiers, and emphasized that reunification was not on the agenda. The French, offended by not having been informed, disparaged the plan as "too rapid" but hoped to contain Bonn by integrating it more firmly into the European Community. The British showed little enthusiasm about a "Fourth Reich" that might reduce their own influence. Solidarnosc spokesmen, even if they accepted the German right to self-determination, missed an unequivocal guarantee of Poland's western border. Small neighbors such as Holland, Denmark, and Czechoslovakia were upset by the prospect of an even larger Germany. Much of the international response was animated by old fears, stemming from German occupation during the world wars. Memories of the holocaust spurred Yitzhak Shamir to denounce unification as frightening to the Jewish people. But there were new concerns as well, revolving around Bonn's growing economic power and potential military neutrality.[62]

Not all governments were completely opposed. Since they considered unity inescapable, American commentators attempted to fit gradual German reconciliation into existing economic and military structures. The European Community leaders were also supportive because of Kohl's effort to put unification into a European framework. Disturbed by the vehemence of international censure of its initiative, Bonn frantically tried to put out diplomatic fires. Chancellery official Horst Teltschik briefed ambassadors; Foreign Minister Genscher shuttled between capitals to allay fears; and Chancellor Kohl gave personal explanations to President Bush and Soviet Prime Minister Silaiev. Despite efforts to calm suspicion by stressing its intention to dampen popular aspirations for unity in the East, Kohl's coup was widely misunderstood as only fanning unification flames.[63]

The Ten-Point Plan turned unification from a topic of debate into a subject of practical politics. Above all, Kohl's proposal responded to the breach in the Wall, which opened the emotional floodgates of unity. The continuing exodus and mass demonstrations demanded a redefinition of relations between the German states. Modrow's concept of a "treaty community" aimed at reconciliation with the West in order to stabilize the GDR, whereas the Ten-Point Plan was designed to use cooperation as a stepping stone to unity. Combining both contradictory intentions in the initial steps, the pragmatic blueprint presented unity in a language of self-determination that evoked popular sympathy abroad. This unprecedented cooperation startled foreign governments, since it threatened the division upon which the European postwar order had been built. The Ten-Point Plan proved vexing because it exposed the discrepancy between international rhetoric in favor of and practical opposition to German unity. Although neighboring cabinets were shocked and dismayed, the unification issue, once raised, would not go away.[64]

A Civic Revolution

The unassailable citadel of post-Stalinism proved surprisingly easy to overthrow. Once Soviet bayonets were sheathed and Stasi operatives curbed, ubiquitous fear began to vanish. When a stalled economy no longer improved living conditions, the social contract between the people and the party dissolved. In their collective exodus, citizens physically escaped from poverty and repression. In the mass demonstrations, critics protested against militarism, ecological waste and lack of human rights. When open debate revealed the full extent of misrule, SED members themselves lost confidence in their party's ability to lead. In the fall of 1989 the gap between rising popular expectations and declining regime performance eroded not just faith in the government but in the entire system. Inadequate responses to mass exits and demands for public voice had undermined GDR loyalty. The palace coup to break Honecker's dictatorial control was but the culmination of this psychological collapse.[65]

With the linchpin removed, the hollow structure crumbled so rapidly that Egon Krenz was unable to stabilize SED control. What started as a tactical retreat from late Stalinist repression to flexible Leninist rule ended up in a communist rout. In yielding to public pressure, the pragmatists Krenz and Schabowski made an unintended but essential contribution by keeping the transfer of power peaceful. Writer Hans Magnus Enzensberger praised these transition figures somewhat ironically as "heroes of retreat."[66] The change of leadership raised difficult challenges of rooting out deep-seated patterns of Stalinist mentality and behavior in the entire population. The quick failure of the pragmatic successors also triggered a power struggle among protagonists of democratic communism and partisans of a reborn civil society.

Was the GDR awakening truly a revolution? To many participants the speed and extent of the changes seemed, indeed, revolutionary. Even Marxists in defending their power rarely denounced the popular awakening as counterrevolutionary. But the frequent use of modifiers such as "gentle," "peaceful," "spontaneous," "Protestant," or "reluctant" suggests an element of doubt. The Krenz government popularized the notion of *Wende* to describe its new course. But the reference to a different tack describes only the shift from one policy to another and fails to address the collapse of the entire system. This understatement has become the leading term in everyday parlance because it left one's own role in the upheaval in the dark. Social scientists increasingly use the technical metaphor of an "implosion." This new circumlocution of the old "collapse" has a neutral ring, because it emphasizes the inevitable crumbling of SED control. But it evades assigning responsibility and ignores the rising from below.[67]

Loaded with emotional overtones, the question of revolution is essentially a matter of definition. Bitter disappointment in the outcome has led many East German intellectuals to distance themselves from the term. But Charles Tilly's historical comparisons suggest that "revolutionary situations" are more diverse than a fixation upon Jacobin terror or Bolshevik takeover suggests. If "revolutions include forcible transfers of power over states," the East German upheaval largely qualifies as revolutionary. Absence of violence, legal transition, and lack of class struggle seem to militate against this view. However, the mass mobilization that compelled the transfer of political power and radical systems change appears to speak for the term. Combining elements of force (the Krenz coup) with compromise (Round Table) and popular reform (Modrow cabinet), the transition to democracy was revolutionary in rapidity, intent, and degree.[68]

The parallels between GDR changes and other Eastern European upheavals suggest a new type of *civic revolution*. Timothy Garton Ash's neologism *refolution*, conflating reform and revolution, does not go far enough in capturing the speed of the transformation in the GDR. Instead of being a party-sponsored renewal from above, this attempt to democratize socialism was propelled by resentment from below. Only the pressure of the streets compelled SED pragmatists to act and to topple post-

Stalinism. Popular discontent gave marginalized dissidents the mass base
to create a broad civic movement that could demand constitutional rights.
Normal East Germans joined the protests primarily in order to improve
their living conditions. Dissident intellectuals, however, challenged SED
control so as to build a civil society of emancipated citizens. In form and
program this unprecedented *Bürgerbewegung* created a new kind of revolution.[69]

Contrary to dissidents' wishes, the civic revolution reopened the national question. Aided by the ideological confrontation of the Cold War,
the Stalinist regime had cemented the division, since it feared for its
survival in open competition with the West. According to Otto Reinhold,
rector of the Party Academy, the GDR "is conceivable only as an antifascist, socialist state, as a socialist alternative to the FRG." The popular
upheaval in the fall of 1989 undercut this rationale for separatism. The
mass flight was a personal reunification on West German soil that created
too many social problems to continue for long. By forcing democratic
concessions and opening the Wall, opposition demonstrations reduced the
disparity between the systems. Honecker's sudden fall removed the main
obstacle to a closer relationship between the Germanies.[70]

The overthrow of post-Stalinism eventually unraveled German division. No doubt Western interference hastened the crumbling of GDR
identity. The reception policy encouraged the flow of refugees even when
newcomers strained social services. Newscasts, opposition contacts, and
reform demands fueled the fire of protest. Political conditions for financial
help wrung concessions in inter-German relations from a reluctant GDR
leadership. But the SED's gradual retreat from power was propelled more
by internal dissent than by outside subversion. Prompted by exodus and
protest, the party's painful disavowal of post-Stalinism started the race
between internal renewal and external reunification. The civic movement
competed with communist reformers for the recasting of the GDR. At the
same time proponents of a treaty community clashed with advocates of
unity via confederation. Who would win this double struggle?[71]

II

THE MASSES
CHOOSE UNITY

4

Searching for a Third Way

In early December 1989 the German Democratic Republic teetered on the brink of chaos. Partisans of unification and advocates of independence began to clash during demonstrations. With "the SED collapsing and governmental structures crumbling," radicalized mobs threatened to take matters into their own hands. Frightened by potential anarchy, moderates looked for a way to bring the opposition into dialogue with the Modrow cabinet. Neighboring Poland and Hungary had avoided bloodshed through an Anglo-American institution that facilitated discussion between opponents—the round table.[1]

Sitting around one table symbolized cooperation. By not specifying power, the circular arrangement facilitated constructive discourse. Avoiding confrontation required mutual respect, joint problem solving, and citizens' input. Proliferating all through the GDR, round tables (*runde Tische*) formalized public dialogue and became the characteristic innovation of the civic revolution. They evoked the revolutionary Soviets of 1917, but by including representatives of the tottering regime aimed less at confrontation than at compromise. With direct participation and prepolitical spontaneity they presented an alternative to Stalinist repression and parliamentary formalism.[2]

Round tables grew out of local disputes between enraged citizens and defensive authorities. When Leipzig protesters demanded input, concerned officials like district secretary Roland Wötzel sought to turn ugly confrontation into orderly consultation. On November 10 the civic movement proposed that fifteen representatives meet with an equal number of government delegates. In separate statements the Social Democrats, Democracy Now, and Democratic Awakening suggested establishing a central *Runde Tisch*. On November 21 Protestant bishops Gottfried Forck and Werner Leich welcomed "intensive debates about the future of the country among all social forces," and offered their church facilities.[3]

One day later, the SED politburo endorsed such talks in order not to be left behind. The government and "other political forces" should engage in formal discussions about "a new election law, free democratic elections and constitutional reform." SDP leader Ibrahim Böhme accepted this "constructive step," and the bloc parties welcomed it as a way of escaping SED control. On November 30 Protestant and Catholic churches invited two representatives of each group to a "round table talk," thereby institutionalizing dialogue. Even without official standing, this forum possessed that "moral-political weight" necessary "to set the course for democratization."[4]

On December 7 the Round Table held its first dramatic meeting. "Out of deep concern for our crisis-ridden country, its independence, and lasting development," the delegates demanded frank "disclosure of the ecological, economic, and financial situation." Claiming neither legislative nor executive power, the *Runde Tisch* insisted on information about important cabinet decisions and on proposing its own recommendations. "As part of public control in our country," it vowed to keep working until free elections were held. To allow time for campaigning, it set their date for May 6, 1990.

The Round Table intended to act as a watchdog on the SED. Instead of governing, it wanted to advise on fundamental issues beyond day-to-day politics. To speed reform, it created four working groups to draw up a new election law, establish fresh rules for associations, draft a new constitution, and solve economic problems. Trying to restore the rule of law, the Round Table above all demanded an investigation of official corruption as well as the dissolution of the hated secret police (AfNS). The opposing forces reached a series of compromises after twelve exhausting hours. Their spirited debates became an important lesson in applied democracy.[5]

The Round Table's composition favored cooperation. As hosts, the church leaders assumed the role of moderators between adversaries and adopted a conciliatory approach. Across the table seven opposition groups (Democratic Awakening, Democracy Now, Green Party, IFM [human rights], Social Democratic Party, and United Left with two participants each and New Forum with three) faced five bloc parties (CDU—Christian, DBD—peasant, LDPD—liberal, NDPD—nationalist and SED with three delegates respectively). When the trade union FDGB and peasant league VdgB demanded seats, the Independent Women's Association (UFV) and a newly founded Green League were also added to keep the delegates balanced at nineteen and nineteen. Though client organizations multiplied SED influence, the bloc parties gradually discovered their own mind and provided the regime critics with a majority.[6]

Primarily a discussion device, the Round Table reached decisions by simple majority vote. It drew its legitimation from articulating reform demands that the government could not afford to ignore for fear of chaos. But self-selection of the represented groups produced great disparities in power, membership, and agendas. Unprepared for responsibility, the fragmented opposition participated in order to democratize the country without actually governing. With the SED crumbling, the Modrow government joined the Round Table in order to broaden its popular base. Though intended as "a preparliamentary discussion," the Round Table in effect inaugurated a kind of "dual rule."[7]

An Alternative Quest

The attempt to renew the GDR led to a widespread search for a "Third Way" between communism and capitalism. Motivated by the failures of "real existing socialism," this quest for an alternate path was conditioned by German division. In neighboring countries, Czechoslovak repression and Polish martial law had shocked intellectuals into abandoning the idea of "socialism with a human face." Yet in East Berlin, dissenters from Robert Havemann to Rudolf Bahro continued to dream of democratizing Marxism. While seeking to escape from the communist frying pan, they refused to jump into the capitalist fire. Among average citizens who were only dimly aware of these antecedents protest instead derived from the frustrations of daily life.[8]

Compared to futuristic party rhetoric, GDR reality was drab and disappointing. Lack of travel created a sense of imprisonment. Scarcity of goods and services produced endless irritation and scheming. Muzzling of expression generated boring uniformity in the media, only undercut by popular wit. Repression reduced public life to conformity without chance for participation. But the East also had compensatory advantages. Even if it came from standing in line together, there was much solidarity. Tutelary bureaucracy created a predictable life without need for decisions. A modest living standard made for relative equality, and many social services such as child-care from infancy were provided without charge. Humanizing socialism meant getting rid of Stalinist abuses without losing evident gains.[9]

The popularity of the Third Way also derived from a profound ambivalence about the West. Most East Germans had little concrete information about the Federal Republic. Television programs, visits of relatives, and care packages painted a picture that both fascinated and repelled. On the face of it, Westerners had everything Easterners lacked. They could move freely all over the world; they lived in abundance, dressed in stylish clothes, and drove fast cars; they liberally expressed their opinions on any subject; and they could protest, vote, and run for office with impunity. As this image seemed too good to be true, intellectuals suspected that something must be wrong with their rich cousins.

Incessant propaganda reinforced these suspicions. The FRG became synonymous with NATO militarism, unemployment, imperialism in the Third World, and drug abuse. Was the West not a "two-thirds society," where the fortunate few lived at the expense of the exploited many? In

Eastern eyes, free travel made for arrogance, wealth created consumerism, glossy media produced shallowness, and parliamentarianism led to apathy. Not willing to becoming a poor copy of a questionable original, opposition leaders and communist reformers looked for an alternate path that would preserve their own sense of identity.[10]

Among artists the dream of a Third Way aroused high hopes. Proud of their contribution to the awakening, writers perceived it as "a rare historical moment in which we hold the power to correct the future." At last able to speak out without censorship, they celebrated the recovery of authentic language, purged of Stalinist doubletalk. Predictably, their "pious wishes" concentrated on free speech and uncensored publication. For some artists like Helga Königsdorf, the awakening of reason was painful, since it posed the question of personal guilt. But it also produced an extraordinary "moment of beauty." For a fleeting instance, socialism seemed an unfulfilled promise, and intellectuals believed they could remake the world.[11]

A realistic utopia proved surprisingly difficult to define. All the writers assumed they should lead the public and hoped for the continuation of massive state support for culture. Especially on the question of unity opinions started to diverge, since many were suspicious of Western consumerism and rejected the FRG as a "freebooter state." Volker Braun pleaded for "another approach which will reach different goals, softer technologies, and a gentler market." Literary reflection captured the excitement of the new dreams without being able to show a practical way. "The daring and honorable, but uncertain and never realized experiment of a democratic socialism" still held intellectuals enthralled.[12]

For the civic movement the Third Way revolved around the realization of direct democracy. Opposition thinkers resented the "hegemony of the SED and the bloc parties" as much as the "excessive might of Western capital." Their resistance experience inspired a strong commitment to human rights, such as free speech, demonstrations, and the like. The first priority was the recovery of a public sphere in which a civil society could emerge, allowing new forms of debate and association that would not be imposed from above. The New Forum aimed at a "grassroots democracy," marked by direct citizen participation rather than by parliamentary forms of representation, supported by the SDP and DA.[13]

The divided opposition offered only hazy suggestions for an alternate society. Although dissidents recognized the need for market incentives, they wanted "clear limits" to the profit motive, set by concerns of equity and ecology. Even when Marxist rhetoric was no longer required, many clung to the vision of democratized socialism from a sense of social responsibility. Church activists particularly emphasized a commitment to pacifism. Most opponents preferred reforming an independent GDR to unification. Remembering their own persecution, they produced a telling critique of Stalinist abuses, but the overwhelming speed of change made it difficult to articulate a coherent vision for the future.[14]

Party intellectuals welcomed the chance to realize socialist goals in a more democratic form. At Humboldt University a small group of Marxist theoreticians around Dieter Klein discussed necessary reforms. Michael and Andre Brie as well as Rainer Land criticized "administrative-centralist" socialism for its "tendency to stagnation and rottenness." Originally written for the politburo, their "paper on renovating" socialism (*Umbaupapier*) argued that bureaucracy, economic planning, and the leading role of the party oppressed the individual. Only "real socialization of property, power and public consciousness" could break the vicious cycle of periodic crises. To reach legitimate decisions, the political system had to be democratized.[15]

These communist critics wanted to rescue socialism by proposing unprecedented changes. The economy needed to be reformed to become competitive. "Economic and social councils" would assure industrial democracy. As a safeguard of GDR independence, foreign policy had to open itself to Western Germany and Europe. The "real socialist, democratic, humanist, antifascist, ecological character of the GDR as *the other German state* not only needs to be preserved but must be created in the first place." In December 1989, Berlin circles hotly debated the rebirth of a radical yet democratic socialism in the spirit of Rosa Luxemburg. But conserving Marxism through self-reform was hampered by an illusory strategy: renewal now had to come from a discredited instrument, the leaders of the SED.[16]

As a double negation of communism and capitalism, the Third Way promised a moral rebirth of politics. Bärbel Bohley believed that East Germans "want something else, something new" that had yet to be defined. While resolved that "things have to change," they rejected mere "surface improvements" such as full store shelves. Thirty to forty-five year olds, especially, responded to the quest for a more humane society. Restoring socialist goals transcended their parents' timid compromises and seemed pure, unselfish, and apolitical enough to usher in a new age. Western critics of capitalism followed the attempt with passionate interest: "The GDR has a unique chance to build a new social system, freed of the Communist version of Socialism and uncorrupted by capitalist principles." Somehow in the historic rupture, the GDR would forge ahead and form a higher society.[17]

The vagueness of the notion allowed disparate groups to imbue it with their own ideas of change. Some SED apparatchiks could endorse concessions as a way to preserve their privileges. Bloc parties were able to abandon Marxism and rediscover their bourgeois roots. Moderate opponents in the Social Democratic Party or the churches could combine parliamentarianism with participation from below. Managers were able to call for autonomy and competition to get state enterprises back onto their feet. Factory workers could also demand representative unions and higher living standards. Since this approach promised to solve their special problems, many East Germans saw it as a path to a better future. Eventually, the Third Way turned into a ubiquitous slogan expressing contradictory hopes to reform post-Stalinist society.[18]

What did ordinary people think about the search for an alternative? The loss of hope ran deeper than anyone imagined since many believed: "The game is up for socialism." The high expectations of the founding years had been shattered by successive disappointments. Once people realized that the SED's "central aim [was] to maintain power" for the party rather than improve life for the many, East German citizens abandoned the dream of a better world. "The entire ideology that had impinged upon me for so many years is . . . just gone." The elderly felt robbed of decades of their life and wanted to enjoy their remaining years. Having suffered so long in "a mummified utopia," many East Germans were unwilling to embark upon another socialist experiment. The practical obstacles were also daunting: "To find a Third Way is something that I consider very difficult."[19]

Instead of stopping halfway, the mood of the disillusioned populace swung to the other extreme. In November 1989 an overwhelming 86 percent still championed socialist reform, 9 percent searched for another path, and only 5 percent preferred capitalist restoration. By early February, however, only 56 percent sought to renew socialism, 13 percent hoped for an alternative system, while already 31 percent wanted to return to capitalism. To critics, continued support for the Third Way by the intellectual opposition underscored "the arrogance . . . of intellectuals as a social class." Unlike his peers, the writer Uwe Kolbe argued: "*We* do not have the right to maintain and continue the rule of a minority by reforming it by our own participation."[20]

Hopes for a Third Way nevertheless continued to dominate Round Table debates. Aside from a few hardliners, most party members and opposition leaders achieved "a fair consensus on what has to be done" to renew the GDR. At a minimum, participants agreed on the importance of restoring human rights; they accepted the need to democratize politics; they understood the necessity of making the economy more efficient through market incentives; and they also clung to some sense of social solidarity. No doubt, these vague aspirations contained many contradictions and the economic concepts remained amateurish. But the search for an alternate path provided the common ideological ground for the debates of the *Runde Tisch*.[21]

Despite shared goals, the Round Table found it hard to reconcile conflicting expectations. Although the government tolerated its "ideas and suggestions" only in order to stabilize the situation, the opposition viewed the Runde Tisch as a fulcrum for overturning SED domination. Different experiences and discourses which divided party reformers from dissidents rendered cooperation difficult. None of the participants could be sure of popular support. The old powers represented authority without credibility, whereas the new forces stood for authenticity without organization. Successive emergencies shifted attention from long-term constitution building to short-term crisis management. At the same time the pull of national unity began to override desires for continued independence, turning the Round Table into the key battleground over the Third Way.[22]

For a Better Socialism

During the first week of December "the revolution approached its climax." Opening the wall failed to stop the exodus, since about two thousand five hundred East Germans left for the West each day! Though the numbers dropped off a bit, opposition demonstrations continued through the rain and snow. In Leipzig, between 150,000 and 200,000 people demanded free elections and an end to communist rule with placards showing Honecker in prison garb. Slogans became more graphic, warning, "Get lost SED—kiss our ass!" In Chemnitz the New Forum called for a general strike to force the party to separate from the state, leave the factories, reduce its apparatus, publish its finances, and dissolve the Stasi, the hated secret service.[23]

Enraged crowds forced their way into Stasi headquarters, when dark smoke pouring out the windows indicated that documents were being burned. On December 4, protesters occupied secret police compounds in most major cities. To preserve the record of repression, aroused citizen groups began to seal off their files. Popular unrest was beginning "seriously to endanger the authority of the state." Near panic, the Modrow cabinet groped for a way to head off domestic anarchy. But the powerful SED was disintegrating through mass resignations and grassroots rebellion. Perceptive observers sensed that "power lay on the street," ready to be seized by any force. Who would have enough will, discipline, and organization to fill "the political vacuum"?[24]

Prime Minister Hans Modrow faced the crisis with more personal support than his predecessors. In spite of an impressive SED career, he enjoyed a reputation of exceptional honesty. He was born in 1928 in a Pomeranian village into the modest circumstances of a baker's family. When the Red Army captured him in 1945, antifascist schooling opened wider horizons and made communism the credo of his life. During the 1950s, training as an agitator in Moscow forged emotional ties to the Soviet Union and led to his rise in the state youth organization FDJ. But Honecker did not appreciate his North German stubbornness and banished him to Dresden as district secretary in 1973.[25]

In the former Saxon capital, Modrow worked hard to rebuild a neglected area, remote from Berlin intrigues. Though faithful to the communist vision, he saw some of its shortcomings realistically and began to voice his doubts in the inner circles. Only ties to the Soviet embassy and a growing reputation in the West kept him from being fired by Mittag in revenge for his economic criticism. As a partial insider, not tainted by corruption and dedicated to duty, Modrow seemed to be the only leader who could salvage a crumbling GDR. He commented tersely, "I know that I have accepted a difficult legacy."[26]

The new government sought to prevent anarchy by responding quickly to the most pressing needs. Since Modrow intended "to serve not one party but the entire population," the coalition members supported his attempt to work toward a better socialism through reforms. In order to prevent violence against the hated Stasi, the cabinet renamed the secret police Office for National Security (AfNS) and began to reduce its size. On November 18, the parliament (*Volkskammer*) set up a committee to investigate official corruption. Issued in early December, its interim report disclosed shocking instances of misuse in building lavish homes, creating private hunting preserves, and the like.[27]

The GDR parliament also denounced "speculators and profiteers" so as to discourage Westerners from buying up basic goods. In order to keep demonstrations peaceful, the cabinet worked out a "security partnership" with the opposition. The December 4 agreement stipulated that marches receive police protection, that authorities and the civic movement renounce violence, and that citizens preserve public records from destruction. Modrow "did not want to pour out the baby with the bathwater," but the civic movement pressed for further change. Across their differences, both sides concurred on "keeping the country governable" so that democratization could proceed.[28]

Reforming the political system was the top priority. Some Stalinist structures were simply abandoned. When the Christian CDU and liberal LDPD left it, the democratic bloc collapsed and the national front faded away. As a signal of good will, the SED also struck its leadership claim from the constitution on December 1. Other institutions could quickly be turned from democratic trappings into instruments of self-government. Even if deputies owed their seats to sham elections, the Volkskammer gradually grew into a working parliament through its frank, televised debates and contested votes. To restore the rule of law, it eliminated political crimes, rehabilitated victims of persecution, and re-established the independence of the legal profession.[29]

Constitutional changes to create new forms of participation required longer legislative debate. In early December special committees of the East German parliament started working on a novel election law, a revised statute for parties and organizations as well as fresh rules for freedom of opinion, information, and the news media. In well-publicized hearings, civic demands for openness clashed with bureaucratic obfuscation from the nomenclatura, intent on preserving vestiges of the old regime. Unlike quick symbolic concessions, the formal process of restructuring took so much time that public patience began to wear thin.[30]

Equally imperative was reviving the stagnant economy. The appointment of the economist Christa Luft as deputy premier promised a rapid transition to "a market-oriented planned economy." First disclosed to a stunned politburo in late October, the situation was desperate though not hopeless: False balance sheets hampered accounting, lack of competitiveness hindered production, sham unionism prevented worker participation, arbitrary investments wasted resources, lagging productivity limited output, and massive subsidies led to unrealistic pricing, while mounting foreign debts and growing deficits threatened the state with bankruptcy. On December 9, managers of the leading state enterprises attacked the bureaucratic planning system as the root of all evil, demanding entrepreneurial flexibility and responsibility.[31]

Modrow tried to repair the economic engine while keeping its motor running. On December 14 the cabinet approved a stabilization program that tried to safeguard material production, shore up the domestic market, support the currency, and maintain foreign trade. Though they prevented a total collapse, such emergency measures failed to change inefficient structures sufficiently. The Volkskammer did begin to liberalize rules for small business. Reformers in the cabinet also started to develop a comprehensive concept of marketization rather than privatization. But for all the talk about joint ventures and Western aid, too little was done to replace outmoded machines or to fill empty counters in the shops.[32]

Rising anger within the party threatened to destroy the SED. The arrest of former bosses such as Günter Mittag and Harry Tisch made loyal members feel "betrayed and abused." Throwing off decades of prohibition, frustrated intellectuals proposed a plebiscite on the renewal of socialism. In early December, journalists and media workers of the Werk für Fernsehtechnik drafted an independent platform: "We withdraw our trust from the party leaders and the supporting apparatchiks, but endorse the present government. Our party's salvation lies in its uncompromising renewal, which would in fact mean its refounding." The precipitous flight of the state secretary for commercial coordination, Alexander Schalck-Golodkowski, deepened the crisis by confirming rumors of shady arms deals and currency manipulations.[33]

Under pressure by demonstrating Berlin party members, the politburo "decapitated itself" and resigned. In doing so, it expelled Honecker with his cronies, and appointed a committee under Herbert Kroker to prepare an extraordinary party congress. Twenty-five uncorrupted persons like district secretary Roland Wötzel, Mayor Wolfgang Berghofer and spy master Markus Wolf denounced the "failure of the party leadership" to develop "a constructive policy of renewal." The SED's third echelon believed that only "a radical reformation of the party" could prevent a split into discredited hardliners, confused pragmatists, and sincere reformers. "The rescue of the party . . . the salvation of the GDR and of socialism in this country" depended on it.[34]

A lawyer named Gregor Gysi chaired the sensitive subcommittee on corruption. Only forty-one years old, he was the son of an intellectual, diplomat, and minister for church affairs of part Jewish descent. From a prominent party family, Gregor had imbibed Marxism as a matter of course. But as a member of the elite he also enjoyed outside contacts and a free personal style. Following in his father's resistance footsteps, Gysi became a well-known lawyer, specializing in defending dissidents. Other attorneys such as Lothar de Maizière and opposition leaders such as Bärbel Bohley testified to his personal integrity. Gysi believed strongly in the humanitarian potential of socialism and worked hard to eliminate repression by expanding human rights.[35]

In the fall of 1989 Gysi quickly achieved public prominence. Advocating the rule of law, he mercilessly criticized the inept travel bill and demanded the resignation of the politburo. When the managerial Berghofer refused the party leadership, the Kroker committee picked Gysi as standard bearer. He accepted in order to reshape the party toward modern socialism and maintain GDR independence. The desperate SED could not have made a better choice, for he proved uncommonly adept at working the media with his biting wit. Little interested in theorizing, Gysi was an instinctive politician who projected the dynamism of a non-Stalinist left.[36]

The decisive congress of 2,753 delegates opened on December 8 in a Berlin sports arena. This dreary hall had none of the usual trappings of power. Many delegates were dejected and feared popular backlash. To break with Stalinism, reform activists of the "WF platform" demanded its "factual refoundation" as a new "socialist party." Though holding the old guard responsible for the crisis, the Kroker commission recommended only a "restructuring of the SED as a modern socialist party" in order to preserve its apparatus and vast wealth. Calling on all "honest comrades," Hans Modrow urged the party to reform in order to save the GDR: "At stake is our country, this German state in which we live." His dramatic appeal sent a signal of hope.[37]

Astutely, Gysi denounced the failure of "administrative centralist socialism." As an alternative to "the rule of transnational monopolies," he offered the popular formula of the *Dritte Weg:* "This socialist Third Way which we seek is characterized by radical democracy and the rule of law, humanism, social justice, environmental protection and the achievement of real equality between men and women." Though deploring corruption, he also defended the sincerity of the party faithful. The sixteen-hour session vented countless complaints. At the critical juncture, Modrow stopped the dissolution of the party with his plea to keep the country governable. Instead of splitting, the SED repudiated its old structures, elected Gysi as chair, and created a hundred-member presidium.[38]

The conclusion of the meeting a week later underscored the incompleteness of renewal. Though several manifestos suggested necessary reforms, they neither confronted past failures nor provided a theoretical foundation to build upon. Manfred Schumann eloquently criticized Stalinism, and Dieter Klein tried to define the Third Way. But Gysi presented a grab-bag election platform for "democratic socialism" that pleaded for GDR independence. The discussion focused on the symbolic issue of the party name. Traditionalists opposed any change, whereas reformers tried for some combination of democracy and socialism, different from the moderate SPD. Hardliners insisted on retaining the discredited initials "SED" out of sentimental respect for old-timers, but reformers pleaded for adding the "PDS" to announce to creation of a reformed Party of Democratic Socialism.[39]

In the short run, the SED-PDS compromise held the remaining 1.7 million members together. But in the long run, the lack of a clear decision was a "self-deception" that created an unwieldy hybrid. Psychological and material reasons prevented either dissolution or a fresh start. Although most of the about 75,000 intellectuals clamored for reform, there remained some two hundred twenty-five thousand old-style apparatchiks who wanted to hold onto their emotional home and their offices. More than half a million members in leading administrative positions and security services also depended on the continued existence of the party. The new statute departed from the cadre system and created a more open structure. But compared to widespread hopes for dissolution, "the mere change of name" seemed to the public "a gross insult."[40]

At the height of the SED crisis, the civic movement refused to seize power. The commitment to nonviolent reform that helped overthrow the post-Stalinist regime in no way prepared opposition intellectuals for taking control. Internal disunity, aggravated by personal rivalries between Bärbel Bohley and Rainer Eppelmann, also rendered cooperation difficult. The grassroots movement of the New Forum attracted over two hundred thousand signatures, but possessed no program. Emerging parties like the Social Democrats and the Democratic Awakening produced elaborate platforms but had a scant following. Clashes over reunification within and between groups did not make agreement easier.[41]

On emerging from illegality, the opposition first wanted to organize its own affairs. In late fall it tried to establish permanent structures to absorb the influx of thousands of new adherents. Though useful for initial mobilization, loose contact networks had to be transformed into firm organizations. Responding to local economic and environmental problems absorbed much of the energy of unpaid volunteers. In order to educate the public through dialogue, groups were busy drafting programs and statutes. Unwilling to make a bid for power, the New Forum and the Social Democratic Party rejected proposals for a general strike. Instead the opposition sponsored an "appeal to reason" that sympathized with anger against corruption and suggested citizen committees be appointed to dissolve the secret police.[42]

As alternative to taking control, the civic movement concentrated its efforts on the central Round Table. Regular participants included some of its most talented figures, such as Ibrahim Böhme and Martin Gutzeit (SDP), Ulrike Poppe and Wolfgang Ullmann (Democracy Now), Ingrid Köppe and Reinhard Schult (New Forum), and Gerd Poppe and Wolfgang Templin (human rights). The SED sent reformists Gregor Gysi and Lothar Bisky, while the block parties deputized second raters (see Table 4). The debates confronted the old nomenclatura with a new counterelite.[43]

The Round Table focused on solving the problems at hand. In con-

TABLE 4. Seating Chart of the Central Round Table, 1989–1990

2 FDGB (union), 3 church moderators and 3 media speakers (no votes)	
2 United Left	3 LDPD (liberal)
2 Social Democratic Party	3 NPD (national)
2 Democracy Now	3 DBD (peasant)
3 New Forum	3 CDU (Christian)
2 Green Party	2 VdgB (peasant)
2 IFM (human rights)	Sorbs (no vote)
2 Green League, 2 Ind. Women's Assoc., 2 Dem. Awakening, 3 SED/PDS	

New forces in *italics*, old bloc parties in roman; Sorbs are an ethnic minority.

trast to parliamentary posturing, it sparked "genuine debate concerning issues of political substance." Much of its work was carried on in sixteen committees, ranging from economics and constitutional issues to gender equality. Since Modrow did not want to decrease governmental influence, he only reluctantly offered logistic support and office space in a "house of democracy." To make sure that the government carried out its orders, the Runde Tisch demanded "the continual presence of a competent cabinet representative" and economic specialist. Because of bureaucratic sabotage and lack of access to the media, the Round Table's first challenge was to establish its own authority by tackling urgent problems.[44]

Initial decisions combined reforming zeal with a commitment to socialist ideals. On December 18 the Runde Tisch deplored the undemocratic structure of the judiciary and demanded the removal of the old justice minister and officials in order to make "the rule of law credible." During the next meeting, the Round Table insisted on clarifying governmental evasions on Stasi dissolution and on postponing the creation of a new security service until after the May election. Out of revolutionary sympathy, it also supported the Romanian revolt. But at the same time, the Runde Tisch emphasized that "the sovereignty and identity of both German states shall not be called into question by anyone."[45]

The Round Table's ideology was curiously ambivalent. With fierce dedication, it attacked the apparatus of Stalinist repression. At the same time it voiced stock leftist sentiments, such as anticapitalism and antiimperialism. For instance, antifascism inspired it to agree with SED arguments against "neofascist tendencies" that sought to buttress GDR sovereignty. From the beginning, the Runde Tisch fought on two fronts: On the one hand, the opposition wanted to speed the "dismantling of old power structures" in order to prevent a return of Stalinism. On the other hand, it joined the government in searching for a democratic form of socialism that could be realized in an independent East German state.[46]

The rising threat of violence compelled cooperation and kept the revolution from spiralling out of control. During the critical Stasi confrontation in early December, both sides showed remarkable restraint. Modrow's hesitant reformism neutralized the hardliners, but it failed to fulfill hopes for fundamental change. Partial renewal by the SED-PDS threw off Stalinist ballast without making the party truly innovative. The tough demands of the civic movement vocalized popular resentment yet were not so radical as to precipitate chaos. More than "a fig-leaf," the Round Table never quite became a revolutionary directorate, but after a rocky start it provided an institutional mechanism for keeping order *and* speeding change. With hundreds of thousands of Soviet and NATO soldiers watching anxiously, people understood that moderation was the only way.[47]

The Turn within the Turn

During the last weeks of November the message of the demonstrations shifted toward German unity. After the fall of the Wall, a few placards started to demand "reunification, [since] it has already begun." By early December dozens of posters called for "One Germany," "Reunification yes, we are one people," "DDR + BRD = Germany," and "We live only once—therefore yes to German unity." Hundreds of black, red, and gold flags appeared with the GDR emblem cut out, reclaiming the national and liberal symbol adopted by the West. As during international soccer matches, thousands of voices shouted *Deutschland, Deutschland* in an intoxicating crescendo.[48]

This *Wende* within the *Wende* signalled the desertion of the masses from the opposition program. Many protesters still warned "No fourth Reich!", supported "neither Stalinism nor capitalism," and continued to urge autonomous renewal. "After hammer and sickle over my neck, I don't want to carry a Mercedes star on my forehead." But immense revulsion against decades of betrayal swept away intellectual fears of "new subjection, another sell-out." Angry choruses of "Get the reds out of the demo!" began to drown out defiant shouts of "DDR!" Once the civic movement created a public space for the articulation of its feelings, the silent majority filled it with clamor for unity. For the populace the social market economy of the FRG beckoned as the quickest way out: "No more experiments—reunification now!"[49]

As a counter to unification pressure, the East German government redoubled efforts to assert its independence. During an early December Warsaw Pact meeting in Moscow, Modrow obtained Gorbachev's backing for the continuation of two German states. "Our allies, especially the Soviet Union but also the other neighbors and partners, count on a sovereign, socialist GDR," the prime minister reported during the SED congress. Signalling flexibility, he welcomed Kohl's "moderate approach" to reunification but suggested expanding cooperation between both states instead of speculating about unity. His advisers suggested that the GDR faced an "existential crisis as a state."[50]

To shore up sovereignty, Modrow strengthened Western contacts. With a surprise visit to East Berlin on December 12, Secretary of State James Baker sought to slow the unification momentum. Though avoiding any commitments, he gave the impression "that a treaty community would find the approval of his government." On the way back from consultations in Kíev, which echoed an earlier Franco-Russian alliance, the French president reaffirmed East German sovereignty even more strongly. The signing of six agreements on economic and cultural cooperation with the GDR demonstrated that France still based its policy on "the continued existence of two German states within the framework . . . of the EC." Yet in discussions with Leipzig students, François Mitterrand intimated that he "would not resist" a popular desire for reunification, if it were expressed in free elections.[51]

In response to changing sentiment, opposition groups and bloc parties reconsidered their attitude towards unification. Most dissidents preferred creating a better world to selling out to the West: "After we have liberated ourselves from the claws of Stalinism, we do not want to surrender to the social injustice of Mr. Kohl's two-thirds society." But on December 7 the Eastern SDP endorsed "German national unity with confederative structures" in a treaty community that would merge both economies with sufficient social safeguards. While the New Forum remained divided, the Green Party and liberal LDPD also began to move toward supporting unification.[52]

On December 14, Democracy Now proposed a "three-step plan for national unity." As an alternative to "reunification" these Berlin intellectuals proposed a fresh merger through political and social reforms. Democratization in the East and greening in the West were to lead to "union in a confederation" that would prepare eventual unity in a "federation of German states." This was the most elaborate scenario for a slow approach to the German question that balanced dissident hopes for Eastern renewal with popular desires for unity. The next day, the Reform Congress committed the SED more clearly to "strive for the unity of the German nation" as well. Not to be outdone, Democratic Awakening also dedicated itself to "overcoming the division" in a federal state.[53]

On all levels of government, relations between the Germanies grew closer. On December 5, Hans Modrow and Rudolf Seiters agreed to create a common currency fund to ease travel by ending Western "welcome money" and Eastern "compulsory exchange." With a couple of hundred DM of legal change in their pocket, GDR citizens could move more freely. West Germans would be allowed to enter without restrictions after the New Year. Structurally similar states like Baden-Württemberg and Saxony suddenly rediscovered old ties. In Berlin mayors Momper and Krack created a "regional commission" that would reconnect the estranged halves of the former capital.[54]

Increased inter-German contacts raised fears abroad. After shunning the East for decades, Bonn cabinet members raced to meet with their counterparts. Economics ministers Helmut Haussmann and Christa Luft agreed to form a joint commission for facilitating Western investment. During the European summit in Strasbourg Chancellor Kohl found it difficult to assuage the neighboring countries' fears. After heated discussion, the community endorsed "German unity through free self-determination" as long as Bonn accepted speeding up the drive for a common currency. To synchronize German unification with European integration, President Richard von Weizsäcker visited the East and warned against a hasty "shot-gun wedding [*zusammenwuchern*]."[55]

The German rapprochement climaxed with Kohl's visit to Dresden on December 19. FRG Ministers Norbert Blüm (social), Helmut Haussmann (economics), Rudolf Seiters (chancellery), and Dorothee Wilms (German affairs) came along to work out practical steps. Modrow and Kohl were on their best behavior, "trying to create a good climate for open talks." Both leaders quickly reached agreement on a joint declaration "about the formation of a treaty community," with negotiations to begin after the new year. When Modrow demanded 15 billion DM to equalize postwar burdens, Kohl rejected such reparations and preferred to speak in terms of "a solidarity contribution."[56]

As sign of good-will, the East German hosts agreed to open the border to Western visitors on Christmas Eve. Subsidiary negotiations on economic issues such as joint ventures and small business contacts, as well as on cultural and other questions made rapid progress. In the concluding press conference, differences surfaced between Modrow's stress on short-run independence and Kohl's emphasis on eventual unity. But the chancellor and the prime minister agreed on the need for self-determination, stability, and financial support. In the formal talks Modrow won Western assurances for closer ties that presupposed the continued existence of the GDR.[57]

The "enthusiastic welcome" of the Dresden people swept aside these carefully laid plans. The unrepentant still warned: "Herr Kohl, you want the best *for* us—but you won't get it *from* us!" The long-suffering populace, however, showed its longing for unity in a dramatic way. When he stepped to the microphone in front of the Frauenkirche, demolished by the fearsome 1945 bombing raid, the chancellor was greeted by a sea of German flags. "Helmut! Helmut!" shouted the excited people, "We need you!" For a leader who had often been booed in the West, this ringing acclaim proved unforgettable. Even simple promises, such as "We shall not leave our fellow countrymen in the lurch," were cheered frenetically. Unresponsive to appeals for reason or references to Europe, the throng exploded when Kohl vowed: "My goal remains—if the historic hour permits—our nation's unity."[58]

Conscious of international anxiety, Kohl kept the tone of the speech moderate. His down-to-earth message of community was designed as much to dampen as to raise hopes of unity. Yet the effect was electrifying. By coming to Dresden, Kohl gave rising but diffuse unification sentiment a personal focus. The media broadcast shots of the crowd response into German living rooms and amplified his triumph. Touching a "national nerve," the strength of popular feelings made the chancellor reconsider East Germany's viability and rethink his timetable. One sad observer noted with only slight hyperbole: "From this day on, the GDR ceases to exist."[59]

During its concurrent congress in West Berlin, the Social Democratic Party also yielded to unification pressure. So as not to miss the national train, a grizzled Willy Brandt had cautioned earlier that "arbitrary division" would not expiate guilt and suggested "we should come together in a new kind of German federation." But speaking for a postnational generation, populist Oskar Lafontaine instead mused about recognizing GDR citizenship and stopping the influx of refugees. Trying to keep the SPD party leadership from disintegrating completely, centrist chair Hans-Jochen Vogel hammered out a compromise that envisaged a gradual progression from treaty community to federal unity.[60]

The Berlin formula put a brave face on a difficult reversal. In the tradition of *Ostpolitik*, the SPD promised "to work for a peaceful Europe in which the German people find their unity in free self-determination." The party also distanced itself from the moribund SED and accepted the fledgling Eastern SDP as a legitimate partner, offering material aid. While Brandt was happy to see "unity grow from below" and Meckel announced the rebirth of social democracy in the East, Lafontaine called for "social justice in both German states." Though it finally responded to the pressure for unity, the moderate Left continued to harbor many doubts that limited its appeal.[61]

The growing momentum of unity also forced the Soviet Union to reassess its opposition. East Berlin's reluctance to reform had long irritated Moscow leaders. Liberal planners began to think the unthinkable and reflect on the advantages of dropping a recalcitrant GDR. Self-determination lay in the logic of perestroika, but the East German *Wende* had restored prospects for fruitful cooperation. Initially, Mikhail Gorbachev refused to consider reunification "a question of actual policy today." But by early December he only warned against forcing the issue: "History shall have to decide what the fate of the continent shall look like in the future."[62]

Before the European parliament in Brussels, Foreign Minister Shevardnadze tried to resolve the problem by defining Russian interests. Alternating between warnings and encouragement, he professed to be willing to recognize the logic of German unification after integration and disarmament were complete. But seven vital questions had first to be clarified, regarding procedures, German frontiers, alliance structures, size of military forces, presence of allied troops, Helsinki process, and European security. Shevardnadze's catalogue established rational conditions for Soviet approval. The German chancellery considered this statement "contradictory" but welcomed the offer of closer dialogue.[63]

As a token of normalization, the GDR opened the Brandenburg gate on December 22. Braving the cold rain, tens of thousands of spectators alternately "laughed and cried" when the politicians walked through the breach in the twelve-foot thick wall. Mayor Erhard Krack talked about peace, while Walter Momper burst out: "Berlin is still divided, but the people are no longer separated and the city has regained its old symbol." Hans Modrow presented the opening as proof of his commitment "to facilitate the meeting of people." The historian Helmut Kohl called it "one of the happiest hours of my life" since he had long dreamt of walking from the Reichstag to the old city center. The mixture of popular joy and official speeches made "the historic step" a television spectacle. The Eastern and Western press celebrated it in rare unanimity.[64]

The festive spirit carried over into the holidays, the first Christmas season to rejoin separated families for over one generation. Some 380,000 West Germans and 765,000 West Berliners visited the East, whereas about 1,200,000 GDR citizens travelled to the West. On New Year's Eve, youths from both sides of the city gathered at the Brandenburg gate in a raucous party. Celebrating with beer and champagne, they danced to rock rhythms, scaled the remnants of the wall, and damaged the monument's crowning statue, the Quadriga. An extraordinary year had turned deadly bullets into harmless fireworks.[65]

Not all East Germans were, however, delighted about the growing momentum of unity. SED-PDS members feared for their privileges or worried about the resurgence of nationalism. Writers and dissidents wanted to shape their own future rather than surrender to the West. On December 19, fifty thousand Berliners demonstrated "for a sovereign GDR, against reunification and a sellout" of their country. In Rostock thirty thousand supporters of the Third Way chanted, "This is our land; we must take its future into our own hands."[66] Though impressive, these counterprotests were less effective than the push for unity, since they lacked a compelling issue.

On December 28, "anti-Soviet and nationalist slogans" mysteriously appeared on a Russian war memorial. The cabinet sharply denounced the scrawls as neo-Nazi tendencies, delighted to have found a popular theme. On January 4, 1990 the SED, bloc parties, mass organizations, some intellectuals and left opposition groups (such as the VL) led 250,000 marchers to Treptow. Passionately, Gregor Gysi called for a united front to keep the Right from "ruining the chance for democratic socialism in the GDR." In order to win back the masses, this old style demonstration played on antifascist fears, protesting "Against reunification and the brown plague!" But the campaign backfired when rumors alleged that the Stasi was actually responsible for defiling the Russian monument.[67]

At the end of 1989, prospects for unification remained clouded. GDR opinion surveys were notoriously unreliable, since pollsters tended to ask loaded questions and the public did not always dare express its true feelings. In the available returns, the Modrow government seemed to be gaining some respect. About half of the respondents approved of the cabinet in contrast to only a third who supported the failing SED. Between a quarter and a half advocated some form of reunification, and even higher numbers favored a treaty community or a kind of Europeanization. In the FRG, feelings of solidarity were coupled with growing concerns about its cost.[68]

The groups supporting and opposing unity were roughly equal in strength. In the East, many ordinary people, the moderate opposition (Democracy Now, Social Democratic Party), and the bloc parties favored a merger. In the West, the CDU/FDP coalition, the centrist SPD, and the majority of the populace supported Kohl's course. But abroad, only the United States was committed to German self-determination, provided Bonn remained in NATO. Equally impressive were the forces arrayed against unity. In the GDR, the Modrow government, the SED-PDS, and many adherents of the Round Table preferred independence. In the FRG, the Greens, the left SPD, and many intellectuals also favored two states. Abroad, the Soviet Union and Poland, but also allies like Britain and France, were more comfortable with the status quo. As François Mauriac had suggested maliciously, they liked Germany so much that they hoped to have more than one. The issue had been joined, but it was unclear how the struggle would turn out.

Renewal or Unity?

Above all, the civic revolution aimed at renewing the GDR. To facilitate democratization, government and opposition borrowed an institution that had succeeded in dampening conflict in Warsaw and Budapest—the Round Table. Yet unlike skeptics in neighboring countries, German reformers stubbornly pursued the dream of a Third Way. Elsewhere the opposition repudiated Marxism-Leninism as a Soviet imposition and returned to religious or liberal values. But in East Germany party and dissident discussions centered on creating a democratic socialism beyond Stalinism and capitalism. Propounded in dozens of position papers in the fall of 1989, the Third Way offered SED reformers and opposition activists "a vision that makes life worthwhile and enables us to accomplish something tangible."[69]

The appeal of the *Dritte Weg* stemmed from the peculiar circumstances of the GDR. The Nazi trauma had discredited nationalism so thoroughly that it could no longer inspire resistance against Soviet rule. Effective repression, backed by a larger number of Russian troops, made for greater party discipline and public conformity than elsewhere. The Stasi expelled anti-communists to West Germany, permitting only a small opposition that was willing to work *within* rather than *against* the system. Deriding capitalism as materialist, the regime's antifascist, humanist stance appealed to idealists concerned with bettering the world. Western critics like Fritz Haug supported Eastern experiments "as projective wish fulfillment" for reforms which they were unable to achieve in their own society.[70]

The failure of this utopian quest was predictable. Mounting economic difficulties and public unrest no doubt contributed. The struggle for power between an eroding government and a rising opposition complicated the process of reform. Conceived as antipolitics rather than politics, the Third Way agenda was clearer on what it opposed than on how to reach positive goals. Frequent intervention of Bonn politicians complicated the process. The media also played a crucial role in the "TV revolution." Adept at touching feelings, network news broadcast gripping pictures of national moments such as the Dresden visit or the Brandenburg gate opening. In contrast to the polished sound-bites of Western professionals, the earnest Round Table discussions appeared amateurish and confused.[71]

When they regained their voice, the silent masses spoke out against the Third Way. Regular citizens who flocked to demonstrations began to articulate their own desire for a clean break with the Red past. Ordinary folk had grown so disillusioned about social experiments that brought repression that they embraced the Western model as "the only hope." Despite their lip service to the people, Marxist observers were dismayed when confronted by actual popular demands. Elated by protest chants, the dissidents had mistaken themselves for the *Volk* and were bitterly disappointed when the people refused to follow their lead. Their anti-Stalinist alliance for civil rights broke down because of the disagreement on the material improvement of daily life. The renewal foundered not just on practical problems but also on the gap between intellectuals and the masses.[72]

Growing momentum toward unity inspired insistent warnings against a greater Germany. Afraid of international backlash, historian Hans-Ulrich Wehler called "unification in one state a highly dubious goal." Progressive intellectuals considered "an undivided Germany either quite unimportant or most undesirable." Typically, novelist Günter Grass condemned unification talk as "so much feeling and so little [critical] consciousness." Interested only in the "cultural nation," the combative SPD member argued that Hitler's atrocities forever forbade the restoration of a national state. Preferring "the slower pace" of the East, Grass asserted that unification would not solve "real" problems such as pollution. Perhaps the Eastern revolution might inspire reforms in the West.[73]

Much of the opposition to unity stemmed from revulsion against Kohl's political style. Time and again, intellectuals resented the chancellor's petit bourgeois "narrow-mindedness . . . incorrigibility [and] offensive arrogance." On December 9, one hundred Western journalists protested against "the megalomaniac policy" of turning the Eastern revolution into Western reunification. A few observers like Peter Schneider welcomed the fall of the Wall and pondered its ironies. Martin Walser, another exception, argued that "for once, German history might yet turn out well." Most of the intelligentsia, however, were committed to a postnational agenda and opposed unity.[74]

During December international attitudes shifted from alarm to attempts to cope with the inevitable. Propelled by public sympathy, the U.S. government took the lead in supporting the "wind of freedom." President George Bush sought to control unification by setting conditions: The East Germans should decide the form; Bonn must remain in NATO and respect Allied rights; unity could only come about peacefully; and existing borders would have to be respected.[75] Poles, Israelis, and other former victims continued to be anxious about the prospect of a greater Germany. But with Soviet resistance softening, the World War II victors decided not to block the momentum toward unity. As long as the Germans proceeded slowly within established norms, they were free to determine the shape of their reconciliation themselves.[76]

5

Abandoning
the Socialist Dream

With the New Year, the mood turned. The elation of the popular rising began to give way to frustration with the difficulties of a new start. During the wonderful fall of 1989, "the people, acting as one, had determined their own fate with imagination and resolve." Led by a courageous opposition, they had overthrown post-Stalinism, restored human rights and created a Round Table. These breathtaking advances signalled "a new historical awakening." Yet during the winter of 1990, the same masses realized "that practically nothing has changed after all, at least not for the better."[1]

Political excitement only aggravated the tribulations of daily life. The continuing exodus created supply problems, rendering even basic foods scarce. Long lines in front of the few stores frayed salesclerks' and customers' nerves. Growing impatient, ordinary people wanted to see tangible improvements in their everyday existence. For the New Year, the government instead promised to continue political reforms: "The GDR needs revolutionary changes. It needs the rule of law. It needs reason and prudence. The liberties that have been won must be solidified." But such appeals no longer moved citizens, confident of their own voice. How much longer would they wait for results?[2]

Public irritation centered on the secret police. The ubiquitous Stasi was hated both as symbol and as instrument of repression. When Hans Modrow insisted on transforming the large ministry for state security (MfS) into a smaller office of national security, enraged citizens occupied Stasi district offices. Though the cabinet used the "danger of neo-Nazi tendencies" to justify the creation of a new "constitutional protection" service, the Round Table insisted that the AfNS be completely dissolved. The generous severance pay for dismissed agents angered the long-suffering public. Moreover, the discovery of a secret service circular call-

ing for a putsch to recapture power inspired opposition threats of obstruction.[3]

The effort to salvage the Stasi by reducing its size was a fiasco. On
January 8, Peter Koch, the official in charge of dissolution, informed a
skeptical Round Table that twenty-five thousand members had been dismissed and 216 local offices closed. But when he was unable to answer
questions about the main computer, the bloc parties called for his ouster
and an alarmed opposition threatened to walk out unless Modrow fully
disclosed his plans within two hours. Because the prime minister continued to advocate a smaller secret police, Berlin construction workers struck
and pulled down the GDR flag. On January 12, Modrow finally gave in,
promised to dissolve the Stasi, and vowed not to form a new force until
after the election.[4]

Unconvinced by this belated reversal, people took matters into their
own hands. When the New Forum called for a protest against the old Stasi
and new "Nasi" (AfNS), about one hundred thousand Berliners gathered
around its infamous headquarters in the Normannenstrasse on January 15.
Defended by high walls and armed personnel, this bloc of forty buildings
in suburban Lichtenberg was the electronic nerve center of repression.
Here were carried out the *s*lugging, *t*hwacking, e*a*vesdropping, *s*pying,
and *i*ncarcerating that the Stasi acronym signified, according to popular
wit. To prevent violence, dissident leaders brought bricks along to seal off
the main entrance.[5]

Suddenly the massive steel gates swung open. Protesters rushed inside, curious and bent on revenge. Astounded by the modern interior,
they smashed doors, ripped open filing cabinets, and threw furniture out
the windows. On the walls they sprayed slogans like "Down with the
SED!" Pent-up anger exploded into uncontrolled violence against property. Posing as demonstrators, Stasi agents carried off incriminating files and
deflected the rampage from espionage and surveillance offices. The
aroused crowd discovered tons of weapons and instruments of torture. Yet
the "ghost of Mielkeville" escaped vengeance, since the essence of bureaucratic oppression proved largely intangible.[6]

The storming of the East German bastille threatened to unleash
chaos. Immediately, the Round Table suspended its discussions and authorized Konrad Weiss of Democracy Now to appeal not to use force.
With blue lights flashing, Modrow rushed to the Normannenstrasse and
implored the unruly mob: "I have come here in my responsibility as
minister president" in order to urge prudence. Opposition leader Ibrahim
Böhme calmed the crowd. Dissidents who had been persecuted there
cordoned off the Stasi fortress, and citizens formed a committee to speed
its dissolution. That same evening half a million protesters demonstrated
in other cities against the SED and called for the elimination of the secret
police.[7]

The occupation of Stasi headquarters was a psychological turning
point. The surprised cabinet desperately warned: "The democracy that

has just begun to develop is in gravest danger." Though order eventually returned, dramatic television footage showed that "the symbol of old power has lost its terror." Forced to back down, the Modrow government seemed either incompetent or, worse yet, duplicitous. The Stasi conflict also signalled that the people were developing a mind of their own, independent of government or opposition. The contradiction between official reform promises and continued police surveillance robbed the renewal of socialism of its credibility.[8]

Economic Failure

The deeper reason for discontent was the failing economy. On January 11 Hans Modrow painted a bleak picture to the Volkskammer. Triggered by the exodus, the downturn in the final quarter had created "a deficit of four billion marks in the plan" and of "five to six billion in the state budget." The same day, a long article in the *Neues Deutschland* disclosed the full extent of the economic debacle. According to secret figures, nominal growth dropped from 4.5 percent to 3.1 percent during the late 1980s, only to stall completely at the end. East Germans were profoundly shocked by this admission of failure that proved official success stories had been untrue.[9]

The self-criticism of the SED discovered many reasons for stagnation. The deterioration of capital stock caused frequent breakdowns of machinery. Without proper incentives and pay, companies created shoddy products. The priority of planning over the market made for inefficiency. Obsolete technology resulting from the GDR's international isolation rendered production antiquated. Prices set by political priorities falsified exchange relationships and inspired mistaken allocations. With its heavy social expenditures, the GDR did not invest enough. In effect, it had been living above its means. In the competition with the dynamic West, such failure to advance spelled political defeat.[10]

Attractive on paper, the planned economy disappointed in practice. Workers had long dreamt of replacing the cruelty of the market with the security of the plan. But Stalin turned this vision into a method of economic development and political control. Following the Soviet example, GDR industrial firms were nationalized into "people-owned-companies" (VEBs) and redirected from consumer needs to investment goods. After the breakup of Junker estates, agricultural land was taken from the peasants and organized into collective farms (LPGs). In the early seventies, trade and services were reorganized into cooperatives (HOs), virtually eliminating the private sector.[11]

The state planning agency defined economic goals, based on political and social priorities. Ignoring price and profit, ministries oversaw individual sectors such as heavy industry and construction, but ultimately the Central Committee's economic section took charge. To outflank capitalism, it created plans designed to prevent periodic crises and maximize growth according to values other than greed. Instead of providing worker power, the planned economy became a kind of state capitalism, with bureaucrats and functionaries in control. This system succeeded in organizing postwar reconstruction and modest growth, but failed miserably in accomplishing the transition to high technology.[12]

On the company level, the planned economy produced organized chaos. Fixated on fulfilling their output target (IWP), managers developed a production mentality that neglected quality and cost. Their decisions had to reconcile often-conflicting party orders, economic imperatives, and local community concerns. They had to cope with permanent shortages and rely on constant improvization to stretch a blanket that was always too short. Individual companies sought to become self-sufficient and produce everything they needed, from nails to machines. Such autarchy led to hoarding of raw materials and bartering between companies. Yet managerial salaries were hardly larger than overtime blue-collar pay.[13]

Workers enjoyed security but had little power. The right to work prevented unemployment but led to poor performance. Lack of pressure and antiquated machinery encouraged low productivity, reaching only one-third of the Western level. Incentives were collective rather than individual, with premiums and prizes given to groups or awarded by rotation. Since there were no local taxes to support infrastructure, the factory had to provide child care, sports facilities, cultural entertainment, and vacation resorts. In spite of production rhetoric, party control created a largely noneconomic economy. Since rewards were based on apparent fulfillment of plans rather than on sales, it was a wonder that anything worthwhile was produced at all.[14]

For consumers, economic planning offered more famine than feast. Unlike neighboring countries of Eastern Europe, the GDR generally enjoyed full store shelves. But all too often shops did not have what buyers really wanted. If there were more than enough shoes, they would be ugly and in the wrong sizes. Since most goods were shoddy, finding the few quality items, largely imported, became an obsession. Pricing without regard for cost aggravated supply difficulties. Subsidies kept staple goods so cheap that people fed bread to farm animals. But durables like television sets or cars were so overpriced that they remained almost out of reach for ordinary people. Service was usually surly, because there was little reason to be pleasant.[15]

To compensate, popular ingenuity developed strategies outside the plan. Scarcity put a premium on personal and political connections. The fortunate few who could offer attractive goods or services bartered in kind. Some of the best houses in town were owned by carpenters, plumbers, and other craftsmen with scarce skills who helped one another on weekends. Too much cash with too little to buy created a black market, for instance in used cars. To siphon off buying power, the government established foreign currency stores and luxury shops, creating a two-class society. Though East Germans could get the basics, obtaining something special took inordinate time and energy.[16]

Günter Mittag's opportunism blocked any chance for greater efficiency. For almost three decades this ambitious planner was "the master of the GDR economy." As young advisor to Walter Ulbricht, he helped launch the "New Economic System" in 1963 that restored some market incentives as a performance guide. When this experiment produced insufficient results, Erich Honecker shunted Mittag aside. In 1971 he shifted priority to consumption and social services under the slogan "the unity of economic and social policy." Initially this communist Keynesianism spurred some growth. But eventually social spending "used more than it produced" and created a growing gap between limited means and unlimited aspirations.[17]

In 1976 a cowed Mittag was recalled as head of the Central Committee's economic section to keep this deficit system running. Since the oil price shock and the arms race made international borrowing difficult, Mittag combined competing firms into 257 state monopolies (*Kombinate*), stressed technological innovation, and centralized power in his own hands. When reality failed to live up to the plan, this devious bureaucrat used indoctrination and censorship to maintain the appearance of success. Aware that excess spending meant ruin, the ailing Mittag silenced his doubts. "Sometimes one has to howl with the wolves and do the right thing anyway."[18]

In the 1980s economic difficulties became critical (see Table 5). The fifteenfold increase in foreign borrowing demanded that two thirds of the hard currency earnings were used just to service the debt. Exports in machinery, optics, or textiles had to be increased, even when they brought decreasing returns and deprived the population. The rate of capital accumulation was cut in half, slowing necessary investments. Within the limited funds, the share of nonproductive investment projects such as housing construction rose from one-third to over one-half. Military and Stasi expenditures also consumed a large amount of resources (16.4 billion Mk in 1989), which could have been used to increase consumer goods.[19]

The consequences of these mistakes were disastrous. Much produc-

TABLE 5. East German Economic Performance, 1970–1987

Year	Foreign Debt (billions of Mk)	Capital Accumulation (percent)	Productive Investment (billions of Mk)	Unproductive Investment (percent)
1970	2.2	19.4	34.4	34.3
1975	11.0	17.1	42.0	41.4
1980	25.3	16.5	46.9	43.1
1985	30.0	12.0	39.6	54.0
1987	34.7	11.4	45.5	49.2

tive stock was ripe for a museum. Two-fifths of the steam boilers and turbines were over fifty years old! As the planners tried to circumvent Western strategic prohibitions (COCOM), questionable investments aggravated the bottlenecks. For instance, the development of computer chips that were cheaper on the world market made little sense. It took 534 East German Mk to produce a 256 Kb chip that cost only 17 Mk abroad! Lagging productivity and increasing price subsidies depressed nominal growth to 2.5 percent in 1987. Hidden by the term "value increase," creeping inflation wiped out all gains, while the external value of the currency dropped by half. Optimistic reports continued to please the planners, but accelerated "the loss of trust" among managers, workers, and consumers. [20]

In spite of frantic countermeasures, the debacle proved inescapable. When the Soviet Union reduced oil supplies from 19 to 17.1 million tons in 1981, the energy base shrank and the hard currency source for exporting refined products dried up. Only the billion DM credit negotiated by the populist Bavarian Prime Minister Franz Josef Strauss in 1983 postponed the day of reckoning. Desperate to increase foreign exchange, the East German government gave State Secretary for Commercial Coordination (KoKo) Schalck-Golodkowski more authority to make secret deals. In cooperation with the Stasi, his trade empire sold anything movable to the West, from dissidents to cobblestones. Instead of going into productive investments, its reported annual earnings of more than 1.5 billion were employed for military purposes. Schalck-Golodkowski's profits were also used to make up civilian shortages by buying bananas or Volkswagen cars. [21]

At the end of 1987 Mittag realized that the game was up. "The East was unable to help," he later admitted, "and I could not turn to the West for comprehensive cooperation because of latent political resistance in our own ranks." Since lowering the living standard would have produced a popular revolt, cutting social expenditures proved impossible. Though advisors like planning chief Gerhard Schürer warned of impending bankruptcy, Honecker persisted in spending more than he earned. His self-deception ended only in 1989 when exodus and protests forced the regime to admit publicly that long-term stagnation had turned into actual decline. [22]

The shocking truth inspired a confused debate about economic reform. The managers of state enterprises hoped for greater independence, harder work, and more realistic pricing. Welcoming international competition, Vice-Premier Christa Luft championed a "socialist market economy" that would introduce incentives while maintaining public ownership. [23] Considering such steps "insufficient," the New Forum sponsored a conference on the creation of a "socioecological market economy." These plans aimed at balancing private initiative with social security for the people, and stressed limited privatization, open competition, and currency convertibility to change the state's role from player to referee. [24]

Western critics called for even more radical change. Minister of Economics Wolfgang Haussmann derided the state monopolies (*Kombinate*) as dinosaurs and claimed that "the planned economy is finished." The head of the Deutsche Bank Alfred Herrhausen demanded "changing the whole system" legally, economically, and politically as a condition for investments that would lead to reunification.[25] But leftist spokesmen stressed that the GDR was not bankrupt and had a "good chance to catch up soon." Trying to maintain independence, the Round Table recommended measures to stabilize production and to initiate the transition to a market economy.[26]

The failure of the planned economy was both structural and political. High reparations to the Soviet Union and unfavorable trade terms with Moscow constituted a big handicap. The lack of "useful raw materials except for salts and lignite" hampered development. Reduced access to Western markets and technology made the GDR dependent upon exchange with less developed Eastern neighbors in the COMECON. The planning process produced more paper reports than useful goods. Without a true performance gauge such as competition, targets grew remote from reality, since statistics were "improved" every step up the ladder. Honecker's economic illiteracy, Mittag's power mania, and Schalck-Golodkowski's secretiveness kept inherent distortions from being corrected and added new mistakes to the list.[27]

In the end, management consisted of continual crisis responses. Solving one problem created another and sacrificed future prospects. Only the 2.5 billion DM annually transferred from Bonn for highway construction or personal visits kept East Berlin solvent. Though the GDR had achieved miracles under trying circumstances, its 1989 per capita GNP was only one-third of the level of the West (11,829 versus 35,856 DM). Afraid of losing power, the SED leaders never dared take the distateful medicine that would break the downward spiral. With $20.6 billion of foreign debt and the COMECON partners switching to hard currency, the ailing economy teetered on the brink of collapse.[28]

Political Crisis

By mid-January, the Stasi confrontation and the economic debacle created a crisis of legitimacy. Alarmed by efforts to restore Stalinist control, demonstrators demanded the ouster of the SED and shouted "Modrow must go!" When the prime minister appealed for "a climate of confidence," the New Forum balked because the communist power monopoly had yet to be broken. Tired of government foot dragging, Western CDU Secretary Volker Rühe pressed the Eastern CDU to "make a clean break" and leave the coalition. With popular hostility rising, the SED was losing its grip. Its vaunted unity had fractured into competing groups of "Communists," "Third Way" partisans, and "Democratic Socialists."[29]

To avoid a power vacuum, Modrow warned against undermining the government and rejected a Round Table "veto right." The unprecedented budget deficit of 17 billion Mk made economic recovery the top priority. To assuage anticapitalist fears, Christa Luft explained the need for "a radical but regulated transition" to a market system. Frustrated that "nothing is moving" in everyday life, citizens were quickly losing confidence. Government disarray, opposition impotence, and popular impatience raised fears that the country might become ungovernable before the promised election.[30]

On January 15, Hans Modrow swallowed his pride and appeared before the Round Table. "It is my special hope that the government remain capable of action through your support." Because the domestic situation was grave, he pleaded for restraint and support. The prime minister asked the opposition for help to keep "work in all areas of the economy proceeding undisturbedly and productively" so that "GDR citizens stay in their traditional home." In exchange, he offered "direct and responsible participation in government through competent persons." Cooperation would allow the civil movement to take part in commissions, negotiations with Bonn, and legislative proposals.[31]

Modrow's speech fundamentally altered relations between the government and the Round Table. With one stroke, the opposition would rise from Round Table criticism to cabinet responsibility. As an inducement, the prime minister suggested that the Social Democratic Party name the deputy minister of the environment, but Ibrahim Böhme declined service in a "transition government." Though the Stasi emergency complicated the situation, media and politicians welcomed the proposal as the beginning of a "constructive consensus." But the offer of power sharing put the opposition groups into a quandary: Should they cooperate in stabilizing the country or refuse and force real reform?[32]

The government had to broaden its base because its central pillar, the SED, was disintegrating. The decision "not to break radically" with the past undermined its public credibility. "Disappointed because many adherents did not notice any changes," about half the original members had left the party by January. Often the old apparatus blocked Gysi's initiatives, thereby creating a Janus face. Overworked reformers had no compelling answers to vexing questions about SED property, labor problems, or German unification. Competing factions proposed programmatic platforms ranging from communist orthodoxy via reform socialism to social democracy.[33]

On January 20, the party presidium met in crisis session. Though intellectuals who called for a Third Way demanded an immediate disbanding, younger members and women sought only a thorough renewal. To safeguard the social achievements of the GDR, the party leaders rejected formal dissolution and instead pushed for further organizational reform and dropped the old letters SED. The next day, however, popular Mayor Wolfgang Berghofer and the entire Dresden leadership resigned. In the partial steps taken so far, these pragmatic managers did not see "any political will in this party to change fundamentally." Since disintegration continued apace, Gysi only succeeded in preserving a core of the Party of Democratic Socialism (PDS).[34]

The Round Table seized on the government's weakness to expand its own authority. The January 18 meeting condemned anti-Stasi violence and reaffirmed "its determination to permit no further delay, dithering, or half-measures" in democratizing the GDR. To make doubly sure, the Runde Tisch created a "working group" with extensive powers for supervising the dissolution of the secret service. In general, the Round Table criticized the cabinet for proposing legislation without its approval, demanded speaking rights in the Volkskammer, and insisted on checking shady real estate deals. Only accelerated reform could maintain stability until the coming elections.[35]

On January 22, a worried Hans Modrow asked for help: "My government needs constructive cooperation with the Round Table" to maintain its legitimacy. Distancing himself from the discredited PDS, the prime minister reiterated his offer of opposition participation in governing. Modrow promised real influence on economic policy and the drafting of laws (such as a better election bill). He urged "all new parties to suggest persons who are ready to join the cabinet" immediately. The Round Table sensed that this grand coalition proposal "put the opposition into the driver's seat." Since it feared losing credibility, the civic movement would accept only under tough conditions that enabled it to achieve its own agenda.[36]

In secret negotiations, the Runde Tisch groped for a solution to the deadlock. During long sessions on January 24 and 26, government and opposition positions fragmented. Among the bloc parties, the Christian Democrats faced mounting internal and external pressure to distance themselves from the PDS so as not to go down with it. Chairman de Maizière felt duty-bound to support "a transitional grand coalition" until the elections. Nonetheless, his party threatened to leave the cabinet unless opposition groups joined the government. Buoyed by favorable but imprecise surveys, the untainted Social Democrats began to think of themselves as the likely election victors. To heighten his own chances, SPD leader Ibrahim Böhme wanted to avoid propping up a failing rival.[37]

Surprisingly, "this survival crisis" converted the dissident opposition. Erstwhile skeptics such as Democratic Awakening and New Forum came around and accepted Modrow's offer. Among smaller groups, Democracy Now, the human rights activists (IFM), the Greens, and the feminists wanted to join, but the United Left refused because it opposed unification. The civic movement demanded "a caretaker government" that would be independent of parties. When the CDU ministers resigned, the SPD gave in and agreed to the proposal of a nonpartisan grand coalition. Astute observers realized that "this means a decisive change in power relationships."[38]

After seven hours of hard bargaining, a tenuous compromise emerged on January 28. The deepening disarray had left little choice. The coalition had become "increasingly fragile," the "economic situation deteriorated alarmingly," public authority was rapidly eroding, and "the population [was] growing more and more uneasy." The agreement was simple enough. The general elections were moved up to March 18. Though the new groups objected that they would stand little chance, the PDS and SPD insisted on an early date in order to shorten the interregnum. Only the local voting was to remain on May 6. Moreover, "a government of national responsibility" would be formed. Each of the eight opposition groups would send one representative to take part in all cabinet decisions as minister without portfolio.[39]

Such general cooptation institutionalized power sharing without administrative responsibility. The civic movement lacked the technical competence to head ministries, but felt capable of exerting political control. SPD and CDU could participate in the government but would not have to shoulder blame. In a show of good will, the cabinet also promised to designate a minister as permanent liaison to the Round Table. Though the Volkskammer still had to approve, this agreement was "a sign of reason" that helped restore some stability. Once an outside critic, the Runde Tisch now took formal charge so as to stave off the bankruptcy of the GDR.[40]

With strengthened authority, the Round Table pushed for further reform. Beyond addressing persistent Stasi problems, it promoted "guarantees for freedom of opinion, information, and the media." On January 29, the Runde Tisch shifted its attention to "questions of ecology and environmental protection." Overriding official denials, Minister Peter Diederich frankly discussed "the ecological crisis" caused by the heaviest sulfur-dioxide emissions in Europe. The unsafe nuclear reactors in Greifswald were harshly criticized. Discussions also touched on "the problems of large-scale animal production, the social consequences of plant closings and the issue of protecting water resources."[41]

As a way out, the environment committee recommended "an ecological transformation." To reverse the threatening catastrophe, society needed to set different priorities. The Round Table insisted on legal measures to stop abuses, better information and research, and more recycling, energy conservation, nonchemical agriculture, landscape protection, and mass transit. The first public discussion of the disastrous extent of environmental degradation aroused much passion. But the comprehensive reform program ignored the collapse of the economy and lacked any means of enforcement to compel obstructionist local businesses and authorities.[42]

Democratizing the 8.5-million-member trade unions was equally difficult. The switch of roles from SED "transmission belts" to workers' advocates made little headway until disclosures of corruption forced the fall of the interim leadership. Though shop stewards organized anticommunist strikes, attempts to create independent unions did not generate much enthusiasm either. The extraordinary union congress convened in late January was stormy. When members voted to disenfranchise the functionaries, the latter changed the rules and ignored the delegates. To restore consensus, the meeting passed an action program to strengthen union power and voted a draft law with a maximum of rights, including the general strike. Since the apparatchiks defended their influence by creating separate unions under the Communist (FDGB) umbrella, union credibility continued to erode.[43]

On February 5, Hans Modrow proudly presented his "government of national responsibility" to the Volkskammer. The grave situation made an unusual coalition among thirteen different parties and groups imperative: "The GDR can no longer be governed, unless responsibility is broadened." The new ministers were an impressive group of committed professionals: Tatjana Böhm (Independent Women's Association), a feminist scholar; Rainer Eppelmann (Democratic Awakening), a pacifist pastor; Sebastian Pflugbeil (New Forum), a nuclear physicist and environmentalist; Mathias Platzeck (Green Party), an ecological activist; Gerd Poppe (Human Rights Initiative), an engineer and social reformer; Dr. Walter Romberg (Social Democrat), a mathematician and disarmament advocate; Klaus Schlüter (Green League), an environmental engineer; and Dr. Wolfgang Ullmann (Democracy Now), a church historian.[44]

Opposition leaders infused the moribund cabinet with fresh legitimacy and novel ideas. In internal discussions, they participated vigorously in the shaping of legislative proposals. But most of the administrative work proceeded behind their backs since they had only small staffs and the party cadres were none too eager to take orders from dissidents. The broadening of the government was both "a line of last defense and harbinger of something new." For the PDS this arrangement preserved a remnant of power through the legitimacy of the opposition. For the civic movement it was the first chance to shape decisions by getting access to state authority.[45]

A key figure in the new coalition was Wolfgang Ullmann. Born in 1929, the pudgy and balding professor of the Protestant academy in Berlin embodied the honesty and openness of reform theologians. Drawing on wide historical reading, this radical scholar sought to set people free: "The emancipated citizen wants to decide himself who plans and rules in the country." As one of the fathers of the Round Table, Ullmann searched for a direct form of democracy that would mobilize "energies of self-organization." Ullmann used the considerable force of his personality to make the televised Round Table debates into "a nursery of democracy." Though he helped dismember the Stasi hydra, his polished rhetoric was more effective at conveying a vision of civil society than at solving the problems of everyday politics.[46]

Action was most urgent but difficult in the deteriorating economy. On February 5, the government disclosed that "1990 production is sinking to the level of 1985." Forced to improvise solutions, the cabinet accelerated internal reforms while seeking external assistance. With a joint venture law, recognition of private property, and realistic pricing, Christa Luft attempted to nudge the unwieldy planning system into a market direction. At the same time, the cabinet called for 10 to 15 billion DM in assistance from Bonn to facilitate the purchase of new machinery and cushion the social shock. Confronted with a failing economy, the Round Table had little choice but to agree with the half-hearted conversion to the market. But in the necessary restructuring, it voiced popular fears of unemployment and demanded special protection for the weak.[47]

Just as the Round Table gained influence, the masses started to desert its policies. In January, "everyone demonstrated only for reunification and against the SED." With the Stasi scare, the opposition could still turn out half a million to protest in Leipzig, Dresden, and Chemnitz. But the common folk gradually sensed that the Round Table pursued the Third Way rather than the improvement of living conditions. Instead of a more humane world, most people wanted prosperity through unification. Confident that "we have the power!" demonstrators began to defect from the civic movement. They intoned a new chant: "Neither brown nor red— Helmut Kohl [is] our bet!"[48]

Opinion polls reflected the shift in the popular mood. By mid-February, 72 percent of Leipzig protesters strongly endorsed unity and 20 percent supported it somewhat less. Many of the marchers were young (averaging 35.5 years), male (72 percent), and working class (39 percent) as well as white-collar (32 percent). The protesters were committed demonstrators; more than half had participated ten times. Though more timid, the general population followed their lead. Between November and February, the share of decided unification advocates doubled from 16 percent to 40 percent, and the proportion of moderate supporters rose from 32 percent to 39 percent. In another survey, two-thirds favored unity and another 16 percent wanted some kind of confederation. Since intellectual dreams for a civil society increasingly clashed with popular desires for a better life, the Round Table's authority began to wane.[49]

Cooperation between government and opposition proved insufficient to end the political crisis. When the SED seemed to be reconsolidating, the public supported dissident demands to dismantle the hated secret police. With the creation of the cabinet of national responsibility, the civic movement succeeded in gaining a share of formal power that allowed it to promote additional reforms. But the people, conscious of their own force, used their new freedom of speech to push for material improvements rather than following the constitutional agenda of the Round Table. Although united against Stalinist oppression, the dissidents and the populace parted ways when they realized that their visions of the future were incompatible.[50]

Newly won freedoms allowed liberal and conservative groups to emerge. Since opposition to Marxism had been forbidden in the GDR, national sentiment had only slowly surfaced in demonstrations. In the New Year, center-right parties dared to form and champion a radical break with socialism. The German Social Union (DSU) denounced Marxism as "the joke of the century." In the South the new groups quickly grew popular, because the common folk were disappointed that "few tangible improvements can be felt in daily life." With another fifty-eight thousand moving to the West in January, time was running out for the GDR: "Hence the demand for the quickest possible unity with the FRG."[51]

Diplomatic Destabilization

Economic collapse and political disarray raised doubts about the continued viability of the East German state. During Vaclav Havel's visit and talks with Western business leaders, Modrow still stressed GDR sovereignty. But the COMECON meeting on January 9 revealed "so many illusions" that the prime minister concluded: "Only an orientation to West Germany was a realistic alternative for us." But this was more easily said than done. In East Berlin the PDS and the Round Table distrusted reliance on Western help. Moreover, in Bonn the FDP and SPD warned against dealing with the SED and pouring money into a bankrupt regime.[52]

Mounting GDR difficulties spurred Helmut Kohl to work on improving the international prospects for unification. During intensive discussions with President Mitterrand, the chancellor dispelled French fears by reiterating his commitment to European integration. In response to the Soviet food shortage, the West German government began sending supplies in order to shore up Gorbachev and soften Russian opposition. Though feminists deprecated "the dreams of old men," the Western parties began to increase contacts with potential Eastern partners in order to prepare for the coming election campaign. East German troubles renewed the momentum toward unity in the first weeks of the new year.[53]

The Eastern turmoil also rendered plans for a treaty community obsolete. When Modrow suggested a visit in February to discuss the project, Bonn responded favorably. To the television public Kohl explained the need for "giving the people a perspective" while he reassured the international community that he had no fixed timetable for unity. But on January 15 the dramatic news of the storming of the Stasi citadel changed his mind. When he realized the depth of East German discontent, the chancellor wanted "to push the SED-PDS out of the government as quickly as possible" and postpone serious talks until after free elections. Unfortunately, Bonn never communicated this shift to East Berlin.[54]

The GDR government presented a draft on "cooperation and good neighborliness" on January 17. As a "new dimension of mutual relations," a treaty community that "opens the way to a confederation" should contain a "consultative commission" and create "an economic association" with a currency link. Since Kohl had privately decided that "concluding treaties with Modrow no longer makes any sense," he decided to put off actual negotiations until after a democratic government was formed. Bonn was willing to encourage reforms and discuss short-term help only in order to stem the refugee tide. When the East Germans pressed for "a fast start to negotiations" and for massive financial help, Minister Seiters turned a deaf ear.[55]

During the same weeks, the Soviet government dropped its veto of German unification. Realists like Edvard Shevardnadze had long understood that the "German problem" needed a more permanent solution, but the emotional trauma of the deaths of 27 million in World War II had prevented any change from the policy of partition. The GDR turmoil triggered a power struggle between Russian hardliners like Central Committee spokesman Valentin Falin and glasnost advocates like Alexander Yakovlev, who were close to Gorbachev. Gradually, enlightened self-interest began to carry the day in the argument that agreement would produce more lasting peace than force. In late January the German specialist Nikolai Portugalov hinted to the tabloid *BILD:* "If the GDR people want reunification, it shall come."[56]

On January 30 Hans Modrow's visit to Moscow brought the political breakthrough. Hoping for continued independence after an SPD election victory, Gorbachev privately criticized Kohl's efforts at destabilizing the GDR. Instead, the Soviet leader welcomed Modrow's gradual approach to unification, since it offered a chance for assuring German neutrality. Ever the supreme realist, Gorbachev grudgingly recognized the futility of opposing popular pressure for unity. Unwilling to use force to stop its momentum, he wanted to channel the process toward weakening the NATO threat. After concluding the talks, Gorbachev announced to a stunned press: "Among the Germans in East and West as well as the four power representatives, there is a certain agreement that German unification has never been doubted by anyone." From right to left, the German media celebrated: "Gorbachev gives in: Unity inescapable."[57]

With Soviet backing, Hans Modrow tried to regain the unification initiative. On returning to Berlin, he invoked the GDR anthem to plead for "Germany, united fatherland." In response to the "understandable pressure of great parts of the population in both states" he sought to "present a perspective which makes peaceful development possible." Expanding his previous ideas, he suggested "the creation of a unified German state" through a federation that would be militarily neutral. To calm international fears, Modrow proposed "a gradual . . . and calculable coming together of both German states." He was now ready to move from association towards "a united fatherland of all citizens of the German nation." The civic movement, the Communist party, and his own family preferred GDR independence. But Modrow appealed to the silent majority of East Germans by proposing a controlled approach to unity.[58]

Moscow's apparent change of course accelerated the momentum of unification. Delighted with "Modrow's capitulation," Bonn objected only to his demand for neutrality.[59] The GDR plan suggested to the FRG chancellor "that political unity might come more quickly than anyone had assumed." As a sign of support for the East, Western financial experts therefore began to urge a reform of the worthless currency. To restart the economy, Ingrid Matthäus-Maier of the SPD proposed "a 'DM-monetary' union between the FRG and the GDR beginning at the latest in 1991." At the world economic forum in Davos Modrow asked the chancellor for aid to stop the decline. Deflecting this request, Kohl instead suggested a potential currency deal.[60]

Spurred by stories of collapse, a new FRG cabinet committee on unification began to discuss scenarios for economic union. To forestall his party rival Lothar Späth, Kohl reluctantly decided to tackle fiscal concerns. On February 6, he surprised the CDU/CSU Bundestag delegation by declaring his intention to enter into "immediate negotiations with the GDR about a currency union and economic reform." Citing demonstration posters, he argued: "If we don't want the people to come to the DM, the DM has to go to the people." On the following day the cabinet accepted quick conversion when Bundesbank president Karl Otto Pöhl bowed to political pressure for using the DM as lever for unity. Kohl ignored warnings about the likelihood of economic disruption and social suffering, arguing "we should not approach this historic decision with a mercenary mind."[61]

Chancellor Kohl's visit to Moscow on February 10 confirmed the Russian reversal. Upset that the GDR was to be swallowed, Soviet hardliner Yegor Ligachev had warned against "a new Munich." In a predeparture briefing Kohl's advisor Horst Teltschik stressed the need "to prevent the impending chaos" in the East by obtaining Russian assent. Reassured by private letter from George Bush that Moscow might relent, Kohl also emphasized "that unity was getting close. He would prefer to have more time, but the momentum was unstoppable." Though concerned about the rush, Gorbachev conceded: "Between the Soviet Union, FRG, and GDR, there were no differences of opinion about unification and the people's right to strive for it." Since the Germans had learned from their past to be peaceful, "they should know themselves which way they want to go."[62]

Taking rapid notes, Teltschik privately rejoiced. "That is the breakthrough! Gorbachev agrees to German unification. A triumph for Helmut Kohl, who shall enter history as the chancellor of unity." Since the West Germans promised economic help, the Russian leader remained surprisingly flexible about his demand for military neutrality. On network news Kohl proudly announced that the Germans could determine the "timing and manner" of unity themselves. Initially, the press was skeptical about this claim, since security issues remained unresolved. Only after the Soviet news agency TASS repeated Gorbachev's assurances did journalists join the chancellor in a toast on the flight home.[63]

Angered by reports of the GDR's imminent bankruptcy, the Round Table decided to fight back. With rare unanimity, it imposed stringent guidelines for unification negotiations. For instance, Bonn needed to "do everything to counter the further destabilization" of the GDR. A Western contribution of 10 to 15 billion DM would facilitate economic reform. Before "giving up financial sovereignty," experts should study the effects of a currency union. A social charter was needed to cushion the transition shock and preserve "the social security of the GDR population." Gradual union ought to remain embedded in European integration and disarmament. "The Round Table opposes any attempt at direct or indirect extension of NATO to the territory of the present GDR." In eight additional letters, the PDS, unions, farmers, ecologists, and others demanded special protection for their respective clienteles.[64]

During Modrow's visit to Bonn on February 13 the slow approach clashed with the fast conception of unification. Arriving with eight Round Table and nine other ministers, the GDR premier was received politely but distantly in the West German capital. To discourage further refugees from coming West, Chancellor Kohl suggested immediate negotiations about a currency and economic union: "GDR citizens will soon possess the most precious thing that the FRG owns, the DM." Modrow accepted commission talks, but presented a memorandum detailing the Round Table's positions. After a quick look, Teltschik thought, "Nothing much can be done with this paper, since many points are quite unrealistic."[65]

When Modrow hinted "that the GDR is facing bankruptcy," Kohl refused to offer aid. "The chancellor is no longer interested in making decisive agreements with a helpless Modrow." The subsequent delegation debates made little progress, since Wolfgang Ullmann provoked his hosts by likening rapid unity to the Nazi *Anschluss* of Austria. In the official press conference, Kohl, in victor's pose, emphasized his currency union offer. In contrast a proud but dejected Modrow stressed the GDR's cultural achievements. To one astute observer the symbolism of this meeting suggested "the unconditional surrender of the GDR to the FRG."[66]

The sobering visit revealed the conflict between "national euphoria and social fear" that bedeviled the unification process. In the West, conservative media celebrated while leftist sheets denounced Kohl's power play. Because of the slowness of reform, the major parties saw Modrow as an undemocratic "bankruptcy administrator" who should not be supported with taxpayers' money. Only the Greens were appalled that the GDR government was treated as if it no longer existed. A leftist "Bremen initiative" called on Bonn to pay 727 billion DM in catch-up reparations to East Berlin. Critical academics warned that currency union would turn out to be a "(bi)national disaster."[67]

On his return Modrow tried to put a good face on his disappointment. He reported to the Round Table: "The most important result of the visit is that the governments of both states have now thrown the switches for a rapid unification of GDR and FRG into a German federation." Monetary preparations were to begin immediately; but economic sovereignty would be relinquished only after the election. The Runde Tisch refused to be reassured, opposed "a fire sale of public property," and reiterated the need for a social charter. The PDS saw its worst fears borne out, and the civic movement worried about dislocations but could offer no alternative. Only the CDU and FDP bloc affiliates welcomed the currency union wholeheartedly.[68]

The disintegration of the GDR created international concern about the implications of restoring German unity. When the elections were moved up, President Bush urged his aides to plan a framework for managing the process. State Department advisers Robert Zoellick and Dennis Ross thought Big Four negotiations too antiquated and thirty-five-nation CSCE discussions too cumbersome. Hence they suggested bringing the four World War II victors together with the two Germanies and detaching the domestic from the international aspects of the talks. When Secretary of State Baker informed the British, his colleague Douglas Hurd initially preferred "four plus zero," but eventually went along. During his Washington visit several days later, FRG Foreign Minister Genscher welcomed the idea, insisting that the Germans work out their internal merger while resolving the external issues with the other powers separately.[69]

Afraid of being overwhelmed by demands, Bonn rejected a general peace treaty. It preferred to keep the fifteen NATO or thirty-five CSCE states out of the negotiations, but would let them ratify the result in a European summit instead. The French, though favoring great power talks, eventually fell into line with Bonn. On February 8, Baker offered deep troop cuts and presented the two-plus-four idea to President Gorbachev, who seemed interested in spite of strong domestic opposition. When Kohl was briefed on the American proposal, he initially objected to "four midwives." But he endorsed the negotiations between the two Germanies and the Big Four during his Moscow visit two days later. Surprisingly, Gorbachev accepted, saying "Nothing [will be done] without the chancellor."[70]

The international framework for unification was hammered out during the Open Sky meeting in Ottawa on February 13. Instead of debating air inspections of military movements, the foreign ministers of the Big Four and the two Germanies worked out the two-plus-four agreement. Constantly shuttling between Douglas Hurd, Roland Dumas, and Hans-Dietrich Genscher, Baker discussed ending the postwar order "with stunning frankness." After a breakfast with his allies, the secretary of state handed Eduard Shevardnadze a piece of paper with the proposed language in his own handwriting. President George Bush phoned Helmut Kohl to emphasize German NATO membership, and the chancellor consulted with Genscher about the time frame of the proposed negotiations.[71]

After he had checked with Gorbachev, Shevardnadze overcame his doubts and gave the green light. Intent on "writing security guarantees for the USSR and all of Europe into this process," Moscow only insisted on reassuring Poland with a promise to respect the concerns "of the neighboring states." The Ottawa formula limited talks to the World War II victors and the German successor states. The press had a double sensation to

report: Troops in Europe would be substantially reduced, and external
negotiations about unity would be ratified by the CSCE. Sure that "decisions would not be taken over German heads," Genscher could boast to
his cabinet: "The result of Ottawa was optimal."[72]

The diplomatic breakthroughs in mid-February were so rapid that
their full implications were difficult to grasp. Coming on top of each other,
Russian approval, the currency union offer, and the two-plus-four agreement transformed German politics. "Never have we been so close to our
goal, the unity of all Germans in freedom, as we are today," Helmut Kohl
proudly called on the Bundestag for "national solidarity." Annoyed at
having been left out, SPD leader Hans-Jochen Vogel shot back: "What is
at stake here is not the absorption of a territory without government," but
unification "with a people that has won its own freedom." Sensitive to
foreign concerns and GDR fears, Hans-Dietrich Genscher stressed the
need for "total equality" and for contributing to European stability.[73]

An impotent Left denounced the impending victory of capitalism over
socialism. Though aware that the GDR could hardly be saved, critical
intellectuals kept polemicizing against a Western takeover without proposing a practical alternative. While financially risky, the currency union
proposal capitalized on the FRG's economic strength and sent the East
German population a signal of hope. To safeguard GDR independence,
Hans Modrow tried to defend the putative interests of the Soviet Union.
But Moscow's surprise acceptance of German unification, and the Ottawa
agreement on the modus of negotiations made it clear that East Germany
was losing international support. From a full-fledged participant, the
GDR was turning into an object of negotiations. The disintegration of
East Berlin would soon transform the talks into one-plus-four.[74]

The Implosion of the GDR

In the first two months of 1990, the East German state collapsed. Although it does not answer the question of agency, the "implosion" metaphor suggests that the GDR crumbled psychologically as a result of economic and political pressures. The bankruptcy of the planned economy,
once acknowledged, rendered attempts to democratize socialism pointless.
By revealing the danger of a Stalinist relapse, the Stasi conflict discredited
the search for a Third Way. The struggle between reform Communists
and civic opposition led to power sharing, but prevented the solution of
mounting problems. Hence the effort to reform the GDR started losing
the race to the rising sentiment in favor of union with the FRG.[75]

Economic collapse and political disarray changed the democratization
movement into a stampede towards unity. "The patience of the masses is
exhausted. They no longer want new social experiments," the sociologist
Heinz Kallabis pondered dejectedly. "They want the living standards of
their brothers and sisters in the FRG. They want them today and not just

tomorrow. They do not want to pull 'the cart out of the mud' alone."
Perhaps unfairly, Honecker's travesty had "discredited the idea of socialism among the broad masses for the near future." During the first few
weeks of 1990, "the last illusions about continuing the separate existence
of the GDR [so as to build] a democratic socialist society foundered on the
hard facts." When the silent majority gave up on renewal, the socialist
"open air museum GDR" had to be closed.[76]

The Eastern implosion dramatically accelerated the rush to unity.
The Bonn government exploited the GDR's loss of legitimacy to urge
quick unification. Exaggerated by media hype, predictions of catastrophe
helped persuade the Soviet Union to drop its most important European
client. Hastened by U.S. pressure, Gorbachev's withdrawal of support for
East Berlin in late January destroyed the GDR's international viability.
Hesitant Western neighbors like France had no choice but to accept the
inevitable by agreeing to a four-power framework that would manage the
merger of the two principals. Popular disaffection weakened Modrow's
hand, forcing him to surrender economic sovereignty and accept Kohl's
currency union scheme.[77]

By eliminating the confederation alternative, the New Year's crisis
reduced the psychological timetable from years to months. Policies that
had seemed extraordinarily daring only a few weeks earlier quickly grew
out of date. The rapidity of change threatened to overtake the ability to
react: "Politicians have neither foreseen recent developments nor do they
control the tempo of events." Frightened by national intoxication, intellectual critics protested against the FRG government's "speed-rush" on the
runaway train to unity: "Pressed into their seats by the acceleration, the
conductors utter shrill shouts of joy." Would the passengers safely reach
the station or would they crash on the way?[78]

The prospect of rapid unity intensified the West German debate
about its legitimacy. Neoconservative spokesman Karl-Heinz Bohrer
scathingly denounced the taboo against nationhood as hysterical "colonial
consciousness." Scorning the Third Way as utopian, he argued that only a
chastened national state could produce a stable identity. Touched at a
nerve, left-wing intellectuals responded vehemently. SPD intellectual Peter Glotz rejected conservative arguments as a falsification of history.
Instead of turning the cultural nation once again into a state, he urged "an
intelligent division of sovereignty" in an integrated Europe. More emphatically yet, Günter Grass held the national state responsible for Auschwitz.
The prominent novelist opposed unity because he believed that it would
lead to another holocaust.[79]

Aside from student radicals, the FRG public did not share these
intellectual scruples. Unity endorsements by prominent citizens, ranging
from soccer stars to industrialists, came closer to reflecting the popular
mood. According to opinion polls, Western support for unification increased from 70 percent to 78 percent between November and February,
with three-quarters favoring aid for the East. Only the acceleration of

events proved unsettling for two-thirds of the respondents. Since a large majority expected unity to be completed in the near future, "the question is no longer whether but only how and with what speed."[80]

The growing likelihood of unification heightened international ambivalence. In most countries popular attitudes surprisingly favored unity. In the United States, 61 percent welcomed unification while only 13 percent rejected it. Support was highest in Italy (78 percent), followed by Spain (73 percent), France and Hungary (each 68 percent), Great Britain (61 percent) and the Soviet Union (51 percent). The Czechs (58 percent) and the Dutch (52.4 percent) were also positive. Only most Poles (64 percent) and Danes (51 percent) were opposed.[81] In contrast, political elites remained skeptical. In America columnist Abraham Rosenthal invoked the "open wounds" of Hitler's victims to argue for postponement. In France, historian Alfred Grosser wanted to preserve the East from Western tutelage. In Russia Eduard Shevardnadze cautioned against "artificial acceleration of unity." In Britain Thatcherites wanted to put off unification for a decade.[82]

The holocaust trauma inspired the most bitter criticism in Jewish circles. Fixated on a bitter past, Israeli Premier Itzhak Shamir emotionally warned against unification as "a danger to Jews." The writer Elie Wiesel predicted that German rehabilitation would obliterate the memory of Hitler's crimes. Only a few moderates like Nazi-hunter Simon Wiesenthal or Jerusalem Mayor Teddy Kollek were ready to risk forgiveness.[83] Eventually, ex-Secretary of State Henry Kissinger, novelist Michel Tournier, and publishing tycoon Lord Weidenfeld calmed elite fears by pointing to the positive record of the FRG. The East was not joining the old Reich but a stable and democratic Western state. Reluctantly, foreign observers began to learn that in the new German math two plus four would equal one.[84]

6

Voting for a Better Life

The parliamentary election on March 18 decided the GDR's fate. For the first time in over half a century, the people could vote their political preference without fear. Since Hitler and Honecker had allowed only acclamation, the unaccustomed freedom of choice raised high and often conflicting expectations. Dissident leader Bärbel Bohley hoped for "the storm to abate" and stability to return. Marxist intellectual Jürgen Rennert wished for "something well-nigh impossible"—the continued existence of East Germany. Writer Helga Schubert, however, desired drastic reforms to revive the economy, restore the old states and prepare for unification: "Hence, I expect the dissolution of the GDR."[1]

The stakes were enormous. This Volkskammer election would not only determine the party in power, but also decide the nature of the political system. At the same time, the ballot was a referendum on the continuation of separate East German statehood. "At issue is a freely elected GDR government which represents the interests of sixteen million" people. East and West Germans as well as foreigners watched the campaign with anxious anticipation. "Events are moving with lightning speed." The novelist Joachim Seyppel wondered: "Will the election bring clarity?"[2]

The outcome of the vote was an open question. During a revolutionary realignment of loyalties, it was exceedingly difficult to predict where voters would turn. Previous free elections, decades removed, could offer little guidance for a contest between Communists, bloc parties and the civic movement. SED hostility to empirical social research had also limited practical experience with constructing representative samples. Because of the dearth of telephones, the use of party members as interviewers, and antiquated procedures, survey results were none too reliable.[3]

Initial polls showed a declining PDS, a fragmented opposition, and a large group of undecided voters. In late January, the Leipzig Central Institute for Youth Research predicted that the reborn SPD would receive an astounding 54 percent of the vote. Other surveys confirmed expectations of a Social Democratic victory with between 36 percent and 44 percent of the vote. Most analysts considered a switch to a milder, democratic form of socialism more plausible than its total repudiation.[4] But by early March a few institutes noted that the bourgeois bloc was starting to close the gap. Strong swings of popular mood and many undecided voters kept everything in flux.[5]

The election result was sensational. When the first prognoses flashed onto the monitors, analysts were stunned and incredulous. One TV commentator had to order a quick *Schnapps* to overcome her shock. At 7 P.M. the major networks officially announced the outcome: "In the first free elections in 58 years [Helmut Kohl's] 'Alliance for Germany' celebrates an overwhelming victory." With an impressive turnout of 93.38 percent, the Christian Democrats (CDU) "gain 192 seats, whereas the SPD only receives 88. Who would have expected that?" The predicted success of the Social Democrats that had drawn Willy Brandt, Oskar Lafontaine, and Hans-Jochen Vogel to Berlin turned into thorough rout.[6]

In the crammed Eastern CDU hall, reporters, party workers, and politicians rejoiced in the unexpected upset. The Bonn SPD headquarters sank into "silence, embarrassment, disbelief, and compulsive attempts to suppress resentment." In the chancellor's bungalow, "the joy is immense, everyone congratulates Kohl," noted Horst Teltschik. "We agree that he experiences a personal triumph" since "his appearances seem to have turned the campaign tide." The CDU had every reason to gloat, since with its allies the Democratic Awakening (DA) and the German Social Union (DSU) it came close to an absolute majority at 48.1 percent. In contrast, the SPD suffered a crushing defeat, winning just 21.9 percent of the ballots cast.[7]

This popular verdict was a clear mandate for unity. In their postmortems, most parties hailed the vote for freedom, social security, and prosperity as a "victory of democracy." After he had won the biggest gamble of his career, a relieved Helmut Kohl thanked East Germans for "choosing a path that leads to a united Germany" by expanding the Federal Republic. Admitting "great surprise," Lothar de Maizière mused that the "unexpectedly favorable result" implied "a high degree of responsibility and popular expectation." The liberal coalition partners could also be gratified that their makeshift alliance gained more than 5 percent.[8]

Challenger Oskar Lafontaine deplored the "miserable outcome." Bitterly, he warned that it would not be easy for the chancellor "to keep his promises." Eastern SPD spokesman Stefan Reiche rationalized that "GDR citizens have decided in favor of the FRG and not for a specific party." The PDS was delighted that an unexpected comeback made it the third strongest party with sixty-five seats. Saddened at the marginalization of the civic movement (under 5 percent), Bärbel Bohley fumed that by electing "money [and] bananas" the people had lost the chance to create something new. The overwhelming vote for quick union with the Federal Republic provided irrefutable domestic and international legitimation for the unification drive.[9]

Parties and Platforms

In GDR politics, elections had a strange history. To broaden the system's legitimacy, the postwar "people's democracy" claimed to be the culmination of progressive traditions. Since the original Communist party (KPD) was small, the Soviet military administration forced its amalgamation with the larger SPD into the Socialist Unity Party of Germany (SED) in 1946. Together with the restored Christian (CDU) and Liberal (LDPD) parties, this SED formed a "democratic" bloc, which it controlled by adding new nationalist and peasant parties (NDPD and DBD) and mass organizations (FDGB, FDJ, DFD, Kulturbund). When the Communists failed to win several local elections, they rigged the outcome by introducing a "united list" for the state-wide balloting in 1950.[10]

SED control turned elections into ritual acclamations. With communist leadership enshrined in the constitution, democratic procedures lost their original purpose of public choice and became mere trappings. To eliminate all risk, seats in the Volkskammer were distributed beforehand. Initially, the SED received 25 percent, the CDU and LDPD got 15 percent each, and the other parties tallied 7.5 percent with the mass organizations dividing the rest. Parliamentary debates could therefore only ratify prior SED decisions. Though critical of bourgeois democracy, the regime maintained periodic ballots as proof of its "democratic" character abroad. At home, nomination rewarded faithful followers and campaigning became propaganda for certain public goals.[11]

During the fall of 1989, the bloc parties began to reject their subservient role. For their members, the Christian and Liberal parties (CDU and LDPD) provided a protected niche that demonstrated loyalty without requiring them to join the SED. For their leaders, collaboration brought public esteem and private wealth. Gathering academics, artisans, and small businessmen, the 113,000-member LDPD sought a liberal image. Chairman Manfred Gerlach was the first to address exodus and dissent: "The GDR needs inquisitive, impatient and curious people" to move forward. "Disagreement is not subversion." Though the LDPD championed reforms to help its clients, it hesitated to break openly with the SED.[12]

The docile CDU appealed to religious and traditional middle class circles. Lacking Western contacts, the 140,000-member party grew restive as a result of the church's sheltering of emigrants and protesters. On September 10, an outspoken "letter from Weimar" called for greater "democracy within the party," more external "profile" and "resolute tackling of social problems." Spurred on by the criticism of the Protestant synod at Eisenach, Christian reformers pushed through "the renewal of the party" and dared to demand "a fundamental change in public life." Seeking to become "an independent and autonomous party," the CDU called for "new elections as soon as possible and a truly democratic election law."[13]

The renewing CDU chose as its unlikely chairman Lothar de Maizière. Born in 1940 into a Huguenot family of jurists and officers, this slight and greying man emulated Prussian virtues. A nerve inflammation had forced Lothar to give up playing the viola as a concert musician. Studying law at night, he became "the sole Christian lawyer in East Berlin." His Protestant sense of duty compelled him to take on dissident cases, which brought him into conflict with the authorities. Church business required contact with the Stasi, which listed him as a secret informant. In 1956 he joined the CDU, yet did not participate actively or have any party career.[14]

When the corrupt CDU leader Gerald Götting resigned, reformers searched for an honest successor. They wanted someone identified with the church, not compromised by office, but experienced in leadership and able to reach out to the masses. As legal advisor to the church and vice-president of the GDR synod, de Maizière seemed to fit the bill. He loathed political backslapping and preferred to stand in the second row, but eventually accepted the draft. Though earnest probity gave him credibility, tenacious righteousness limited his appeal. His courageous call to "break open encrustations" came to symbolize Christian hopes for reform.[15]

The most vigorous of the new competitors was the SPD. Unlike the tainted bloc parties, the Social Democrats had made a fresh start. Since they drew on regional traditions as well as popular sympathy for Willy Brandt's and Helmut Schmidt's *Ostpolitik*, they became a dangerous challenger to the SED. But without a union base, these leftist pastors and employees possessed no organization, publication, or infrastructure. Though the party claimed about one hundred thousand members in mid-February, it lacked any practical tools for political work, such as offices or cars, copiers or telephones. The Social Democrats' greatest asset was their name.[16]

Recognition by the Western SPD as primary partner boosted the confidence of its Eastern counterpart. During its congress in January, the party quickly reversed its initials from the new SDP to the traditional SPD. Based on the principles of "freedom, justice, and solidarity," its program aimed at human rights, a democratic state, gender equality, etc. But the SPD found it difficult to define an "ecologically oriented market economy" and to endorse unification "within a European peace order." Such programmatic vagueness was the result of its collective leadership, in which only the charismatic Ibrahim Böhme stood out. Distancing itself both from the bloc parties and the opposition, a confident SPD rejected SED feelers and aimed "at power in this country."[17]

The civic movement preferred to remain a grassroots group. The New Forum saw itself as "a political platform for all citizens who strive for more direct participation, independent of existing parties." Instead of restoring parliamentarianism, it wanted to empower civil society to control the state. Through local mobilization, Jens Reich hoped to "rebuild government from below" and prevent the ossification of representation through voter alliances and independent deputies. The official program defined the *Neue Forum* as "state-wide citizen's initiative," consisting of local, factory, and issue-oriented groups.[18]

The New Forum refused to become a regular party. A stormy delegate meeting in Leipzig clung to the "principle of self-organization" and halted the transformation half-way. Angered by this "illusion," southern dissidents split off and formed a German Forum party (*Deutsche Forumpartei*), which joined the liberal camp. In order to straddle the divide, the remainder decided to "organize democratic involvement outside parliament," while also running candidates for election. Strong on citizens' rights, this intellectuals' movement ignored gender tensions and remained skeptical toward unity. At the same time it failed to develop practical alternatives to parliamentary democracy.[19]

The bloc parties' lack of credibility inspired new groups to form on the right. Since other Westerners rejected them, the Democratic Awakening (DA) gradually turned into a Christian people's party. In lengthy debates this fifteen thousand-member group, led by the lawyer Wolfgang Schnur, followed popular sentiment and shifted toward a market economy and unification. When leftists like Friedrich Schorlemmer resigned, the party moved towards the center. The DA sought to become a fresh alternative to the reforming but tainted CDU.[20]

The influence of the Bavarian Christian Social Union (CSU) in Saxony inspired the founding of a *Deutsche Soziale Union* (DSU) in February. This unabashedly promarket and prounification party, led by pastor Hans-Wilhelm Ebeling, appealed to more conservative voters. The Bonn CDU watched the twenty-five thousand-member group uneasily as it threatened to fashion a national competitor in its own camp.[21] Finally, liberal circles created an Eastern Free Democratic party (FDP) as a market advocate and a fresh alternative to the SED-tainted Liberals (LDPD). After decades of uniformity, East Germans faced a bewildering choice, ranging from moribund GDR parties to new opposition foundations and imports from the West.[22]

The coming elections forced a consolidation of the competing groups. Confusion was greatest on the center-right. Though it possessed the right name, organization, and membership, the reforming CDU was discredited by having played the recorder (*Blockflöte*) in the SED band. The untainted DA appeared promising but unproven. As a regional offshoot of the Christian Social Union, the aggressive German Social Union seemed unlikely to attract a majority. Lacking an obvious partner, the Bonn CDU fretted over which party to endorse. When he realized that he needed the old CDU *and* the new forces to win, party secretary Volker Rühe sought to combine both in a "German Alliance."[23]

With only six weeks remaining, Chancellor Kohl personally intervened to "craft an electoral alliance in the GDR." Overcoming his reluctance, he met the prickly Lothar de Maizière, duplicitous Wolfgang Schnur, and thoughtful Hans-Wilhelm Ebeling and urged the recalcitrant CDU, DA, and DSU to cooperate. The large SPD lead in opinion polls helped convince Western conservatives and Eastern reformers to embrace the CDU in an "Alliance for Germany" on February 5. Though preserving their identities, the three parties hoped to win the election and form a government. Godfather Helmut Kohl was "quite delighted" at last to have a group strong enough to compete for power in the East.[24]

Facing a similar problem, the Liberals adopted the same solution. In early February, the compromised LDPD updated its program and elected the engineer Rainer Ortleb as chair. Encouraged by Otto von Lambsdorff, the Eastern Free Democratic Party negotiated with the Deutsche Forumpartei and the reforming Liberals (LDPD). The resulting "Alliance of Free Democrats" saw itself as "a strong liberal middle" between socialists and conservatives. In harnessing Hans-Dietrich Genscher's popularity, the Liberals favored market economics and unification. They faced a tough challenge, because the SED had virtually destroyed their clientele of artisans, small businessmen, and professionals.[25]

The civic movement was less successful in creating a united front. The Western Greens refrained from intervening in the East in order to preserve its "independent political and economic path." A projected opposition alliance foundered when the Social Democrats deserted in the hope of winning alone and vitiated any chance of a dissident majority. Without Western support, the thirty thousand-member New Forum, small Democracy Now, and Human Rights Initiative (IFM) created their own front, called *Bündnis 90*, on February 7. As "corrective to the parties," this opposition alliance propagated participatory democracy and social solidarity. More committed to gender equality and ecology, the Independent Women's Association (UFV) and the Green Party formed a fourth electoral alliance in mid-February. The original revolutionaries entered the campaign divided but proud.[26]

The competing groups nonetheless cooperated in creating a new election law. On February 20 the revived parliament adopted Round Table recommendations for a more democratic procedure. Public observers and judicial review were to stop traditional SED abuses. Instead of folding ballots in open view, citizens were to use a closed booth to mark their choice. Civic movement objections prevented a "winner-take-all" format and led to proportional representation. To give outsiders a chance, no minimum share was required for seats. Any group with more than 0.25 percent of the vote would be represented in the four hundred-member Volkskammer. Not only parties, but loose civic associations and electoral alliances were allowed to run. Only neofascists were prohibited.[27]

These reforms created a simple, participatory election system, "without grave faults." An astounding twenty-four groups, ranging from the Beer Drinkers' Union to the United Left, registered before the deadline. Behind the confusing labels lay a triple choice: Voters could endorse a reformed GDR with the PDS or back unification with the other groups. Citizens could support grassroots democracy with the civic movement or favor a return to parliamentary government with other parties. Finally, electors could choose slow unification with the SPD or opt for rapid unity with the Alliance for Germany or the Liberal Bloc.[28]

Election Surprise

The course of the campaign determined the outcome of this pivotal election to an unusual degree. With so many East Germans changing their allegiances, it became crucial to get one's message across. The PDS enjoyed an enormous advantage in mass membership, media control, and government authority. Complaining about "unfair working conditions," the opposition insisted on live TV coverage of Round Table debates from early January on. Since concessions in the form of office space, cars, and phones remained paltry, the Bonn government demanded "equal opportunity for all political groups."[29]

Breaking the PDS monopoly proved difficult. Some newspapers offered an opposition page and electronic media began to produce election spots for the new parties. But only in January did the New Forum graduate from mimeographed news sheets to its own weekly, called programmatically "The Other" (*Die Andere*). In February the passage of free speech and association laws finally safeguarded fresh viewpoints and organizations. Even if its leaders were released from work, the opposition had to campaign on a playing field that was steeply tilted against it. Only the erosion of PDS control and more realistic reporting eventually evened the odds somewhat.[30]

As compensation, some groups called in Western help. The SPD, Alliance for Germany, and Liberal Bloc received copiers and cordless telephones, benefitted from professional consultants, and welcomed prominent speakers from Bonn. These parties could use FRG media to broadcast their views. Afraid of being drowned out, Bärbel Bohley "harshly condemned" outside assistance that kept Easterners from finding their own voice. "Before we knew what had happened, Western politicians arrived and put out slogans which the disoriented people largely accepted." Playing on GDR resentment against "imperial subjection," the PDS warned against "Ko(h)l"-onization.[31]

On February 5, the Round Table rejected outside interference. Voting twenty-two to nine, it demanded that parties "renounce guest speakers" from the West for the sake of fairness. Incensed, the Eastern CDU denounced the prohibition as "massive intrusion into the substance of the campaign." Arguing that "the future of our country and its people can no longer be separated from the behavior of political forces in the FRG," it promised to ignore the ban. In rare unanimity, the other Western parties also rejected any restraint as one-sided. But among opposition groups without PDS or FRG ties, this failure to comply left a bitter aftertaste.[32]

Inequity and inexperience produced an exasperating yet exhilarating campaign. Without precedent or infrastructure, everything had to be improvised. Voting freely for the first time in two generations created great excitement. People were "incredibly hungry" for information, devouring even makeshift flyers and small print. In the grey cities, colorful posters, balloons, and information stands looked like alien imports. Though announcements were often torn down, opponents belittled, and confrontations grew rough, there was little violence. The Leipzig Monday demonstrations turned into "quite normal campaign" events with hand-outs, speeches, and flag-waving.[33]

The early election date caused a furor of political activity. With rapid political changes, platforms quickly became outdated. Faced with a myriad of practical obstacles like lack of paper, volunteers drove themselves to exhaustion. For Western professionals, the unusual level of public acclaim worked like an intoxicating "fountain of youth." Eastern amateurs, however, often resented the tutelage of arrogant outsiders. Campaign styles varied astoundingly between different groups. Drab PDS material competed with homely opposition handouts, only to be overshadowed by slick Western brochures. The incongruities of the campaign mirrored the clash of Eastern and Western political cultures for the allegiance of the GDR.[34]

The ruling PDS tried to run away from its Stalinist past. To fend off the anticommunist onslaught, the SED successor presented itself as a new party of reform: "We stand firm [for] a democratic socialism for the GDR." Trying to prevent the implosion of its state, the program sought to Europeanize unification and maintain as many East German "achievements" as possible. After shrinking to 650,000 members, the ruling party projected a youthful style with its charismatic chairman, and fresh slogans like "progressive, productive, and pro-GDR" and "don't worry, take Gysi." Membership demand forced "honest Hans" Modrow to run as lead candidate so as to turn his popularity into votes.[35]

During the campaign the PDS tried to define a post-power role for the Communist elite. Since popular hatred rendered victory unlikely, the party had to prepare for an unaccustomed opposition role that would place it to the left of the SPD. As guardian of GDR security, the PDS fanned anticapitalist fears that unification would mean unemployment, higher rents, loss of pensions, and the like. The party also appealed to Eastern defiance against a takeover by the West. By mobilizing the remaining faithful in the nomenclatura and bureaucracy, it tried to keep the unity advocates from gaining a two-thirds majority. In anticipating defeat, Modrow made the best of a bad show: "A strong opposition for the weak."[36]

After its revolutionary elation, the civic movement found the campaign sobering. Disunity, a late start, and lack of means muffled its voice, but integrity, enthusiasm, and creativity provided a chance. The microbiologist Jens Reich likened dissident groups to "mushroom spores." Transient, growing underground, they might pop up anywhere. The Bündnis 90 drew strength from imaginative local sheets like the *nez*, the new Erfurt "paper for an alterna(t)ive journalism." Ranging from mimeographed handouts to small weeklies, they criticized the Stasi, lampooned authorities, warned against annexation, and announced the countless workshops of the dissident network.[37]

With simple graphics and witty wordplay, the opposition emphasized its grassroots character. To East Germans, the repetitive slogan "citizens for citizens" sounded catchy and irreverent. On the one hand the civic movement attacked the ruling party, charging that the PDS was in *princi*ple still *de same*. On the other hand, it warned that the "Bonn elephant circus" threatened to crush Eastern independence. Since the populace worried about economic survival, postmaterialist appeals for "social solidarity of independent citizens" found little resonance. The Green-feminist alliance was even less visible but could rely on its single-issue constituencies.[38]

The Social Democrats campaigned as odds-on favorites to take power. They had a head start in mobilization, the popularity of their elder statesmen, help from neighboring states, and media sympathy. But the SPD had to overcome disorganization, small membership, and doubts about Oskar Lafontaine's reservations against unity. Advertising professionals produced tons of printed material, especially handbills that were easy to read and focused on simple themes. Calling itself "Sympathetic, Practical, and Democratic," the SPD invoked its grand tradition while trying to appear "future oriented." As the alternative to "the old forces" and the CDU steamroller, it promised "to manage unification with dignity and decency," providing unity without social cost.[39]

The personality-oriented SPD material featured the photogenic Ibrahim Böhme. Handouts portrayed the handsome lead candidate as "the last GDR prime minister" with "a sense of justice and integrity." The Leipzig election congress endorsed a timetable for unity that combined European integration with the development of common German institutions and GDR reforms. Among the Western speakers, the main drawing card was ex-chancellor Willy Brandt, who made ten appearances in the final two weeks. Rejecting PDS feelers, the SPD tried not to be tarred with the socialist brush and to avoid overconfidence. Billing itself as the "social and European conscience of unity," its honest campaign lacked inspirational spark.[40]

Trying to catch up, the Alliance for Germany ran more aggressively. A strange mixture of old and new faces, it claimed the middle ground and capitalized on the Bonn government's prestige. Since it was vulnerable to charges of opportunism and Western domination, the Alliance employed an even more professional approach. With ample funds, its flood of hand-

bills addressed special topics from aging and ecology to educational reform, family values, health services, market economics, social security,
and urban decay. Its posters were even glossier and more plentiful. Alliance campaign tactics were also dirtier. A favorite handout with the letters
"PDSPDPDSPD . . . " suggested that a vote for the SPD would be tanta-
mount to reelecting the Communists.[41]

CDU slogans concentrated on a few simple themes. They promoted
"a turn around into the future," marked by "freedom and unity" as well as
"prosperity for all." Elaborate election papers denounced socialism,
pushed rapid unification, and focused less on the dour de Maizière than on
the upbeat chancellor: "Helmut Kohl gives us hope for a better future."
While the Democratic Awakening (DA) and the German Social Union
(DSU) attempted to maintain separate profiles, the CDU-run Alliance for
Germany machinery promoted rapid unity within the Basic Law, the
immediate introduction of the DM, privatization, a social safety net, and
cultural reform. Facing an uncertain future, many East German citizens
were willing to listen to promises of a better life.[42] The Liberal Bloc used
its Eastern "lost sons" like Genscher to promote a market economy.[43]

Except for the question of the Polish frontier, foreign policy was
virtually absent from the campaign. Since the CDU believed it needed
every refugee vote in the upcoming federal election, the chancellor refused
to go beyond the 1976 Warsaw treaties in guaranteeing Poland's western
border. Though only a united Germany could legally decide its frontiers,
Kohl's reluctance was politically unwise. The "pointless border quarrel"
not only alarmed the Polish public but also unsettled foreign skeptics
about the intentions of a united Germany. Washington and Paris exerted
pressure on Bonn to yield gracefully, but the chancellor dragged his feet
because of domestic concerns.[44]

The frontier issue gave the opposition ammunition and threatened to
split the coalition. When Genscher's FDP demanded a clear commitment,
CDU hardliners were miffed. In the East, unification critics in the PDS
and the civic movement used Kohl's insensitivity to cast doubt on Alliance
credibility. Maladroit efforts to tie German guarantees to a Polish renunciation of reparations and greater rights for the Silesian minority only
increased the furor. On March 6, the coalition confrontation finally produced a face-saving compromise: an immediate joint parliamentary declaration to be followed later by a bilateral treaty. Though irritations lingered, the problem failed to derail the East German campaign.[45]

In the final weeks, Kohl's six personal appearances turned the tide. In
campaign stops at Erfurt, Chemnitz, Magdeburg, Rostock, Cottbus, and
Leipzig the chancellor addressed about one million people—almost 10
percent of the electorate! A flawless presentation made his towering figure
appear statesmanlike. Alliance leaders Ebeling, de Maizière, and Schnur
preceded him and denounced the disasters of socialism. With excitement
at a fever pitch, Kohl smiled at the innumerable flags and shouts of "Hel-

mut, Helmut" that drowned out PDS boos. Speaking with a folksy Palatinate accent, the CDU leader conveyed studied moderation, but the eager crowds took comforting rhetoric for firm promises.[46]

The chancellor's speeches conjured up a vision of instant prosperity. When the necessary laws were passed, "thousands of entrepreneurs" would come to invest "and quickly build, together with you, a flourishing land." Seeking to dispel fears, Kohl reassured pensioners, the unemployed, and small savers that they would be supported by the "proven safety net" of the West. Unification would not be annexation, but liberation from suppression and want, a gateway to a better life. "At stake is your home," he concluded. "At stake is our German fatherland, at stake is a common future in Europe." The optimistic message that darkness was coming to an end hit home. Tens of thousands shouted with joy. One placard prayed: "God protect our chancellor, the architect of German unity."[47]

Kohl's vague promises created a blinding national euphoria, and the fearful masses embraced hope. Intellectuals resented "the arrogance" with which the West "takes political and economic possession of the GDR," but normal people "were simply fed up. We were tired of always shutting up" and of just eating "moldy celery." They were "sick of the poisonous air, the stinking [river] Pleisse, the derelict houses, and no longer wanted to live as wingless birds." Afraid of sliding back into Stalinism, they expected Kohl to "help us quickly out of our mess. We hoped that with his help our country would return to prosperity." According to the disgusted poet Thomas Rosenlöcher, ordinary people saw unification as the culmination of their revolution: "If they choose what they always wanted, they find themselves, the West in the East."[48]

On election eve, a worried Left sought to stop the growing momentum of the Right. In its final meeting, the Round Table urged safeguards for the right to work, sexual equality, education, health, and housing. The media circulated a rumor that Wolfgang Schnur was a Stasi informant, forcing him to resign. West Berlin radicals demonstrated against "national intoxication." To stop "the annexation of one German state by another," the Soviets warned against Bonn's "massive interference in GDR internal affairs." With time running out, Jens Reich predicted a tie: One third for the SPD, one third for the Alliance and the rest for the others to split. For a brief moment, East Germany teetered between an oppressive past and an uncertain future.[49]

Last minute opinion shifts made the result a genuine surprise. A high turnout of nine out of ten voters underscored the intensity of the campaign. Gaining over 48 percent and 192 seats, the Alliance for Germany parties almost reached an absolute majority (see Table 6). Compared to earlier expectations, the SPD was the big loser with only 21.9 percent and 88 seats. Although the PDS fell from power, it did much better than anticipated with 16.4 percent and 66 seats. With 5.3 percent and 21 seats

TABLE 6. East German Election Results, March 18, 1990

| Parties | Totals | | Regional Totals (%) | | | | | |
	Seats	Percent	Berlin	Brandenburg	Mecklenburg	Saxony	Saxony-Anhalt	Thuringia
PDS	66	16.4	30.0	18.4	22.4	13.3	14.0	11.2
SPD	88	21.9	35.0	28.9	23.9	15.1	23.6	17.4
Bündnis 90	12	2.9	6.4	3.3	2.3	3.0	2.2	2.0
FDP	21	5.3	3.0	4.8	3.6	5.7	7.7	5.6
CDU Alliance	192	48.1	21.6	38.5	39.3	57.7	47.8	60.2
Others	21	5.0	4.0	6.1	8.5	5.2	4.7	3.6

126

the Liberal Bloc barely reached its goal. A disappointed Bündnis 90 garnered only 2.9 percent while the Greens got merely 1.9 percent. This electoral debacle marginalized the dissidents.[50]

In regional terms, the conservative Alliance swept the deprived south from Saxony to Thuringia. The Left won pampered Berlin and did well in the north, such as Brandenburg and Mecklenburg. Surprisingly, the CDU triumphed in industrial areas while falling short in service and agricultural regions. Contrary to Marxist orthodoxy, 58 percent of the workers voted Right, compared to 47 percent of white-collar employees and only 32 percent of the intellectuals. The Left dominated the cities, but the small towns became Alliance territory. PDS and dissidents drew from the same young, secular, and intellectual clientele. The SPD failed to reach its traditional labor constituency and fell between all chairs. The Liberal Bloc did best in commercial cities in the mid-south. Workers, the elderly and the religious endorsed a drastic change, but farmers were in less of a hurry, and intellectual elites clung to the legacy of the GDR.[51]

The meaning of the verdict was unmistakable: "Most important, the result of the first free GDR election is a victory for democracy, which about 80% of the voters chose." Impartial commentators interpreted the outcome as a personal triumph for Helmut Kohl. "The chancellor has won. He sensed better than anyone else that the majority of East Germans only wanted to join a united Germany as quickly as possible." A chagrined Left derided the vote as a materialist grab for money and a desertion of socialist ideals. The "magnetism" of the Western currency proved irresistible, since it promised to repeat the postwar miracle in the East. "Most voters thought the strong chancellor in Bonn would bring the hoped-for DM and economic revival."[52]

The Right celebrated the result as a ringing endorsement of the "social market economy." As "the only clear alternative to socialism," the CDU managed to capture the longing for freedom and prosperity better than its competitors. Resentment against "real existing socialism" tarnished the indecisive SPD with the same brush. Foreign observers read the outcome as a plebiscite "for quick unity," citing Article 23 of the constitution, and surveys confirmed rapid union as the dominant motive. Concerns about the precise form of the merger lingered, but this overwhelming democratic legitimation "further accelerated the rapid tempo of German unification."[53]

The hard-fought campaign precipitated an extraordinary reversal of feelings towards socialism and sovereignty. Many East Germans had long cultivated a double consciousness. Nightly emigration via television created potential allegiances to Bonn parties. This virtual membership could now be actually expressed in a free ballot. By embracing quick unity, East Germans repudiated their troubled everyday selves and sought refuge in a larger national identity. After years of frustration, they "wanted to get rid of the feeling of inferiority" and cease being "second class Germans." No doubt the lure of the glittering West, amplified by a media blitz, also played a considerable role.[54]

Ordinary East Germans did not fall for Kohl's slick promises. People wished to improve their lot in a broader sense that included the environment and health: "It was touching [to see] how these hopeless people were so full of hope that at least their children, grandchildren or great-grandchildren would be able to experience better times." Disappointed intellectuals railèd: "Many have evidently only changed leaders from Honecker to Kohl; instead of the dictatorship of the party, they chose the power of money." But during the expectant March days, the masses believed they had simply picked the quickest way to better their lives.[55]

The Grand Coalition

Democratizing the GDR in order to dissolve it was an intimidating challenge. Unsure whether he wanted this "great responsibility," Lothar de Maizière placed top priority on establishing a functioning government. Since he needed a two-thirds majority for constitutional changes, the weary winner appealed to the Free Democratic and Social Democratic parties to form "as broad a coalition as possible." Without gloating, he promised to achieve unity quickly and "as well as possible." The new cabinet faced formidable problems. According to the Alliance, it needed to "conclude a currency, economic, and social union," restore the states that had been dissolved in 1952, embed unification in European integration, observe existing treaties, and remove the remnants of the Wall.[56]

The Bonn government hoped the Conservative victory would stop the costly influx of refugees and calm social fears. Responding to intense Western pressures, Kohl appealed to East Germans: "Stay home and help to rebuild this beautiful land together with us." Because of the spiralling cost, the Bonn cabinet decided to cancel financial incentives to refugees with the onset of the currency union. Foreign policy advisors worried that the two-plus-four negotiations had yet to agree on an international framework and resolve security disputes. "An enormous mountain of tasks lies before us."[57]

Forming the first free government proved more difficult than expected. In a drastically altered environment, the GDR parties met and discussed the next steps with their Western allies. In a seven-hour session, the CDU nominated a reluctant de Maizière to head its parliamentary delegation. After consulting with the Christian Social Union, the German Social Union, jubilant about its sizable vote, refused to join a common parliamentary group and be absorbed by the CDU. Only the Democratic Awakening, disappointed with its lack of success, accepted closer association. Prompted by Count Lambsdorff, the liberals transformed themselves into one party and absorbed the crumbling nationalists of the NDPD.[58]

With Helmut Kohl's blessing, de Maizière decided to run for prime minister. As a first step, he renewed his coalition offer to the FDP and SPD. Initial contacts showed much common ground between the Alliance and the Liberals, who together held 213 of 400 seats. For a dejected SPD, Ibrahim Böhme vowed not to enter a cabinet with a most unfair opponent, the rightist DSU. But he left the door open a crack by promising to cooperate in practical matters. In spite of such rebuffs, the CDU continued to court the SPD in order to gain a two-thirds majority necessary for constitutional changes. At the same time the PDS tried to draw the Social Democrats and civic movement into a veto minority.[59]

The SPD could not make up its mind. Going into opposition with the Communists was as distasteful as jumping on the Kohl bandwagon. The bruising campaign had left much resentment, especially among young and southern members, making radical Social Democrats reluctant to alienate these critical voters. But if it wanted to cushion unification socially, the SPD "had to swallow the toad" and cooperate with the antisocialist DSU. Moderates also wanted to "stiffen the GDR government's back" in dealing with Bonn. The Western Social Democrats were little help since they sent conflicting signals. Unable to decide, the Eastern party elected Ibrahim Böhme as legislative chair and approved "informational talks" with all groups, except for the PDS and DSU.[60]

The coalition negotiations dragged on over ten days. On March 21, SPD and CDU leaders met to get acquainted and survey the terrain. Gradually "the fear of being embraced by an [unloved] partner" waned, and the desire "not to shirk political responsibility" took over. Chances for agreement rose when Oskar Lafontaine publicly dropped his opposition and several union leaders urged the SPD not to refuse. On March 27, the SPD decided to talk, provided the Polish frontier was recognized, East Germany was kept out of NATO, and property rights remained untouched. Though de Maizière grew visibly impatient, SPD parliamentary chairman Richard Schröder claimed that the talks were having "positive results."[61]

On April 4, a bare majority of SPD Volkskammer deputies authorized further negotiations. Though the presidium rejected a coalition by twelve to six votes, the parliamentary group was "impressed, that *Herr* de Maizière wants to pursue a GDR policy."[62] The main obstacle was the nationalist DSU, which had mounted nasty antisocialist attacks. To expedite agreement, its leader Ebeling lamely apologized for the harshness of his campaign statements. Once this issue was resolved, the SPD drove a hard bargain. In the 24-member cabinet it demanded seven ministries, especially the posts in foreign affairs, labor, and the interior. Continuing divisions among the Social Democrats themselves made progress between the election antagonists even more difficult.[63]

A change in SPD leadership finally brought the breakthrough. In late March the weekly *Spiegel* alleged that Ibrahim Böhme was a Stasi collaborator, forcing him to suspend his party offices. A talented but unsteady communicator, he was a chameleon in a pinstripe suit, eager to fit in and be popular. According to secret police files, the long-time dissident had not just been a pitiful victim but a nasty perpetrator. Though many SPD members refused to believe it, he had continued to submit intelligence reports while leading the party! Moreover, he remained skeptical about entering a coalition with the CDU.[64]

His successor, the bearded opposition theologian Markus Meckel, was a more independent man. Expelled from high school, he could only attend a Protestant seminary, where he wrestled with the ideas of Prussian philosopher G. F. W. Hegel. Believing in the "vision of a humane socialism," he became active in environmental groups and led annual peace seminars. But Meckel differed from other religious dissidents in understanding the importance of power. This country pastor was the moving spirit behind the refounding of the Eastern SPD as a political party, "a kick in the shin of the SED." Tempted by potential influence as foreign minister, the brusque and outspoken Meckel came to embrace a grand coalition with the CDU.[65]

The new leadership quickly concluded the talks. On April 9 marathon sessions reached agreement on personnel and policies. Although GDR citizens had grown tired of the wrangling, the fifty-page coalition agreement was considered "a respectable achievement." Directed at "prosperity and social justice," the common program aimed at "implementing freedom and the rule of law" and promised "rapid and responsible realization of German unity after negotiations with the FRG on the basis of Article 23." In foreign policy, the parties tried to integrate unification into the European order with border assurances, an overarching security structure, and disarmament.[66]

The coalition's domestic agenda was equally ambitious. The unequal partners vowed to restore the states, cleanse the judiciary, abolish the secret police, and clear up the SED past. "The conclusion of a currency, economic, and social union is one of the most urgent tasks." During the transition, incomes, pensions, and rents were to receive priority. Specific measures spelled out the contours of a "socially and ecologically oriented market economy." New rules for privatization, competition, and taxation would improve performance while protecting the maltreated environment. An omnibus list that combined many CDU and SPD wishes, this agreement was designed to cushion the shock of the rapid transition from the GDR to a radically different West.[67]

On April 12 the Volkskammer confirmed the new cabinet. Lothar de Maizière was comfortably elected prime minister with 265 votes to 108, with nine abstentions. As the largest party, the CDU claimed eleven ministries whereas the SPD was allotted seven. The FDP received three portfolios, the DSU two, and the DA one. Aside from the premiership, only economics (Gerhard Pohl) and education (Hans-Jochen Meyer) were important CDU posts. In Markus Meckel (foreign affairs), Walter Romberg (finances), and Regine Hildebrandt (labor), the SPD had several strong personalities in the government. The DSU obtained the ministry of the interior (Peter-Michael Diestel), the FDP occupied justice (Kurt Wünsche), and the DA received defense (Rainer Eppelmann).[68]

This was a lawyers' and pastors' cabinet. Containing four women and fifteen Ph.D.s, it reflected a new elite. Although professionally competent, most ministers were political neophytes with little experience. De Maizière viewed his government "as an administrator in difficult times, as advocate of the well understood interests of all people in our country." In a symbolic break with the past, the first free parliament apologized for the holocaust to Jewish and Slavic victims, the suffering inflicted on Russia during World War II, and GDR participation in the repression of the Czech Spring in 1968. Most important, it affirmed the inviolability of the Polish frontier.[69]

The grand coalition faced a problematic legacy. The preceding Modrow government had taken pride in limiting "the damage of the failure of the command economy" and in preventing chaos by holding elections and welcoming unity. The last Communist cabinet, however, had permitted a whitewash of all personnel files, made former Stasi agents into teachers, and turned a blind eye to shady financial and real estate deals. Compromised by concessions to the old guard, its half-hearted reforms provided little guidance for the transition to a more democratic regime.[70]

Before its dissolution, the Round Table tried to distill the legacy of the civic revolution in a draft constitution for a united Germany. Lengthy discussions with legal experts produced a document with comprehensive and adjudicable rights for social services, direct democracy, and recommendations for slow unification. In the spirit of the Third Way, its 136 paragraphs expanded newly won civil rights into social entitlements for housing, work, or education and stressed direct citizens' involvement. Since voters had overwhelmingly rejected the civic movement, the Round Table document of late April could only suggest an alternative framework for civil society.[71]

In his first address to the Volkskammer, de Maizière promised to "realize unity." Paying hommage to the "peaceful revolution," the prime minister vowed, "After decades of repression and dictatorship, we want to create freedom and democracy under the rule of law." Endorsing quick currency, economic, and social union, he intended to fight for Eastern interests, such as a one-to-one exchange rate: "Unity must come as quickly as *possible*, but its conditions must be as good, reasonable, and progressive as *necessary*." To restore GDR pride, he claimed: "We bring into [this union] our land and our people, we offer our achievements and labor, our training and gift for improvisation."[72]

The prime minister's speech was a proud agenda for several years of reform. He committed himself to creating the legal, fiscal, and structural preconditions for conversion to a "social market economy," while safeguarding the environment as well as social welfare. De Maizière demanded a clean-up of the communist debris from housing to education, from sports to health. His inaugural address culminated in the promise that unification would enhance peace: "German unity shall strengthen

European community." This was not a scenario for rapid surrender, but a wide-ranging catalogue of renewal, leading to a negotiated merger of equal partners.[73]

The impressive coalition program earned widespread respect in East Berlin. All sides in the Volkskammer agreed in substance with de Maizière's attempt to combine the gains of the civic revolution with aspirations for unification. Even Marxist skeptics could not "deny the new head of government's dignity, courage and ethical principles." The civic movement criticized the SPD entry into a grand coalition as a "diminution of democracy," but the assertion of GDR interests struck a sympathetic cord.[74]

In Bonn, the CDU was delighted with the affirmation of rapid unity and market economics. Kohl alone sulked as he had expected more verbal gratitude. SPD candidate Lafontaine applauded the plea for solidarity but demanded that the West German parliament be involved in future decisions on unification. Only the Greens claimed that "de Maizière's program seems to have come directly from the chancellery." The media emphasized the "credibility and dignity" of the agenda, although some conservative circles found it too leftist in tone. With decisions postponed until the formation of a legitimate Eastern cabinet, the Western government was relieved that official negotiations could now begin.[75]

The Eastern vote improved the international climate for acceptance of unification. Before the election, Soviet Foreign Minister Shevardnadze complained about Western destabilization of the GDR. President Bush worried about German commitment to NATO during Kohl's Camp David visit, and Mitterrand supported Polish demands for immediate border guarantees. But the popular verdict lessened foreign pressure for a general peace treaty and made it possible to confine Polish border discussions to a single two-plus-four meeting. The election, giving incontrovertible proof of self-determination, muted foreign opposition to the currency union and rapid unification as stipulated in article 23.[76]

The grand coalition made it easier for Bonn to justify unity abroad. In an *Izvestiia* interview Kohl assured Moscow that he would keep Soviet security needs in mind. Before the European commission the chancellor argued that "German unity would accelerate European integration." Bowing to East Berlin's preferences, Soviet advisor Portugalov indicated flexibility on the issue of German neutrality, as long "as war no longer emanated from German soil." Even Margaret Thatcher dropped her opposition to unity, if NATO survived. Though none of these thorny issues was yet resolved, the parallel policies of both German cabinets increased prospects for favorable results.[77]

A National Revolution

The March election decided the contest between socialist renewal and national unity. After the overthrow of Stalinism, the "unification landslide" was the second surprise of the GDR upheaval. As explanation, conservative commentators pointed to the incoherence and impracticality of Third Way programs, discredited by Stasi abuses. Political analysts stressed the erosion of Modrow's credibility and the Round Table's economic naivete. Dissident intellectuals attributed the desertion of the masses to the lure of Western consumerism. Marxist critics blamed the "unconditional surrender" on false promises by the Bonn government. In a condescending gesture, the ex-Green Otto Schily pulled a banana out of his pocket on national television.[78] This fruit came to symbolize the Eastern desire for all those little things that were ubiquitous in the FRG but unattainable in the GDR.

The failure of "real existing socialism" was so complete as to bury all democratic socialist alternatives. "Now that these goals have been negated by practical social developments," a Marxist sociologist reflected, "bourgeois society in its modern guise also becomes reality for us." This was not a simple counterrevolution, but a dialectic "negation of the negation," leading to a more advanced "social market economy." Since the first free elections produced a similiar reversal all over Eastern Europe, there was a great deal of logic in the popular choice of the antithesis to the failed regime. The divided East Germans could most quickly accomplish this general switch to capitalist democracy by embracing unity.[79]

In the winter of 1990, the revolution turned national. Ironically, the achievement of civil rights enabled mute antisocialist forces to re-emerge. The equation of Stalinism with Soviet domination added an antiforeign dimension to the unrest. Encouraged by Western politicians, popular protest shifted its aims and character. After regaining free expression, mass aspirations switched to the unfinished national business. Though accelerating its speed, the campaign kept this turn to unity orderly and free of internal or external bloodshed. Because of Gorbachev's realism, the Russian occupier yielded without using force. Helmut Kohl guided the unification steamroller from the outside, and the election outcome ratified quick unity by plebiscite.[80]

The consequences of the national choice were revolutionary. Restoring a "social market economy" hardly appeared futuristic. But unification meant a more drastic overturning of the political, economic, social, and cultural order than gradual internal reform would have achieved. Unity implied the dissolution of the GDR as a separate state, moving the populace lock, stock, and barrel from the Eastern to the Western camp. The merger required a more fundamental break in the continuity of individual lives and collective institutions than anyone could imagine. In contrast to slow internal reforms in other Eastern countries, external unification was the most radical attempt at transition to capitalist democracy.[81]

Left-wing intellectuals denounced the switch to unity as a "national annexation movement." Hoping to stop the run-away train with manifestos, they were bitterly disappointed in the people's vote. Wedded to a Leninist conception, literati complained that the repudiation of socialism made for "an aborted revolution." Construing unity as a capitalist relapse, they predicted it would turn the GDR from "a state company into a DM colony." Proponents of a civil society mourned the missed opportunity to establish a postmaterialist alternative. Awareness of the holocaust trauma made foreign critics view unification with alarm. Especially the 1968 generation of the Western student revolt "related to national traditions and history primarily in negative terms."[82]

In a curious inversion of prior chauvinism, progressive opinion deemed any German identity taboo. To a Marxisant elite that had learned the lessons of the past too well, the mass switch to unity seemed an "orgy of nationalism" that would end in imperialist intoxication. Especially among Western radicals, the election surprise inspired diatribes that sought to inform Easterners of the dire consequences of their choice. Often correct in predicting material complications, these shrill warnings fell on deaf ears, since they expressed Western self-hate. To leftist critics, the revolution had forfeited its legitimacy by turning national. Only a few moderates like Peter Schneider and GDR-born Monika Maron defended the validity of the majority vote.[83]

Unexpectedly but inexorably the civic awakening grew into a national reunion. With Stasi suppression of all conservative opposition, unification hopes had gone underground. On an individual level, the mass exodus indicated the strength of the desire for a better life. Though dissident leaders did not talk of unity in the heady October days, aspirations for material improvement inspired the masses to demonstrate for civil rights. After the fall of the Wall, longings for the Western lifestyle, which they could at last see with their own eyes, erupted with elemental force. The inchoate hope for unification became a longing not only to overthrow the Communist dictatorship but also to avoid further experiments in reforming socialism toward the Third Way.[84]

The return of parliamentarianism propelled the revolution's national turn. The election broke the deadlock between old guard and new forces in the Round Table. The campaign allowed former bourgeois parties to regain credibility, new conservative groups to spring up, and Bonn politicians to harness shifting sentiment to their own cause. Through the balloting, the mobilized masses repudiated the civic movement because people felt these reforms would not go far enough in improving their lives. "They voted for the surest path to freedom and prosperity." In voicing the wishes of the silent majority, the election completed the surprising transition from civic rising to national revolution.[85]

III

THE EASTERNERS
JOIN THE WEST

7

Uniting the Currencies

The monetary merger was the "first big step toward unity." Popular frustration with "worthless [GDR] currency" made conversion to the Western DM imperative. Though experts warned of the fiscal risks, the breakdown of the command economy seemed so complete that only a switch to a market system promised recovery. The weekly exodus of four thousand people had to be stopped, if necessary by transferring Western prosperity to the East. The impending bankruptcy of the GDR treasury required drastic measures, and much needed FRG support would become more effective if the entire system were changed.[1]

Political reasons also urged a speedy approach. Monetary issues belonged to those domestic matters that the two-plus-four agreement left to Germans to decide. The nineteenth-century precedent of the Prussian *Zollverein* suggested that a customs union could pave the way for political unification. In short, politicians believed that the introduction of the DM would create "the economic precondition for growing together into a united Germany." Because it combined practical help with symbolic change, Prime Minister de Maizière welcomed the currency union as "a chance" for a fresh start.[2]

East Germans awaited the DM with mixed emotions. For weeks the media were full of complicated advice, trying to explain the technical aspects of conversion. The public was confused and wary. For the optimists, the prospect of hard cash was "an intoxicating joy." Long-held dreams could be realized at last: "Many [were thinking], now I am finally free, I can start to buy things . . . go everywhere, and will no longer be humiliated." Most wishes were "exceedingly modest," like getting a mirror or some records. Grander desires aimed at purchasing a color television set or a shiny new car: "Eating decently, [visiting] a disco or a whorehouse, that's all possible now."[3]

To the pessimists, the change appeared threatening. Unsure how far their pay or pension would reach, they resolved to restrain themselves. "First I have to see how my other expenses develop." With jobs no longer secure, many intended to hold onto their new banknotes, wondering, "Will we . . . become unemployed?" As reassurance, the Bonn government sponsored a cartoon to give advice featuring "smart Ludwig" Erhard, the inventor of the DM. Though experts failed to dispell their worries, people looked forward to having a choice and meeting Westerners "on equal terms." Even if the consequences were unpredictable, "on balance there was much relief that the GDR system [was] gone."[4]

The magic moment came at midnight on July 1. For weeks Western banks signed up Eastern offices of the state banks as local affiliates. Under cover of darkness, the Federal Reserve Bank trucked 28 billion DM in six thousand tons of notes and five hundred tons of coins to its fifteen regional headquarters. Precisely at 12:00 A.M. the Deutsche Bank branch office at Berlin Alexanderplatz opened its doors. Manager Rüdiger Wrede called "the historic occasion" an "initial step toward unity." Outside, thousands of eager East Germans pushed to get in. As the first through the door, the truck driver Hans-Joachim Corsalli was welcomed with champagne and a 100 DM savings account.[5]

Other towns celebrated the coming of the hard currency with fireworks or rock concerts. The tumult subsided when frantic tellers began to catch up. On Sunday morning ten thousand offices with thirty thousand employees disbursed the new cash all through the GDR. On average, customers took out only 833 DM to buy a few things, vacation in the West, or live on for the next couple of weeks. Hoping they were standing in line for the last time, most were relaxed and optimistic. Bundesbank president Otto Pöhl felt gratified: "I had expected more technical problems in this unprecedented operation."[6]

The currency union transformed Eastern lives. Most visibly, economic unity meant the end of the hated intra-German frontier. On July 1 interior ministers Schäuble and Diestel agreed to suspend passport controls, opening the border just in time for summer vacation trips. After decades of division, Germans could again move freely wherever they chose. The monetary merger also required the destruction of old GDR money. Even if they had struggled to obtain East-marks before, few people wept when their aluminum chips were melted down or their bills stored in secret salt mines. The colorful FRG banknotes looked bigger and the coins felt more solid.[7]

The arrival of the DM also meant the introduction of thousands of Western laws and practices. These new rules restructured business activity and social relations. It would take time for Easterners to get used to paying income or value-added taxes and receiving social security checks. The "currency gamble" exposed the moribund command economy to fierce competition as well. To ease the transition, the Bonn government appealed to business leaders "to invest in the GDR now" and to create new jobs. Financial experts like Helmut Schlesinger worried about the risks, and dissident spokesmen warned of "the social costs of the rapid start." But confident in the market, Helmut Kohl spread optimism: "Together, we will make it."[8]

DM Appeal

The separation of currencies had played an important part in the division of Germany. After the 1945 collapse, the Weimar Rentenmark and Nazi Reichsmark continued to be used in all occupation zones. But with goods scarce and money abundant, the Mark lost most of its value. When the Russians kept running the old printing presses, Western powers decided to reform the money in their territory. Fearing capitalist influence, the Soviet Military Administration (SMAD) hastily introduced its own bills on June 23, 1948. This conversion was supposed to serve the "interests of the working people . . . social justice and the . . . most rapid restoration of a peace-time economy."[9]

To reduce cash in circulation, the SMAD devalued the Eastern currency at 10:1. The only exceptions were for a 1:1 exchange of the first 70 Mk per capita and better rates for insurance policies (3:1) or small savings (5:1). To the chagrin of the population, the high prices initially remained unchanged. In Berlin, two currencies competed chaotically, creating a bonanza for black-market profiteers. Eventually the East German authorities asserted control, using their money to shield industrial expropriation and agricultural collectivization. Because forcible change was associated with the new bills, older people never quite accepted the Eastern Mark.[10]

The Western currency reform was a greater success. A similar tenfold devaluation, this conversion wiped out old debts, and favored owners of real property. Overnight, store windows filled with goods and the dormant economy sprang back to life. Though it was more war-damaged than the East, the West had an easier start. In contrast to over 100 billion Mk of reparations delivered to the Soviet Union, the FRG paid only 75 billion DM restitution and debts, on three times the population base. Once the Western Allies stopped dismantling industries, the capital stock was relatively new, management aggressive, and labor willing.[11]

Despite food rationing and initial unemployment, the *Währungsreform* (currency reform) sparked a postwar economic miracle. Credits of the European Recovery Program, commonly known as the Marshall Plan, stimulated rebuilding. The steel demand of the Korean War turned the shaky expansion into a solid boom. Finally, the daring free-market policies of Ludwig Erhard gradually lifted state controls on production and foreign exchange. The Western DM slowly advanced from a 1:4.2 to a 1:1.6 exchange rate with the U.S. dollar and became the leader in the European Monetary System. Celebrated in conservative rhetoric, this currency reform became a founding myth of the FRG that exerted a powerful pull on the East.[12]

In contrast, the weakness of the command economy rendered the GDR Mark nonconvertible. In the 1950s, the currency split had certain advantages for building socialism. Fiscal separation protected infant industries from the capitalist competition of the West. Independence allowed fundamental economic and social reforms that aimed at a more egalitarian society. Autonomy also facilitated redirecting trade from traditional Western markets to the COMECON states of the East. As it did not reflect real buying power, the artificial exchange rate required stringent massive controls that invited circumvention by a black market.[13]

By the 1960s, the separate currency produced fatal disadvantages for the GDR. Domestically, nonconvertibility created a constant scramble for foreign exchange in order to gain access to outside goods. Internationally, the Eastern Mark's lack of value hampered trade, since partners preferred barter to receiving cash. During the 1980s the amount required to earn one Western DM rose from 2.2 to 4.4 Mk, an effective devaluation by half! Chronic *Devisen* (currency) shortages also gave Shalck-Golodkowski's official foreign trade empire much of its power. By cutting the GDR off from the world market, the currency separation not only made the economy uncompetitive, but also created a valuta dependence on the West.[14]

The prized DM became an escape route from Eastern scarcity. Though basic food and clothing were abundant, overpriced durables like color television sets were hard to get. Forever standing in lines, consumers had to wait over a decade for a subcompact car that cost one year's wage. Because of its inaccessibility, the Western DM was a magic wand that made shortages disappear. Hard currency opened the doors to the fabled Intershops, which sold the latest in liquor, perfume, fashions, and power tools unavailable elsewhere. At a moment's notice, Western money would produce a plumber, ready to fix a faucet that might have kept dripping for years.[15]

Western currency conveyed many advantages. With a travel permit, valuta allowed one to attend a conference that would have remained out of reach. As a result, institutions invented elaborate stratagems to generate hard currency. Individuals either received it from Western relatives, earned it by internationally marketable skills, or gained it in reward for exceptional loyalty. As unofficial exchange medium, the DM was more coveted in the East than in the West. At home, its possession created a social divide between the fortunate few and the unfortunate rest. Abroad, its humiliating lack spurred much resentment and a sense of GDR inferiority.[16]

The modest prosperity of the East could not compete with the ostentatious wealth of the West. A GDR family with two children earned only about half as much disposable income as its FRG counterpart (2,074 Mk versus 4,118 DM). Because of heavy subsidies, Easterners paid less for housing and public transport (only 7.3 percent of their earnings) and food (21.9 percent). But little luxuries like alcohol and coffee (8.7 percent) or furniture and electronics (23.0 percent) ate up a larger share of their household budget. Though the range was small, nominal income rose about one quarter during the 1980s, with 45 percent of families earning over 2,000 Mk per month.[17]

Almost everyone possessed a refrigerator and a washing machine. But only one-half of the households had some kind of a car or color television set. With few attractive goods to buy, people annually saved 6 percent of their income, putting about 10,000 Mk per person into the bank (a total of 159.79 billion by 1983). Though two-thirds of the people lived in apartments, available space had slowly increased to a respectable level of 27.7 square meters per person. More than four-fifths of the flats had a bath and three-quarters possessed an inside toilet; but less than one-half enjoyed central heating and only 16 percent had a telephone. Since buildings were crumbling and products shoddy, Western currency promised access to more modern and reliable goods like computers, microwaves, or VCRs.[18]

Cut off from contact, Easterners formed an exaggerated image of the consumer society of the West. Travel restrictions made it hard for most people to judge whether the rosy tales of Eastern retirees or the disparaging accounts of the party faithful were accurate. Returning travelers exaggerated Western wonders while those left behind criticized what they had never seen. Compared to the utilitarian and none too solid GDR goods, those few available FRG products looked glamorous and durable. Presents from visitors and holiday packages reinforced images of wealth by providing proof of Western superiority. This "scarcity syndrome" made the DM appear as a passkey to a charmed world of affluence.[19]

With Western newspapers and magazines largely unobtainable, electronic media filled the information gap. Since they considered FRG newscasts generally more accurate than their own managed releases, most Easterners watched Western channels. Their image of daily life was also subtly formed by the opulent settings of regular shows, ranging from sit-coms to police dramas. Though limited to about an hour in early evening, commercials reinforced their fantasies. The eye-catching and witty ads portrayed a consumer paradise in which all problems disappeared when one used the right shampoo. Major brandnames, such as West cigarettes or Tchibo coffee, were well established in the GDR even before they became available. In the absence of real experience, the imaginary world of Western television stars like Kojak and Schimanski colored attitudes.[20]

The SED tried to immunize the populace against the lure of the West. Schools, media, and organizations doggedly struggled to create "socialist personalities." As an antidote to consumer temptation, the party constructed a frightening image of capitalism. Exaggerating defects into a caricature, propaganda painted a world of fat owners exploiting weary laborers. The *Neues Deutschland* headlined FRG unemployment increases to show socialist superiority. Eastern TV pictured drug addicts and criminals in order to emphasize GDR order. East Berlin magazines were filled with stories on homeless indigents so as to illustrate the security of life in a communist society.[21]

As official philosophy, Marxism-Leninism provided "scientific" proof of the perniciousness of capitalism. Proud of its antifascist record, the SED tried to tar West Germany with a brown neo-Nazi brush. During the Cold War arms race, Eastern propaganda also emphasized NATO militarism in contrast to its own commitment to peace. Though its excesses robbed this rhetoric of credibility, especially among intellectuals, such ideological attacks created deep-seated reservations about bourgeois democracy. As a result, East Germans were both fascinated and repelled by the glitter of the West.[22]

The border opening tipped the balance from socialist security toward capitalist risk. The warm welcome given to the Eastern millions showed that the Western cousins also had a heart. The first encounter with abundant and attractive consumer goods triggered shopping mania. In a veritable buying binge (*Kaufrausch*) Easterners strove to share in the long-denied wealth. Suppressed longings surfaced in a cathartic rush. Incredible as it seemed, a new, fuller life suddenly appeared possible. Though the writer Stefan Heym criticized this materialist scramble as demeaning, decades of deprivation created an unstoppable urge. On returning from the technicolor West, travelers felt the familiar East to be a disappointing black and white.[23]

Discouraging economic news did the rest. During the last quarter of 1989, industrial production contracted 4.2 percent and construction dropped 18.2 percent compared to a year before. This downturn from stagnation to decline convinced managers, workers, and even politicians that salvation lay in switching to a social market economy. When Christa Luft's paradoxical effort to introduce competitive incentives without converting to capitalism failed to produce visible results, Bonn's currency union offer looked like the only way out. Although PDS intellectuals warned about likely unemployment, the impatient masses wanted to join the DM economy without delay.[24]

Ironically, Eastern calls for help decreased Western willingness to sacrifice. Though Bonn liked using economic influence to obtain its aims, the FRG public wanted unification without cost. By January more than half of West Germans considered the refugee transition subsidies excessive. In mid-February 55 percent expected more losses than gains from unity. While three-quarters favored general support for the East, only one-half were willing to share the expense. By March 75 percent of Western citizens as well as most managers explicitly rejected raising taxes for unification.[25]

Caught between Eastern hopes and Western reluctance, Helmut Kohl scrambled for a course that did not require additional funds. So as not to ruin his re-election chances, he vowed that unification could be funded out of economic growth without personal sacrifices. Hans-Dietrich Genscher argued more honestly that "national unity cannot be gotten for nothing." Speaking for the East, Lothar de Maizière pleaded that division could only be overcome by sharing the expense. Similarly, the critic Jürgen Habermas warned against the arrogance of a "DM-nationalism." The currency union drew overwhelming support in East (91 percent) and West (76 percent) precisely because it promised quick unity without imposing heavy costs.[26]

The State Treaty

The form of the monetary merger sparked much controversy. Financial experts like Bundesbank President Karl Otto Pöhl, politicians like Economics Minister Helmut Haussmann, and businessmen like the chairman of the Bundesverband der Deutschen Industrie Tyll Necker favored a gradual approach. Proceeding in discrete steps would make it possible to create preconditions for revival such as privatization, real cost pricing, budgetary restraint, and convertibility of the Eastern Mark. Beginning with a fixed Mk to DM exchange rate such as 4:1 would protect the transformation of the Eastern economy and make it more competitive by keeping its goods cheap.[27]

In a gradual scenario, the Western DM would be introduced as the crowning achievement at the end. Bankers warned unanimously that comprehensive reforms were necessary before conversion. "Quick currency union cannot solve the structural problems of the GDR." Most economic research institutes opposed "taking the second step before the first." Predictably, the Greens claimed that "rapid monetary merger means annexation of the GDR by the FRG." The PDS and the Round Table warned that haste would exacerbate the collapse. But public impatience left no time for gradualism. Even if it might be wrong, a quick currency union became politically inevitable.[28]

The case for rapid conversion to the DM was largely psychological. Following Eastern wishes, Western Social Democrat Matthäus-Maier suggested currency reform as "a signal for staying" in the GDR. After some hesitation, the chancellor backed this speedy strategy, since unification required unorthodox measures. The popular myth of the Western currency reform of 1948 was a powerful argument as well. The success of Ludwig Erhard's gamble suggested that hard currency would trigger a "business big bang" and become "the starting gun for an economic miracle in the GDR." Rising refugee numbers indicated that Easterners were no longer willing to wait.[29]

The reason for fast action was "above all its political effect." The quick introduction of the DM would reassure the East that "we are ready to take a decisive step towards German unity." Though Pöhl and Waigel eventually swallowed their scruples, currency union was a double risk. For the West transfer payments and consumer demand raised the specter of inflation. For the East shock therapy threatened widespread bankruptcies. But Helmut Kohl persuaded his reluctant cabinet to override expert objections in order to channel GDR hopes toward unification:

"Because of the dramatic events I now consider this path both possible and necessary."[30]

Public emotions focused on the exchange rate. The low unofficial course of 10:1 made more than half of the Westerners favor a 2:1 conversion. The advantage of equal internal buying power led almost all Easterners to prefer a 1:1 exchange. Requiring more Mk to obtain one DM would keep Eastern wages down, reduce pent-up buying power, and decrease the debt load. Cutting costs would make GDR products cheaper and industries more competitive. A higher conversion would offer the public more purchasing punch, preserve accumulated savings and make Western goods more accessible. Lack of Eastern productivity (only one-third of the West) suggested a lower rate, whereas modest GDR wages (merely one-half of the FRG's) might permit a higher course.[31]

The choice lay between consumption and production. The SPD, the trade unions, the CDU social committees, and East Germans in general called for a more favorable rate to preserve wealth. Financial experts, the Bundesbank, business leaders, the FDP and the entrepreneurial wing of the CDU suggested a lower course so as to avoid unemployment. Trying to please both, chancellor Kohl played for time while suggesting sympathy for savers. Responding to opposition criticism and popular pressure, the GDR cabinet demanded parity as a matter of self-respect. Lothar de Maizière warned that cutting wages in half would lead to "unbearable" social tensions and might endanger unity.[32]

The finance ministers involved in the bargaining could not have been more different. Beetle-browed and feisty Theo Waigel represented the West. As chief of the Bavarian Christian Social Union (CSU), he was a professional politician, skilled in media use. A Catholic conservative, he tried to reconcile southern particularism with German patriotism. Afraid of the potential costs for the public treasury, he only gradually accepted a fast-track monetary merger out of a sense of "national solidarity." For the sake of fiscal stability, he preferred Bundesbank control to the risk of supporting an independent GDR currency.[33]

The haggard and thoughtful Walter Romberg spoke for the East. As a political neophyte, this mathematician had advised the Protestant church on disarmament and joined the SPD because of its social conscience. When Meckel claimed the foreign ministry, Romberg was put in charge of GDR finances since he knew how to read a balance sheet. To keep Easterners from becoming "second class citizens," he articulated their economic fears. For "psychological reasons" he advocated a 1:1 exchange rate and insisted on cushioning the union with unemployment insurance and retraining measures. Intent on "negotiating hard," Romberg was not about to "surrender the GDR."[34]

Both sides struggled intensely over the proper exchange rate. Various interests mounted vociferous campaigns to sway public opinion. The central bank, industrial circles, and financial advisers continued to demand a 2:1 course for the sake of competitiveness. Labor Minister Norbert Blüm pleaded for a generous social union to "help and improve the GDR." Oskar Lafontaine accused the chancellor of "gross deception" regarding the future costs. About one hundred thousand disgruntled citizens demonstrated for parity in East Berlin. Conflicting signals kept experts from making much technical headway. In private talks, Waigel, Lambsdorff, Pöhl, Blüm, and Schäuble eventually hammered out a compromise.[35]

On April 23, the Bonn cabinet suggested differentiated rates as a solution. In the interest of DM stability and GDR jobs, wages and salaries would be converted at 1:1, savings under 4,000 Mk at 1:1, and larger amounts at 2:1. Debts would be transformed at 2:1, and foreign accounts exchanged at 3:1, while pensions were set at 70 percent of average pay. Though it lacked compensation for price increases and larger payroll deductions, this 1.5:1 over-all course split the difference between converting running costs at parity and cutting fixed expenses in half. Kohl and de Maizière were relieved to be able to keep their word without endangering economic growth. The opposition, experts, journalists, and East Germans slowly resigned themselves to the compromise.[36]

International reaction to the currency plans was surprisingly mild. Though financial experts worried about the stability of the DM, foreign diplomats remained preoccupied with security issues. The U.S. administration ignored critical editorials about Bonn's growing economic strength and provided diplomatic support. Constant consultations with President Mitterrand also made the French leadership more sympathetic to the German cause. In a special report, the European Community summit in Dublin welcomed the monetary merger and rapid unification via Article 23 "without reservations." At the same time officials began to prepare the agenda for the two-plus-four talks.[37]

Only the Soviets made difficulties. Complying with Modrow's parting request, Moscow demanded that inter-German negotiations leave four-power regulations concerning "de-Nazification, demilitarization, and democratization" untouched. Concretely, it insisted that all pre-1949 changes in "property and land" be upheld. When Western conservatives wanted to undo the expropriation of Junker estates, Lothar de Maizière warned: "No political group in the GDR will ever accept this." Ironically, this Soviet intervention facilitated compromise by excluding the psychologically touchy issue of ownership rights from the inter-German talks.[38]

Monetary agreement emerged on May 2. As a step towards economic union, the currency deal tried to reconcile DM stability with Eastern marketization. Still critical, Romberg demanded compensation for increasing costs, higher pensions, and better conversion of savings, but Waigel shot back: "Our offer is the upper limit of what we can accept." The technical talks between state secretaries Hans Tietmeyer (West) and Günter Krause (East) confirmed the main outlines, but modified important details. As anticipated, wages, salaries, and pensions would be exchanged at 1:1, debts were to be converted at 2:1, and foreign accounts transformed at 3:1.[39]

The most important change stipulated that savings would be treated according to a graduated scale. Children under 15 were entitled to 2,000 DM at parity, adults under 60 to 4,000 DM and senior citizens to 6,000 DM. Günter Krause justified favoring older people because they had to live on their savings and would not be able to earn new cash. Helmut Kohl was pleased with "the immense achievement," which came just in time for local balloting in the East. Moderates were satisfied, and the left could claim to have won some concessions for savers. The man in the street realized that "more could not be done."[40]

The local election of May 6 was a referendum on the currency union. One year after the fraudulent GDR vote, it offered a chance to build democratic structures from the bottom up. Though the exodus had declined from 73,700 to 24,600 between January and April, the public continued to worry about the conditions of the economic merger. Attacking the planning as undemocratic, PDS chair Gregor Gysi and civic movement leader Wolfgang Ullmann played on social fears. But the cabinet blamed unemployment on the command economy and promised that no one would be worse off than before. In decaying cities like Dresden local issues also loomed large.[41]

Instead of repudiating the March vote, the May ballot confirmed and corrected its verdict. This time, only 75 percent of the electorate went to the polls. The CDU noticeably declined but remained the largest party with 34.4 percent of the popular vote. Surprisingly, the SPD failed to profit, also dipping slightly, and the PDS dropped further to 14.6 percent. But small parties gained, with farmers capitalizing on resentment and local groups, Liberals, Greens, and New Forum advancing as well. Berlin remained a PDS stronghold, while Leipzig chose Hanoverian Hinrich Lehmann-Grube as mayor for the SPD. According to Horst Teltschik, "the chancellor is very pleased with the result," because it kept unification on track.[42]

The treaty was finally signed on May 18. Though the Eastern SPD pressed for further concessions, Theo Waigel refused to yield. When several hundred thousand union members demonstrated their concern, Labor Minister Norbert Blüm responded that "nobody in the GDR needs to be afraid." While the GDR deficit held up agreement, the hard bargaining forced improvements in pensions and social supports. After much wrangling the Western states agreed to share half the cost of a "Fund for German Unity," which would generate 115 billion DM to finance unification. Western critics like CDU maverick Kurt Biedenkopf welcomed these changes that compelled the FRG to do its part.[43]

The ceremony in the Gobelin Hall of the Palais Schaumburg in Bonn radiated a "moving and joyous" mood. Confident that the FRG could bear the economic burden, Kohl announced, "What we experience here is the birth of a free and united Germany." Full of hope, de Maizière hailed the deal as "a solid timetable for the introduction of an ecologically oriented social market economy." If people seized their "unique chance" with pioneer spirit, everyone would be better off than before. With the SPD ambivalent, the PDS and Greens railed against "subjection" and "expropriation." The Berlin civic movement sarcastically staged a mock burial of GDR identity in "the hard DM family vault in Bonn."[44]

Considering the haste of its creation, the State Treaty uniting the GDR and FRG was an impressive document. Its thirty-eight paragraphs and appendixes spelled out the terms of Eastern integration into West Germany. Praising the "peaceful and democratic revolution," the preamble justified the currency, economic, and social union as "a first significant step towards the achievement of political unity according to Article 23." By joining the "social market economy," the GDR accepted "the free, democratic, federal, legal and social order" of the Basic Law. The currency section reiterated the exchange agreement and spelled out Bundesbank control. The economic provisions called for "liberating market forces and private initiative." But they remained vague on competitiveness, European Community integration, and environmental protection.[45]

Extensive passages promised social safeguards. The treaty introduced labor law, welfare support, and private health care, as well as contributory retirement, health, accident, and unemployment insurance, with start-up funding by Bonn. The concluding budget stipulations tried to eliminate the GDR deficit by privatizing enterprises, cutting multiple subsidies, and reducing personnel expenses. Limiting credit to 10 billion DM, plus 7 billion for privatization, the West promised 22 billion DM transfers in 1991, hoping to make the East self-sufficient through new customs and taxes. Long appendixes demanded the abolition of socialism, the introduction of private enterprise, the formation of free unions, reform of the legal system, and the passage of enabling legislation.[46]

The ratification struggle provided some comic relief. After the Western SPD won state elections in the Palatinate and Lower Saxony, it controlled a majority in the Bundesrat, which had to approve the treaty. Intent on improving his chances for the federal campaign, chancellor candidate Oskar Lafontaine rejected the agreement in order to embarrass his rival Kohl. The SPD presidium demanded additional support for industrial competitiveness, environmental protection, control of SED property, and involvement in decision-making. Nevertheless, the chancellor offered to talk with Social Democratic leaders so as to keep the opposition divided. Disagreeing with Western radicals, the Eastern SPD supported ratification in a heated Volkskammer debate.[47]

To top the confusion, Lafontaine proposed accepting the treaty in the Bundesrat while rejecting it in the Bundestag. When the government conceded a number of improvements regarding ecology, questionable property and speculation, SPD moderates forced their candidate to give in. In order not to disappoint Eastern hopes, the SPD presidium called the agreement "inevitable and necessary." Though two hundred thousand Berliners demonstrated against the treaty, the Volkskammer approved it by 302 to 82. On June 21, the Bundestag ratified it by a larger margin of

445 to 60. One day later the Bundesrat followed suit. The "greatest experiment of financial history" could begin.[48]

The last days before conversion were hectic. East Germans thronged into the banks to establish separate accounts for every family member and pick up exchange applications. Drab stores suddenly blossomed with colorful sales, seeking to dispose of their GDR goods at any price. In order to stock up before things became more expensive, people tried to spend their last East-marks. The unforeseen buying spree depleted supplies, leading to food shortages, since wholesalers stopped shipping in order to reap higher returns at a later date. Western salesmen crowded Eastern hotel lobbies, hustling to sign up outlets for FRG chains.[49]

Even a skeptical Lothar de Maizière noticed "something like a frontier spirit." Approvingly he added, "we need that." Western managers spread optimism. The Federal Industrial Association (BDI) argued: "The economic starting point could hardly be better for the accomplishment of the enormous entrepreneurial and political tasks" of the currency union. Bundesbank vice-president Helmut Schlesinger believed that "the GDR has a better chance than any other Eastern country." But state companies began to dismiss workers, trying to trim labor costs. In spite of official pep talks, people were "confused and insecure" about how they would be able to manage.[50]

The State Treaty marked a decisive advance for unity. For the civic movement, this GDR close-out sale seemed to "dispossess the revolution." For the silent majority, Kohl's vision of "prosperity and security" promised the achievement of their original aims. Although the populace was hardly consulted, and the parliaments only allowed to vote on the finished product, the treaty was not quite a *Diktat*. Drawn up by Bonn bureaucrats and financial experts, the draft evolved through hard bargaining within the coalition, with the SPD and the states, inside the GDR cabinet, and between the two governments. Not surprisingly, the result reflected the power disparity between a crumbling East and an assertive West.[51]

With the economic union, the GDR was in effect joining the FRG. Lack of time and precedent made for legal declarations of intent that sketched a general direction of change rather than spelling out every detail. The treaty's philosophy was Ludwig Erhard's liberal faith in the magic of the market, supplemented by the "unique chance" of Western help. In essence, the agreement ended GDR economic sovereignty and destroyed the last dreams of a Third Way. Its fiscal demands and existential risks could only be justified if they advanced unification. Westerners worried about "who will foot the bill," while Easterners wondered whether the takeover would be "an end or a beginning."[52]

Creative Destruction

The first steps into capitalism were exhilarating and frustrating. Over the weekend, the stores did fill with shining Western goods. Where there had been useful but uninspiring Eastern products, attractively packaged items from all over the European Community beckoned. With colorful advertising, dusty displays suddenly turned into tempting vistas of material bliss. Competing for the first time, salespersons tried to be polite and a few actually smiled! Instead of buying in a frenzy, as critics had feared, cautious customers preferred to window shop. Before they parted with their hard money, most wanted to compare cost and quality.[53]

What they saw was shocking: Without subsidies, food and other basics had doubled or tripled overnight. It was cold comfort that durables like walkmen or dishwashers also drastically dropped in price. Behaving like the worst capitalists, many retailers "shamelessly abused their monopolies." Unsure about their own future, four-fifths of East Germans wanted to save their "new money." Heeding the politicians' warnings, the public only bought necessities and satisfied a few frustrated desires. On both sides of the counter, new roles of seller and buyer had to be learned, but "jumping into the cold water" was less frightening than many had feared.[54]

On initial contact, the market economy hardly seemed very social. After the first restocking, store shelves quickly emptied once again. Underestimating the bad roads and lack of phones, Western suppliers failed to deliver many of the promised goods. Eager managers, unused to calculating costs, often overcharged in order to make a quick profit. When goods cost more than in the FRG, astute consumers simply drove across the border to shop in discount stores, finding themselves standing in line once more. To lower prices by competition, the GDR cabinet lifted the remaining trade barriers, dismantled the HO and Konsum trade monopolies and invited cheap Western retailers like ALDI.[55]

An unexpected rejection of GDR products aggravated the chaos. Tempted by glossy ads, East Germans indiscriminately preferred Western goods to their own familiar wares. FRG chains also systematically displaced Eastern products via exclusive contracts with their new affiliates. While local cherries rotted outside Potsdam, Berlin stores offered fruit flown in from Washington State. Protesting farmers poured milk into the streets and factories produced towering inventories that no one wanted to buy. The government tried to help with credits and export subsidies. Though some consumers and producers profited, more people found the change unsettling.[56]

After the excitement subsided, many East Germans felt worse off than before (see Table 7). Not only apparatchiks who lost their privileges, but also ordinary people began to grumble about the effect of the currency union. When travel and luxuries were finally within reach, money dried up. Half of the savings beyond the minimum were lost, decreasing average wealth by about 3,500 DM per capita. When they received their first paycheck, workers experienced a take-home shock. With new income taxes, insurance and retirement contributions, Western deductions were almost twice the customary amount. As a result, net income actually declined by 15 percent.[57]

TABLE 7. Social Impact of the Currency Union, 1990

	GDR	Change	FRG	Difference
Income				
Gross pay	1,170 Mk	none	3,000 DM	+ 1,830 DM
Net pay	1,000 Mk	− 150 DM	2,200 DM	+ 1,350 DM
Expenses				
Food	822 Mk	+ 106 DM		
Industrial products	838 Mk	− 226 DM		
Services	166 Mk	+ 128 DM		
Monthly total	1,826 Mk	+ 8 DM		
Rent (as percent of income)	3%	+ ?	20%	+ 17%
Per capita wealth	11,022 Mk	−3,500 DM	40,747 DM	+33,225 DM
Income dissatisfaction	44%		19%	

Even if an average market basket cost about the same, many items of daily consumption increased alarmingly. Higher charges for eating at home and going out were not offset by cheaper tobacco, coffee, or alcohol. While clothes, furniture, or electronics grew more affordable, services, repairs, and leisure activities became more expensive. Absurdly low rents had to rise to Western levels, if buildings were to be repaired and maintained. Utilities also raised their prices considerably. Since they started with less, Easterners were more dissatisfied with their earnings. New Western unions like the IG Metall agitated for an across-the-board supplement of 250 DM. When local strikes wrested concessions, some incomes began to grow.[58]

Splashes of fresh color marked the Eastern metamorphosis. The old GDR had been a strangely grey land. Endless collective farms abutted on villages where the clock seemed to have stopped decades ago. While inner cities decayed, faceless prefabricated apartments sprouted in the outskirts, close to smoke-belching industries. After conversion bright umbrellas welcomed motorists to new fast-food stands, selling FRG beer and the mass-circulation daily *BILD*. In meadows and courtyards, flapping flags announced used or new Western cars, promising speed and comfort to those weary of the bone-jarring Trabant.[59]

Big private banks dispensed the essential DM and courted depositors from makeshift offices in containers. Making up for deprivation, video-parlors emerged everywhere, dealing in Hollywood dreams and sexual fantasies. In the town markets, itinerant peddlers displayed Western wares from bright T-shirts to deafening rock music. Slowly, bakeries and butchershops restored their owners' names and renewed pride in their craft. Here and there a new coat of paint spruced up a house, punctuating the drab facades. Thousands of attempts to set up business seemed to herald the promised revival. But would small initiatives be enough to restart the stalled command economy?[60]

For business, conversion to capitalism meant a tough struggle for survival. It was easy to restore a traditional name, turning the machine-tool company "VEB October Seventh" once more into the "Niles Werkzeugmaschinenbau, GmbH." But managers, used to orders from above, found operating on their own extremely difficult. They faced inherited problems such as worn-out machinery that produced shoddy goods with too much labor. Eventually cut in half, old debts created by state financing swallowed a prohibitive share of current cash. Overstaffing, imposed by full employment, needed to be reduced by painful lay-offs. Peripheral activities, stemming from excess centralization, had to be spun off as independent auxiliaries (transport) or shed entirely (social services such as day-care).[61]

The new challenges of competition were even more frightening. The revaluation of the currency raised prices and made many products uncompetitive. The rejection of GDR goods, breakdown of Eastern trade, and arrival of Western rivals destroyed traditional markets. The reluctance of FRG banks to lend to moribund businesses hampered liquidity and pushed many needlessly into bankruptcy. The withdrawal of capitalist partners from earlier cooperation plans and the unreliability of self-styled consultants added to the confusion. Without Western accounting, many firms could not even tell if they were profitable.[62]

The GDR cabinet struggled to find ways of making order out of this chaos. The Round Table had suggested a trusteeship for preserving public property and fostering the transition to a market economy. Turning state enterprises into joint stock companies would make them profitable while keeping the "people's wealth" (*Volkseigentum*) from being squandered. On March 1, the cabinet founded the Treuhandanstalt, a holding company that was to divide the nationalized assets—totalling some 600 billion Mk—into federal, state, and local parts ($1/4$); compensation for claims ($1/4$); people's shares ($1/4$); collateral for savings ($1/10$); and foundations (the rest). But the staff converted only 170 companies in three months.[63]

To speed marketization, de Maizière restructured the Treuhand on June 19. Though dissidents objected to "public expropriation," the new charter called for reduced state involvement and "privatization as quickly and thoroughly as possible." By breaking up the state monopolies, the Treuhand would make companies competitive and preserve old jobs or create new ones. Profits not used "for transforming the economy and balancing the treasury" would be distributed as public shares. On July 1, this trust became the largest state holding in the world with eight thousand companies, forty thousand plants, 6 million employees, and sixty-two thousand square kilometers of farms, forests, and other real estate.[64]

The unprecedented conversion of a planned economy required unorthodox managers. Since Easterners lacked market experience, the Treuhand needed proven entrepreneurs, "capable of riding such a monster." Detlev Rohwedder was an excellent choice as its head. Born in Thuringia, this Western SPD economist successfully combined government and business careers. As state secretary under socialist and liberal economic ministers, he specialized in energy and structural policy. In the early 1980s, he had saved the deficit-ridden Hoesch steel concern through drastic restructuring. Now Rohwedder tried to attract experienced managers who considered making inefficient companies competitive a personal challenge.[65]

The Treuhand was a paradoxical hybrid between the public and private spheres. Its staff combined some top-flight entrepreneurs, unsuccessful managers looking for a second chance, and disappointed socialist planners. Rohwedder tried to create a small holding company that would make only strategic decisions, but the task of running thousands of companies bloated personnel to some three thousand members and required decentralization into regional offices. Sparing the politicians from making hard choices, this trusteeship organization used bureaucratic control to foster capitalist competition.[66]

Privatization was the top priority. In converting, the Treuhand tried to combine the contradictory objectives of extracting profits and saving jobs. Aversion to costly subsidies and the need to cover the GDR deficit strengthened the resolve to sell public property. But finding buyers was more difficult. When they learned how deplorable conditions actually were, investors quickly lost their enthusiasm. Even an official estimate that 32 percent of Eastern companies could survive without help, 54 percent required massive aid, and the rest would have to go under turned out to be far too optimistic.[67]

Obstacles to investment were high. Sometimes old managers conspired with local bureaucrats to keep Westerners out. At other times, legal disputes about ownership deterred capital outlays. Moreover, ecological devastation created fears of costly clean-ups. When COMECON trade with the Eastern neighbors collapsed, the GDR became unattractive as a place of production. With eager refugees, Western businesses could supply Eastern needs from their home base without risky commitments. In competitive bidding, a few productive firms quickly attracted suitors, but many Kombinate had to be divided into marketable and moribund parts. Other companies were beyond salvaging and had to be shut down. By privatizing instead of reconstructing, the Treuhand became the angel of death for many industries.[68]

Using profitability as the standard for decision caused much destruction. In spite of massive protests, firms that could not compete on the world market, like the camera producer Pentacon, were quickly closed. Since the GDR fostered single product monopolies, the failure of one industry such as copper mining devastated an entire region like the Mansfeld area. The petrochemical factories around Buna and Leuna were so ecologically damaged that no investor would risk buying into them. Only by coupling salvage with the sale of the lucrative Minol gas stations could any jobs be saved. In the beginning, lax Treuhand procedures led to scandalous deals such as the giveaway of the light-bulb producer NARVA and the ruination of competitors such as the state airline Interflug.[69]

Political pressure sometimes saved the day. When demand dried up, the outdated Trabi and Wartburg car factories shut down. But VW and Opel invested several billion Deutsche Mark in new East German auto manufacturing plants in Zwickau and Eisenach. Similarly, the original Zeiss optical works at Jena could not survive competition with their Western offshoot in Oberkochen. When ex-premier Lothar Späth persuaded Thuringia to help, the Treuhand committed billions to their rescue. Western investors struggled fiercely for Eastern consumer industries like insurance, food, retailing, power generation, and media where good profits could be made. Except in the case of a few hundred management buyouts, salvage required the dismissal of workers, outside control, and credit dependency.[70]

The redirection of foreign trade imperiled the transformation. In COMECON barter, the GDR had specialized in producing trains, ships, and machine tools while receiving raw materials such as oil, finished products like trams, and fruits and other foods. The Soviet revaluation of the transfer ruble from 1:4 to 1:2 destroyed virtually all profits from this trade. Once they had access to European Community products and DM to pay for them, East Germans refused to buy inferior East European goods. Political turmoil and economic collapse in Russia and the Communist bloc decimated orders so that exports fell by 60 percent. Since hundreds of thousands of jobs depended on products not marketable in the West, the Bonn government tried to preserve a remnant of trade with favorable loan guarantees.[71]

The influx of cheaper and better food products from the EC was the other side of the same coin. When unappealing collective farm products could no longer be sold, agriculture began to collapse. With tender Western veal available, who wanted to eat fatty Eastern pork? While the collective farms struggled with heavy debts and uncertain land ownership, Bonn interest groups tried to restore inefficient family farms. The European Community welcomed the accession of the GDR, but its competitive market required export industries to shrink and farmers to improve product quality in order to survive. Would they get the chance?[72]

The social impact of the transition was devastating. Most people were awed by the momentous changes, greeting acquaintances with a sigh and asking, "Do you still have a job?" A growing minority found itself out of work. By December 1990, unemployment rose to 642,200, or 7.3 percent. This figure was kept at an artificially low level by underemployment: 1.8 million people (20.5 percent) worked reduced hours in order to be retrained. About 460,000 of the elderly were mercilessly pushed into early retirement. Women, who had virtually all been previously employed (90 percent), were especially vulnerable, since their industries (textiles) or service roles seemed dispensable. When dismissed, they found it difficult to get work, because insolvent companies abandoned child care. The young also had greater problems in landing a first job.[73]

In spite of generous support from the West, the DM conversion heightened social inequality. Some go-getters profited from capitalism. Soon flashy entrepreneurs drove fast cars and spent their new gains with abandon. Most people somehow muddled through by balancing increased costs with new savings. But many others were left behind. Time and again trade unions tried to mount collective protests. Small firms went under without much noise. Only when large factories were threatened did strikes attract enough attention to force politicians to intercede. Even in the best cases, a mere fraction of the jobs was saved. While the Treuhand took the blame, the cabinet counseled patience and funded unemployment compensation or retraining schemes.[74]

In Schumpeter's phrase, marketization wreaked "creative destruction." Socialist monopolies, subsidies, hidden unemployment, and low productivity had to be destroyed for a capitalist market to emerge. The introduction of hard currency dramatically transformed patterns of consumption and trade. The Treuhandanstalt excelled at breaking up the mammoth Kombinate. By August 1991, it had already privatized 3,378 of 10,334 companies. Banks, insurance agencies, power companies, retailers, food chains, hotels, and newspapers led the way. But the once proud GDR industries such as chemicals, ship-building, textiles, and electronics were harder to sell. Hundreds of hopeless cases like the Soviet-German uranium combine Wismut had to be shut down entirely. By December 1990 almost two million jobs had been lost.[75]

The Treuhand found new economic life much harder to create. Until mid-1991, privatization had safeguarded about six hundred thousand jobs in competitive industries. Easterners contributed little, since they could only afford to start small businesses or shops. Western big business buyers promised they would pour in 70 billion DM in investments. Government spent tens of billions to repair infrastructure—roads, transit systems, phone lines and the like. But to the East German people, the conversion seemed initially more destructive than creative. Dissidents wondered whether they had overthrown "the Stalinist dictatorship" in order to return to crude "Manchester capitalism."[76]

Market Shock

Neoliberal faith in the market inspired the currency union. Because of the success of his 1948 currency reform, Ludwig Erhard had urged that future reunification "must take place by means of the market economy." As a believer in private initiative, he considered "widespread fears about tragic material effects on individual lives unfounded." Though he conceded the need for initial government help, the father of the economic miracle predicted that "German reunification will unleash forces" that planners could not imagine. Forgetting the state's role in the transition to economic freedom, his later followers mythologized the power of the market.[77]

This misunderstanding of the economic miracle led Bonn to trust blindly in competition. Following liberal orthodoxy, the cabinet refused to steer the transition, leaving the decisions to the Treuhand instead. Western reluctance to pay the costs of unification misled Helmut Kohl into promising that he would not raise taxes. While the Eastern economy was collapsing, Western politicians repeated assurances that the revival was just around the corner. Unsure of their predictions, they launched a propaganda campaign to encourage the rise of small business. Unfortunately, the post-1948 takeoff did not repeat itself in 1989. Without supportive policy initiatives, the market failed to work its magic.[78]

Skeptics predicted all along that the shock would be severe. Marxists forecast that economic annexation would bankrupt state enterprises and throw half the people out of work. Social Democrats worried that competition would damage the elderly, women, youth, and the handicapped. The civic movement stressed that Western colonization would reinforce the Eastern sense of inferiority and passivity. Such prophecies of doom fell on deaf ears since they came from opponents of unity and failed to present a persuasive alternative.[79]

Criticism of mistakes in implementation had more effect. The muckraking *Spiegel* exposed the scandalous dispersal of the assets of the GDR foreign trade empire to former Stasi operatives. Business columnists scored the give-away of the prestigious Interhotels to the Western Steigenberger hotel chain. Leftist politicians complained that the Treuhand made life-and-death decisions based only on immediate profitability. Slowly these criticisms led to corrections. A parliamentary committee began to investigate Schalck-Golodkowski's mysterious commercial deals. Flagrant abuses like the Western oligopolies' control of power production were contested in court. In the spring of 1991, the Treuhand board was enlarged to include Eastern state and labor union representatives. After regional review commissions and temporary employment programs (ABM) were set up, the trusteeship made salvaging firms a higher priority.[80]

Crash conversion ultimately produced chaos. The pessimists who forecast deindustrialization were more correct than the optimists who predicted growth. Most indicators pointed to collapse. Declining by 13.4 percent in 1990, the Eastern GNP contracted another 20.0 percent during 1991. Industrial production fell by two-thirds within two years, while prices increased 12 percent in 1991. The labor market disintegrated. With one million already unemployed and another 1.6 million on reduced hours, the Eastern economy lost 1,830,000 more jobs. Even if GDR peculiarities like hidden unemployment and unusually high female employment are taken into account, the loss of half the workforce was an unprecedented disaster.[81]

There were also a few positive signs. Eastern investment grew from

48.3 to 88.3 billion DM between 1990 and 1992. As a result of union
pressure and social support from the West, real income actually rose about
28 percent between 1989 and 1991. During the same period about 175,000
new businesses were founded that promised to create more jobs. With the
belated Eastern Recovery Program of March 1991, the Bonn government
transferred an incredible 135 billion DM from the West during that year
alone. Despite the immense downturn, the people did not revolt. Joining
one of the world's strongest economies suggested reasons to hope that a
revival would eventually come.[82]

The currency union required a double transition. To begin with,
command production had to be converted into a social market system.
Even before the civic revolution, the GDR economy had reached the end
of its rope. Consuming its infrastructure and polluting its environment, it
could not meet international competition and began to stall. Joining the
FRG was bound to cause severe dislocation because it merged an economy
of the second world with one of the first. Popular pressure for quick action
eliminated the possibility of a gradual changeover, as carried out by other
East European countries. Hasty privatization made a crisis well-nigh inescapable.[83]

At the same time, the economy needed to move from high industrial
to postindustrial patterns. Following the Stalinist model, the GDR had
developed a labor-intensive smokestack production, typical of the second
phase of industrialization. Painful struggles in mining and shipbuilding
had reoriented the West to tertiary high-technology and service pursuits.
The currency union forced the GDR not just to adopt capitalist organization, but also to shift to postindustrial patterns at the same time. The
neoliberal rejection of structural policy unnecessarily deepened the market
shock and increased the eventual cost, but the rapid merger also called
forth an unparalleled amount of help. The disruption of the currency
union was the price of regaining political unity.[84]

8

Negotiating Accession

The transition to unity aroused widespread anxiety. Conservatives could not wait to get rid of the hated GDR, but leftists wanted to slow the merger with the West in order to cushion the shock. On June 17 the Volkskammer and the Bundestag met to commemorate the 1953 uprising and ponder the appropriate way to proceed. Praising the civic revolution, Protestant church leader Manfred Stolpe warned that it would take time to unite the estranged parts. Even if their "differences no longer divide, unification will become more difficult if they are not taken into account."[1]

An impatient German Social Union (DSU) disregarded this advice and demanded that the GDR join the FRG "on this very day." Caught by surprise, Prime Minister Lothar de Maizière refused to be stampeded in the ensuing Volkskammer session. "First we must negotiate another not inconsiderable state treaty" so as to create a legal framework for the merger of East and West Germany. "And then the two-plus-four process will have to reach a result acceptable to all sides." Since daunting domestic and diplomatic problems had yet to be resolved, the speed and shape of unity depended on the completion of these tasks.[2]

The "miracle of Moscow" broke the foreign political deadlock. On July 15 an optimistic but nervous Kohl met with a "a friendly and serious" Gorbachev in the Soviet capital to discuss the terms of German unity. Well prepared and trusting each other, both leaders tried to heal the wounds of World War II by bringing "Russia and Germany together again." Offering economic help, Kohl proposed a comprehensive cooperation treaty, once "we have overcome the current obstacles together." While the German chancellor stressed the "dramatic deterioration" of the GDR, the Russian leader flexibly acknowledged that NATO was beginning to transform from a military into a political alliance.[3]

This meeting of minds suggested compromise. If Bonn accepted its current frontiers and renounced nuclear, biological and chemical (ABC) weapons, it would recover full sovereignty. Provided that alliance structures were not extended eastward during the transition, "Gorbachev quite calmly and earnestly agrees that Germany can remain a NATO member." As soon as Soviet troop withdrawal was regulated by separate treaty, four-power control could be lifted. "What a sensation! We had not expected such clear assurances from Gorbachev," Kohl's advisor Horst Teltschik commented. "For the chancellor this conversation is an incredible triumph. . . . I am witnessing a historical moment!" To his media spokesman Johnny Klein, Kohl confided elatedly, "It's all in the bag."[4]

A change of scenery facilitated the solution of the remaining problems. The subsequent trip to the presidential dacha in the Caucasus mountains relaxed the atmosphere. On July 16 the full delegations agreed to trade Bonn's support of Soviet entry into Europe for Moscow's acquiescence in German unification. To document the new quality of relations, Kohl reiterated his treaty offer and his hope for complete independence and membership in the Western alliance. Seeking to meet Russian security concerns, the chancellor promised to hold off extending NATO structures temporarily and to refrain from stationing nuclear arms in the East.[5]

In exchange for financial help, the Soviets agreed to withdraw their forces within four years. During this period Western troops might remain in Berlin. Assured that GDR economic commitments would be observed, the Russians also accepted the extension of NATO protection to GDR territory. When negotiations threatened to stall over the size of military cuts, Gorbachev settled for an effective halving of the combined forces to 370,000 men. "The great goal has been reached!" The German visitors were delighted that the security compromise removed any doubt about the return of their full sovereignty. "All questions have been solved amicably. What a success!"[6]

The scope of the Caucasus agreement stunned the public. TV shots of relaxed statesmen strolling along mountain streams had suggested unusual cordiality. But when Gorbachev and Kohl announced the results of their talks, "the surprise [was] immense." Since it settled every two-plus-four dispute, the eight-point summary surpassed all expectations. Russian, German, and international journalists reacted with "a mixture of incredulity, astonishment, and increasing joy." Almost unanimously, the media praised "Kohl's coup" as a historic breakthrough.[7]

The Germans made significant financial promises, renounced former Eastern territories, and conceded deep military cuts. In return the Russians swallowed their fears and reversed decades of divisive policy. With new realism about their declining power, they offered to withdraw troops, allow NATO membership and grant "full and unimpaired sovereignty." Foreign observers were the first to comment that the Caucasus agreement meant the end of postwar Soviet hegemony. Unlike the punitive peace of 1918 or 1945, this was a settlement among equals that removed the rubble of the past to inaugurate a better future. The Caucasus deal also finished "the task of an independent foreign policy of the GDR."[8]

Dimensions of Partition

Rejoining East to West Germany required healing the wounds of division. The most hated symbol of partition was the border. For 1,378 kilometers an ugly scar disfigured the landscape, dividing the GDR from the FRG. To keep its people in, the SED regime had built a formidable fortification that was open at only a dozen crossing points. On land, the frontier consisted of a broad forbidden zone, an inner barrier, a plowed and mined strip, watchtowers and searchlights, a jeep track, self-triggering shrapnel, and electrified outer fences. On water, shore barriers, nets and patrol boats discouraged the foolhardy. Thousands of privileged troops with hundreds of trained German shepherd dogs guarded this prison wall against escape.[9]

Following historical accident, the jagged frontier cut across villages, streets, rail lines, and bridges. The death strip ran through valleys and hillsides, severing forests, fields, and meadows. The border ruptured personal relations, kinship ties, and ancient communities and created economic blight. On the Eastern side, people were forcibly dispossessed and resettled. On the Western end, viewing platforms looked out over a forbidden land where time seemed to stand still. Only hawks and hares prospered.[10]

As a by-product of partition, soldiers were everywhere. In an area half the size of Texas, more troops and deadly weapons confronted one another than anywhere else in the world. About 1.4 million Warsaw Pact and NATO soldiers faced each other across the Fulda gap in the heart of Germany. They were armed with 21,000 tanks, 7,400 pieces of artillery, 2,250 combat aircraft and 900 helicopters. More than 2,000 nuclear warheads were aimed at Central European soil. It was in large part this concentration of arms that had spawned a broad peace movement in both Germanies.[11]

Hemmed in by Soviet and U.S. enclaves, Germans felt as if they lived in occupied territory. Especially during the summer, slow-moving military convoys tied up traffic on the *Autobahn*. Sudden sonic booms from low-flying fighter planes jangled citizens' nerves. During maneuvers tanks tore up fields and rattled through cobblestoned streets while helicopters clattered overhead. In the East, vast areas were cordoned off for exercises. Russian troops were penned into their barracks without chance to fraternize. In the West, there was more contact between civilians and the military. But separate U.S. towns sprang up, complete with schools, baseball fields, and country-western radio stations. The Cold War had produced a parallel military world.[12]

Separation also limited legal sovereignty. Even if it rarely touched on daily lives, the incomplete authority of the two successor states created practical problems and hurt German pride. As a result of defeat, both were subject to military restrictions (no ABC weapons). In the former capital of Berlin, people were not even masters in their own house. Although the Eastern part of the city became the GDR capital, the Western sectors could not obtain full political rights in the FRG. For military reasons, Lufthansa was not even allowed to fly to West Berlin. Transit problems also needed to be taken up with the four powers before being resolved with the GDR.[13]

Without a peace treaty, the former victors still held responsibility for the fate of Germany as a whole. In economic and political questions, the GDR and FRG played an increasingly important role in the Warsaw Pact and COMECON and NATO and the EC respectively. East Germans resented the remnants of four-power rights on Berlin as a limitation of their own independence. To self-assured West Germans lingering restrictions seemed irksome and anachronistic. Incomplete sovereignty made Bonn assume the contradictory stance of an economic giant acting like a political dwarf.[14]

Division created two of everything. Germans had to have two governments, embassies, armies, air forces, and navies. Two different flags waved over competing national teams, and two anthems greeted the winners during sporting events such as the Olympic games. Two cultural establishments with academies, orchestras, museums, and publishing houses drew on the same past to propagate the consciousness of two antagonistic countries. Two national railroads and post offices served their respective territories. Both sets of institutions were negatively fixated on each other, because each drew its justification for existing from combatting the dangerous influence of the other.[15]

As a result, much public money was wasted in mutual one-upmanship. In prestigious projects such as the commemoration of Berlin's 750th anniversary, East and West competed for the most impressive ceremony. Ideological confrontation engendered intolerance; dissidents could be marginalized and unceremoniously told to go to the other side. In quarrels over protocol the intense competition often verged on the comical. But the jockeying had a serious undertone. At stake was the claim to represent the best traditions of Germany as a whole. The two successor states were like adolescent siblings, close kin but locked in bitter rivalry.[16]

Partition was most obvious in the political realm. The two Germanies developed their common heritage in distinctive ways. While Third Reich crimes inspired a communist antifascism in the East, they justified a democratic capitalism in the West. In theory, East Berlin rejected any connection to the unsavory past, whereas Bonn claimed continuity, even if it meant paying restitution to Nazi victims. In practice, GDR uniforms and institutions resembled Prussian authoritarianism more than FRG practices that modified republican traditions. While older Western symbols possessed popular legitimacy, newly invented Eastern representations such as the hammer and compass emblem looked somewhat artificial.[17]

Institutions and attitudes gradually grew further apart. In the East, the primacy of the SED eroded the functioning of the multiparty system. The creation of fifteen administrative districts in 1952 suppressed the tradition of federalism. The transfer of power to the party and Kombinate also interrupted the practice of local self-government. In the FRG the youth revolt of 1968 transformed political culture to real grassroots participation and postmaterialist values. Stifled by Stasi repression, East Germans distrusted their institutions and remained locked in traditionalist preferences for leadership and delegation. By developing different elements of a common legacy, separation produced two distinctive political cultures.[18]

Division gradually made daily lives different. Many "secondary virtues," such as hard work, honesty, and living habits like Sunday's *Kaffeeklatsch*, remained similar. But four decades of partition created divergent life styles. Compared to affluent Westerners, most Easterners remained poor. In contrast to bewildering FRG freedom, GDR choices were circumscribed by the tutelary state. Unlike the stratified, competitive West, Eastern society was formally egalitarian and cooperative. Lacking the cosmopolitan ease of the Bonn elite, the East Berlin nomenclatura appeared a bit provincial and crude.[19]

Easterners worked longer hours, used mass transit, lived in dilapidated apartment buildings, and had to stand in line. But they also sent their children to free nurseries, vacationed in trade union resorts, paid less for cultural entertainment, and showed solidarity in need. Constant comparison with the glossy West created a widespread sense of inferiority. But socialism also nourished a defensive pride in athletic success, leadership in the Soviet bloc, and claims to be the tenth largest industrial power. Despite relatives' visits and care packages, living patterns grew apart so that separate societies gradually began to emerge.[20]

The cultural community also started to crack. Though the *Kulturnation* still shared one German tongue, lack of communication made the spoken language increasingly dissimilar. Marxist phrases, new realities, and popular humor created a GDR patois that outsiders found hard to understand. The printed word developed different styles as well. Drab Communist publications bored their readers and attracted little interest in the FRG. The colorful Western products that fascinated Easterners remained largely inaccessible to them. While critical Eastern authors were widely printed in the FRG, only "progressive" Western writers were available in the GDR.[21]

Media and fiction depicted different worlds. The problems of real existing socialism diverged more and more from the anxieties of postindustrial affluence. While most Eastern writers promoted an antifascist anticapitalism, many Western authors engaged in postmodern word plays in exotic settings. Only a few novelists on both sides like Christa Wolf, Martin Walser, and Peter Schneider still talked about unity. The GDR attempt to propagate a "socialist nation" had little success and the "constitutional patriotism" advocated by Western intellectuals retained a somewhat provisional ring. Although the aims of the two regimes were not fully realized, decades of division created different self-images and identities.[22]

In many ways the provincial East appeared more "German" than the international West. Although the enormous fields of the collective farms were new, development had touched the GDR landscape less than the bustling FRG. Dominated by church steeples and with high-rises relagated to the outskirts, many towns seemed hardly changed in the past half-century. The unmistakable Eastern smell that blended lysol disinfectant with lignite dust and body odor also seemed a throwback compared to the soaped and perfumed aroma of the West. As a result of constant waiting for trams, surly officials, or store clerks, time flowed more slowly under socialism than under hectic, money-making capitalism.[23]

In the East, space also seemed more confined, intimate, and controlled. Fast-moving *Autobahnen* and trans-continental jet travel created larger horizons in the West. Enforced public conformity made privacy more prized in the GDR than in the showy FRG, where success required an audience for self-display. Decades of oppression rendered Easterners more authoritarian in outlook and docile in behavior than their assertive and individualistic cousins. Since material pleasures were rare, the life of the mind loomed larger, allowing books, plays, concerts, and exhibitions to be savored. Many visitors found in the GDR a more sympathetic world of older virtues that had somehow been lost in the up-to-date FRG.[24]

Decades of division had deeply estranged the Germanies. In spite of national rhetoric, each side was profoundly ignorant of the other. While travel restrictions limited Eastern access to the West, lack of comfortable accommodations and confiscatory exchange rates inhibited the reverse flow. Western research on the GDR was a small and embattled social science specialty that had much difficulty in obtaining hard data. Eastern investigations of the capitalist world served polemical purposes and were kept out of the public eye. Though leaders met at official occasions, the political classes knew next to nothing about life in the other system.[25]

Personal contacts could not bridge the gap. Pensioners who were allowed to travel were an important source of news in the East. Businessmen with GDR contacts told tall tales in the West. Some Protestant clergymen cultivated ecumenical ties and a few intellectuals maintainted academic contacts. Unusual politicians with GDR roots or special sensitivity, like Erhard Eppler, established close relations, even with opposition figures. Assuming they were still basically alike, both sides embraced hostile stereotypes. GDR intellectuals railed against capitalist "elbow-society," while FRG spokesmen inveighed against "Stalinist repression." This legacy of rivalry abroad and alienation at home made unification a daunting challenge.[26]

Diplomatic Breakthrough

The World War II victors held the international keys to unity. Accustomed to Cold War stability, the four powers were surprised by the civic revolution and viewed Bonn's unification drive with suspicion. The return of the German problem posed unexpected risks: If the Big Four opposed self-determination, they might have to use military force. If they tried to slow its momentum, frustrated Germans might take matters into their own hands. Only if they conceded the restoration of unity would they be able to influence its conditions. Meanwhile the smaller neighbors could only watch anxiously and hope for the best.[27]

National interests differed considerably on unification. Washington could afford to be generous, as it only wanted to preserve NATO and free trade. Paris vacillated between historic suspicion of a stronger neighbor and newfound friendship. London did not relish abandoning the last vestiges of its imperial past. With twenty-seven million World War II victims, Moscow was deeply troubled by the prospect of losing its Western bastion. Bonn wanted, above all, to avoid a general peace treaty that might become "a second Versailles." Tirelessly, Kohl and Genscher reiterated that they would not go it alone. By stabilizing the center, unification would "not create but solve a problem concerning all of Europe."[28]

On May 5 the two-plus-four negotiations began in Bonn. FRG leaders had carefully prepared the ground by consulting with their Western allies and Eastern neighbors. In order to speed the talks, Foreign Minister Genscher invoked Thomas Mann: "We do not want a German Europe, but a European Germany." Representing the civic revolution, Markus Meckel vainly tried to establish an independent East German stance favoring neutrality. U.S. Secretary of State Baker challenged the meeting to find "a formula to end all remaining four-power rights and duties and to transfer them to a completely sovereign Germany."[29]

Under pressure from angry generals, Eduard Shevardnadze suggested "decoupling" the internal from the external aspects of unity. Though he privately considered unity inevitable, he publicly cautioned that any solution would "have to take the domestic situation in our country into account." While Genscher was willing to give ground, Kohl eventually balked, as he did not want to remain subject to foreign controls. In spite of "serious differences" in security questions, the ministers resolved to speed up the timetable. Genscher felt encouraged by the good start: "All participants agree that the process of German unification can take place and that no temporal limitations are put in its way."[30]

The Germans campaigned hard to wear down Russian resistance. Neither Bonn nor East Berlin wanted to turn the GDR into another independent Austria. Soviet opposition to NATO membership threatened to transform the two-plus-four negotiations into a confrontation of one against five. Afraid of provoking a veto backed by 380,000 troops, Bonn tried to dispel Moscow's fears by promising to meet its security needs. In Geneva, Windhoek, Brest, and Münster, Hans-Dietrich Genscher ceaselessly reiterated to Eduard Shevardnadze that the competing alliances needed to be developed into cooperative structures, preferably within the framework of the CSCE.[31]

Through diplomatic channels, Chancellor Kohl "proposed the idea of a comprehensive bilateral treaty." Ending past enmity, a general settle-ment would put future relationships on a constructive footing. Prodded by Bonn, East Berlin, though more sympathetic to Soviet wishes, also ex-pressed its own desire for quick currency union. During his Moscow visit, Lothar de Maizière assisted in the "first-class funeral" of the Warsaw Pact and supported NATO membership as well. As a tangible token of good-will, Kohl unceremoniously responded to Soviet financial difficulties by offering a five billion DM credit. Bonn diplomats, pleased that such ef-forts were improving the climate, announced, "We are on the right track."[32]

Close consultations with Western allies produced a common stance. During the fifty-fifth Franco-German summit, Chancellor Kohl stressed that German unification and European unity were two sides of the same coin. President Mitterrand slowly warmed to Bonn's historic chance. Be-fore the Atlantic Alliance, European Community, and other audiences, the German leaders denounced German neutrality as "old thinking." In-stead of upsetting the balance, NATO membership would enhance Eu-ropean security by maintaining proven multilateral ties. Even if Western insistence failed to overcome the reservations of Soviet hardliners, the united front increased the pressure for compromise.[33]

During a mid-May visit to Washington, Kohl reiterated his loyalty to NATO. To meet Soviet wishes, he emphasized "that the alliance must adapt itself to the circumstances." Thanking the American president for his vital support during the past difficult months, the chancellor called Bush "a stroke of luck for the Germans." Kohl pleaded that helping Gor-bachev was in the West's own interest and underlined the importance of American military presence in Europe. To explain the breathtaking speed of unification, the chancellor compared his situation with that of "a peas-ant who wants to bring in his crop because a thunderstorm might threat-en."[34]

The Polish border dispute had to be resolved first. Kohl's foot-dragging had created unnecessary doubt about German sincerity. To calm popular fears in its new western provinces, the Warsaw government kept pressing for a treaty before unification. In rejecting concessions, Bonn argued that an initialled draft would be less binding than a legislative resolution. "Only a future united German government can finally recog-nize the frontier in a legally binding manner through a treaty with Po-land." Since he needed their votes in the general election, Kohl tried to prepare conservatives for the inevitable by arguing that failure to recog-nize the Polish border would make unification impossible.[35]

In a special briefing, the chancellor implored skeptical leaders of Ger-man refugees expelled from Poland to listen to reason. With all allies demanding acceptance, responsible Germans had no choice but to accept the World War II borders. "Recognition of the Oder-Neisse-frontier" was an inescapable precondition for "the chance to realize the dream" of unity. Over a few negative votes, the Bundestag and Volkskammer adopted a resolution on June 21 that promised "to affirm the border between a united Germany and the Republic of Poland through an international treaty in perpetuity." While Polish leaders were still not entirely satisfied, the German public was relieved and the international community reassured.[36]

The second session of the two-plus-four negotiations convened on June 22 in Berlin. In a symbolic gesture the ministers watched the demolition of the Allied border crossing, called Checkpoint Charlie. Then Shevardnadze surprised his colleagues by proposing a draft treaty on "fundamental principles for a final legal settlement with Germany." Preliminary consultations had produced unanimity that the new borders would comprise the FRG, GDR, and Berlin. As a guarantee of peace, Germany would renounce nuclear, biological, and chemical weapons. But the Russians further insisted that all GDR and FRG agreements be extended "for a transition period of five years." To preserve its victory, Moscow demanded reducing German troops to a token force of 250,000 men.[37]

The Soviet proposal provoked heated opposition, because it took back prior concessions. Already during his Washington visit in early June, Gorbachev had conceded to Bush that alliance membership was "a matter for the Germans to decide." The perplexing idea that united Germany belong to both NATO and the Warsaw Pact appealed only to the neutralist Meckel. Secretary of State Baker objected that Bonn should not be "singularized" by having its sovereignty reduced. Genscher insisted that there be no "open questions" left and suggested redefining relations between the blocs. Shevardnadze's hint that his draft was not Gorbachev's view but a "politburo statement" aroused hope that a solution would be found before the November CSCE conference. Since domestic Soviet opposition had yet to be overcome, the Berlin round produced "no breakthrough, but tolerable prospects."[38]

Compromise required improvement in the military and economic climate. Following Moscow's hints, Bonn suggested as solution that NATO needed to change its threatening character. In early June, Kohl urged Bush to "send a message . . . which would help Gorbachev." Two weeks later, the American President took the initiative and proposed a declaration that would make the alliance posture less offensive. A delighted Genscher wanted to transmit a "clear political signal" to Moscow by revising alliance strategy. In order to overcome objections by Russian hardliners, NATO leaders met in London on July 5 to show their commitment to change.[39]

In conciliatory words, President Bush extended "the hand of cooperation" to the former enemy. Concretely NATO offered to abandon the doctrine of forward defense, use nuclear weapons only as "a last resort," withdraw atomic artillery, and establish consultations with the Warsaw Pact. German leaders were pleased with the spirit of the "London Declaration." The shift of emphasis from defense toward politics succeeded in helping Soviet reformers by allaying the military suspicions of the hard-line faction of NATO's intentions. The subsequent World Economic Summit in Houston also resolved to "strengthen democracy" in the East. Though lack of funds and business skepticism prevented the granting of fresh credits, the group of seven leading industrial nations endorsed aiding the transition toward a market economy.[40]

After the Nazi defeat, Moscow had been able to choose among three alternatives. In a one-Germany solution, social strife might drive the entire country into the Communist camp. In the GDR version, occupation and support of the SED could create a puppet state. In an Austrian variant that would repeat the state treaty of 1955, relinquishing the East might gain neutrality and economic cooperation. When the Economic Miracle spoiled the first option, Moscow settled for its second choice and occasionally flirted with the third. With perestroika, liberal advisers began to argue that "German unification lay in the Soviet national interest." Stalinism could only be reformed at home by ending confrontation abroad and moving Russia back into Europe.[41]

Western concessions and internal reform facilitated the Soviet reversal. Between June 1989 and July 1990 the Soviet government shifted from GDR support to an Austrian approach and reluctantly recognized the German right to self-determination. Only after the Twenty-eighth Communist Party Congress defeated the hardliners could Gorbachev's reformers act more freely. Orthodox Leninists and Soviet generals put up much "bitter resistance" against the surrender of Germany. But after heated debates Shevardnadze's conviction that "it is impossible to found one's own security on the division of another country" won out. The chancellor's visit would show how much Moscow could get in return for its new flexibility.[42]

Detailed preparation and personal sympathy produced the diplomatic breakthrough. Remembering the suffering of World War II, Gorbachev and Kohl seized the historic opportunity to improve Russo-German relations. To the amazed media, they announced agreement on controversial two-plus-four issues: (1) "German unity comprises the FRG, GDR and Berlin." (2) "At the moment of its merger, united Germany receives its full and unlimited sovereignty." (3) Bonn would remain in NATO, able to decide freely "to which alliance it wants to belong." (4) A bilateral treaty would regulate "troop withdrawal from the GDR which shall be completed within three to four years."[43]

The remaining points focused on military matters: (5) During the transition, "NATO structures shall not be extended" to the East but territorial forces would be allowed. (6) As long as Soviets are present, "troops of the three Western powers shall remain in Berlin." (7) In the Vienna disarmament talks, the FRG would declare its obligation "to reduce armed forces within three to four years to the strength of 370,000 men." (8) Finally, "a united Germany shall renounce production, possession and control of ABC weapons." Grateful for removing the security obstacles, Kohl promised to explore "further possibilities of economic and financial cooperation."[44]

The Caucasus agreement was the "single point at which the Cold War ended." Rising above emotional traumas, Kohl and Gorbachev realistically redefined their national interests. The combination of contentious issues into a comprehensive package made compromise possible. Gorbachev artfully argued, "The FRG has not gotten part of what it wanted and we have not achieved some" aims either. But the Soviets "had capitulated on the single most troublesome and dangerous issue of the Cold War." Conceding more than the Germans dared to hope, Moscow abandoned decades of division and accepted German unification. Gorbachev broke with hallowed taboos and promised to withdraw Russian troops, restore German sovereignty, and permit NATO membership.[45]

In return Kohl offered inducements that would aid the Russian reform process. The cooperation treaty replaced antagonism with friendly relations. Conventional disarmament and renunciation of ABC weapons would reduce the security threat and allow military expenditures to be cut. Payments for troop withdrawal, fresh credits, and Western expertise would assist in rescuing the ailing Soviet economy. Though Communist hardliners denounced the deal as "one of the most hated developments in Soviet foreign policy," Moscow preserved enough elements of neutralization (neither Western troops nor nuclear arms in the GDR) to salvage some of its pride.[46]

Bonn and East Berlin acclaimed this "fantastic result." A tired but happy Kohl explained "the breakthrough in regulating the external aspects of German unification," admitting, "I have been fortunate." The CDU/CSU was naturally pleased with the coup, and FDP chairman Lambsdorff lauded the deal as "a very successful day for German foreign policy." SPD spokesman Horst Ehmke was pleased that the government had adopted some opposition positions. Only the Greens demanded the withdrawal of NATO allies as well. East German Premier Lothar de Maizière was also satisfied, but Foreign Minister Meckel seemed chagrined by the extent of Russian concessions, which rendered his own office superfluous.[47]

At home and abroad, the press celebrated. Headlines proclaimed, "Gorbi sets all of Germany free," "Lucky Kohl," and "Unity on Credit." The media praised the chancellor for "achieving his lifelong goal" and becoming "a political giant." Even foreign papers were impressed with Kohl's "greatest accomplishment." International approval undercut domestic opposition to unity by robbing it of the argument of foreign hostility. Even if Western leaders were miffed at having been excluded, this favorable response accelerated the pace of diplomatic and domestic negotiations.[48]

A few days later, the Paris two-plus-four meeting approved the Cau-

casus deal. Bonn quickly assured its uneasy allies that it was not embark-
ing on a "separate path" with Moscow that would replicate the Rapallo
treaty of 1922. The Soviet-German talks had produced so much progress
that the external and internal aspects of unification could now proceed
synchronously. Almost euphorically Shevardnaze signalled that the comprehensive settlement with Bonn made Moscow willing to relinquish its
four-power rights. Hence already the third two-plus-four conference
started drafting a final document that would substitute for a peace treaty.[49]

Discussions in the French capital focused on guaranteeing the Polish-
German frontier. When Warsaw demanded that Bonn's sovereignty be
postponed until ratification of a border treaty, an offended Genscher
countered that the multilateral agreement would provide "final recognition." Unwilling to allow Poland to hold up matters, the meeting issued a
statement claiming that "the border question has been solved to the satisfaction of all sides." James Baker declared that "we are on the way to a
sovereign and united Germany as well as a stable security context for
Europe." Though German revanchists grumbled, Kohl promised to work
toward full reconciliation as precondition for European peace. In overriding the Polish veto, the meeting removed the last diplomatic obstacle to
unity.[50]

Germans were relieved by such unexpected international approval.
The common folk viewed foreign policy as grand theater, an entertainment without direct relation to their own lives. They followed the international moves of statesmen on TV or in the papers much as they cheered
for sports teams. Though many Western citizens still found it too fast,
Kohl's unification policy steadily gathered support against SPD criticism.
A solid two-thirds majority favored NATO membership, and less than
one-tenth opposed recognition of the Oder-Neisse frontier. The international success also noticeably boosted the re-election chances of Chancellor Kohl's government. Between June and August, the CDU-led coalition
regained the opinion lead in the West (see Table 8).[51]

Easterners were similarly surprised by the diplomatic settlement.
Even after the Warsaw Pact was discredited, almost nine out of ten preferred a European security system to extending the Atlantic Alliance
eastward. Fearing for its jobs, an overwhelming majority preferred neutrality and opposed the restoration of the Reich borders of 1937. To counteract "the open arrogance" of West German power, Meckel worked for an

TABLE 8. Eastern and Western Party Preferences, 1990 (Percentages)

| | East | | | | | West | | | | |
	Feb.	Apr.	June	July	Aug.	Feb.	Apr.	June	July	Aug.
CDU	13	32	35	33	37	41	40	42	43	43
SPD	53	26	26	30	25	41	40	40	39	38

over-arching security structure that would transcend the military blocs. But the crumbling of the GDR and unexpected Russian concessions rendered his suggestions irrelevant. The diplomatic breakthrough strengthened Bonn's hand in the accession negotiations with East Berlin.[52]

The Unification Treaty

An orderly transition required a second state treaty between the two Germanies. In the March election East Germans had rejected the slow process of a constitutional convention and stepped onto the fast track, joining the existing system of the FRG. The precedent for using Article 23 of the Basic Law was the accession of the Saar as a tenth state after the plebiscite in 1956. Against the wishes of Chancellor Adenauer the population of this coal-mining region under French occupation voted overwhelmingly to return to Germany. To avoid "a legal vacuum," Western regulations had to be introduced quickly but sensibly into the East. Since transition rules touched on countless interests, their precise shape triggered a long struggle.[53]

The Bonn cabinet proposed a minimal approach that would alter its proven practices as little as possible. Minister of the Interior Wolfgang Schäuble saw "no reason for changing the Basic Law" except for a few modifications, such as dropping the now superfluous Article 23. But the SPD adopted the aspirations of the civic movement and demanded "a widening and deepening of the democratic substance of the new republic." The Social Democrats proposed adding principles like the right to a job, worker codetermination, direct democracy, more federalism, multiculturalism, and gender equality to the constitution. The unification talks faced the challenge of fusing two incompatible legal systems and meshing opposing political cultures.[54]

The negotiators shared a basic pragmatism despite their different experiences. The Western spokesman was Interior Minister Wolfgang Schäuble. Born in the Badensian university town of Freiburg in 1942, he was a soft-spoken lawyer. A long-time CDU legislator, he rose to head the chancellor's office in 1984 and became minister five years later. Above all, Schäuble was an efficient organizer and problem solver. More credible than other party politicians, he was even mentioned as Kohl's potential successor. As the civic revolution was beginning to unfold, he had begun to worry about its implications and to advocate unity.[55]

His Eastern counterpart was Parliamentary State Secretary Günter Krause. Only thirty-one years old, he hailed from the Saxon-Anhalt city of Halle, where he had been an outstanding student. An engineer by training, he taught computer science at the Technical College in Wismar. Even before 1989 he had dared to promote market economics, since he was impressed by the superiority of Western technology. As an untarnished newcomer, Krause became chair of the CDU delegation in the Volkskammer and a vigorous proponent of "clearing up the debris" of the SED. Though pressure often made him polemical, this adaptable technician of power optimistically promoted a rapid union.[56]

Bonn had begun to prepare the unification treaty long in advance. In February 1990, Schäuble created a working group on "state structures and public order" within the cabinet committee on unity. Germinating ideas, this bureaucratic nucleus prepared various scenarios. By March it submitted a first draft to the states and the cabinet, sketching positions for accession legislation. During April, the Interior Ministry produced "discussion elements" that contained all the essential features of an agreement. Already within his own camp, Schäuble had to "juggle many balls" to gain agreement among ministries such as justice, finance, and foreign affairs.[57]

East Berlin was slower to start deliberations, since Lothar de Maizière preferred a longer transition period. Though overworked, Günter Krause drafted his own proposal that detailed many "concrete concerns" of GDR citizens. The negotiators exchanged texts on May 29, and the West presented another version on June 23. Less confrontational than Kohl, Interior Minister Schäuble drew in the opposition by keeping the SPD majority in the Bundesrat informed. In increasingly public meetings with the CDU, cabinet, states, and Bundestag, he tried to build a consensus. But such consultations transformed his minimalist outline into an omnibus text, loaded down with special requests.[58]

On July 6 the first negotiating session convened in East Berlin. Voicing Eastern hopes, Lothar de Maizière asked that the document be called "unification treaty." Since "division can only be overcome by sharing," GDR interests needed to be fixed in a legal agreement. Though accession required no treaty, Schäuble was ready to negotiate because he understood that "Easterners want to be able to find themselves in a united Germany." In order to finish by the end of the summer, the GDR premier proposed a simple approach, consisting of a preamble, specific provisions, and detailed appendices. Surprisingly, he emphasized "symbolic questions of unity," such as name, flag, anthem, and capital of the united state.[59]

"This is the accession of the GDR to the FRG and not the reverse." Schäuble countered with benevolent paternalism: "We have a good Basic Law that is proven. We want to do everything for you. You are cordially welcome. We do not want to trample coldly on your wishes and interests. But this is not the unification of two equal states." De Maizière also pleaded for restructuring the Treuhand and for new constitutional goals. Though many issues remained open, the Eastern and Western approaches were remarkably similar. Schäuble was relieved that things had gone well: "The start was a success."[60]

Slowly, outlines of agreement began to emerge. Through July, the Eastern and Western ministries prepared lists of changes and cleared them with each other as well as the European Community. In fact on transferring their own rules, the labor, finance, and justice departments proposed immediate conversion to Western law. Though retaining GDR codes would have reduced disruption, East Berlin surprisingly yielded, insisting only on enumerating exceptions. The second round of talks in early August revealed much common ground. Both sides agreed on revising the preamble to the Basic Law, striking Article 23, and adding a "paragraph 143" to permit legal differences during the transition. However, tough problems such as rules for civilian service, revenue sharing, the location of the capital, and creation of a reconstruction ministry remained unresolved.[61]

When the SPD felt left out of drafting proposals and of setting an election date, the talks broke down. Undeterred, Wolfgang Schäuble continued discussions with his own delegation and reached further compromises. Berlin would be designated as capital without specifying the seat of government. A new Article 5 stipulated that the disputed constitutional issues had to be settled within two years. In spite of the unwillingness of Western states to share their rich revenues, the new states would gradually be phased into obtaining their portion of sales tax receipts. Starting out with only 55 percent, the East would receive the full amount in 1995.[62]

Political confusion complicated preparations in East Berlin. Though uninformed about the East, Bonn bureaucrats realized that orderly accession required a credible partner. Overstressed GDR negotiators worried that strikes and continued rumors about Stasi activities would make public order disintegrate. Faced with economic collapse, the GDR representative Günter Krause warned time and again: "We cannot make it alone. . . . We will only get going when we have also completed political unity." Because of many neophytes in the cabinet, the de Maizière government often seemed to perform like a "group of amateur actors." Threatening disorder left no time for gradual transition but led to excessive haste.[63]

In late July, the Eastern FDP left the coalition in a dispute over the election date. When two of its ministers were dismissed because of criticizing the negotiations, the SPD followed suit on August 19. Chairman Wolfgang Thierse threatened to reject the treaty unless financial conditions were improved, land reform safeguarded, a new constitution elaborated, and conscientious objection and abortion allowed. Ideological differences, Western interference, and the impending election created clashes about the preferred path to unity. These quarrels took up much time and weakened the negotiating position of the East. Schäuble could only hope that the inexorable approach of unity would compel agreement in the end.[64]

On August 20, the final round of negotiations began under a cloud. An enraged Western SPD demanded that central points be changed and reopened many issues that had already been dealt with. To keep the treaty from failing, Wolfgang Schäuble warned that a Bundestag "conversion law" would be even more time consuming, expensive, and confusing. The talks succeeded in tying up loose ends, setting differential dates for transition rules, keeping the door open for constitutional change, and debating financial burdens. But these final compromises left many details to be filled in by later legislation.[65]

The continuing disputes resulted in a treaty that was legalistic and vague. Since SED victims deserved to be recompensed but funds were short, Article 17 promised "appropriate indemnification." According to Article 36, radio and TV were to become independent and regional, though institutional arrangements remained unclear. Specific ministries rather than a central office would reduce excessive public service personnel, who would be retrained during a waiting period (*Warteschleife*). In the costly area of ecology, Article 34 promised that Western standards would be introduced. Although a more flexible approach might have speeded recovery, bureaucrats created elaborate rules on transition practices.[66]

When the document seemed ready for initialing, new obstacles arose. On August 24, Günter Krause signalled agreement: Negotiations had produced a draft that contained provisions for "the approximation of laws," secured conditions for "GDR reconstruction," and offered "special measures" for conversion to a market economy. Because ratification required Social Democratic approval in the Bundesrat, Kohl reluctantly invited the leaders of the major parties to the chancellery on August 26. In a lengthy session, SPD chairman Hans-Jochen Vogel demanded improvements in property issues, state finances, abortion law, and constitutional reform.[67]

Specific working groups pressed on to clarify the remaining points. The touchy question of the future capital required a further debate, and could be decided by the Bundestag alone. When the GDR designated October 3 as the accession date, this day was accepted as a new national holiday. Complicated maneuvers produced a compromise on the number of votes in the Bundesrat that would guarantee the larger states a veto. Against local government objections, the negotiators also turned most of Eastern power generation over to three FRG companies that were big enough to make the necessary investments. The final controversies involved competing interests in the West rather than objections by the East.[68]

The most emotional issue was abortion. In the East, women were able to terminate pregnancies on demand within the first trimester (*Fristenlösung*). In the West, a fetus could be aborted only if a physician decided that medical, psychological, or social conditions warranted it (*Indikationslösung*). Secular definitions of women's rights clashed with Catholic teachings on the protection of unborn life. While the SPD saw unification as a chance to extend choice to the West, some CDU circles wanted to impose pro-life restrictions on the GDR. Unable to reconcile these views, the draft stipulated that the previous rules should continue in each area until the Bundestag passed a new law for the entire country.[69]

The FDP broke this tenuous compromise by switching sides. The Liberals shifted from treating abortions according to where a woman lived (*Wohnortprinzip*) to where they were performed (*Tatortprinzip*). To save the agreement, CDU legislators reluctantly swallowed the locality principle, but the SPD objected to shortening the transition period with different laws to two years. On August 30 the Socialists accepted a compromise for Article 31 of the unification treaty that promised women "help instead of punishment." Though they remained irreconcilable, the antagonists realized that nobody would understand the failure of the treaty over the abortion issue (paragraph 218).[70]

Another hurdle was the question of property. Once again, incompatible principles created an impasse. Righting old wrongs of expropriation required committing new injustices which would take hard-won possessions from their new owners. Satisfying the West meant alienating the East. In formal statements, the Soviet Union and GDR had insisted that the pre-1949 "land reform" not be undone. But the Basic Law gave priority to restoration of property over compensation for illegal losses. Since ownership disputes hindered investment, litigation had to be curbed so as to create jobs. Local governments also requested the return of community property.[71]

When it affirmed limited restitution, the unification treaty aroused heated objections from all sides. Landed interests in the Western FDP and CDU were so eager to overturn the postwar expropriations on GDR territory that they appealed to the Supreme Court, which turned them down. The SPD and the East German government preferred compensation, because it would leave present ownership untouched. In the end, however, the FDP's legal arguments in favor of restoration prevailed. While Westerners could live with the compromise, East Germans were horrified by the prospect of future claims.[72]

The last obstacle was the poisonous Stasi legacy. To keep revenge in check, Schäuble wanted to punish only crimes against persons, letting spies who merely gathered information go free. But protests against a "Stasi amnesty" stopped the pardon of transgressions related to German division. The one hundred-eighty km long Stasi files with unsavory material on six million people sparked even greater controversy. To protect personal privacy and public order, the treaty severely restricted their use. The civic movement deplored collective amnesia concerning SED crimes, construed control by the Federal Archives as dispossession, and opposed cooperation with Western secret services.[73]

On August 24 an agitated Volkskammer demanded wider access to the Stasi files. The GDR parliament called for "political, historical, and judicial investigation," and preservation in Eastern depositories. Public pressure forced Eastern Pastor Joachim Gauck and Western Undersecretary Hans Neusen to work out a last minute compromise: The GDR should put a special deputy in charge of the archives; a five-person board with three Easterners would supervise his work; files would be kept decentralized in the East; and data might be used only for rehabilitation, vetting officials, and prosecuting crimes. Arousing heated emotions, the Stasi dispute was a symbolic struggle over control of the GDR's past.[74]

The final ceremony was almost anticlimactic. On August 31 an exhausted Günter Krause and Wolfgang Schäuble signed the mammoth treaty in the festive Crown Prince Palace in East Berlin. Pleased with its "balance," Premier de Maizière hailed the agreement as "one of the most important treaties of German postwar history." The tough negotiations had brought clarity about property claims, conditions for investment, the transfer of social security, future state funding, ecological improvements, renewed federalism, and cultural support. A deeply moved Schäuble called it a "day of joy and confidence" that would bring unity in an orderly way. "We have created a solid and stable foundation for our community."[75]

The governing parties were delighted that "the last hurdle has been overcome." The opposition accepted the result, satisfied that it had "corrected mistakes." Although the Greens felt excluded, a skeptical PDS resigned itself to the inevitable. The press welcomed "the end of a laborious process" as "a historic day for Germany." In East and West, newspapers praised the great step and paid tribute to the Herculean effort that went into "this bureaucratic achievement." Only intellectual critics wondered whether they should celebrate.[76]

The document was a marvel of "German perfectionism." The preamble set as its purpose "the completion of German unity in peace and freedom as an equal member of the international community." In forty-five paragraphs, the text spelled out the accession date, constitutional changes, the merger of the legal systems, administration and judiciary, public property and debts, social issues, cultural questions, and implementation provisions. In an additional nineteen chapters, the FRG ministries specified endless details. All the fine print swelled the final copy to more than a thousand pages![77]

For the FRG, the adjustments were minor. The document announced six modifications of the Basic Law, beginning with alterations in the preamble to strike the unification mandate. For the GDR the treaty spelled out a plethora of changes in laws, rules, and regulations. In effect, it systematically superimposed a democratic legal system upon a communist order. To reduce transition difficulties, the appendixes specified the nature and duration of exceptions as well as the manner of convergence. In a number of contentious questions, the document simply deferred solution to a united German legislature at a future date. The speed and thoroughness of this legal blueprint for unification were impressive.[78]

The treaty was better than detractors allowed and worse than supporters claimed. Much left-wing criticism sprang from illusory premises. The wish that East and West would meet halfway ignored the impossibility of combining dictatorship with democracy. The hope that negotiations would proceed between equals overlooked the disintegration of the GDR. The desire that unity would bring previously stalled reforms disregarded parliamentary majorities. Some right-wing praise was similarly exaggerated. The blessings of a proven legal order were undermined by the lack of a competent bureaucracy in the East. The advantages of an extensive social safety net were vitiated by inequalities of coverage. Transferred Western funds were consumed by massive Eastern deficits.[79]

The agreement made a crucial contribution by forcing an unruly stream into predictable channels. Some compromises solved ancient problems, but haste also produced mistakes that triggered new conflicts. Though allowances for exceptions cushioned the shock, special interests destroyed valuable Eastern institutions such as public health clinics. In spite of hard bargaining, Bonn's preferences won all too often over East Berlin's sensibilities. The treaty effectively incorporated the GDR into the FRG. Yet many skeptics wondered: Would extending Western patterns produce a truly united Germany?[80]

An Orderly Transition

A key challenge of unification was to keep the transition orderly. With emotions running high, the people might take matters into their own hands. Foreign observers feared that "provocations" against Soviet garrisons would unleash widespread bloodshed. The civic movement tried to focus public anger on the SED in order to force domestic reforms. Western elites wanted to channel protest into established institutions, since they associated citizen participation with radical violence. The de Maizière government sought to direct popular hopes toward unification.[81]

The desire to control the process governed external and internal negotiations about the conditions for unity. The danger of military clashes prompted the international community to work out a procedure for unification. To pre-empt unilateral steps, the diplomats created the two-plus-four framework for negotiating multilateral solutions. Concern over violence also spurred domestic antagonists to find compromises regarding contentious issues of accession. Both Germanies preferred a unification treaty to a Western "transition law" with little chance for Eastern input.[82]

Another constraint was the press of time. Critics coined the neologism of *tempocracy* to decry the lack of reflection caused by the rapid changes. The Bonn cabinet blamed the need for haste on East German impatience. At the same time Kohl repeatedly used popular expectations as a rationale for shortening deadlines and advancing the timetable. The decision to conclude talks before the November CSCE conference eliminated much maneuvering room for Soviet opposition to NATO membership. Similarly the designation of December 2 as the joint election date tightened the schedule and forced compromise.[83]

The participants yielded to the acceleration as if mesmerized by its speed. The demand to keep both sets of negotiations synchronized further increased their tempo. Supported by the Gulf crisis, the argument of a fleeting international "window of opportunity" shortened the time horizon. The virtual fiscal collapse of the GDR after the currency union compelled Lothar de Maizière and Oskar Lafontaine to switch from gradual transition to immediate accession. The partly real but partly contrived time pressure contributed heavily to pushing through solutions within three short summer months.[84]

Great power negotiation fit a remodeled Germany into the European house. After half a century of division, other countries realized that reintegrating Eastern into Western Europe required rejoining the Germanies. Based on the FRG's good behavior, the World War II victors did not insist on a general peace treaty and asked the vanquished to be present at the conference table. The two-plus-four format combined great-power responsibility with German participation. While Genscher's diplomacy transformed the line-up into five versus one, American leaders strove for general consensus.[85]

In contrast to Bismarck's wars, the second unification received foreign consent. Bonn politicians like Theo Waigel could take pride: "Never before has German unity come in peace and freedom, with the neighbors' approval." Even left-wing critics admitted that Soviet concessions "surpassed all expectations." The result balanced removal of postwar restraints (such as Russian occupation forces) with maintaining Western ties to NATO and the European Community. The settlement transformed central Europe from a Cold War battleground into an arena of East-West reconciliation. By quelling fears of a Fourth Reich, diplomats hoped to turn Germany from a trouble spot into a pillar of stability.[86]

The unification treaty was the result of corporate politics. Its provisions were hammered out between East and West, the federal government and states, and the coalition and opposition. Unlike the currency union, it drew on a GDR draft and incorporated SPD amendments. To the chagrin of the civic movement, however, the deliberations remained confined to the elite, and the people were relegated to the role of spectator. Intellectuals' hopes for more new departures were disappointed, since the pressure for quick solutions postponed broader constitutional discussions. Left out of insiders' talks, Greens and dissidents could only criticize from the sidelines.[87]

The provisions of the treaty turned unification into a bureaucratic process. In effect, the unification agreement (*Einigungsvertrag*) inserted a bankrupt Eastern system into a functioning Western state. To reduce the uncertainties of transition, the Germans adopted a predictable procedure, specified in countless rules. To resolve difficult conflicts, an army of lawyers codified compromises in innumerable regulations. Instead of inspiring national town meetings, insistence on an orderly and swift transition produced a voluminous legal compendium. The complexity of re-unifying two estranged states took the process out of the public's hands and turned it over to distant bureaucrats.[88]

9

Forging Unity

The GDR vanished on October 2. Hammer and compass emblems disappeared from official buildings, leaving blank façades. Enough red flags for an entire parade piled up in garbage cans. East German embassies closed their doors, leaving not even janitors behind. Ministries stood deserted while skeleton crews sealed files and wrote dismissal notices. With a grand tattoo the People's Army turned its command over to the former archenemy. The Volkskammer met in final session "to write its own obituary." With 164 laws in 181 days, the freely elected parliament had "fulfilled its task of completing German unity in self-determination."[1]

On the eve of accession the popular mood was "strangely split. Hope and fear, concern and curiosity, resignation and tentative optimism" alternated. Three-quarters of the Westerners were glad to see unification come. Even if Easterners expected a turbulent transition, many were happy to escape the anarchy of the interregnum. The revolutionaries of the previous fall were "a bit sad" about the unexpected result of their rising. Though resentful of their cramped lives, intellectuals looked back at the dissolving GDR with a touch of nostalgia. Only a brisk trade in memorabilia recalled forty-one years of a separate state.[2]

The union was celebrated with quiet dignity. In the Berlin Schauspielhaus, Leipzig conductor Kurt Masur dedicated Beethoven's *Ode to Joy* to freedom: "We are one people [who] are becoming one state." Lothar de Maizière announced the end of the GDR: "It is a farewell without tears. . . . What was for most only a dream is becoming reality." Throughout the evening hundreds of thousands of spectators gathered in front of the old Reichstag building by the Brandenburg Gate. Waving black-red-gold flags, they peacefully awaited the historic moment. It seemed hard to believe that the national anthem's promise of "unity, justice and freedom" was about to be fulfilled.[3]

Suddenly, unity came. Fourteen athletes hoisted a huge flag sixty meters square. The freedom bell began to toll, and a crescendo of shouts arose. President von Weizsäcker vowed: "In a united Europe, we want to serve world peace." Enormous fireworks lit up the sky. All over the country, people danced in the streets. But the public was more pensive and subdued than raucous. Only a few skinheads shouted *Sieg Heil* while anarchists demonstrated for a republic called Utopia. "Half confident and half afraid," many Easterners were glad to be Westerners at last.[4]

A national holiday marked the reunion of the Germanies. On October 3, Catholic Bishop Karl Lehmann urged the political leaders during a thanksgiving service in the Marienkirche, "Now that the wall of stone has tumbled, the barrier in our heads must also come down." The festivities climaxed in the Berlin Philharmonic Hall. Grateful to the East Germans, allies, and neighbors, President von Weizsäcker noted with pride: "For the first time Germany finds its lasting place in the circle of Western democracies." He warned that material equity required sharing and that psychological reconciliation needed tact. "We have found the form of unity. Now we must fill it with substance and life."[5]

Outside, the festivities were more down to earth. Throngs of visitors packed the boulevard Unter den Linden all the way to the Alexanderplatz. Rock music echoed from the walls, the smell of grilled sausages wafted through the air, and children carried balloons. This *Volksfest* was friendly and relaxed until ten thousand defiant radicals demonstrated against unity, chanting, "Shut up Germany!" Anarchist militants expressed their disgust by battling with the police. Except for this jarring note, the first day in united Germany produced "a harmonious festival."[6]

This peaceful, civil celebration revealed a new public spirit. Under the Kaiser, Hitler, and Honecker, national holidays had been martial affairs. So as not to rouse old ghosts, this time there were "neither parades nor gun salutes, neither marching columns nor torchlight processions, but hurly-burly and carnival" instead. Politicians made sober speeches, and the media played classical music to foster "quiet joy." Weimar's Republic Day and Bonn's Unity Day had never taken hold, since they remained starchy official affairs. This was an attempt, with unpretentious fun, to make the new holiday truly popular.[7]

Most people were awed by the breathtaking changes and concerned about the challenges ahead. There was "no national intoxication, no excess, certainly less beer than after winning the soccer world cup." Though "everyone stayed put, many [Easterners] no longer felt at home," since the country had changed under their feet. Caught between an end and a beginning, they were happy to have escaped the repressive GDR, but had not yet arrived in the FRG. Only Leftists and intellectuals refused to rejoice. This sobriety and folksiness signalled a new democratic style for the united Germany.[8]

The Burden of History

To get this second chance, Germany had to come to terms with its troubled past. Since memories shape attitudes, every decision during unification was debated in terms of prior analogies. Neighboring countries never tired of recalling imperial transgressions or Nazi atrocities. Whenever there was a dispute, foreign politicians reawakened deep-seated stereotypes of the Boche or the Hun. Former victims kept digging up Third Reich atrocities that many burghers would rather forget. Anniversaries of wars necessitated unending public apologies. In Bonn and Berlin, history was a source not of pride but of constant embarrassment.[9]

German historical culture was deeply fractured and ambivalent. Successive changes of street signs exemplified this instability. In this century, the names of Kaiser Wilhelm II, Weimar president Friedrich Ebert, and Nazi Führer Adolf Hitler would designate the same road, only to be replaced by FRG founder Konrad Adenauer or GDR leader Walter Ulbricht. Historians quarreled about whether and how to preserve painful memories. But simple people wanted to stop beating their breasts. The popular preference for amnesia and the insistence by intellectuals on guilt were opposite responses to the same disturbing legacy.[10]

The standard for debates about unity was Imperial Germany. As the first national state, the Second Reich (1871–1918) left a conflicted legacy. Popular memory recalled it as "the good old days," the legendary *gute alte Zeit* when the world was still in order. Its supporters argued that it ended centuries of division, created a federal empire and gained international respect. They glossed over its newness by fostering instant tradition and appropriating medieval imperial symbols. Profiting from growing prosperity, the *Kaiserreich* represented the rule of law, academic renown, and municipal reform.[11]

Critics viewed the Empire as a repressive system that persecuted Catholics, Socialists, and other minorities. Foreigners associated the blustering "Kaiser Bill" with imperialism and the naval race. The Second Reich was discredited by its coresponsibility for World War I, enshrined in the treaty of Versailles' War Guilt Clause. Hence the first national state produced contradictory images of prosperity and aggression. Its new nationalism had succeeded in gaining the loyalty of most Catholics, Socialists, and Jews. But its militarism also spawned widespread fears and brought into question the legitimacy of a united German state.[12]

The Nazi trauma seemed to justify division beyond appeal. The failure of the Weimar Republic had suggested that Germans might be unsuited for democracy. Among the general population, the early Third Reich left subterranean recollections of peace and prosperity. But among its victims, Hitler's later horrors confirmed wartime anxieties and indelibly associated Greater Germany with human misery. At home, the SS state came to mean ruthless dictatorship and bloody warfare that did not spare civilians. Abroad, the Nazi regime became associated with renewed aggression and immense loss of life. In critical memory both combined in the concept of an unparalleled holocaust that engulfed Jews, Slavs, Gypsies, and other people throughout Europe.[13]

The Third Reich created the widespread belief that German unity must be ended once and for all. The safety of the neighboring countries compelled vigilance against another bid for hegemony. At the same time, Nazi abuses of this claim in Austria and the Sudentenland served to discredit future appeals to the right of self-determination. After 1945 many intellectuals like Günter Grass argued that the Auschwitz crimes morally barred unity. Jewish survivors expanded the anguished resolve "Never again!" into a perpetual prohibition of another national state. Though German leaders continually professed special "historical responsibility," the Nazi past made partition seem to be an essential barrier against a return of barbarism.[14]

Initially the GDR experiment appeared to have solved the German problem. The new communist state claimed to represent "a better Germany" of antifascism and social equality. This progressive alternative attracted émigrés such as playwright Bertold Brecht, poet Johannes Becher, and composer Hanns Eisler. The "workers' and peasants' state" alleged to have learned history's lessons once and for all and espoused communist internationalism. But after the Cold War abated, East German shortcomings could no longer be excused as the price of innovation. Dissidents realized that the SED was using resistance to fascism to cement a new tyranny.[15]

Eventually, the failure of the GDR nonetheless reopened the national question. Stasi repression seemed to undermine the moral legitimacy of separate statehood and validate the theory of totalitarianism that equated Nazi with Stalinist excesses. The general collapse of communism eroded leftist acceptance of division as the cornerstone of peace. Other revolutions in Eastern Europe suggested that German unification might provide a bridge for returning Poland, Czechoslovakia, or Hungary to the West. By discrediting the "two-state theory" as justification for partition, the implosion of the GDR created negative incentives for unity.[16]

West German success provided a more attractive alternative. The Bonn republic saw itself as a provisional continuation of German statehood until the severed East could be rejoined. The Basic Law avoided the mistakes of the Weimar constitution, revived federal self-government, and incorporated Western traditions. While critics charged that Nazi patterns persisted, the FRG made resolute efforts to come to terms with the "brownshirt" past. The spectacular boom of the social market economy gradually won the population over to democracy. To escape its troubled past, Bonn embraced the West and anchored itself in multilateral organizations such as NATO and the EC.[17]

Ultimately Konrad Adenauer's "magnet strategy" proved correct. Postponing any attempt to secure immediate reunification, the FRG founder put priority on building a Western state that might eventually attract the East. The youth rebellion of 1968 and its pacifist, ecological, and feminist movements further democratized institutions and living patterns. Reactions to occasional scandals such as the *Spiegel* affair only proved that its citizens and neighbors accepted the FRG to an unparalleled degree. Some intellectuals worried that democratic commitment would continue to be fragile as long as the country remained divided. But when the Eastern experiment failed, the Western model was available as positive substitute.[18]

In spite of Bonn's stability, fears persisted abroad. The minutes from Prime Minister Margaret Thatcher's consultation with leading British and American historians at Chequers illustrate historical apprehensions. Written down by her advisor Charles Powell, its discussions presented an appalling digest of the stereotypes of German national character. Teutonic traits supposedly consisted of "anxiety, aggressiveness, arrogance, ruthlessness, complacency, an inferiority complex [and] sentimentality." Nonetheless, the assembled experts agreed that the Germans had changed so much that past transgressions no longer justified present misgivings. The key message was unmistakable: "We should be nice to the Germans."[19]

Foreign apprehension of the Teutonic threat was slow to disappear because it was focused on the past rather than the present. During the summer British Secretary for Industry Nicholas Ridley characteristically denounced the creation of a joint European monetary policy: "This is all a German racket designed to take over the whole of Europe." Though allusions to Hitler merely voiced what many thought, an outcry against hate-mongering forced his dismissal. More sympathetic to the new Germany, the general public overrode the skepticism of policy elites. Though deep-seated, historical anti-German anxieties could complicate but not prevent unity.[20]

Unification presented a chance to break the national taboo. To prevent the resurgence of nationalism, intellectuals had fashioned partial Eastern or Western identities that rendered any references to the nation highly suspect. While Eastern progressives kept dreaming of a more humane socialism, Western leftists clung to their cherished cosmopolitan provincialism. Critics like Western SPD theorist Peter Glotz cited earlier chauvinist excesses to predict disasters if their post-national blueprint for the future were abandoned. The democratic legitimacy of the East German wish for unity fundamentally changed the terms of this debate. Without fear of derision, historian Thomas Nipperdey could now argue that self-determination was the delayed fulfillment of the revolutionary aspirations of 1848.[21]

Supporters claimed that only unity could end the "collective anomaly" of self-hate. Bonn political scientist Hans-Peter Schwarz argued that Germans might for the first time live in a democratic state with accepted borders: "After a long Odyssey, the country has returned to itself."

Though risky, merging the Eastern and Western experiences offered the possibility of regaining normalcy. "FRG citizens will not lose their identity," he claimed, "but at most their collective identity neurosis." Unification did not have to lead to a resurgence of chauvinism, but might at long last present an opportunity to heal the wounds of history. As the most successful German regime, the FRG had a right to shape the character of the new state.[22]

Unification offered a return to and an escape from history. The debate about the legitimacy and form of unity was saturated with references to the past. Such allusions were inevitable, since prior experiences provided the only vocabulary in which it could be discussed. For older supporters, "reunification" meant returning to a natural state, resuming a national course. For younger skeptics, "new-unification" implied the joining of two disparate societies that could hardly be more different. Ultimately the debate about the frightful past facilitated a more hopeful present. Painful lessons learned from earlier mistakes helped prevent unilateral German actions or dictatorial Allied responses. More positive recent experiences suggested that the risks of unity could be reduced by embedding it in international treaties and domestic agreements. In historical perspective, unity was both a homecoming and a departure.[23]

Precipitous Union

The last weeks before unity passed in "strange haste." When economic erosion forced the East to move up its accession date, time pressure once again increased. Officials scrambled to meet deadlines and tie up loose ends. The two-plus-four talks had to be concluded, the unification treaty ratified, the political parties merged. The old order crumbled quickly, but the new authority was slow to arrive, creating a never-never-land. This state of suspension attracted both helpful idealists and shady profiteers.[24]

The coming change evoked mixed feelings. Easterners awaited the magic moment "with concern but without fear." Sad about the disappearance of their state, dissidents took pride in the democratic awakening. Cabinet members were pleased to be the architects of unity. Westerners gradually began to realize that their accustomed routines were about to change. The well-known sociologist Niklas Luhmann mused about "the end of the Federal Republic," famous for its economic energy and culture of protest. Ironically those intellectuals who had criticized Bonn for years discovered how much they had grown to like it, just when it was about to disappear.[25]

The date of accession created endless controversy. Article 23 implied that diplomatic and domestic negotiations had to be completed and Eastern states be restored first. Unwilling to wait that long, the right-wing DSU pressed for immediate action. Brandenburg church leader Günter Krusche also counselled that "it would be good if this vacuum were ended soon." But Eastern SPD chairman Wolfgang Thierse argued for a slow pace that would postpone the merger until 1991. The left-wing opposition of Bündnis 90 and PDS also wanted to draw the process out in order to ease the transition. These differing priorities kept the cabinet from agreeing on a day.[26]

Caught in the middle, Prime Minister de Maizière temporized. Although the public clamored for an early union, he refused to be rushed because his coalition was committed to a gradual approach to unity. Lothar de Maizière was determined to clean up East Germany first, and preferred to "enter unity securely and fairly" at a later date. Resisting Bonn's pressure for rapid accession, he suggested the day of the federal election in early December as a compromise. The GDR electorate soon grew disgusted with this incomprehensible parliamentary maneuvering.[27]

The accession dispute ruptured the East German coalition. On July 24, the impatient Liberals left the cabinet. A week later de Maizière panicked, fearing that "his country could collapse economically and sink into general chaos." During a visit with Kohl at the Wolfgangsee, he suddenly proposed moving accession and the federal election up to the date of state balloting—October 14. Afraid of being disadvantaged by a short campaign, the SPD first refused an early election but then tried to outdo the CDU by suggesting September 15 as the merger date. Schäuble angrily rejected this move as "sowing new confusion," since the CSCE had to ratify the unification treaty beforehand. In frustration, the SPD disavowed its parliamentary leader Richard Schröder and bolted from the government.[28]

Accelerating disintegration finally forced the politicians to compromise. Public impatience with this disarray compelled the CDU to give ground, the SPD to reconsider, the Bündnis 90 to mediate. Seeking to maintain "a certain dignity," de Maizière suggested October 9, the anniversary of the Leipzig demonstration. When this proposal proved unacceptable, the CDU cut the Gordian knot. In a dramatic night session on August 23, it suggested October 3 as the earliest date, and 294 of 363 Volkskammer deputies agreed. After endless wrangling, all parties were relieved that "the path is free."[29]

Moving up accession created "enormous time pressure" to complete the diplomatic framework. After the Gulf conflict displaced the unification issue from the headlines, drawing up a Soviet-German treaty for economic cooperation became easier. But when Kohl phoned on September 7 and offered eight billion DM to house troops returning from the GDR, Gorbachev demanded a much higher price. To calm Russian fears, the chancellor vowed not to station foreign troops or hold NATO maneuvers in the East. Three days later Kohl called back, increased his offer to 12 billion DM for relocation support and added 3 billion more in interest-free loans.[30]

Visibly pleased, Gorbachev accepted the compromise. Specific agreements would regulate relations during the transition period and organize the withdrawal of Soviet forces. The bilateral rapprochement culminated in a general treaty on "good-neighborliness, partnership, and cooperation." Seeking to "give their mutual relationship a new quality," it guaranteed frontiers, promised neutrality, and strengthened cultural ties. In the cabinet, the chancellor noted with satisfaction, "The door stands wide open for a future of good relations, new partnership, and comprehensive cooperation with the Soviet Union."[31]

The bilateral treaties facilitated the conclusion of the two-plus-four agreement on September 12. Although the basic outlines were already in place, many details had yet to be resolved in the Moscow talks. When Douglas Hurd objected to the prohibition of NATO maneuvers on GDR territory, a frantic Genscher woke James Baker at 2:00 A.M. to work out a compromise. A supplemental protocol left a united Germany to decide the matter "in a reasonable and responsible way." Another stumbling block was Shevardnadze's reluctance to give up four-power rights by October 1. Only a reminder that Soviet magnanimity would engender German financial generosity persuaded him to yield.[32]

These compromises allowed the exhausted ministers to sign "the treaty on the final settlement with respect to Germany." Convinced that unification was "a significant contribution to peace and stability in Europe," the seven substantive paragraphs restated the detailed provisions of the Caucasus agreement. Since the treaty improved Russian security, a subdued Shevardnadze welcomed it as "wrapping up the results of World War II." Happy about his crowning achievement, Genscher claimed that the solution "of the external elements of German unification" opened a new chapter of European history. The media hailed the "eight months' miracle" with unrestrained enthusiasm.[33]

Renewed Stasi controversy, however, threatened to block approval of the unification treaty. To keep the archives from being turned over to the West, two dozen dissidents occupied the former headquarters at the Normannenstrasse on September 4. Calling on citizens to protect their files, Bärbel Bohley and other protesters started a hunger strike to keep personal documents out of FRG secret service hands. Though Schäuble did not want to renegotiate, he agreed with Krause on a supplementary letter to clarify conditions. On September 18, additional provisions "described the archiving of Stasi files more precisely, facilitated requests for information by victims," and prohibited routine access by the West German Secret Service (BND).[34]

Moral outrage and political expediency kept the Stasi issue alive. In late September, allegations shook the Volkskammer that a handful of ministers and more than sixty deputies were informal Stasi agents. When the civic movement and SPD pressed for disclosure, an unholy alliance of CDU and PDS blocked publication of their names. Confronted with evidence in closed session, several politicians tearfully resigned. To combat growing rumors, Prime Minister de Maizière denied that he had informed on the church. The Stasi problem proved intractable, since ever more East German writers, clergymen, and politicians were discovered to have been compromised.[35]

Ratifying the unification treaty provoked much controversy. In the Bundestag, disagreement focused on the costs of unity. For the CDU, Wolfgang Schäuble explained that the document intended to make the "great, dramatic changes . . . bearable for the people." After helping to produce the text the SPD had to agree, but it sought to blame the government for tax increases.[36] In the Volkskammer, de Maizière defended the treaty as a "good basis" for reconstruction and as guarantor of "citizens' rights" after the GDR was gone. Though it was "no dream result," Thierse promised that the SPD would vote for it. The PDS denounced it as an "*Anschluss*-accord" and dissidents deprecated it as "a collective emigration" ticket.[37]

In spite of heated debate, the GDR accession agreement was approved on schedule. In the final discussions, the parties positioned themselves for the federal election campaign. In a sweeping attack, SPD candidate Oskar Lafontaine deplored Kohl's "catastrophic mistakes" in economic policy. "What is this man talking about?" Schäuble replied, "He has forgotten to say yes to unity." Since the FDP supported the treaty, only the Greens mourned the "lost chances." Ignoring refugee objections, the Eastern and Western deputies favored unification overwhelmingly. The Volkskammer accepted with over 80 percent, the Bundestag approved with over 90 percent and the Bundesrat was unanimous.[38]

On the eve of union the political parties merged. Already in August the Eastern Liberals (BFD) had joined the smaller Western FDP, electing Count Lambsdorff as chair and Rainer Ortleb as deputy. As market advocates, the Free Democrats ignored the bloc party's compromised past. On September 27, the Eastern SPD also fused with its Western counterpart after 354 days of independence. Though they had only thirty-five thousand new members and neither property nor apparatus, these proud Social Democrats were reluctant to give up their identity. Although Easterners were not always happy with Oskar Lafontaine's populism, they endorsed him as candidate and elected the fiery Wolfgang Thierse as their representative to the leadership.[39]

The CDU was the last to unite on October 1. After absorbing the Democratic Awakening and peasant groups, the Eastern party was a large and prosperous organization, tainted only by its prior collaboration with the SED. The triumphant Christian Democrats re-elected Helmut Kohl as chair with a GDR-like majority of 98.5 percent. But his deputy Lothar de Maizière vowed to advocate "a keener social conscience" in the conservative camp. Since they represented a smaller territory, Easterners in effect joined existing political organizations of the West without transforming them to suit their needs. In every case, they could only hope to add a few new notes to a familiar melody.[40]

Additions to the Bonn cabinet completed the political transition. On October 4, an enlarged Bundestag met to swear in five new ministers without portfolio. Sabine Bergmann-Pohl, Günter Krause, and Lothar de Maizière (CDU) as well as Rainer Ortleb (FDP) and Hans-Joachim Walther (DSU) represented the new GDR constituencies. With another 144 deputies, the Federal parliament swelled to an unwieldy 663 members, retaining a large government majority. Most newcomers were technical professionals (38 engineers, 16 doctors, 15 scientists, and 12 economists) rather than humanists (13 teachers, 8 clergymen, and 7 lawyers). These Easterners formed a new political elite.[41]

The creation of a united government switched priorities to completing internal unity. Chancellor Kohl urged Germany to "become one economically and socially" as quickly as possible. To repair the enormous physical and spiritual devastation, he cautioned, "we shall have to make sacrifices." His rival Oskar Lafontaine retorted sharply: "Whoever talks about sacrificing must say the truth and that means tax increases." Gregor Gysi warned against diminishing Eastern self-esteem and creating "second class citizens." For the civic revolutionaries, Wolfgang Ullmann recalled that constitutional issues remained unresolved. All speakers agreed that psychological reconciliation would require patience and tact.[42]

Unification advocates sought to justify the rapid merger in celebratory discourse. For the new national holiday, Helmut Kohl, Lothar de Maizière, and others created an official success story: "The reunification date of October 3 is a day of joy and gratitude for all Germans." In Cold War terms, their stylized narrative claimed that "dictatorship and tyranny, repression and division have finally been overcome." The CDU, FDP, and large parts of the SPD celebrated unity as the fulfillment of the mandate of the Basic Law. Most people old enough to remember one Germany viewed unification as a return to a natural state. Optimists praised the civic revolution as one of the "grandest chapters of German history."[43]

The celebration rhetoric tried to establish a founding myth for a united Germany. "Without nationalist excess," it paid tribute to Adenauer's and Erhard's legacy of friendship with the West. Claiming that "the people determined the speed of unification," its partisans congratulated themselves on maintaining an orderly process. Their positive account acknowledged "the enormous challenge" of creating psychological harmony, but sought to shore up confidence in Eastern recovery. Countless official pronouncements reassured the world that Germany wanted "lasting understanding and reconciliation" as well as European integration.[44]

In contrast, critics warned of unsolved problems in a catastrophic counterdiscourse. Many intellectuals felt "sad that the process of democratization was broken off in the spring and replaced by quick unification." The leftist SPD, PDS, Greens, and the civic movement saw the merger as a catastrophe. To younger people who had grown up with division, unification seemed deeply unnatural. In postmaterialist code words, they argued that unity would not solve the problems of ecological devastation, gender inequality, North-South tension, and the like. Dissidents who had fought against Stalinism mourned "the definitive end of a long-buried utopia" that cut short their search for the Third Way.[45]

The pessimistic version denounced unification as an "overly hasty *Anschluss.*" Skeptics also regretted the triumph of an FRG deeply flawed by intolerance of radicals and foreigners. They railed against the victory of Western capital and predicted exploitation and colonization for the East. Moderate voices like Oskar Lafontaine's cautioned that "the difficult and time-consuming process of social unification is only just beginning." The Left refused to celebrate and felt "somewhat anxious instead." From the debacle of its reform hopes, the catastrophic discourse sought to salvage an opposition rhetoric.[46]

Foreign commentary on unification tried to find a middle ground between old fears and new hopes. In early October, the suspension of occupation rights and CSCE approval of the two-plus-four treaty attracted much media coverage. While American and French opinion was generally favorable, British and Russian statements remained guarded. Drawing on historical anxieties about German power, critical voices continued to predominate in Israel and Poland. But most analysts sought to leave behind propaganda clichés. Like a Dutch critic, they grudgingly accepted the inevitable: "No matter what we may think, [unification] is a reality."[47]

Surprised by their own approval of unity, international observers were concerned but resigned. On the whole, "sympathy and acceptance outweighed the bad memories." In Washington, the Bush administration claimed some of the credit for "victory in the Cold War." In Paris, columnists regretted the loss of French predominance. In London, congratulations had a "bittersweet" ring. In Moscow, amazement about Soviet concessions mingled with hope for a better future. Smaller neighbors found "little reason to celebrate with the Germans." Most foreign commentators strove for a hortatory stance that combined acceptance with vigilance.[48]

The marriage metaphor became the image of the unequal union. Physical differences between the massive Kohl and the frail de Maizière symbolized the disparity between East and West. In biting cartoons unification critics suggested a capitalist rape of the socialist GDR. An obscene underground flyer pictured Bonn as a lecherous old wolf, about to pounce on East Berlin, depicted as Little Red Riding Hood. When the helpless girl asks the fake grandmother why she has such a big member, the beast replies: "The better to unite with you." Less crudely, drawings of an impetuous Kohl as groom wooing a prickly de Maizière as bride conveyed a similar message of sexual subjugation.[49]

Ironically, unity advocates used the same picture to make the opposite point that the union was propelled by GDR collapse. One cartoon showed two figures in wedding clothes approaching a civil ceremony. The Eastern woman holds an empty purse up to the Western man, saying, "Helmut, I need more household money!" A macabre American drawing represented a worried Genscher figure, carrying the GDR economy across the threshold as a bride—only to realize that it was a corpse! Less polemically, the Social Democrat Egon Bahr likened unification to an arranged marriage with "later love not impossible. The celebration was really nice, but now we must get to know one another."[50]

Democratic Legitimation

The completion of unification required democratic legitimation. From the outset, the managers of power rejected a constitutional plebiscite as an unnecessary complication, but both governments had planned to consult the population beforehand so as to gain approval for the merger. Unfortunately, the rapid collapse of the GDR forced accession before elections could be held. Since the civic revolution started as a movement for greater participation, this reversal of the sequence left a bitter aftertaste. Critics charged not without justification: "Many aspects of this [process] have nothing or almost nothing to do with democracy."[51]

By coming at the end, the first nationwide ballot profoundly shaped the timing and character of the unification process. Many observers complained that the federal election politicized issues excessively. Instead of being decided on their own merits, problems were approached from a partisan perspective. This preoccupation with short-term advantage produced mistakes such as the vacillation about the Polish frontier. When the cost of unity became a campaign issue, the government refused to discuss necessary sacrifices since it did not want to raise taxes. Who would win, the pragmatic managers of unity or its intellectual critics?[52]

In the East, voters needed to elect five state governments first. The civic movement had demanded ending SED centralism so as to bring government back to the people. Restoring the *Länder* would resume older traditions and make Eastern structures compatible with Western federalism. It might reorient identities from the shattered GDR to regions considered psychologically as "home." Since with about seventeen million inhabitants the entire East had only as many people as the Western state of North-Rhine Westfalia, the optimal number of units was hotly debated. Though fewer *Länder* would have been fiscally stronger, public sentiment compelled the recreation of five different states. Instead of inventing new entities, recombining existing GDR districts was the quickest solution.[53]

With five million people, the "free state" of Saxony seemed viable. At half that number, Brandenburg and Thuringia also had strong historic roots. But Mecklenburg-Vorpommern was poor and had only two million inhabitants, while Saxony-Anhalt, populated by three million, combined former Prussian provinces with a small erstwhile duchy. East Berlin would have to be merged with its Western half. The prior capitals of Dresden, Potsdam, and Erfurt quickly reasserted themselves. But only after much controversy did Magdeburg win over Halle and Schwerin beat out Rostock. About fifteen counties held plebiscites to determine their allegiances. Economically less than an ideal arrangement, the resulting states restored pre-1952 territorial entities.[54]

The state election campaign was sluggish. East Germans were tired of voting and were losing faith in politics. Since most GDR politicians were tarnished by the Stasi, the candidates for state governor were either unknowns or imported from the West. Peter Michael Diestel (Brandenburg), Josef Duchac (Thuringia), Gerd Gies (Anhalt), and Alfred Gomolka (Mecklenburg) of the CDU, as well as the SPD's Reinhard Höppner (Anhalt), and Manfred Stolpe (Brandenburg) had little experience. The CDU only called on one outsider, Kurt Biedenkopf (for Saxony), but the SPD had to draft Friedhelm Farthmann (for Thuringia), Anke Fuchs (for Saxony), and Klaus Klingner (for Mecklenburg) from the West.[55]

This time, resources and media coverage were more equal. Yet the bloc parties CDU, FDP, and PDS still enjoyed material advantages over the new SPD, Bündnis 90, and DSU. Job losses, price rises, and rent increases made the economy the overriding issue. While Lafontaine predicted the worst, Kohl was radiating optimism, pretending that all was well and whatever was not, would become well. The collapse of old loyalties made identity another theme. While the left appealed to GDR nostalgia or internationalism, the right reassured with regional and national rhetoric. In spite of lack of interest, the political stakes were high. At issue was control over Eastern state houses and the Bundesrat majority.[56]

The result was another smashing victory for Helmut Kohl. Though polls had predicted a conservative trend, the October 14 success surprised by its magnitude. While the CDU and SPD competed for state leadership, the smaller parties struggled to surmount the 5 percent hurdle. After the absorption of Democratic Awakening (DA) and the peasant party (DBD), the CDU became the largest party in four of the five Eastern states. Though the Social Democrats (SPD) advanced everywhere, they captured only Brandenburg. The PDS continued to decline, the Free Democrats (FDP) gained from the CDU, the civic movement hung on, but the German Social Union (DSU) disappeared. By consolidating the March triumph, the state elections renewed the mandate for the CDU (see Table 9).[57]

TABLE 9. Eastern State Election Results, October 14, 1990

Party	Brandenburg Vote	Seats	Mecklenburg Vote	Seats	Saxony Vote	Seats	Saxony-Anhalt Vote	Seats	Thuringia Vote	Seats
CDU	29.4	27	38.3	31	53.8	92	39.0	48	45.4	44
SPD	38.3	36	27.0	21	19.1	32	26.9	27	22.8	21
PDS	13.4	13	15.7	12	10.2	17	12.0	12	9.7	9
FDP	6.6	6	5.5	4	5.3	9	13.5	14	9.3	9
Bü90	6.4	6	—	—	5.6	10	5.3	5	6.5	6

Election postmortems tried to explain the CDU success. Surveys revealed that Easterners were more concerned with unemployment (86 percent) and the economy (75 percent) than with abortion (58 percent) or ecology (40 percent). Though fewer people cast their ballots (70 percent), they voted for the CDU as more economically competent than the rival SPD (35 percent to 11 percent). Volker Rühe praised "the gigantic win for the CDU," and Wolfgang Thierse blamed the SPD's disappointing showing on popular "faith in miracles." A gratified Kohl acknowledged high expectations and promised: "My friends and I shall try to live up to this responsibility." While the Left consoled itself with the Brandenburg victory, the Right celebrated another "triumph of the chancellor."[58]

Building state governments from scratch proved difficult. Lack of facilities and equipment hampered decisions; meeting rooms, telephones, and copiers had to be improvised. At the same time, neophyte parliamentarians needed to acquire experience with forming democratic coalitions. In Brandenburg Stolpe negotiated patiently to gather a "traffic light" majority of the "red" SPD, the "yellow" FDP, and the "green" Bündnis 90 members. In Mecklenburg, Gomolka persuaded an SPD member to switch parties and provide the CDU-FDP alliance with a tenuous one-vote majority. In Saxony the CDU majority allowed Biedenkopf to rule alone. Gies in Saxony-Anhalt and Duchac in Thuringia governed with the FDP.[59]

The creation of effective administrations was an even greater challenge. Officials who had served under the SED needed to learn modern bureaucratic procedures. As sponsors, Western states helped with personnel, machines, and advice. For example North-Rhine Westfalia adopted Brandenburg and Baden-Württemberg supported Saxony. The East was not always appreciative. When *Wessis* upset their routines, *Ossis* resented the innovations as arrogant interference. With only minimal revenues, the new states lived by transfers from Bonn that often had strings attached. Crucial economic decisions were made by the Treuhand in Berlin. In spite of their dependence, parliaments and administrations gradually took hold and the states provided a new regional identity.[60]

The most popular governor was Manfred Stolpe. A fifty-four-year-old lawyer, the Brandenburg premier was a Protestant administrator who had negotiated for the church with the SED and secret police. A flexible mediator, Stolpe had a conciliatory temperament, instinctively seeking common ground. Though he did not belong to any party, he accepted an SPD draft so as to help rebuild Brandenburg. With his experience, he understood the problems of transition and tried to restore popular self-confidence. His administration possessed a social conscience and pursued a progressive course. Even mounting evidence of his extensive dealings with the Stasi hardly shook his popularity.[61]

Similarly successful was the Saxon premier Kurt Biedenkopf. The sixty-year-old jurist was a Western import with some Eastern ties. A brilliant thinker, he had served as CDU general secretary and North-Rhine Westfalian leader until his outspoken criticism angered chancellor Kohl. When the Saxon CDU was deadlocked between hacks and reformers, it turned to this visiting professor at Leipzig University. The diminutive academic gained widespread affection with his political experience, economic competence, and courage to stand up to Bonn. Both premiers saw rebuilding as a chance for new departures and called for greater sacrifices by the West.[62]

The final test of unification was the federal election for the Bundestag. Since it would decide power in Bonn for years to come, the form and timing of the voting created much controversy. Though FRG law mandated balloting by January 1991, the GDR government wanted to postpone it. Wolfgang Schäuble proposed three models: early accession would make a joint vote possible in December; an election treaty could regulate conditions and allow a merger immediately afterward; or separate balloting could be held simultaneously. After much wrangling, the Volkskammer agreed to a compromise that combined rapid union with a formal agreement.[63]

Interests also clashed on the 5 percent hurdle for representation in the Federal parliament. To suppress smaller rivals, the SPD and FDP wanted a uniform requirement for proportional voting, arguing that a united country demanded one standard. Fearing to be shut out, the PDS and DSU clamored for a separate count, and the civic movement rejected any barrier. On August 3, both sides signed an election treaty that extended Western regulations to the East. By threatening the coalition, the FDP forced through a uniform 5 percent clause, modified by the possibility of joint lists. When the Supreme Court declared this approach unfair on September 29, procedures reverted to the original CDU proposal of counting votes separately in East and West.[64]

The campaign turned into a plebiscite on unity. Westerners were eager for a chance to express their opinion on the historic merger. Not only had the opposition SPD led the ruling CDU in surveys through 1989, but it also beat the coalition in several state elections during 1990. The government played the unification card to trump the post-materialist causes of gender and ecology, in which its critics held a stronger hand. By making the vote a "chancellor election," the CDU tried to cash in on Helmut Kohl's unusual popularity as the architect of unity. The talented populist Lafontaine, who criticized unity and aroused social fears, seemed like "the wrong man in the wrong place at the wrong time."[65]

Although it determined who would control the new Germany, the contest lacked suspense. Poll after poll showed Kohl personally leading Lafontaine by 15 to 20 percentage points and the CDU-FDP coalition with a substantial advantage over its challengers. With the outcome of the main race predictable, only the results of the smaller parties were in doubt. Would the FDP top the 10 percent mark, the Greens survive, the

PDS decline further, or the far Right get in? In the final days the race began to tighten because of conservative overconfidence. A socialist-liberal-green surge might yet deny the government an absolute majority.[66]

The Social Democratic opposition faced an uphill struggle. The public doubted SPD competence to deal with diplomacy or economics, but gave it credit for commitment in the areas of ecology and social security. The candidate Oskar Lafontaine was both an asset and a problem. The Saar premier was an unorthodox polemicist, young and glamorous. But this Europeanized bon vivant had little appeal in the East. On the campaign trail, Lafontaine earned applause as a critic of unity. Deploring Kohl's "high-handedness and arrogance," he warned against "hiding the costs of unification" and predicted that tax increases were inevitable. Addressing Western concerns, the program promised the creation of an "ecological, social and economically strong" Germany.[67]

The SPD campaigned as the youthful alternative, showing "a new way." Posters sported attractive graphics with a rose motif and displayed the catchy slogan "It'll work with us." Unions, feminists, artists, and intellectuals made ringing endorsements of "more democracy." The dispirited party, however, found it hard to convince itself that "the SPD can win." Especially in the East, voters were tired of socialist rhetoric. Despite his personal magnetism and acerbic wit, Lafontaine stirred little enthusiasm with prophecies of doom and demands for sacrifice. Fighting desperately, the SPD hoped that "the tide has turned during the last weeks."[68]

The CDU tried to capitalize on unity. The Christian Democrats mounted "a chancellor campaign," convinced "that we are unbeatable with it." For the first time in his career, Helmut Kohl enjoyed the advantage of greater popularity than his challenger. Tall and massive, this consummate politician succeeded by being underestimated by his enemies. Through rubbing shoulders with ordinary people, he instinctively sensed the mood of the masses. As an incumbent, Kohl acted the statesman and simply ignored his opponent's attacks. Unlike the fear-mongering SPD, the CDU reassured with promises of freedom, prosperity, and security. Its slogan was "Yes to Germany—yes to the future."[69]

Controlling the media spotlight, the ruling party employed traditional campaign methods. Its vague program supported tightening asylum law and opposed abortion. Preferring continuity to change, the CDU emphasized "security and prosperity in all of Germany." The Christian Democrats produced simple flyers in bold letters. Posters featuring the chancellor claimed "together we will make it" and stressed government competence. In interviews and appearances Kohl promised prosperity without spelling out financial sacrifices. To win this crucial election the CDU glossed over the problems of unification and radiated confidence.[70]

The outcome produced few surprises. For once, the polls proved correct. Though the CDU peaked in October, the SPD managed to gain little ground, and the small parties remained marginal. When the votes were counted on December 2, the CDU/CSU had triumphed over three

TABLE 10. Federal Election Results, 1983, 1987, 1990
(percent of popular votes and seats in FRG Bundestag)

	1983	1987	West	East	Total	Number of seats
			1990			
CDU/CSU	48.8	44.3	44.1	43.4	43.8	319
SPD	38.2	37.0	35.9	23.6	33.5	239
FDP	7.0	9.1	10.6	13.4	11.0	79
Greens/Bündnis 90	5.6	8.3	4.7	5.9	3.9	8
PDS/DKP	.2	—	.3	9.9	2.4	17
NPD/Reps	.2	.6	2.6	1.6	2.4	—

dozen competitors with 43.8 percent. Even with fewer votes than in previous elections, the Christian Democrats held their Western constituency and built a solid bastion in the East. The FDP maintained its position and profited from Genscher's popularity and the reluctance of middle-class voters to give Kohl too much authority (see Table 10).[71]

In contrast, the SPD made its most disappointing showing in years, because of its weakness in the new states. The antiunification Western Greens dropped out of the Bundestag altogether since they refused to join the civic movement in one electoral list. But the Eastern Bündnis 90/Greens just got into parliament because of the separate count. For the first time since 1949, Communists returned with the PDS as a result of their regional support in the East. But the new Right of NPD or Reps failed to overcome the 5 percent barrier. In reunited Berlin, the CDU surprisingly won (39.3 percent) over the SPD (30.5 percent), PDS (9.7 percent), and FDP (9.3 percent). An elated Kohl praised "the best result for a party since there have been free, secret and direct elections in Germany."[72]

The government won by mobilizing its constituency. While net shifts between parties were small, numerous individual voters switched. In the West, the FDP gained from all camps while the Greens lost support across the board. In the consolidating East, the PDS lost adherents to the SPD while the FDP drew most from the CDU. Though receding in its strongholds, the CDU ran well in Bavaria (51.9 percent), Saxony (49.5 percent), Baden-Württemberg (46.5 percent), Rhineland-Palatinate (45.6 percent) and Thuringia (45.2 percent). Still attracting Catholics, farmers, and older people, the Christian Democrats managed to extend their appeal to middling towns and workers in the East.[73]

The unification issue overrode all other concerns. The public considered the CDU/FDP coalition more competent in this vital question. The decline in voter participation to 78.5 percent in the West and 75.1 percent in the East hurt the SPD. The Social Democrats lost some labor support and drew mostly younger, urban, and white collar voters. The SPD managed to retain only the Saar (51.2 percent), Bremen (42.5 percent), North-Rhine Westfalia (41.1 percent), and Hamburg (41.0 percent). The conservative pollster Elisabeth Noelle-Neumann suggested that unusual feelings of gratitude for unity dominated the election. Since Kohl and Genscher had worked the miracle, victory was their "reward for unity."[74]

The landslide was a "confirmation of Kohl's German policy." In TV interviews, party leaders tried to put a positive spin on their performance. Kohl was overjoyed by "the clear electoral mandate," which cemented his control over the CDU and his hold on power. For the Liberals Count Lambsdorff gave Foreign Minister Genscher much of the credit. The civic movement was relieved to have survived, and Gysi promised a "left alternative politics" for the PDS. Though he took solace in the support of the young, a dejected loser Lafontaine refused the SPD party leadership. To reverse the defeat, realists among the Greens continued to plead for a more constructive policy.[75]

The chancellor's victory cup contained some bitter drops. The expected "unification bonus" remained small and FDP gains would make the junior partner less tractable. The press commented, "as brilliant as the coalition victory was, as difficult the challenge will be for Kohl, Genscher, and Lambsdorff in years to come." In spite of campaign denials, getting East Germany back on its feet would demand "many sacrifices from Western citizens." The "clear leadership mandate for the CDU/CSU and FDP" might yet become a heavy responsibility. In a more general sense, the unmistakable vote legitimized unity democratically. "The people have ratified and confirmed the process of German unification by plebiscite."[76]

A Social Revolution

Joining the West was a "gigantic social experiment" for the East. Accession required the new states to undo decades of communist structures so as to restore prior common patterns. Unification also forced Easterners to replicate the postwar Western modernization in a few months. A one-party dictatorship had to be transformed into a pluralist parliamentary democracy. A planned economy was supposed to metamorphose into social market capitalism. A servile judiciary needed to evolve into a defender of civil rights. An indoctrination apparatus was expected to become a free education system. . . . Virtually all aspects of life had to change.[77]

This double transformation was nothing short of revolutionary. Begun under Modrow, the transition accelerated under de Maizière and reached full steam under Kohl. To the people trying to cope, this liberation was a shattering experience. A very few institutions, such as the church, could remain intact, if they had escaped corruption by the regime. Though most East Germans welcomed change, they resented being "reconstructed" by superior bureaucrats and by *Wessi* outsiders. Through its national turn, the civic rising from below produced an unintended effect. The imposition of the Western system on the East in the final stage of the German upheaval recalled the classic Prussian pattern of "revolution from above."[78]

The change was especially unsettling in the workplace. In contrast to leisure-oriented Westerners, Easterners defined themselves via their jobs. For almost three-fifths of the workforce, incorporation in the West fundamentally disrupted security and stability. Half a year after accession, one-fifth of the workers (21 percent) had moved to a new position, partly through commuting westward (4 percent); one-sixth (16 percent) worked reduced hours; and the remainder were either unemployed (8 percent) or had retired prematurely (10 percent). For virtually everyone, unification disbanded job collectives, upset comfortable routines, and severed social ties.[79]

For those fortunate enough to hang on, work became far more demanding. Tough competition called for greater effort so that going through the motions no longer sufficed. Succeeding in a merciless market required new skills, performance pride, and an ethic of responsibility. Better supplies and newer machines eliminated some bottlenecks. Yet the faster pace proved so exhausting that many Eastern workers refused to apply to Western companies. For the survivors, assertive unions managed to reduce hours to about forty per week and to raise pay to roughly half of FRG scales. Energetic souls thrived on the fresh opportunities. But many workers felt dazed and lost in the strange capitalist world.[80]

The postcommunist transition unleashed a fierce redistribution struggle. The GDR's lower-middle-class pattern of wage equality coupled with party privilege quickly crumbled. Ideological purges dissolved the nomenclatura, lack of funds reduced the state apparatus, competition threatened inefficient managers, and unemployment displaced redundant employees. After a few months, this restratification produced a variety of losers: The politically compromised were dismissed, older workers went into early retirement, many women lost their jobs, and much manual labor became superfluous. Unity shattered many of the pillars of the "Socialist estate society."[81]

Others profited from the transformation. A new political elite emerged out of the bloc parties and dissidents. The highly trained and well connected had a better chance to retain their jobs. Some independents succeeded in setting up their own businesses. Skilled workers gained employment in some of the new companies. Finally, the young and flexible quickly internalized the new rules. This restructuring restored a social pyramid topped by politicians, the propertied, and the remaining professionals. By rewarding performance, this competitive climate overturned ideological hierarchies and increased social inequality. Instead of being boringly predictable, the future suddenly became exciting and insecure.[82]

The social revolution created "a crisis of meaning." The system's transformation posed embarrassing questions about one's prior role and devalued virtually all cultural capital. The rapid advent of capitalist democracy rendered formal techniques of dealing with the SED regime as well as informal survival strategies such as compliance, passivity, or privatism worthless. Overnight, East Germans had to learn new regulations for legal procedures, health insurance, child support, and the like. To function effectively in a Western society, the new citizens also had to acquire the unwritten rules of initiative, public speech, and responsibility.[83]

People responded to this challenge according to their prior experience. Some incorrigible or idealist Marxists clung nostalgically to a vanishing GDR identity. Previous opportunists flip-flopped completely and embraced the new master code without fully understanding it. Those who had maintained a certain reserve toward the SED adapted more selectively to the novel order. Prior dissidents easily joined the critical subculture of the FRG. Many Westerners failed to understand this difficult reorientation process. From hour to hour, Easterners alternated between a feeling of liberation and a sense of victimization. Only the future could tell whether the "social mega-experiment" of unification would ultimately succeed.[84]

Conclusion

The New Germany

A single year transformed the face of Germany. Between the fall of 1989 and 1990, the GDR, the most stable member of the Soviet bloc, disappeared. The very symbol of the Cold War, the Berlin Wall, collapsed, to be sold off piece by piece. The Stasi octopus that struck terror into dissidents' hearts dissolved into mounds of incriminating files. Socialist promises of prosperity for all had failed miserably, leaving ruined industries and polluted soil behind. German division, so long at the center of the East-West conflict, went down with them.[1]

Unification profoundly reshaped the center of Europe. Where the GDR and FRG had confronted one another, a single country reemerged with the same name and anthem. In ideological competition, the "free democratic order" vanquished the Communist utopia. Without a single shot being fired, the Warsaw Pact crumbled and NATO extended its territory to the East. The "social market economy" with its higher living standards proved more attractive than socialist planning. Utterly unexpected, German unification perplexed participants and observers alike. Reeling from its speed, everyone wondered how this stunning change could have come about.[2]

The joint country was smaller and less threatening than before the world wars. But the increase of 41,817 square miles made it the third largest state on the continent with about 137,931 square miles. Reunification of the divided city restored Berlin as a metropolis of 3.5 million and moved the center of gravity toward the East. The addition of 16.34 million people pushed the German population up to 78.42 million, the most numerous in Europe. GDR accession made the populace younger (17 percent under 15), more Protestant (42 percent), and more atheist than it was in the old FRG. The gain of another 12 percent in output increased the joint GNP to about $2 trillion (by 1992). Though GDR trade disintegrated, the new Germany remained the second biggest exporter in the world, after the U.S. but before Japan.[3]

It took time to get used to a united Germany. To catch up with reality, geographers hastily created new maps and post offices dropped the separate prefixes from their mailing codes. Critics exaggerated the increase in Bonn's power, and adjoining countries worried about the larger neighbor in their midst. But apologists argued that many resources would be consumed by Germany's struggle with the problems of internal unity. Efforts and costs required by reintegration might turn out to be much greater than predicted. After decades of self-effacement, growing into larger international responsibilities could prove difficult. How would the new old Germany turn out?[4]

Dynamics of Unification

The German upheaval has left a kaleidoscope of bewildering images. In the summer of 1989, daring refugees dominated media reports. During the fall, peaceful demonstrators filled the screen. Then Honecker's overthrow, Krenz's promises, and the toppling of the Wall made the news. In the winter, the picture shifted to "honest" Hans Modrow and the heated debates of the Round Table. During the spring cameras focused on Helmut Kohl's rallies and on Lothar de Maizière's surprise victory. In the summer journalists covered the currency union and the first DM purchases. Then Gorbachev and Kohl's Caucasus breakthrough stole the spotlight from the less exciting unification treaty talks. In the fall, reporters zeroed in on the union ceremony and the federal election campaign.[5]

The media partly clarified and partly obscured the drama. Highlighting crisis moments provided an illusion of information that left more complicated developments in the dark. In the East, the journalistic rebellion against decades of censorship speeded the disintegration of communist power. In the West, the human interest focus prepared the emotional ground for unification. Because of such spotty reporting, participants had difficulty understanding the process. The unexpected trajectory from civic rising to unification created instant legends of "heroic protest" and also of an "aborted revolution." Ambivalent commentators found the events at once compelling and threatening.[6]

Many aspects of unification suggested a celebratory account. The dramatic exodus and peaceful protests stirred powerful emotions in East and West. Popular demands for human rights and attempts to create a civil society evoked much support abroad. Even skeptics considered the fall of Honecker overdue and the floundering of his successors inevitable. Intellectuals sympathized with the idealism of the Third Way, even if such dreams could not revive the ailing economy. Though dissidents criticized Bonn's interference, the election verdict for unity looked legitimate. Foreigners noted with relief that the shift to unification lacked nationalistic fervor.[7]

The moderation of the participants helped unification to appear a "grand success." Although experts warned of a debacle, the quick introduction of the DM was a necessary response to popular wishes in the East. In contrast to Cold War confrontations, the Soviet settlement and the two-plus-four treaty were not imposed but negotiated. Although the unification treaty was much criticized, it did permit an orderly accession of the five new states. By confirming the loss of the eastern provinces, the reunification of the East created the most "Western" Germany in history. Unlike Bismarck's conquest of central Europe, the second merger was remarkably nonviolent, democratically legitimated, and internationally accepted.[8]

Other features supported a catastrophic view. The protesters who stayed behind denounced those who left for the FRG as materialists. All too often Western politicians dismissed Eastern dissidents as wooly-headed and ineffective. The population viewed Krenz's strained attempts to modernize the SED as flagrant opportunism. Those who wanted to salvage a socialism with a human face considered the implosion of their state unnecessary and the result of conspiracy. Losers denounced the March vote as a stolen election, based on false promises of prosperity. By threatening established interests and ideologies, the upheaval necessarily provoked much scorn.[9]

Though pointing out its defects, the chorus of criticism failed to halt the union. Partisans of slow constitutional reform deplored rapid accession through Article 23 of the Basic Law as hasty. Marxist skeptics castigated the currency union as capitalist and predicted economic disaster. Disarmament adherents decried the negotiations with tottering Moscow as a one-sided Western power play. The original revolutionaries also disparaged the unification treaty for producing a mountain of red tape. Intellectuals mourned the loss of Eastern identity and complained about cultural colonization. These objections pointed to the precipitous, neoliberal, and bureaucratic character of the unequal union. In the hasty process, such positive and negative elements were inextricably intertwined.[10]

Four extraordinary developments came together to produce German unity. Most fundamental was the collapse of communism in Eastern Europe. When it finally came, Soviet disintegration was unstoppable because it occurred simultaneously on several fronts. The command economy failed to master the transition from labor-intensive smokestack industries to tertiary services and information technology. Stagnating living standards belied Marxist promises and disappointed the working class. Intellectuals perceived a widening gap between the antifascist, humanitarian ideology and the privileged state of the nomenclatura. Disclosures of corruption undermined the moral credibility of the regime's emancipatory claims.[11]

In the long run, the veneer of socialist internationalism could not hide the reality of Russian military occupation. The contradiction between pacifist claims and arms race practices troubled church circles and the young. Finally, the rhetoric of democratic centralism no longer convinced people to accept one-party dictatorship and Stasi repression. The postponement of the communist utopia to a distant future made popular loyalty to the regime vanish. Polish and Hungarian deviations from orthodoxy encouraged GDR reformers and led to a failure of nerve in the politburo. Ultimately, the Soviet decision not to intervene doomed the SED.[12]

In the GDR the assault on post-Stalinist rule took the form of a civic revolution. The mass exodus challenged the inflexible gerontocracy and created economic bottlenecks. Dissident demands posed a political danger as unprecedented demonstrations gained popular support. Debates among party intellectuals about reforms to democratize socialism dissolved ideological orthodoxy. Calls for the creation of a civil society were both restorative and futuristic. Reformers wanted to recapture liberal civil rights and to forge ahead to an ecological, feminist, and pacifist society. The growing but nonviolent ferment triggered a chain reaction that overthrew post-Stalinism.[13]

Against its own wishes, the democratic awakening undermined the legitimacy of the GDR as a separate state. Krenz's palace coup to oust Honecker vainly sought to safeguard Leninism by more flexible means. Modrow's appeals for a democratic socialism failed to halt the downturn of the command economy. Round Table power-sharing provided a respite by offering legitimacy and fulfilled restorative aims by returning to parliamentarianism. But the dissenters could not translate the Third Way into a workable blueprint and failed to achieve their postmaterialist goals. Supported by millions of aroused citizens, the civic movement nonetheless succeeded in revolutionizing GDR politics.[14]

The pull of unity distinguished the German case from the East European pattern. Instead of being divisive, appeals to common nationality allowed the GDR to speed up the transition by acceding to the FRG. The public space won by protests gave long suppressed patriotic feelings a chance to re-emerge. Clamor for reunification did not arise from old-style Pan-Germanism, but a realization that the quickest path to a better life led through Bonn. Against PDS opposition and dissident doubts, the March election legitimized rapid unification and passed the initiative to the FRG government. Though Western political leaders were quite unprepared for the challenge, they responded to the call out of a sense of historic solidarity.[15]

Careful management of domestic sentiment in the West secured support for unity. The elderly, the Right, and former refugees still harbored a sense of national responsibility. But most of the young, the Left, and intellectuals thought postnationally. To implement Article 23 of the Basic Law, the Bonn cabinet developed a two-step approach, beginning with a currency union and culminating in an accession treaty. Kohl and Genscher hammered out the terms of unity in top-level consultations and infused them with restorative political philosophy. Only an unquestioned sense of national community could justify a transformation so painful and costly.[16]

International approval was a result of East-West détente. Loss of sovereignty in 1945 had kept the Germans from determining their own destiny, and, by dividing the four victorious allies, the Cold War froze the postwar division in place. By 1989 a hesitant Soviet-American rapprochement, based on personal trust between Mikhail Gorbachev and George Bush as well as Eduard Shevardnadze and James Baker, improved relations enough to render a settlement feasible. While U.S. leaders pressed for German unification, Washington's public restraint facilitated Moscow's concessions. Since the Cold War had cemented division, the easing of East-West tension symbolized by progress in disarmament was an indispensable prerequisite for success.[17]

Reconciliation efforts through *Ostpolitik* helped reduce East European fears of German hegemony. Bonn's integration into NATO and the European Community reassured Western neighbors. Genscher's predictable policy also created a foundation of respect. By depicting German division as an obstacle to a common European house, he convinced neighbors that further integration required unification. Traditional high politics between government heads and foreign ministers produced the framework for unity. The results of bilateral negotiations were embedded in multilateral settlements. The transformation of the international situation facilitated the success of the two-plus-four diplomacy that led to the end of the Cold War and made German unity possible.[18]

The most striking feature of unification was its ever-increasing speed. After decades of stagnation, any change had to seem unsettling as well as liberating. While opponents bemoaned the loss of control, supporters tried to seize a limited "window of opportunity." In the trajectory from revolt to unity, the course of events accelerated several times. The first breakthrough during October and November 1989 led to the triumph of the civic revolution. Between the peaceful Leipzig demonstration and the destruction of the Wall, popular pressure toppled the post-Stalinist system and began to democratize the GDR. The initial acceleration created an unstoppable impetus.[19]

The second speed-up, in January and February 1990, brought about the collapse of the East German state. The storming of Stasi headquarters, opposition entry into the government, Soviet approval of confederation, and the two-plus-four framework shifted the focus to unification. The third acceleration in July and August 1990 determined the terms of unity. The currency union, the Caucasus agreement, and the union treaty spelled out the economic, international, and domestic conditions of accession. While Honecker's overthrow reduced the timetable from decades to years, the collapse of the GDR shortened deadlines to months, and the summer breakthroughs made unity a matter of weeks.[20]

Time pressure was partly genuine and partly contrived. The original impetus came from the people inside the GDR. Refugees and dissidents took the lead in toppling the hated SED regime. Initially Bonn hesitated about how to respond. With the ten-point plan chancellor Kohl tried to channel popular hopes toward the West. Instead of renewing the GDR, the silent majority opted for unification and elected the rehabilitated bloc parties and newcomers to manage the transition. The diplomatic, financial, and legal negotiations transferred control to the FRG cabinet, which determined the subsequent process.[21]

Western patronage turned East German impatience from an authentic force into an argument for concessions abroad. Economic failure, dissolution of order, and loss of authority rendered the crisis of the GDR real enough. Since other regimes had survived worse circumstances, the collapse was ultimately psychological: The people gave up on reform, and the international community abandoned support for separate statehood. All the talk about East German disintegration shifted concern from whether to allow unity to how to accomplish it most quickly. By the spring of 1990, reunification had acquired a sense of inevitability.[22]

The German upheaval produced a triple revolution. To make up for earlier failures, the civic movement echoed the liberal, national, and social aspirations of 1848 and 1918. Propelled by resentment of SED repression, the initial phase, in the fall of 1989, concentrated on regaining the civil rights that had been central to bourgeois liberalism. Motivated by hopes for a better life, the second phase, in the spring of 1990, focused on restoring the unity that had been lost because of the nationalist excesses of the Third Reich. Inspired by the need for internal reconciliation, the last phase, in the following fall, brought social transformation from above that tried to Westernize the East.[23]

Each stage had different actors and agendas. Dissenters initiated the first steps with their attempt to create a civil society within democratic socialism. The silent majority took center stage in the second phase with its wish to join the social market economy of the West. The Kohl government dominated the third period with its effort to export Western institutions and restore a united state. Led by the dissidents, the popular rising against the post-Stalinist state was a revolutionary process that took an unexpected national turn. By fundamentally transforming the East and the international situation, the ensuing rebuilding also produced a revolutionary result. Like earlier German attempts, the 1989–1990 revolution strangely combined revolutionary and national with restorative elements.[24]

The rush to German unity was quite unplanned. Unification surprised participants, because the Nazi defeat and the holocaust had rendered the national state taboo. The Wall virtually cut in half communication between East and West Germany after 1961. In opinion polls reunification dropped as the "most important question" from more than 40 percent to one percent by the 1970s. In spite of cross-border ties, a sense of cultural community, and the mandate of the Basic Law, two-thirds of West Germans considered unity "impossible" in the 1980s. Only the surprising collapse of the GDR revived a chance for unification and rendered its appeal irresistible.[25]

Shared history made reunification a logical course. Even the SED founders considered independence second best and preferred a unified communist country. To the Eastern population, unity appealed as the most radical solution to their troubles. In the West, an embattled Kohl government played the national card in hopes of recouping its sagging electoral fortunes. To make the restoration of a single state palatable at home and abroad, Bonn offered a chastened nationalism that balanced a strengthened federalism with continuing European integration. Since the younger generations in East and West were developing separate identities, unification came at the last moment when it was still politically possible.[26]

After Unity

Inner unification proved more frustrating than outer union. The accession of the new states merely transferred external problems to the inside, without really resolving them. When East came face to face with West, both realized how different they had become. Living standards, institutional patterns, and personal attitudes were much more disparate than anyone had anticipated. Wits quipped that the Germans never felt more apart than when they were united. As Lafontaine had predicted, the domestic plains were more laborious than the diplomatic peaks. Unforeseen obstacles continually extended the timetables of internal unification from months to years, and from years to decades.[27]

The problems of transition were partially inevitable and partially self-inflicted. On the one hand, the legacy of the SED, such as its proud industries, was in worse shape than imagined. Many of the GDR's well-hidden secrets like the disastrous pollution of air, water, and soil were now finally exposed. On the other hand, mistakes of the rapid merger such as the restitution of property to its former owners also hampered rebuilding. Moreover, the conservative management of unification had consistently understated the cost and complexity of the changes that would be necessary. Though politicians pointed out that new roads, phone lines and shopping centers were being built, "the united country [sank] into depression."[28]

At the root of many difficulties lay the economic decline of the East. The collapse of industrial production and loss of about half the jobs were "an unmitigated disaster," far deeper than the Great Depression. Only the extension of the Western "safety net" of unemployment insurance and retraining measures prevented a social explosion. The failure of East European trade, the excessive conversion rate, and the restitution of property hindered recovery. The Threuhand's priority on privatization successfully dismantled state monopolies but paid too little attention to preserving core industries. Outside investment lagged because production could be expanded with less risk elsewhere. The union push for wage equality with the West in four years raised Eastern labor costs too quickly.[29]

The Kohl-Genscher government was slow to react because it had promised not to raise taxes for unity. Only in March 1991 did the CDU/FDP coalition launch an "Eastern recovery" program that imposed an income-tax surcharge of 7.5 percent and resorted to public borrowing to raise investment incentives. Belatedly, Bonn realized the need to transfer an annual 150 billion DM to the new states for years to come. Though construction and services began to revive, agriculture collapsed and traditional industries continued to disintegrate. Repair of communist damage required endless Western contributions, and public borrowing choked off the boom by keeping interest rates high. When the upturn had not yet begun by the spring of 1993, politicians agreed on new sacrifices enshrined in a "solidarity pact" to salvage the East.[30]

Restructuring East German institutions also proved exasperating. Research and teaching in the Academy of Sciences and the universities were a case in point. Initially reformers tried to democratize departments from the inside while cynics merely relabelled Marxism-Leninism as political science. Subsequently, state governments dissolved ideologically tainted areas like "the communist world system" over protests against "intellectual decapitation." Though they had produced some fine work, GDR institutions were overstaffed, harbored Stasi informers, and sheltered incompetent hacks. To revitalize scholarship, honor committees screened collaborators, Westerners evaluated academic quality, and bureaucrats assessed fiscal viability.[31]

This painful reconstruction produced mixed results. Stasi informants were quickly fired. Most older scholars retired prematurely and many younger colleagues became unemployed, surviving on temporary makework schemes (ABM). Academy institutes were dissolved, but some promising projects were transferred to newly created smaller centers. In the universities, rehiring for all positions was supposed to renew faculties. Entire departments in the social sciences and humanities were replaced by Western scholars, but the sciences and medicine largely escaped unscathed. Imposed from the outside, this draconian approach confused students and left a trail of bitterness. Nonetheless cultural institutions continued to function on a reduced scale.[32]

Toughest of all was psychological reconciliation. Easterners struggled with a loss of identity, "living in two worlds, but not feeling at home in either one." Trying to adapt, they vacillated between self-pity and nostalgic defiance. With so many new demands placed upon them, they were disoriented and "simply stressed out." They resented even helpful advisers as arrogant *Besserwessis* who knew everything better. Westerners failed to understand why *Ossis* were not more grateful. Prosperous FRG citizens resented paying the costs or showed patronizing sympathy. Even after the physical barriers were gone, the wall in people's heads continued to loom large. It would take much patient learning to tear it down.[33]

Vying for cultural hegemony in the united state, intellectuals polemicized across the former frontier. Conservatives proclaimed ideological victory while Leftists mourned the fall of their Marxist utopia. Western critics accused privileged writers like Christa Wolf of unnecessary complicity with the SED regime. Disclosures of Stasi collaboration among dissidents poisoned the air. Wolf Biermann's revelations turned poet Sascha Anderson from a hero into a traitor of the Prenzlauer Berg scene. Pastor Gauck's Stasi archive charged Brandenburg prime minister Manfred Stolpe with informing on the Protestant church. In a "double reckoning," debates about communist abuses began to rival reflections about the Nazi past.[34]

These post-unification challenges caught the population by surprise. Germans had forgotten that Bismarck's unification had also been fraught with bitter domestic conflicts. Easterners hoped to enjoy immediately all the comforts that had taken the FRG four decades to build. Westerners did not want to abandon their accustomed ways and became nostalgic for the tranquility of their prior life. The haste of accession left a trail of unresolved questions such as the abortion issue and the revision of the constitution.[35] The Basic Law's mandate of equal living conditions compelled massive outlays for the East that required real sacrifices from the West and threatened its consensus, built upon the expectation of distributing economic gains. These vexing transition problems tested political maturity and fundamentally reshaped the agenda of domestic politics.[36]

The new Germany also found it hard to define its international role. Unification physically moved the FRG from the West back to the center of Europe. Whereas the Soviet empire and state dissolved, Germany gained territory, population and economic potential. Though old fears lingered, Eastern neighbors expected aid and the Western partners looked for leadership. FRG policymakers were unprepared for these challenges, since they were used to clothing their interests in moralistic rhetoric. Repudiating Nazi power mania (*Machtversessenheit*), Bonn had adopted a nonconfrontational style that pretended might no longer mattered (*Machtvergessenheit*).[37]

The return of sovereignty brought an end to this escape from responsibility. Unity eliminated excuses for acting like "an economic giant and a political dwarf." Unfortunately, just when external demands increased, unification costs strained the country's resources and focused energies on its internal problems. The coincidence of Soviet collapse and German unity put Bonn in a position once again to dominate the continent. The possibility of the European hegemony for which the Kaiser and Führer had vainly striven now fell into Kohl's lap. Used to its multilateral role in NATO and the European Community, Germany was not sure whether it wanted to assume more responsibility.[38]

The response to the Gulf War illustrates this reluctance. The Near

East conflict erupted before Bonn had time to redefine its international stance. The Basic Law prohibition against the use of armed force outside the country now became an acute embarrassment. The accession of the East reinforced Western pacifism. Hundreds of thousands demonstrated not against the aggressor Saddam Hussein but against American help for Kuwait. When mediation failed, Genscher withdrew into sullen silence. Chagrined leftists denounced the immorality of the war, and only a few intellectuals like Hans-Magnus Enzensberger spoke out for Israel.[39]

A confused government tried to recover its credibility by frantic travel and DM-diplomacy. The FRG poured twelve billion dollars into the UN war chest and dispensed additional funds in the Near East. Moreover, it stationed eighteen fighter jets in Turkey against possible Iraqi attack. Western capitals denounced Bonn's scruples as ingratitude and irresolution. Afterwards an uneasy public debated changing the constitution to allow military deployment. The cabinet advocated joining all UN-sponsored actions, but the opposition preferred to offer only peace-keeping troops. Ingrained antimilitarism made returning to the use of force difficult.[40]

Regional responsibility also proved exasperating. Putting aside their historic hostility, East Europeans called on the FRG for assistance. Intellectuals rediscovered German culture and institutions as models for their postcommunist transition. But minority disputes and refugee resentment slowed the ratification of cooperation treaties with Warsaw and Prague. German investors were damned if they did and damned if they didn't. Whereas managers welcomed DM infusion to modernize industries, former communists denounced economic imperialism. The financial drain of rebuilding the new states slowed German involvement further East.[41]

Bonn's role in the breakup of Yugoslavia was even more controversial. Hosting six hundred thousand Slovenian and Croatian workers, Germany sympathized with their aspirations for self-determination. But the bloody legacy of Nazi abuse in World War II tied FRG hands. As sponsors of the South Slav state, Western politicians overlooked Serbian repression of other ethnic groups. When EC efforts to keep the country together foundered, Genscher vigorously pushed for diplomatic recognition of the separatist republics. Though Brussels and Washington eventually followed his lead, they were annoyed that he had forced their hand. If the Germans asserted themselves, they were attacked for resorting to Nazi tactics, if Bonn held back, it was accused of lacking leadership.[42]

The road to a united Europe turned out to be rockier than expected. Helmut Kohl pushed for further integration as compensation for national unity. Intellectuals embraced Europe since it "quiets the Germans' fear of themselves and the neighbors' fear of the Germans." After lengthy preparation, the business community hoped to profit from the completion of the interior market in 1993. But reality failed to live up to the European dream. In contrast to the elites, ordinary citizens viewed the EC as "bureaucratic, centralist, and undemocratic." Brussels could not decide whether to widen the community by admitting wealthy Western countries or their poor Eastern cousins.[43]

The European Community also struggled over how to direct the market toward political union. The Maastricht summit in late 1991 proposed a package solution. Bonn accepted the completion of a currency union in exchange for increased political cooperation. The Danish defeat threatened the Maastricht treaty until French approval rescued the accord. But the British and Italian decisions to drop out of the European Monetary System showed the difficulties of creating a joint currency before a common polity. Not well informed by the cabinet, the German public resented having to give up their DM. By restoring a national state and exacting enormous costs, unification noticeably cooled their enthusiasm for Europe.[44]

Unity also altered German relations with the United States. In Bonn, gratitude for American support reinforced friendly rhetoric: "Our most precious diplomatic asset is the alliance with the U.S." The White House, however, worried about losing its influence over a united Germany. Though relieved by its generous aid to Russia, Washington was disappointed at Bonn's reaction to the Gulf War, and irritated by its policy toward Yugoslavia. U.S. leaders were also chagrined that Kohl failed to overcome French resistance to lowering agricultural subsidies. The Eastern drain on resources caused Washington to snicker, but resurgent nationalism raised fresh concerns about stability.[45]

The end of division considerably changed power relationships. After absorbing the East, Germany would be stronger and less docile than before. Outside observers worried about signs of Bonn's "new assertiveness," such as the FRG's claim for a permanent Security Council seat at the United Nations. American troop reductions in Europe would mean a larger German role in NATO or in continental defense efforts such as a Franco-German Eurocorps. Internal commentators warned instead against a moralistic reluctance to engage in power politics and to accept greater military responsibility abroad. In order to become "a regular nation state," the sociologist Wolf Lepenies advised Germans to become "self-confident enough" to pursue their own interests but remain "modest enough to do it with self-restraint and civility."[46]

The German response to these domestic and international challenges has been uncertain. Because of false expectations, the unification shock was severe. The internal cleavage between East and West shows few signs of abating. The external stance of the larger state continues to be embattled. Feeling overburdened, politicians have been slow to react to the wrenching changes. Chancellor Kohl hesitated to admit his mistakes and the SPD only gradually changed its policies concerning asylum and the military. To restart the economy Saxon Premier Kurt Biedenkopf implored, "We must accept Eastern reconstruction as a task for all Germans."

The historian Christian Meier warned that material and spiritual integration would require the "re-creation of a nation." Democratic stability depends upon how Germany deals with this unexpected task.[47]

In Search of Identity

Unification has reopened the age-old question, "What is a German's fatherland?" The merger of the two successor states provides a definitive territorial answer. Though smaller, more homogeneous and Western than earlier Germanies, the Third Republic has yet "to find its internal balance and its external role." The Right is elated by the return to unity and calls for "a new patriotism," characterized by duty and sacrifice. Despite a disquieting resurgence of xenophobia, only an extremist fringe looks back to lost glories. Moderate conservatives have embraced the social market economy and parliamentary democracy. They are happy about the return of sovereignty, and advocate a measured power policy, conscious of international commitments.[48]

The Left remains troubled by the implications of unity. Radicals feel vindicated by problems of transition and have some reason to fear the rise of a new nationalism. Progressives seek to transform the new country into more of a civil society and prefer a moral internationalism that warns against considering Germany a "normal" state. Claiming that unification threw women out of work and muffled their voice, feminists warn against a "remasculinization" of German society. Presented with these contradictory alternatives, the unequal amalgam of old and new citizens faces a defining moment. In Thomas Mann's terms, "the Germans have the choice." Will they become more nationalist or remain cosmopolitan? They have yet to decide.[49]

The debate over the capital illustrates this identity dilemma. Unable to choose between Bonn and Berlin, Kohl postponed the decision until June 20, 1991. Without party constraints the Bundestag engaged in a memorable debate. Berlin partisans passionately argued for the traditional center of the Reich. They recalled the decades of promises to the divided city and argued that moving government would send a signal of hope to the East. Equally vehement, advocates of Bonn insisted that their city represented a democratic break with the troubled past. Concerned about probable economic losses, they stressed the enormous costs of the transfer. The provisional solution had taken root and symbolized Germany's commitment to the West.[50]

The fronts of the capital controversy cut across party lines. Generally, older, Eastern, and moderate politicians favored going back to the river Spree. Instead, younger, Western, and leftist deputies wanted to stay on the Rhine. Since the Berlin lobby expected to lose, it offered a compromise that would only move the top ministries and leave a substantial presence behind. With an emotional peroration the architect of the unification treaty Schäuble tipped the scales: "In truth, Germany's future is at stake." To everyone's surprise, Berlin won out by a bare seventeen votes. Cynics quipped that Kohl and the PDS had provided the majority. United Germany opted for historical continuity without giving up its new democratic ties to the West.[51]

The question who should be a German also dominated the asylum debate. As latecomer among nations, Germany based citizenship on ethnic descent and rejected an immigration policy. But its constitutional guarantee of asylum made the FRG a favorite target for refugees from Eastern Europe and the Third World. During 1992 alone 438,000 newcomers arrived, while 250,000 ethnic Germans resettled and East Germans continued to move West. Aggravating the housing shortage and the public deficit, this large influx created widespread resentment, which brought rightist fringe groups such as the NPD and the Reps some electoral success. Conservatives welcomed ethnic remigrants but wanted to keep other foreigners out while the Left pursued precisely the opposite policy. This ideological stalemate prevented any action to stem the rising tide of immigration.[52]

Feeling overwhelmed by unification, many citizens resorted to xenophobia. Especially young people, disoriented by the transition, blamed their problems on foreigners. The collapse of the Eastern youth organization FDJ closed clubs and meeting places, while new standards in school and the danger of unemployment raised the pressure. Bored teenagers turned into "skin-heads," adopting the forbidden symbols of a Nazi past without really understanding them. Western neo-Nazi sects preaching German superiority exploded into violence against foreigners. Vietnamese and Turkish guest workers became easy targets when chauvinistic adults cheered and the police failed to intercede. Ugly incidents erupted almost daily during 1992, totalling 2,200 with seventeen people dead. International observers experienced an alarming sense of deja vu.[53]

Outrage over the bloodshed finally triggered a mass response. In the fall of 1992 concerned citizens organized demonstrations in favor of their foreign friends. In major cities like Munich, Hamburg, and Berlin hundreds of thousands marched with candles in their hands to protest against xenophobia. Embarrassed politicians and business leaders belatedly condemned chauvinism so as to improve the German image abroad. In lengthy negotiations the CDU and SPD worked out a compromise that would only accept truly persecuted asylum seekers and keep economic refugees out. Taking their clue from public revulsion, law enforcement officials prosecuted offenders with such determination that incidents began to drop off in the spring of 1993. In a wide-ranging debate politicians also began to discuss changing the basis of German citizenship from descent to residence.[54]

Has unification solved the German problem at last? The recovery of a national state does offer a second chance to lay the old Teutonic troubles to rest. The enlarged Federal Republic promises to settle the succession of regimes from the Second to the Third Reichs firmly on the model of Western parliamentary democracy. Voluntary acceptance of the shrunken borders also confirms the territorial limits of Germany without future revisionism in the East. Twice burnt by failed bids for hegemony, a democratic and satiated Federal Republic is likely to exercise its power more prudently than in the past. This restraint should end the hoary exceptionalism (*Sonderweg*) and allow the reunited country to become a normal European state.[55]

Yet sighs of relief may be premature. The unexpected trajectory from revolution to unification has created new peculiarities in its turn. The unequal union revives historic differences between East and West. Unification has yet to produce material equality or psychological self-assurance. The larger Germany has restored the structural imbalance that troubled European affairs during the past century. The Berlin republic is too big to fit harmoniously with its neighbors and too small to dominate them outright. Though the return of unity has laid old troubles to rest, ex-chancellor Helmut Schmidt cautions perceptively that Germans "are not yet a normal people." The surprises of the unification process should caution against straightline predictions for the future. In the national narrative, the GDR-FRG merger has closed the section on postwar division. But unity also opens up new, let us hope less traumatic, chapters to come.[56]

Notes

Introduction

1. Egon Krenz, *Wenn Mauern fallen. Die friedliche Revolution* (Vienna, 1990), 180ff. Because of space constraints, the notes are highly selective. Only references to direct quotations, important information, or significant interpretations have been included.

2. Elizabeth Pond, "A Wall Destroyed: The Dynamics of German Unification in the GDR," *International Security* 15 (1990): 35–66.

3. Günter Schabowski, *Das Politbüro. Ende eines Mythos* (Hamburg, 1990), 134 ff. Cf. Cordt Schnibben, "Diesmal sterbe ich, Schwester," *Spiegel* 44, no. 41 (1990): 102–9; and letters by Krenz and Schabowski, *Spiegel* 44, no. 43 (1990): 103.

4. Heinz J. Kuzdas, *Berliner MauerKunst* (Berlin, 1990); and Robert Darnton, *Berlin Journal, 1989–1990* (New York, 1991), 76 ff.

5. Gerd Meyer, "Die westdeutsche DDR- und Deutschlandforschung im Umbruch," *DA* 24 (1991): 273–85; Michael Howard, "1989—eine neue Zeitwende?" *EA* 14 (1989): 440–41.

6. Klaus Tenfelde, "1914 bis 1990—Einheit der Epoche," *APZG* B40 (1992): 3 ff.

7. See videos on unification, such as the four-part series produced by the magazine *Der Spiegel*.

8. Jürgen Habermas, *Die nachholende Revolution* (Frankfurt, 1990); and Günter Grass, *Deutscher Lastenausgleich. Wider das dumpfe Einheitsgebot* (Berlin, 1990).

9. Thomas Nipperdey, "Die Deutschen dürfen und wollen eine Nation sein," *FAZ*, 13 July 1990; Jürgen Kocka, "Revolution und Nation 1989," *Tel Aviver Jahrbuch für deutsche Geschichte* 19 (1990): 479–99; Udo Wengst, ed., *Historiker betrachten Deutschland* (Bonn, 1992); and the forthcoming study by Charles Maier.

10. Gert-Joachim Glaessner, *Der schwierige Weg zur Demokratie. Vom Ende der DDR zur deutschen Einheit*, 2d rev. ed. (Opladen, 1992); Gary Marks, "Rational Sources of Chaos in Democratic Transition," in *Comparative Perspectives on Democracy*, ed. Gary Marks and Larry Diamond (Beverly Hills, 1992); and Gary Geipel, ed., *The Future of Germany* (Indianapolis, 1990).

11. Timothy Garton Ash, *The Magic Lantern* (New York, 1990); Volker Gransow, "DDR—Bocksprung in die Zivilgesellschaft," *BfdiP* no. 12 (1989); and Ralf Dahrendorf, *Reflections on the Revolution in Europe* (New York, 1990).

12. Cees Noteboom, *Berliner Notizen* (Frankfurt, 1991), 123, 197 ff.

13. Konrad H. Jarausch, "Divided by Words: Constructing German Unification as History" (MS, Stanford, 1992).

14. Konrad H. Jarausch, "Towards a Social History of Experience," *CEH* 22 (1990): 237 ff.

15. Rainer Tetzner, *Leipziger Ring. Aufzeichnungen eines Montagsdemonstranten* (Frankfurt, 1990); Wolfgang Schneider, ed., *Leipziger Demontagebuch* (Leipzig, 1990); and Hartmut Zwahr, *Ende einer Selbstzerstörung. Leipzig und die Revolution in der DDR* (Göttingen, 1993).

16. Jens Reich, *Abschied von Lebenslügen* (Berlin, 1992); and texts in *When the Wall Came Down: Reactions to German Unification*, ed. Harold James and Marla Stone (New York, 1992), 165 ff.

17. Sigrid Meuschel, *Legitimation und Parteiherrschaft. Zum Paradox von Stabilität und Revolution in der DDR* (Frankfurt, 1992).

18. Noteboom, *Berliner Notizen*, 197 ff; Volker Gransow and Konrad H. Jarausch, eds., *Die deutsche Vereinigung: Bürgerbewegung, Annäherung und Beitritt* (Cologne, 1991).

19. For a theoretical justification, see Michael Geyer and Konrad H. Jarausch, "The Future of the German Past: Transatlantic Reflections for the 1990s," *CEH* 22 (1990), 193 ff.

20. Material in the GDR government and SED party archives that became accessible after the completion of this account has confirmed its conclusions. For fuller citations of the new sources see Konrad H. Jarausch, *Die Eilige Einheit. Ein historischer Versuch* (Frankfurt, 1994).

21. Carl-Christoph Schweitzer et al., eds., *Politics and Government in the Federal Republic of Germany* (Leamington Spa, 1984), 6 ff; and Ingo von Münch, *Dokumente des geteilten Deutschland* (Stuttgart, 1968), 32 ff.

22. Dennis L. Bark and David R. Gress, *A History of West Germany*, vol. 1 (Oxford, 1989), 21 ff.

23. Christoph Klessmann, *Die doppelte Staatsgründung* (Göttingen, 1982); and Klaus von Dohnanyi, *Das deutsche Wagnis* (Munich, 1990), 54 ff.

24. Piotr Abrassimov interview, *Spiegel*, Aug. 17, 1992; Hans Magnus Enzensberger, "Katechismus zur deutschen Frage," *Kursbuch* 4 (1966): 1–18. Cf. Hans-Peter Schwarz, *Die Ära Adenauer, 1949–1957* (Wiesbaden, 1981).

25. Peter Longerich, *"Was ist des Deutschen Vaterland?" Dokumente zur Frage der Deutschen Einheit 1800 bis 1990* (Munich, 1990), 196–97; Bundesministerium für gesamtdeutsche Fragen, ed., *Die Bemühungen der Bundesrepublik um Wiederherstellung der Einheit Deutschlands durch gesamtdeutsche Wahlen* 2 (Bonn, 1958): 246 ff.

26. Michael Lemke, "'Doppelte Alleinvertretung.' Die nationalen Vereinigungskonzepte der beiden deutschen Regierungen," *Zeitschrift für Geschichtswissenschaft* 40 (1992): 531–43; and Heinrich August Winkler, "Nationalismus, Nationalstaat und nationale Frage in Deutschland seit 1945," *APZG* B 40 (1992): 12 ff.

27. J. Rühle, ed., *13. August 1961. Die Mauer von Berlin* (Cologne, 1981), 93 ff; Julii A. Kvizinskii, *Vor dem Sturm. Erinnerungen eines Diplomaten* (Berlin, 1993), 178 ff.

28. Willy Brandt, *People and Politics: The Years 1960–1975* (Boston, 1978); and Armin Mitter and Stefan Wolle, *Untergang auf Raten* (Munich, 1993), 367 ff.

29. J. Nawrocki, *Die Beziehungen zwischen den beiden Staaten in Deutschland* (Berlin, 1986), 99 ff; and Willim E. Griffith, *The Ostpolitik of the FRG* (Cambridge, 1978).

30. Nawrocki, *Beziehungen*, 113 ff; and James A. McAdams *Germany Divided: From the Wall to Reunification* (Princeton, 1993), 3 ff.

31. Annual reports of the Federal Government, *Zur Lage der Nation* (Bonn, 1984); BPA, ed., *Dokumentation zu den Innerdeutschen Beziehungen. Abmachungen und Erklärungen*, 12th rev. ed. (Bonn, 1989).

32. Ilse Spittmann, *Die DDR unter Honecker* (Cologne, 1990); Wilfried Loth, *Ost-West-Konflikt und deutsche Frage* (Munich, 1989); and Carl-Christian Kaiser, "Der General ging unter die Decke," *ZEIT*, Sept. 4, 1992.

33. Bernard Gwertzman and Michael T. Kaufmann, eds., *The Collapse of Communism* (New York, 1990); and Christiane Lemke and Gary Marks, eds., *The Crisis of Socialism* (Durham, N.C., 1992).

34. Wolfgang Rüddenklau, *Störenfried. DDR-Opposition 1986–1989* (Berlin, 1992), 259 ff; Gransow and Jarausch, *Deutsche Vereinigung*, 55–56.

35. "Enno von Loewenstern, "Wessen Selbstbestimmung?" *Welt*, July 7, 1989; "Bonn: Fischers Aufruf Angriff auf die Verfassung," *Welt*, July 29. Cf. Wolfgang Seiffert, *Die Deutschen und Gorbatschow. Chancen für einen Interessenausgleich* (Erlangen, 1989), 204 ff.

36. Fritz Haug, *Versuch beim täglichen Verlieren des Bodens unter den Füssen neuen Grund zu gewinnen* (Hamburg, 1990), 18 ff; Elizabeth Pond, *After the Wall: American Policy Toward Germany* (New York: 1990).

37. See photoreportages such as Klaus Liedtke, ed., *Vier Tage im November* (Hamburg, 1989); or Brigitte Beier et al., eds., *9. November 1989. Der Tag der Deutschen* (Hamburg, 1989).

38. Willy Brandt, ". . . was zusammengehört." *Reden zu Deutschland* (Bonn, 1990); "East Germany Opens Frontier to the West for Migration or Travel; Thousands Cross," *NYT*, Nov. 10, 1989.

39. For a more critical look, see taz, ed., *DDR Journal zur Novemberrevolution* (Berlin, 1989); and Walter Momper, *Grenzfall. Berlin im Brempunkt deutscher Geschichte* (Munich, 1991), 144 ff.

40. Rolf Badstübner, "Der 9. November 1989 und die Mauer," *Weltbühne* 84 (1989): 1484 ff; Michael Stürmer, "Die Deutschen in Europa," *EA* no. 24 (1989): 721 ff.

41. Noteboom, *Berliner Notizen*, 99 ff; and texts in Ulrich Wickert, ed., *Angst vor Deutschland* (Hamburg, 1990).

42. Peter Schneider, "Man kann ein Erdbeben auch verpassen," *GPS* no. 20 (1990): 1–21; and Konrad H. Jarausch, "Towards a Post-Socialist Politics," in Lemke and Marks, *The Crisis of Socialism*, 228 ff.

Chapter 1

1. "Bonn Closes Office to Would-Be Émigrés," *NYT*, Aug. 9, 1989; "Protest mit den Füssen," *ZEIT*, Aug. 11.

2. "Westward Tide of East Germans Is a Popular No-Confidence Vote," *NYT*, Aug. 22, 1989; Serge Schmemann's reports from Budapest, *NYT*, Sept. 5, 6, 7, 9; and "Mein Gott, vielleicht geht's diesmal gut," *ZEIT*, Aug. 25, 1989.

3. "East Berlin Faults Bonn for Exodus," *NYT*, Sept. 12, 1989; Guyla Horn, *Freiheit, die ich meine* (Hamburg, 1991), 308 ff.

4. "Hungary Allows 7,000 East Germans to Emigrate West," *NYT*, Sept. 11,

1989. Cf. Ilse Spittmann, ed., *Chronik der Ereignisse in der DDR*, 3d rev. ed. (Cologne, 1990), 1–4; and the tendentious reports in *BILD* of Sept. 12, 1989.

5. "Smiles from the Guards in Hungary," *NYT*, Sept. 12, 1989; and "Thousands Swell Trek to the West by East Germans," ibid.

6. "Mitteilung des ADN," *ND*, Sept. 11, 1989; and Ligachev interview, Sept. 18, BPA Dok 1989, IX: 337A.

7. "Schwache Moskauer Schützenhilfe für Ostberlin," *NZZ*, Sept. 14, 1989; stories by Craig Whitney and Serge Schmemann, *NYT*, Sept. 12 and 13.

8. H. Merker, ed., *Grundgesetz für die Bundesrepublik Deutschland vom 23. Mai 1963* (Stuttgart, 1963), 16 ff; D. Müller-Römer, ed., *Die neue Verfassung der DDR* (Cologne, 1974), 78 ff.

9. Hartmut Wendt, "Die deutsch-deutschen Wanderungen," *DA* 24 (1991): 386–95.

10. Manfred Stolpe, *Schwieriger Aufbruch* (Berlin, 1992), 146–47; and Wendt, "Die deutsch-deutschen Wanderungen," 390–91.

11. Böttger, ed., "DDR Verordnung über Reisen und Ausreisen," *DA* 22 (1989): 108 ff; Roland Pechmann and Jürgen Vogel, *Abgesang der Stasi* (Braunschweig, 1991), 129 ff.

12. Matthias Ott, *Deutschland—Ein Ausreisemärchen* (Koblenz, 1989); and Armin Mitter and Stefan Wolle, eds., *Ich liebe Euch doch alle! Befehle und Lageberichte des MfS* (Berlin, 1990), 28. Cf. Richard Hilmer and Anne Köhler, "Der DDR läuft ihre Zukunft davon," *DA* 22 (1989): 1386–87.

13. Böttger, "DDR Verordnung über Reisen und Ausreisen," passim.

14. Figures from Henry Krisch, *The German Democratic Republic* (Boulder, 1985), 80–81.

15. Andreas Graf, "Probleme und Beurteilung der DDR-Geschichtswissenschaft," in *Zwischen Parteilichkeit und Professionalität—Bilanz der DDR Geschichtswissenschaft*, ed. Konrad H. Jarausch (Berlin, 1991), 35 ff.

16. Evangelischer Pressedienst, *Problem Ausreisewelle: 'Herr Pfarrer, was sagt denn die Kirche?'* (Frankfurt, 1989), 2, 5; Stolpe, *Schwieriger Aufbruch*, 145 ff; Rüddenklau, *Störenfried*, 228 ff.

17. Figures from Fischer Weltalmanach, *Sonderband DDR*, 135; Mitter and Wolle, *Ich liebe Euch*, 82 ff; Reinholt Andert and Wolfgang Herzberg, *Der Sturz: Honecker im Kreuzverhör* (Berlin 1990), 57–58, 90–91. For further material on the exodus see BA SAP, IV 2/2.039, vol. 307.

18. DPA release, Jan. 19, 1989 and numerous other documents in BPA Dok 1989, I. Cf. *Welt*, July 6.

19. Evangelischer Pressedienst, *Problem Ausreisewelle*, 10, 12.

20. Jens Glüsing and Joachim Nawrocki (*ZEIT*, Aug. 18, 1989) used the word *Torschlusspanik* (gate-closing panic) to describe this feeling. Siegfried Grundmann, "Aussen- und Binnenmigration der DDR 1989," *DA* 23 (1990): 1424–25.

21. Axel Schützsack, *Exodus in die Einheit. Die Massenflucht aus der DDR 1989* (Melle, 1990), vol. 12 of *Deutschland Report*.

22. BPA bulletin, Sept. 12, BPA Dok 1989, IX: 190–91; Minister of the Interior Horvath, *Stern*, Sept. 7; and Horn, *Freiheit*, 317 ff. For the diplomatic maneuvers see BA SAP, IV 2/2A, vols 3238 ff.

23. Heinrich Bortfeldt, *Von der SED zur PDS* (Bonn, 1991), 52 ff; Günter Schabowski, *Das Politbüro. Ende eines Mythos* (Reinbeck, 1990); "Der Medienrummel und die Realitäten," *ND*, Sept. 13, 1989; "Zu einer zügellosen Hetzkampagne der BRD," *LVZ*, Sept. 5.

24. Mitter and Wolle, *Ich liebe Euch*, 151–52; "Menschenhandel," *LVZ*, Sept.

19, 1989; "Bürger zur BRD-Hetzkampagne," *LVZ*, Sept. 25, "Mitteilung von ADN," *ND*, Sept. 16/17; "Ich habe erlebt, wie BRD-Bürger 'gemacht' werden," *ND*, Sept. 21.

25. "East Germans Swell Embassy in Prague," *NYT*, Sept. 29, 1989; John Tagliabue, *NYT*, Sept. 30; and Darnton, *Berlin Journal*, 65 ff.

26. "East Germans Get Permission to Quit Prague for West," *NYT*, Oct. 1, 1989; Serge Schmemann, *NYT*, Oct. 2; Genscher interview with *ZDF*, Oct. 1, and BPA bulletin, Oct. 4, BPA Dok 1989, IX: 383 ff; "Humanitärer Akt," *ND*, Oct. 2; Schabowski, *Politbüro*, 68–69; and Schützsack, *Exodus*, 36–37.

27. "Sie haben sich selbst aus unserer Gesellschaft ausgegrenzt," *ND*, Oct. 2, 1989; and "Unvereinbar mit den Regeln des internationalen Rechts," *ND*, Oct. 5. Cf. Genscher interview, Oct. 2 and other statements, BPA Dok 1989, IX: 403 ff.

28. "Zur zeitweiligen Aussetzung des pass- und visafreien Verkehrs zwischen der DDR und CSSR," *ND*, Oct. 4, 1989; "Information über erste Hinweise . . . ," Oct. 4, 1989; and Mielke order, Oct. 5, in Mitter and Wolle, *Ich liebe Euch*, 192 ff; Zeno and Sabine Zimmerling, eds., *Neue Chronik DDR* (Berlin, 1990), 1: 67–68, hereafter *NCDDR*.

29. Letter of conference of Protestant church leaders to Honecker, Sept. 2, 1989, *NCDDR* 1: 20 ff; Bishop Leich to Honecker, "Änderungen längst überfällig," reprinted in *FR*, Sept. 11, 1989; Krenz, *Wenn Mauern fallen*, 34.

30. "Wortlaut des Amnestie-Beschlusses," *SDZ*, Oct. 28, 1989; Spittmann, *Chronik der Ereignisse in der DDR*, 9 ff; Schützsack, *Exodus*, 40 ff.

31. Cf. Annegret Hahn et al., eds., *4. November '89* (Frankfurt, 1990), 98 ff; "Entwurf des Gesetzes über Reisen ins Ausland," *ND*, Nov. 6, 1989; "DDR-Bürger verliessen die Botschaft der BRD in Prag," *ND*, Nov. 8.

32. "Christa Wolf, 'Wir bitten Sie, bleiben Sie doch!'" *SDZ*, Nov. 10, 1989; Krenz, *Wenn Mauern fallen*, 166 ff. For the background of the decision see BA Po, DC 20, I/3, vol. 2867.

33. "Hinweise auf wesentliche motivbildende Faktoren," Mitter and Wolle, *Ich liebe Euch*, 141 ff; Dieter Voigt et al., "Die innerdeutsche Wanderung und der Vereinigungsprozess," *DA* 23 (1990): 733 ff.

34. Anna Köhler, "Ist die Übersiedlerwelle noch zu stoppen?" *DA* 23 (1990): 425; Infas survey, Sept. 12, 1989, BPA Dok 1989, XII: 537–38; and Hilmer and Köhler, "Der DDR läuft die Zukunft davon, *DA* 22 (1989): 1385.

35. Siegfried Grundmann and Ines Schmidt, "Wanderungsbewegungen in der DDR 1989," and Ines Schmidt, "Zur Übersiedlung aus Berlin," *Berliner Arbeitshefte und Berichte zur Sozialwissenschaftlichen Forschung* no. 30 (1990).

36. Mitter and Wolle, *Ich liebe Euch*, 82 ff; and Voigt et al., "Die innerdeutsche Wanderung," *DA* 23 (1990): 733 ff.

37. Andert and Herzgerg, *Sturz*, 58; Schabowski, *Politbüro*, 59; and Krenz, *Wenn Mauern fallen*, 170 ff.

38. "Was die Kirchen der DDR am meisten bewegt," *Problem Ausreisewelle*, 8. For the broader problem of migration, see Dirk Hoerder's lecture at the German Historical Institute, October 1992.

39. Bundesminister des Inneren, *Wegweiser für Übersiedler aus der DDR* (Bonn, 1989).

40. "Sie sollen gleich fühlen, dass sie zu Hause sind," *FAZ*, Oct. 2, 1989; Wolfgang Käppler, "Übersiedler in der Bundesrepublik Deutschland," in *Fachtagung zur psychischen Situation von DDR-Übersiedlern*, ed. Brüsewitz-Zentrum (1985).

41. Karin Wagner, "Psychische Schwierigkeiten von DDR-Übersiedlern,"

Fachtagung, 20 ff; and Volker Ronge, "Die soziale Integration von DDR-Übersiedlern in der BRD," *APZG* B 1–2 (1990): 39 ff.

42. Kristina Pratsch and Volker Ronge, "Ganz normale Bundesbürger?" *DA* 22 (1989): 904 ff; Hilmer and Köhler, "Der DDR läuft," 1387–88; and Köhler, "Ist die Übersiedlerwelle," 427 ff.

43. Richard Hilmer and Anne Köhler, "Die DDR im Aufbruch," *DA* 22 (1989): 1389 ff; Gerd Herdegen, "Aussiedler in der BRD," *DA* 22: 912 ff.

44. Infratest survey, Sept. 1989, BPA Dok 1989, III: 424 ff; and other surveys, BPA Dok 1989 XII: 578 ff; "Das Fass läuft über," *Spiegel*, Sept. 18; and Hans-Peter Baumeister, ed., *Integration von Aussiedlern* (Weinheim, 1991).

45. "Kohl nimmt Flüchtlinge in Schutz," *FAZ*, Sept. 4, 1989; Paul Bocklet, ed., *Aussiedler, Gastarbeiter, Asylanten. Zu viele Fremde im Land?* (Düsseldorf, 1990); and Klaus Bade, ed., *Ausländer, Ausiedler, Asyl in der Bundesrepublik Deutschland* (Hannover, 1990).

46. Rainer Bohn et al., *Mauer Show. Das Ende der DDR, die deutsche Einheit und die Medien* (Berlin, 1992), 7 ff.

47. Alfred Grosser, "Ein Wunschzettel voller Widerprüche," *ZEIT*, Oct. 27, 1989; "Was steckt hinter der 'Frontberichterstattung'?" *ND*, Aug. 10; and Wolfgang Herles, *Nationalrausch* (Munich, 1990), 45–46, 53–54.

48. See the essays in Reinhard Appel, ed., *Helmut Kohl im Spiegel seiner Macht* (Bonn, 1990). The Bitburg affair was a foreign policy blunder: Kohl invited President Reagan to visit a military cemetery that contained SS graves.

49. "Unsicher wie jedermann," *ZEIT*, March 6, 1992; Genscher interview and "Der Eimer ist voll," *Spiegel*, May 4.

50. Horst Ehmke interview with *NP*, Aug. 15, 1989 and statements of other politicians, BPA Dok 1989, IX: 238 ff, 358 ff.

51. "Schäuble: Ausreise sorgfältig überlegen," *KSA*, Nov. 10, 1989; Schützsack, *Exodus*, 45 ff; and Herles, *Nationalrausch*, 63 ff.

52. Helmut Kohl declaration, July 11, 1989, Horst Teltschik's interview, *GA*, July 6; and Hans Klein's dossier on the German question, Aug. 8, BPA Dok 1989, II: 431, 458, 464.

53. Martin Walser interview, *SDZ*, Aug. 23, 1989; Freya Klier interview, *AAZ*, Sept. 16; and Bund der Vertriebenen press release, July 6, BPA Dok 1989, III: 898.

54. State Secretary Ottfried Henning interview, *Nordwest-Zeitung*, Aug. 26, 1989; "Falsche Angst vor Veränderung," *FAZ*, Aug. 10; and "Nachdenken über deutsche Einheit," *SDZ*, Aug. 12.

55. See the dialogue between Egon Bahr and Stefan Heym, *SDZ*, Aug. 28, 1989; and the forthcoming book by Hans Büchler on this topic.

56. Hans Klein declaration, July 28, BPA Dok 1989, II: 462–63.

57. Dregger column, *AAZ*, Sept. 29, 1989; Hans Klein interview, *Passauer Neue Presse*, Sept. 13; "Wiedervereinigung geht nicht aus Urknall hervor," *Welt*, Sept. 29.

58. Egon Bahr, *Stern*, July 13, 1989; Helmut Schmidt, *ZEIT*, July 14; Norbert Gansel, "Wenn alle gehen wollen, weil die Falschen bleiben," *FR*, Sept. 13; Willy Brandt, *BILD*, Sept. 21; and Oskar Lafontaine, "Das Gespenst des Vierten Reiches," *Spiegel*, Sept. 25.

59. Joschka Fischer interview, *Saarbrücker Zeitung*, Sept. 9, 1989; statements by Hermann Kant, Lutz Rathenow, Rainer Schedlinski, and others in *RM*, Sept. 15.

60. Gennadi Gerassimov interview with the BBC, Sept. 12, 1989 and other

statements, BPA Dok 1989, IX: 333 ff; Julii Kvitsinski interview with *NRZ*, Oct. 26 and other statements, BPA Dok 1989, III: 1159–60.

61. François Mitterrand interview with *SDZ*, July 27, 1989, and other statements, BPA Dok 1989, III: 1129 ff.

62. Vernon Walters interview with German TV, Sept. 3, 1989, BPA Dok 1989, III: 1135; Henry Kissinger *ARD* interview and other statements, ibid., Oct. 13, 1149 ff; George Bush interview, *NYT*, Oct. 25. Cf. Wolfgang-Uwe Friedrich, *Die USA und die deutsche Frage 1945–1990* (Frankfurt, 1991), 369 ff.

63. Bronislaw Geremek interview with *BILD am Sonntag*, Sept. 3, 1989, and other views, BPA Dok 1989, III: 1136 ff; Jacques Delors interview with French TV, Oct. 22, 1157 ff.

64. TV discussion about Genscher's role, Sept. 27, 1989, BPA Dok 1989, II: 28–29; Hans Klein press release, July 28, BPA Dok 1989, III: 462.

65. Compare Helmut Kohl's interview with *BILD*, Sept. 14–16, 1989; Hans-Dietrich Genscher's interview with *Spiegel*, Sept. 25; "Vogel gegen Wiedervereinigungsgerede," *Welt*, Oct. 4; and Egon Bahr, "Einheit und NATO sind unvereinbar," *Vorwärts*, Oct. 1.

66. TV discussion between Oskar Lafontaine, Volker Rühe, Stefan Heym, and Günter Grass, Sept. 20 1989, BPA Dok 1989, III: 1094; survey in *BUNTE*, Oct. 12; and "Hornhues: Grosse Chance zur Wiedervereinigung," *Welt*, Oct. 13, 1989.

67. Horn, *Freiheit*, 326 ff; Infas refugee survey, Sept. 1989; Volker Bergsdorf, "Staunend vor offenen Türen," *RM*, Oct. 27.

68. "Sie haben den Schlußtrich gezogen," *Morgen*, Nov. 18/19, 1989; and "Das Ausreise-Phänomen," *Sinn und Form* 24 (1990): 197–210; Wolfgang Fritz Haug, *Versuch beim täglichen Verlieren des Bodens unter den Füssen neuen Grund zu gewinnen. Das Perestroika Journal* (Hamburg, 1990), 47 ff.

69. "Flucht junger Menschen trifft DDR hart," *TS*, Oct. 8, 1989. Cf. Schabowski, *Politbüro*, 33, 62 ff, 134 ff, 166.

70. Rüddenklau, *Störenfried*, 356 ff; Andert and Herzberg, *Sturz*, 90 ff; Krenz, *Wenn Mauern fallen*, 166 ff.

71. "Refugee Crisis Awakens Poland's Anxieties about Germany," *NYT*, Sept. 21, 1989; Kohl quote from Günter Hofmann, "Politik geschieht anderswo," *ZEIT*, Oct. 27, 1989.

72. William Pfaff, "The Capstone of European Security," *International Herald Tribune*, Sept. 20, 1989; and Conor Cruise O'Brien, "Beware, the Reich Is Reviving," *London Times*, Oct. 31.

73. Andert and Herzberg, *Sturz*, 90; Hans-Dietrich Genscher interview, "Ein Prozess der europäischen Selbstbesinnung," *ZEIT*, Oct. 20, 1989.

Chapter 2

1. Rainer Tetzner, *Leipziger Ring. Aufzeichnungen eines Montagsdemonstranten* (Frankfurt, 1990), 7; Wolfgang Schneider, *Leipziger Demontagebuch* (Leipzig, 1990), 10 ff, Hans-Jürgen Sievers, ed., *Stundenbuch einer deutschen Revolution* (Zollikon, 1990), 29 ff.

2. Neues Forum Leipzig, *Jetzt oder nie—Demokratie* (Leipzig, 1989), 31 ff; and Rüddenklau, *Störenfried*, 298 ff.

3. Mitter-Wolle, *Ich liebe Euch*, 174 ff, 191–92; Neues Forum, *Jetzt oder nie*, 39 ff; and Stasi videotape of Oct. 2 demonstration.

4. Tetzner, *Leipziger Ring*, 7 ff; Schneider, *Leipziger Demontagebuch*, 17; Sievers, *Stundenbuch*, 66 ff.

5. Schneider, *Leipziger Demontagebuch*, 17, and Mielke orders of Oct. 8, and later report in Mitter and Wolle, *Ich liebe Euch*, 200 ff, 216 ff.

6. Pastor Peter Zimmermann's statement at Leipzig symposium, June 7, 1991; and Zwahr, *Ende einer Selbstzerstörung*, 79ff. Cf. Krenz, *Wenn Mauern fallen*, 134 ff; "Feuerts Magazin leer bis zur letzten Mumpel," *taz*, Oct. 24, 1989.

7. Krisch, *The GDR*, 129 ff; Hermann Weber, *Die DDR 1945–1986* (Munich, 1988), 156 ff.

8. Christiane Lemke, *Die Ursachen des Umbruchs 1989: Politische Sozialization in der ehemaligen DDR* (Opladen, 1991), 9 ff.

9. Mielke interview, *Spiegel*, Aug. 31, 1992; David Gill and Ulrich Schröter, *Das MfS. Anatomie des Mielke-Imperiums* (Berlin, 1991); Karl Wilhelm Fricke, *MfS intern. Macht, Strukturen, Auflösung der DDR-Staatssicherheit* (Cologne, 1991).

10. Mitter and Wolle, *Ich liebe Euch*, 54–55, 72 ff, 108 ff. See Suhl committee, *Genossen! Glaubt's mich doch!* (Suhl, 1990); and Roland Pechmann and Jürgen Vogel, *Abgesang der Stasi* (Braunschweig, 1991).

11. Albrecht Schönherr, "Weder Opportunismus noch Opposition," *ZEIT*, Feb. 14, 1992; Richard Schröder, "Nochmals: Kirche im Sozialismus," *ZEIT*, 28 Feb.; and Gerhard Besier and Stephan Wolf, eds., *"Pfarrer, Christen und Katholiken." Das MfS der ehemaligen DDR und die Kirchen* 2d ed. (Neukirchen, 1992), 17–103. For state-church issues see BA SAP, IV B2/14, vol 42ff.

12. Stefan Bickardt, ed., *Recht ströme wie Wasser* (Berlin, 1988); Gerhard Rein, *Die protestantische Revolution, 1987–1990* (Berlin, 1990); Stolpe, *Schwieriger Aufbruch*, 87 ff; and Josef Schmid," Die politische Rolle der evangelischen Kirchen in der DDR in den achtziger Jahren," in *Von der Illegalität ins Parlament*, ed. Helmut Müller-Enbergs et al. (Berlin, 1991), 342 ff.

13. Friedrich Schorlemmer, *Träume und Alpträume* (Berlin, 1990), 12 ff; Markus Meckel peace manuscripts, 1984 to 1989; Rein, *Protestantische Revolution*, 19 ff; Mitter and Wolle, *Ich liebe Euch*, 20 ff, 56 ff; Rüddenklau, *Störenfried*, 28 ff.

14. Manuscript newsletter from Leipzig, Rush collection; Wolfgang Templin and Reinhard Weisshuhn, "Initiative Frieden und Menschenrechte," *Von der Illegalität*, 148 ff; Rüddenklau, *Störenfried*, 51 ff.

15. Rüddenklau, *Störenfried*, 68 ff, 171 ff; Stolpe, *Schwieriger Aufbruch*, 152ff; Mitter and Wolle, *Ich liebe Euch*, 17 ff, 66 ff; and Rein, *Protestantische Revolution*, 42ff. For responses to the opposition see BA SAP, IV 2/2.039, vol. 312.

16. Rüddenklau, *Störenfried*, 178 ff; DPA release, Apr. 26, BPA Dok 1989, I; "Eine 'Arche'—viele Noahs," *FAZ*, Nov. 6, 1989: and Menge, *Revolution in der DDR*, 39ff.

17. DPA and AP releases, May 9, BPA Dok 1989, I; Mitter and Wolle, *Ich liebe Euch*, 42 ff, 72 ff, 93–94, 97 ff, 108 ff, 139–40; and Pechmann, *Abgesang*, 40 ff, 82 ff, 104 ff, 126 ff. See also Krenz's reports in BA SAP, IV 2/2.039, vol. 230.

18. See *Wahlfall 89* (Berlin, 1989); and Menge, *Revolution in der DDR*, 85–86; Rein, *Protestantische Revolution*, 135 ff; Rüddenklau, *Störenfried*, 288 ff.

19. AP release, June 7, 1989, BPA Dok 1989, I; "Die DDR-Opposition geht an den Start," *taz*, Aug. 15; Mitter and Wolle, *Ich liebe Euch*, 46 ff, 113 ff.

20. Mitter and Wolle, *Ich liebe Euch*, 113 ff, 153 ff; Pechmann, *Abgesang*, 160

ff. By mid-September Rainer Eppelmann claimed 500 grass roots groups, *Welt*, Sept. 16, 1989.

21. Markus Meckel interview, June 20, 1991; Mitter and Wolle, *Ich liebe Euch*, 153, 161–62; Th. Ammer and J. Kuppe, "Politische Zielvorstellungen wichtiger Oppositionsgruppen in der DDR," in Gesamtdeutsches Institut, *Analysen, Dokumentationen und Chronik zur Entwicklung der DDR* (Bonn, 1990), 14 ff, 46 ff.

22. Interview with Karsten Voigt, Aug. 28, 1989; Arndt Noack interview, Oct. 9; and Hans-Jochen Vogel's report, Oct. 17, BPA Dok 1989, XVI: 261 ff, 273 ff, and 278 ff.; Stefan Reiche, interview, *Abendzeitung*, Oct. 26; and *Von der Bürgerbewegung zur Partei. Die Gründung der Sozialdemokratie in der DDR*, ed. Dieter Dowe (Bonn, 1993), 89ff.

23. Vereinigte Linke, "Böhlener Platform," and other documents in *Die Aktion* no. 60/63 (Jan. 1990): 936 ff; and *taz* interview, Sept. 23, 1989. Cf. Ammer and Kuppe, "Politische Zielvorstellungen," 31 ff, 76; and Jan Wielgohs, "Die Vereinigte Linke," *Von der Illegalität*, 283 ff.

24. "Aufbruch 89—Neues Forum" (flyer, Sept. 1989); and Neues Forum circular, Oct. 1, 1989, NF Archive. Cf. Jens Reich interview, Sept. 12, 1989, BPA Dok 1989, XVI: 153 ff; Rolf Henrich, *Der vormundschaftliche Staat. Vom Versagen des real existierenden Sozialismus* (Reinbeck, 1989).

25. Dirk Philipsen, *We Were the People: Voices from East Germany's Revolutionary Autumn of 1989* (Durham, N.C., 1992), 227 ff; Neues Forum, ed., *Die ersten Texte des Neuen Forums* (Berlin, 1990); Mitter and Wolle, *Ich liebe Euch*, 153 ff, 170–71, 177, 184 ff; and Marianne Schulz, "Neues Forum," *Von der Illegalität*, 11 ff.

26. "Aufruf zur Einmischung in eigener Sache" and "Thesen für eine demokratische Umgestaltung in der DDR" (Sept. 1989); and *Demokratie Jetzt: Zeitung der Bürgerbewegung*, no. 1 (Oct. 1989), DJ Archive.

27. Demokratie Jetzt, ed., *Bürgerbewegung Demokratie Jetzt. Programm, Aussagen* (Berlin, 1990); Philipsen, *We Were the People*, 210 ff; and Jan Wielgohs and Helmut Müller-Enbergs, "Die Bürgerbewegung Demokratie Jetzt," *Von der Illegalität*, 105 ff.

28. Edelbert Richter interviews, Sept. 15, 1989, BPA Dok 1989, XVI: 390 ff; Edelbert Richter, *Erlangte Einheit. Verfehlte Identität* (Berlin, 1991), 15 ff; and Schorlemmer, *Träume*, 115 ff.

29. Mitter and Wolle, *Ich liebe Euch*, 156, 178 ff; *NCDDR* 1: 40 ff; and Ammer and Kuppe, "Politische Zielvorstellungen," 21 ff, 69.

30. "Standortbestimmung der Fraueninitiative 'lila offensive,'" Sept. 26, 1989, in Zimmerling Archive; essays by Gislinde Schwarz and Ina Merkel as well as "Geht die Erneuerung an uns Frauen vorbei?" in *Aufbruch—Frauenbewegung in der DDR*, ed. Cordula Kahlau (Berlin, 1990).

31. Texts in Kahlau, *Aufbruch*, 27 ff; and Anna Hampele, "Der Unabhängige Frauenverband," *Von der Illegalität*, 221 ff.

32. Grüne Partei, "Gegen Ellbogenfreiheit, Verschwendung, Wegwerfmentalität," in taz, ed., *DDR Journal zur Novemberrevolution* (Berlin, 1989), 85.

33. "Erklärung der Grünen Partei," Nov. 25, 1989, Zimmerling Archive, as well as Wolfgang Kühnel and Carola Sallmon-Metzner, "Grüne Partei und Grüne Liga," *Von der Illegalität* 166 ff.

34. Rüddenklau, *Störenfried*, 112 ff; Pechmann, *Stasi Abgesang*, 147 ff.

35. Eppelmann interview in *We Were the People*, 236 ff; Richter, *Erlangte Einheit*, 20f; Besier, *Pfarrer*, 40–41, 325 ff; and Rainer Eppelmann, *Wendewege. Briefe an die Familie* (Bonn, 1992), 2 ff.

36. Bohley interview in *We Were the People*, 131 ff, 293 ff; portrait in Ernst Eilitz, *Sie waren dabei* (Stuttgart, 1991), 27 ff.

37. Mitter and Wolle, *Ich liebe Euch*, 208 ff; and "Security Forces Storm Protesters in East Germany," *NYT*, Oct. 9, 1989.

38. Jens Reich interview, Oct. 5, 1989, BPA Dok 1989, XIII: 132–33; and Rolf Henrich interview, *Sbl*, Oct. 13.

39. Rainer Schedlinski, "Die DDR wollte den Vergleich," *RM*, Oct. 6, 1989; Manfred Stolpe, "Ein deutsches Sommertheater," *Spiegel*, Sept. 25; and Bärbel Bohley interview, Nov. 6, BPA Dok 1989, IX: 328.

40. "Die Protestanten in der DDR gehen aus der Kirche auf die Strasse," *FAZ*, Sept. 27, 1989; Walter Friedrich and Hartmut Griese, eds., *Jugend und Jugendforschung in der DDR* (Opladen, 1991), 135 ff.

41. Hubertus Knabe, "Politische Opposition in der DDR," *APZG* B 1/2 (1990): 21 ff; Ammer and Kuppe, "Politische Zielvorstellungen," 13–14, 19–20, 23; and Erhart Neubert, "Eine protestantische Revolution," *DA* 23 (1990): 704 ff.

42. Darnton, *Berlin Journal*, 95 ff; Richter, *Erlangte Einheit*, 31 ff; Pechmann, *Stasi Abgesang*, 217 ff.

43. Berlin *Gedächtnisprotokolle*, MS at the Umweltbibliothek, partly reprinted in *Oktober 1989. Wider den Schlaf der Vernunft*, ed. Ulrike Bresch et al. (Berlin, 1990), 46–70; Daniela Dahn and Fritz-Jochen Kopka, *Und diese verdammte Ohnmacht. Report der unabhängigen Untersuchungskommission* (Berlin, 1991); and *Schnauze! Gedächtnisprotokolle 7. und 8. Oktober 1989* (Berlin, 1990).

44. Alexander Zwahr narrative on Oct. 2 and 9, Hoover Institution; and Hatmut Zwahr, "Die Revolution in der DDR," in *Revolution in Deutschland?* ed. Manfred Hettling (Göttingen, 1991), 122–43.

45. Mitter and Wolle, *Ich liebe Euch*, 139–40, 220, 216 ff, 221–22, 227–28; Eckard Bahr, *Sieben Tage im Oktober. Aufbruch in Dresden* (Leipzig, 1990); *Schnauze!* 133 ff; Tetzner, *Leipziger Ring*, 22 ff; Schneider, *Demontagebuch*, 48–49; and Neues Forum, *Jetzt oder nie*, 115 ff.

46. Erich Honecker, *Zu den dramatischen Ereignissen* (Hamburg, 1992); and Bernd Lindner, "Die politische Kultur der Strasse als Medium der Veränderung," *APZG* B 27 (1990): 16–28.

47. Franziska Wende, *Die Zeit ist reif! Revolutionserlebnisse einer Leipziger Postbotin* (Amberg, 1990); and Heinz Kallabis, *Ade, DDR! Tagebuchblätter* (Treptow, 1990); Darnton, *Berlin Journal*, 96 ff.

48. Slogans from Tetzner, *Leipziger Ring*, 15–44; Neues Forum, *Jetzt oder nie*, 79–220; and Schneider, *Demontagebuch*, 41–97.

49. Sievers, *Stundenbuch*, 77 ff. and *LVZ* reports, Oct. 17 ff.

50. Peter Marcuse, *A German Way of Revolution* (Berlin, 1990), 37 ff; numbers for other towns from *NCDDR*, vols. 1 and 2.

51. Leipzig estimates by Karl-Dieter Opp, "DDR 1989. Zu den Ursachen einer spontanen Revolution," *KZSS* 43 (1991): 302 ff. The Stasi claimed 140,000 during Oct. 16–22; 540,000 during Oct. 23–29 and 1,350,000 between Oct. 30 and Nov. 5th, Mitter-Wolle, *Ich liebe Euch*, 234–35, 248–49.

52. Peter Förster and Günter Roski, *DDR zwischen Wende und Wahl. Meinungsforscher analysieren den Umbruch* (Berlin, 1990), 159 ff; Dieter Rink and Michael Hofmann, "Oppositionelle Gruppen und alternative Milieus in Leipzig im Prozess der Umgestaltung in Ostdeutschland," *DA* 24 (1991): 940 ff; Hans-Joachim Maaz, *Der Gefühlsstau. Ein Psychogramm der DDR* (Berlin, 1990).

53. "Dialog, Besonnenheit und aufeinander zugehen!" *LVZ*, Oct. 13, 1989, and dozens of subsequent articles.

54. Mitter and Wolle, *Ich liebe Euch*, 223 ff; Neues Forum, *Jetzt oder nie*, 101–4, 110–13, 123 ff, 133–36, 144–45, 153–54, 159 ff. Cf. Tetzner, *Leipziger Ring*, 27–28, 34, 37–38.

55. Walter Janka, "Manchmal heisst schweigen so viel wie lügen," taz, *DDR Journal* 1: 60–61, 65.

56. Texts of Jürgen Rennert, Joachim Walther, Günter de Bruyn, and Stefan Heym in *Oktober 1989*, 147–62.

57. Annegret Hahn et al., eds., *4. November 1989. Der Protest, die Menschen, die Reden* (Frankfurt, 1990). For the SED's preparations, see BA SAP, IV 2/2A, vol. 3254.

58. Markus Wolf, *In eigenem Auftrag* (Munich, 1991), 221 ff; Mitter and Wolle, *Ich liebe Euch*, 242 ff; and reports in *taz, TS, BZ*, and *ND*, Nov. 5, 1989.

59. "Unglaubliches ist geschehen," *ZEIT*, Sept. 29, 1989, and articles on Oct. 6, 13 and 20 ff. Cf. Gunter Holzweissig, "DDR-Presse im Aufbruch," and Anneliese Holzschuh, "Die Medien proben die Pressefreiheit," *DA* 23 (1990): 220 ff, 231 ff.

60. "Wir schalten um," *ZEIT*, Nov. 10, 1989. Cf. "Police and Protesters Clash Amid East Berlin Festivity," *NYT*, Oct. 8. and 9.

61. "Viele Forderungen, aber noch kein präzises Programm," *SDZ*, Nov. 3, 1989; "So leicht ist die SED nicht zu entmachten," *RM*, Nov. 3; Herbert Werner (CDU) release, Sept. 22; Helmut Lippelt, Oct. 10 in BPA Dok 1989, XVI: 120–21.

62. Herles, *Nationalrausch*, 44 ff; and BPA Dok 1989, XXII for reactions.

63. Kohl interview with *BILD*, Oct. 6, 1989 and other statements, BPA Dok 1989, XXII: 78 ff. For the speech see *FAZ*, Nov. 9.

64. Maaz, *Gefühlsstau*, 145 ff; Helga Schubert, "Wessen Strasse ist die Strasse," *DA* 25 (1992), 60–61; Christian Weber, *Alltag einer friedlichen Revolution. Notizen aus der DDR* (Stuttgart, 1990), 19.

65. Susanne Lohmann, "The Dynamics of Regime Collapse: A Case Study of the Monday Demonstrations in Leipzig," *Graduate School of Business Research Paper* 1225 (Stanford, 1992); John S. Conway, "How to Serve God in a Post-Marxist Land? East German Protestantism's Contribution to a Peaceful Revolution," *Journal of Religious History* 6 (1990): 126–39.

66. Jürgen Habermas, *Die nachholende Revolution* (Frankfurt, 1990), 177 ff; Ash, *Magic Lantern*, passim; Dahrendorf, *Reflection*, 100 ff.

67. Thomas Schmid, *Staatsbegräbnis. Von ziviler Gesellschaft* (Berlin, 1990); and Volker Gransow, "From Cold Civil War to Civil Society in Germany" (MS, Berlin 1990).

68. Mitter and Wolle, *Ich liebe Euch*, 204 ff, 225 ff, and 236. Cf. Weber, *DDR*, 211 ff; and Zwahr, "Die Revolution in der DDR," *Revolution in Deutschland*, 122 ff.

69. Martin Walser, "Kurz in Dresden," *ZEIT*, Oct. 20, 1989; A. Grosser, "Ein Wunschzettel voller Widersprüche," *ibid.*; "Kein Weg zurück," *ZEIT*, Nov. 3; "Auf einmal lösten sich die Zungen," *ibid.*; and "Die führende Rolle als Fiktion," *taz*, Oct. 25, 1989.

Chapter 3

1. Andert and Herzberg, *Sturz*, 66 ff; Krenz, *Wenn Mauern fallen*, 85 ff; Schabowski, *Politbüro*, 73 ff, and *Der Absturz* (Berlin, 1991), 238 ff.

2. *ND*, Oct. 7 and 8, as well as *NCDDR* 1: 73 ff; Wolf, *In eigenem Auftrag*, 186 ff; and "Mutige Zeiten erwarten Sie," *Spiegel*, Sept. 9, 1991, 107–108. See also the material in BPA Dok 1989, XIII.

3. Krenz, *Wenn Mauern fallen*, 32 ff, Schabowski, *Politbüro*, 80 ff and *Absturz*, 245 ff; Hans Modrow, *Aufbruch und Ende* (Hamburg, 1991), 18 ff; Andert and Herzberg, *Sturz*, 2–3; and Günter Mittag, "Das geht so nicht weiter!" *Spiegel*, Sept. 9, 1991, 84–85.

4. Horst Ehmke interview, Oct. 12, 1989, and other statements in BPA Dok 1989, XVII: 49 ff; Bärbel Bohley, "Keine Wende durch die SED-Erklärung," *MP*, Oct. 13; Kurt Hager, "Bewahren und erneuern," *SDZ*, Oct. 13; Wolf, *In eigenem Auftrag*, 197 ff; and "Im festen Bündnis lösen wir die Aufgaben mit dem Volk und für das Volk der DDR," *LVZ*, Oct. 14.

5. Andert and Herzberg, *Sturz*, 29 ff; idem, *Zu dramatischen Ereignissen*, 7 ff; Krenz, *Wenn Mauern fallen*, 141 ff; Mittag, "Das geht nicht," 84–85; Schabowski, *Politbüro*, 99 ff, and *Absturz*, 259 ff; Mielke interview, *Spiegel*, Aug. 31, 1992; Wolf, *In eigenem Auftrag*, 208 ff; and Karl W. Fricke, "Honeckers Sturz mit Mielkes Hilfe," *DA* 24 (1991), 5 ff.

6. "Wie Erich Honecker und sein Politbüro die Konterrevolution erlebten," *Spiegel*, Apr. 16–30, 1990; and Heinrich Bortfeld, *Von der SED zur PDS* (Bonn, 1992), 74 ff.

7. For Western press reaction, see BPA Dok 1989, XVII. It took until Oct. 19 for the *LVZ* to announce "Egon Krenz elected as General Secretary."

8. The term Stalinism originated among Trotskyites. See the dozens of entries under "Stalinismus" in the East Berlin city library catalogue and the archives of the *LVZ*.

9. Weber, *DDR*, 12 ff; and Jarausch, introduction to *Zwischen Parteilichkeit und Professionalität* (Berlin, 1991), 13 ff.

10. Landolf Scherzer, *Der Erste. Protokoll einer Begegnung* (Rudolstadt, 1988).

11. Günter Simon, *Tisch-Zeiten* (Berlin, 1990), 6 ff; Stolpe, *Schwieriger Aufbruch*, 115 ff. Cf. Krisch, *GDR*, 30 ff; and Gert Glaessner, ed., *Die DDR in der Ära Honecker* (Opladen, 1989).

12. Hermann Weber, "Aufstieg und Niedergang des deutschen Kommunismus," *APZG* B 40 (1991): 25 ff.

13. Kremlinology examined minute shifts in ideology as clues to political change instead of reflecting on its function in general. Cf. Wolfgang Leonhard, *Das kurze Leben der DDR* (Stuttgartt, 1990).

14. Krenz, *Wenn Mauern fallen*, 74 ff; Schabowski, *Politibüro*, 154 ff.

15. "Unfähig den Wandel zu begreifen," *Spiegel*, Oct. 2, 1989; Gert Glaessner, *Der schwierige Weg zur Demokratie* (Opladen, 1991), 55 ff.

16. Andert and Herzberg, *Sturz*, 103 ff; Schabowski, *Absturz*, 110 ff; and Peter Przybylski, *Tatort Politbüro. Die Akte Honecker* (Berlin, 1991), 36 ff.

17. Simon, *Tisch-Zeiten*, 11 ff; and Mittag interview, *Spiegel* (1991) 37: 88 ff. Dieter Staritz, "Ursachen und Konsequenzen einer deutschen Revolution," in *Sonderband DDR*, ed. Fischer Weltalmanach (Frankfurt, 1990), 13 ff.

18. Simon, *Tisch-Zeiten*, 14 ff. Christa Wolf, *Kassandra*, 2d ed. (Darmstadt, 1983) and Jürgen Seifert, "'Kassandra' und 'Marmor-Klippen,'" in *DDR—Ein Staat vergeht*, ed. Thomas Blanke and Rainer Erd (Frankfurt, 1990), 48 ff; and Christoph Hein, *Die Ritter der Tafelrunde* (Frankfurt, 1989).

19. Jürgen Kuczynski, *Dialog mit meinem Urenkel* (Berlin, 1983); Markus Wolf, *Die Troika. Geschichte eines nichtgedrehten Films* (Berlin, 1989); Jens-Uwe Heuer,

Demokratie und Sozialismus (Berlin, 1989). Cf. Wolf, *In eigenem Auftrag*, 64 ff, 75 ff.

20. "Hätte es ohne Stalin Hitler gegeben?" *Sputnik* (October 1988): 135 ff; and Bortfeld, *Von der SED*, 20 ff, 36 ff.

21. Wolf, *In eigenem Auftrag*, 26 ff; and Honecker, *Zu dramatischen Ereignissen*, 16 ff. For the politburo discussions see BA SAP, IV 2/2.039, vols 76–77.

22. Krenz, *Wenn Mauern fallen*, 11 ff; Schabowski, *Absturz*, 267 ff; Modrow, *Aufbruch*, 17 ff; Heinz Kallabis, *Ade DDR! Tagebuchblätter, 7. Okt. 1989 bis 8. Mai 1990* (Treptow, 1990), 7 ff; and for Western press reaction, BPA Dok 1989, XVII.

23. Krenz, *Wenn Mauern fallen*, 9 ff; Ernst Eilitz, *Sie waren dabei. Ostdeutsche Profile* (Stuttgart, 1991), 38 ff.

24. Eilitz, *Sie waren*, 38 ff; and Franziska Wende, *Revolutionserlebnisse einer Leipziger Postbotin* (Amberg, 1990), 34 ff.

25. Text in *ND*, Oct. 19, 1989. Cf. "Vor uns ein Riesenberg Arbeit," *LVZ*, Oct. 19 and 20; Krenz, *Wenn Mauern fallen*, 146 ff. For Krenz's own thinking see BA SAP, IV 2/2.039, vol. 88.

26. Schabowski, *Absturz*, 272 ff; Modrow, *Aufbruch*, 20 ff; Wolf, *In eigener Sache*, 207–208; Haug, *Perestroika Journal*, 96–97; opposition comments in BPA Dok 1989, XVII: 303 ff.

27. Christa Wolf speech, Nov. 4, 1989, *TschüsSED*, 38 ff; Neues Forum declaration, Oct. 23, *NCDDR* 2: 16; Kallabis, *Ade, DDR!* 15–16; and statements by Rühe, Lafontaine, Kohl, and others in BPA Dok 1989, XVII: 291 ff. See "Egon Krenz—ein Reformer?" *Spiegel*, Oct. 23.

28. Krenz, *Wenn Mauern fallen*, 146 ff; "Arbeiter in mehrstündigem Gespräch mit Egon Krenz," *LVZ*, Oct. 20; journalist and artist resolutions in *NCDDR* 2: 7 ff; Schabowski, *Absturz*, 276 ff.

29. Krenz speech in *ND*, Oct. 25, 1989; Demokratie Jetzt resolution in, *DJ* no. 3 (1989); lawyer resolution in *BZ*, Oct. 27; Schabowski, *Absturz*, 279 ff; and phone conversation with Kohl in *BILD*, Oct. 27; Cf. also *NCDDR* 2: 17 ff, and for other material see BPA Dok 1989, XVII: 400 ff.

30. Kallabis, *Ade, DDR!* 23 ff; "Der Straatsrat der DDR verkündete Amnestie," *LVZ*, Oct. 28, 1989; "Positionen der CDU zu Gegenwart und Zukunft," *NZ*, Oct. 28; Gerlach interview with *Junge Welt*, Oct. 31; *NCDDR* 2: 28 ff; and Schabowski, *Absturz*, 288 ff.

31. Simon, *Tisch-Zeiten*, 136 ff; Kallabis, *Ade, DDR!* 26 ff; "KPdSU und SED: Erneuerung mit Kraft zum Erfolg führen," *LVZ*, Nov. 2, 1989; Krenz, *Wenn Mauern fallen*, 149 ff; Modrow, *Aufbruch*, 21–22; Wolf, *In eigenem Auftrag*, 218–19. See also BA SAP, J IV 2/2A, vol. 3252 and IV 2/1, vol. 704.

32. Simon, *Tisch-Zeiten*, 136 ff; "Funk- und Fernsehansprache von Egon Krenz an die Bürger," *LVZ*, Nov. 4/5, 1989; Krenz, *Wenn Mauern fallen*, 150–51; *NCDDR* 2: 54 ff; Wolf, *In eigenem Auftrag*, 220–21.

33. "Politbüro nach Rücktritt von ZK neu gewählt," *LVZ*, Nov. 9, 1989; other material in *NCDDR* 2: 76 ff. Cf. Krenz, *Wenn Mauern fallen*, 153–54, 176 ff; Schabowski, *Absturz*, 302 ff; Kallabis, *Ade, DDR!* 33 ff; and Wende, *Revolutionserlebnisse*, 42–43. For the crisis see BA Po, DC 20, I/3, vol 2866 and BA SAP, IV 2/1, vol 706.

34. Michael R. Beschloss and Strobe Talbott, *At the Highest Levels: The Inside Story of the End of the Cold War* (Boston, 1993), 134. Exodus figures from Bundesminister des Innern and unemployment statistics from the Bundesanstalt für Arbeit, Hoover Institution. For the decision cf. BA Po, DC 20, I/3, vol. 2867 and BA SAP, IV 2/1, vol. 707.

35. "Die SED wird sich ändern, aber nie aus der Verantwortung stehlen," as well as "Schritte der Erneuerung," *LVZ*, Nov. 11/12, 1989; Kallabis, *Ade, DDR!* 36 ff; Wolf, *In eigenem Auftrag*, 232 ff; and Bortfeld, *Von der SED*, 105 ff.

36. Neues Forum flyer, November 12, 1989; "Volkskammer beriet über die politische Lage in der DDR," *LVZ*, Nov. 14; survey in *NCDDR* 2: 93; Wolf, *In eigenem Auftrag*, 243 ff, 271 ff.

37. "Aussenseiter im Inneren der Macht," *ZEIT*, Oct. 6, 1989; *NCDDR* 3: 5; and Eilitz, "Hans Modrow," *Sie waren dabei*, 70 ff.

38. "Wille zur Erneuerung der sozialistischen Gesellschaft hat Millionen Bürger erfasst," *LVZ*, Nov. 18/19, 1989; Modrow, *Aufbruch*, 27 ff; Heinz Arnold, *Die ersten hundert Tage des Hans Modrow* (Berlin, 1990), 16 ff; Konrad Weiss statement in *NCDDR* 2: 94.

39. Walter Janka, *Schwierigkeiten mit der Wahrheit* (Reinbeck, 1989); Schabowski, *Absturz*, 312 ff; Thomas Falkner, "Die letzten Tage der SED," *DA* 23 (1990): 1750 ff; and Bortfeld, *Von der SED*, 90 ff.

40. Daniela Dahn and Fritz-Jochen Kopka, eds., *Und diese verdammte Ohnmacht* (Berlin, 1991); Stadtjugendpfarramt, ed., *Gedächtnisprotokoll. Tage und Nächte nach dem 7. Oktober 1989* (Berlin, 1989).

41. Kallabis, *Ade, DDR!* 48 ff; Peter Kirschey, *Wandlitz/Waldsiedlung—die geschlossene Gesellschaft* (Berlin, 1990); Krenz, *Wenn Mauern fallen*, 156–57 ff; Schabowski, *Absturz*, 320 ff; and Volker Klemm, *Korruption und Amtsmissbrauch in der DDR* (Stuttgart, 1991).

42. "SED-Politbüro und ZK zurückgetreten," and "Tumultartige Szenen bei der Kundgebung vor dem ZK-Gebäude," *LVZ*, Dec. 4, 1989. Cf. Thomas Rosenlöcher, *Die verkauften Pflastersteine* (Frankfurt, 1991), 34; and Weber, *Alltag einer friedlichen Revolution*, 22; Bortfeld, *Von der SED*, 129 ff.

43. Krenz, *Wenn Mauern fallen* 158; and Schabowski, *Absturz*, 324 ff.

44. "Rede von Egon Krenz auf der 9. Tagung des ZK der SED," *LVZ*, Oct. 19, 1989; "Das Zimmer in dem ich lebe und wohne," *LVZ*, Oct. 21/22; "SDP gegen Diskussion über Wiedervereinigung," *SDZ*, Oct. 28; and Schabowski, *Absturz*, 327 ff.

45. "Telephongespräch zwischen Egon Krenz und Helmut Kohl," *ND*, Oct. 27, 1989; "Es ist nichts wiederzuvereinigen," *FAZ*, Nov. 2; "Referat von Generalsekretär Egon Krenz," *LVZ*, Nov. 9. Cf. Gesamtdeutsches Institut, ed., *Analysen, Dokumentationen und Chronik zur Entwicklung in der DDR von September bis Dezember 1989* (Bonn, 1990), 169 ff and Krenz, *Wenn Mauern fallen*, 214 ff.

46. "Eine Nacht und ein Tag hüben und drüben an der Bornholmer Brücke," *ND*, Nov. 11/12, 1989; "DDR-Bewohner sind für die Wiedervereinigung," *MM*, Nov. 13; and "Immer mehr wollen Wiedervereinigung," *MM*, Nov. 20. Other polls argued that only one-quarter of East Germans favored unification.

47. "Weiteres Telephongespräch Egon Krenz—Helmut Kohl," *ND*, Nov. 13, 1989; "Interview mit dem Regierenden Bürgermeister von Berlin [West]," *ND*, Nov. 18/19; Modrow, "Wille zur Erneuerung der sozialistischen Gesellschaft," *LVZ*, Nov. 18/19; and Modrow, *Aufbruch*, 41. For GDR-FRG relations see BA SAP, IV 2/2.039, vol. 328.

48. Horst Teltschik, *329 Tage* (Berlin, 1991), 12 ff; Helmut Kohl speech, Nov. 16, 1989, and material in BPA Dok 1989, XXII: 771 ff; Herles, *Nationalrausch*, 77–78.

49. "Nicht Kleinmut und Kleinlichkeit," *RM*, Nov. 17, 1989; "Sagen, was ist," *Spiegel*, Nov. 20; and Brigitte Seebacher-Brandt, "Die Linke und die Einheit," *FAZ*, Nov. 21.

50. "Dregger: Der Weg zur Wiedervereinigung," *FAZ*, Nov. 15, 1989; "Ausser staatlicher Einheit alles möglich," *TS*, Nov. 22; "Bin ein Gegner von der Phrase der Wiedervereinigung," *WR*, Nov. 24. For the parties see BPA Dok 1989, II: 589 ff, 681 ff.

51. Modrow interview, Nov. 18, 1989, BPA Dok 1989, II: 836; "Grenzöffnung ist keine Wiedervereinigung," *ND*, Nov. 20; "Für unser Land," *LVZ*, Nov. 19.

52. "Für euer Land, für unser Land," *BfdiP*, January 1990, 123–24. Cf. Wolf, *In eigenem Auftrag*, 285–86; Haug, *Perestroika Journal*, 162 ff.

53. Teltschik, *329 Tage*, 42 ff. See Herles, *Nationalrausch*, 83 ff.

54. For the full text, see BPA Dok 1989, V: 1 ff. For an abbreviated translation see Adam D. Rotfeld and Walter Stützle, eds., *Germany and Europe in Transition* (Oxford, 1991), 120 ff.

55. Karl Kaiser, *Deutschlands Vereinigung. Die internationalen Aspekte* (Bergisch Gladbach, 1991), 37 ff.

56. Kohl interview with GDR TV, Dec. 12, 1989. Cf. the other explanations in BPA Dok 1989, V: 20ff.

57. Herles, *Nationalrausch*, 83 ff; Hornhues (CDU) press release, Nov. 28, 1989; Ehmke interview, Nov. 29; and other material in BPA Dok 1989, V: 39 ff. Cf. "Kurz wehte der Atem der Geschichte im Bonner Wasserwerk," *FR*, Nov. 30.

58. Lafontaine interview, Dec. 3; press release by the Greens, Nov. 30 and other responses in PBA Dok 1989, V: 39 ff. Cf. Haug, *Perestroika Journal*, 162 ff.

59. "Eine Vision, die uns der Einheit näher bringt," *MP*, Dec. 13, 1989; "Der Bonner Stufenplan," *FR*, Nov. 29; "Endlich wird nachgedacht," *Welt*, Nov. 29; "Vor einem finsteren Wahlkampf," *taz*, Nov. 29; "Kohl nutzt die Stunde," *FAZ*, Nov. 30; "Zehn Punkte für ein Miteiander," *ZEIT*, Dec. 1.

60. Modrow interview, Nov. 30, 1989; Krenz interview, Nov. 28; Ingrid Koeppe interview, Nov. 28; Jens Reich interview, Nov. 29, in BPA Dok 1989, V: 109 ff; and "Sprecher der DDR zu '10-Punkte-Programm zur Deutschlandpolitik' von Kanzler Kohl," *ND*, Nov. 29; and de Maizière interview, Dec. 4, BPA Dok 1989, V: 124–25.

61. Günter Kunert interview, Nov. 30, 1989, BPA Dok 1989, V: 123; "DDR bekundet 'Interesse' an dem Vorschlag einer Konföderation," *FAZ*, Nov. 30; "Zwiespältiges Echo der DDR auf Kohls Vorstoss," *NZZ*, Dec. 1; Förster und Roski, *DDR zwischen Wende und Wahl*, 53; Kallabis, *Ade, DDR!* 57–58; and Wende, *Revolutionserlebnisse*, 71–72.

62. "Moskau: Kohl will der DDR Bedingungen diktieren," *SDZ*, Nov. 30, 1989; "Supermächte zeigten Kohl die kalte Schulter," *FR*, Dec. 1; "Die Siegermächte warnen Bonn," *Spiegel*, Dec. 11; government press releases, and other documents in BPA Dok 1989, V: 30 ff.

63. Beschloss and Talbott, *Highest Levels*, 135 ff; "Deutscher Wille zur Einheit wird Thema der Weltpolitik," *Welt*, Nov. 30, 1989; "Bonn in der deutschlandpolitischen Offensive," *NZZ*, Dec. 1. Cf. reports in BPA Dok 1989, V: 138 ff, 311 ff and articles in *BfdiP* no. 1 (1990).

64. Ulrich Wickert, ed., *Angst vor Deutschland* (Hamburg, 1990).

65. Albert O. Hirschman, *Exit, Voice and Loyalty: Responses to Decline in Firms, Organizations, and States* (Cambridge, 1970).

66. Hans Magnus Enzensberger, "Die Helden des Rückzugs," *FAZ*, Dec. 9, 1989. Cf. Rolf Reissig, "Der Umbruch in der DDR und das Scheitern des 'realen Sozialismus'," in *Das Ende eines Experiments*, ed. Gert Glaessner and Rolf Reissig, (Berlin, 1991), 12 ff.

67. As examples see only Jörg Swoboda, ed., *Die Revolution der Kerzen* (Opladen, 1990); Neubert, "protestantische Revolution," 705 ff; Opp, "spontane Revolution," *KZSS* 43 (1991) 302 ff; Joachim Warbeck, *Die deutsche Revolution 1989/90* (Berlin, 1991), 13 ff, and Sigrid Meuschel, "Revolution in der DDR," in Ilse Spittmann and Gisela Helwig, eds., *Die DDR auf dem Weg zur deutschen Einheit* Cologne, 1990), 3 ff.

68. Charles Tilly, "Europe's Changing Revolutions, 1492–1992," *New School for Social Research Working Paper* (New York, 1991); Philippe Schmitter, "The Consolidation of Democracy and the Choice of Institutions" (MS, Stanford, 1992); and Glaessner and Reissig, *Das Ende eines Experiments*, 7 ff.

69. Ash, *Magic Lantern*, 14, 136 ff; Dahrendorf, *Reflections on the Revolution*, 8 ff; Darnton, *Berlin Journal*, 9 ff; Habermas, *Die nachholende Revolution*, 179 ff. Cf. Rosenlöcher, *Pflastersteine*, 35–36.

70. Reinhold speech of August 19, 1989, in *BfdiP* (1989), 10: 1175.

71. Rosenlöcher, *Pflastersteine*, 58.

Chapter 4

1. "SED Führungsrolle nicht mehr verfassungsmässig verankert," *LVZ* Dec. 2, 1989; "Vor innerdeutscher Vertragsgemeinschaft," *NZZ*, Dec. 8.

2. Ash, *Magic Lantern*, 17 ff; Uwe Thaysen, *Der Runde Tisch. Oder: Wo blieb das Volk?* (Opladen, 1990).

3. Notice in *NZ*, Nov. 21, 1989; *ND*, Nov. 23; Krenz interview, *ND*, Nov. 24; Ibrahim Böhme interview, Nov. 23, BPA Dok 1989, XIX: 168 ff; Erhard Neubert interview, *taz*, Nov. 24.

4. "Erstmals Runder Tisch," *LVZ*, Dec. 2, 1989; Neubert interview, *taz*, Nov. 24; Uwe Thaysen, "Der Runde Tisch," *ZfP* 21 (1990): 71–72. For the SED's attitude see BA SAP, J IV 2/2A, vol. 3263.

5. "Beschlüsse des Rundtischgespräches am 7/8. 12. 1989" (typescript Berlin, 1989), now reprinted in Helmut Herles and Ewald Rose, eds., *Vom Runden Tisch zum Parlament* (Bonn, 1990), 23–26.

6. Kallabis, *Ade, DDR!* 70; Thaysen, *Runder Tisch*, 39 ff, 120 ff.

7. Haug, *Perestroika Journal*, 185 ff. There were also topical round tables for youth, environment, and the like. Other later applicants for seats like the DSU only obtained observer status.

8. Robert Havemann, *Dialektik ohne Dogma. Naturwissenschaft und Weltanschauung* (Hamburg, 1964), and Rudolf Bahro, *Die Alternative. Zur Kritik des real existierenden Sozialismus* (Cologne, 1977). See Andre Brie in Philipsen, *We Were the People*, 270 ff.

9. Essays in Hubertus Knabe, ed., *Aufbruch in eine andere DDR* (Hamburg, 1989); Fritz Damm, ed., *Wir dekorieren! 40 Jahre politischer Witz in der DDR* (Frankfurt, 1990).

10. For the psychological dynamics cf. John Borneman, *After the Wall: East Meets West in the New Berlin* (New York, 1991).

11. Helga Königsdorf, *1989 oder ein Moment der Schönheit* (Berlin, 1990), 58 ff.

12. Volker Braun, Günter de Bruyn, and others in Michael Naumann, ed., *Die Geschichte ist offen . . . Schriftsteller aus der DDR über die Zukunftschancen ihres Landes* (Hamburg, 1990).

13. Essays by Erhart Neubert, Reinhard Schult, Ludwig Mehlhorn, Hans-Jürgen Fischbeck, and Konrad Weiss in Knabe, *Aufbruch in eine andere DDR*, 141 ff.

14. Friedrich Schorlemmer and others in Peter Neumann, ed., *Träumen verboten. Aktuelle Stellungnahmen aus der DDR* (Göttingen, 1990); and Sebastian Pflugbeil in *We Were the People*, 312 ff.

15. Essays by Michael Brie, Rainer Land, et al., in *Aufbruch in eine andere DDR*, 181 ff; Andre Brie, *We Were the People*, 172 ff; Rainer Land and Ralf Possekel, "Intellektuelle aus der DDR" (MS, 1992).

16. Rainer Land, ed., *Das Umbaupapier. Argumente gegen die Wiedervereinigung* (Berlin, 1990); and Dieter Segert, Jürgen Kuczynski and others in "Aufbruch? Umbruch? Ende?" special issue of *Marxistische Blätter* no. 12 (1989).

17. Bohley, *40 Jahre DDR*, 5 ff; Bernd Aischmann et al., eds., *"Menschen wichtiger als Macht . . ." Briefe an Hans Modrow* (Berlin, 1990), 17 ff. See Lutz Niethammer, "Das Volk der DDR und die Revolution," in Charles Schüddekopf, ed., *Wir sind das Volk!* 251 ff; and Haug, *Perestroika Journal*, 123 ff, 171 ff.

18. Letters by Arno Dittmer, Jan. 6, 1990; Petra Sitte, Jan. 23, and others, Aischmann et al. *Briefe an Hans Modrow*, 57 ff; interviews with Runki, Evelyn Schmidt, and others in Clement von Wroblewsky, ed., *"Da wachste eines Morgens uff und hast 'nen Bundeskanzler"* (Hamburg, 1990), 31 ff; and Werner Bramke in *We Were the People*, 262 ff.

19. Interviews in Bärbel Bohley et al., eds., *. . . und die Bürger melden sich zu Wort*, 52 ff. For popular sentiment see Lutz Niethammer, *Die volkseigene Erfahrung. Eine Archäologie des Lebens in der Industrieprovinz der DDR* (Berlin, 1991).

20. Figures from Förster-Roski, *DDR zwischen Wende und Wahl*, 56–57; and Uwe Kolbe, "Gebundene Zungen. Ein offener Brief," in Naumann, *Die Geschichte ist offen*, 85 ff.

21. Wroblewsky interview with Eva Kunz, *Und da wachste*, 62 ff. See Walter Süss, "Mit Unwillen zur Macht. Der Runde Tisch der DDR in der Übergangszeit," *DA* 24 (1991): 470 ff.

22. Modrow, *Aufbruch*, 65 ff; Günter Kunert, "Tagtraum," *Die Geschichte ist offen*, 97 ff; Land-Possekel, "Intellektuelle," 38 ff.

23. "Die Macht liegt auf der Strasse," *Spiegel*, Dec. 11, 1989; Schneider, *Leipziger Demontagebuch*, 103 ff; Haug, *Perestroika Journal*, 179 ff.

24. Wolf, *In eigenem Auftrag*, 294; Gregor Gysi and Thomas Falkner, *Sturm aufs grosse Haus* (Berlin, 1990), 90 ff; *NCDDR* 3: 27–28; New Forum, *Stasi Intern*, 21 ff; Gill-Schröter, *MfS*, 177 ff; and Kallabis, *Ade, DDR!* 74–75.

25. "Hans Modrow," in Eilitz, *Sie waren dabei*, 70 ff; and Günter Gaus, "Hans Modrow," *Deutsche Zwischentöne* (Hamburg, 1990), 115 ff.

26. Modrow interviews, Nov. 14 and 15, 1989, BPA Dok 1989, XIX: 6 ff; "Der Reformer geht einen schweren Gang," *SDZ*, Nov. 17; Arnold, *Die ersten hundert Tage*, 22 ff. For Modrow's measures see BA Po, DC 20, I/3, vols 2870 ff.

27. Wolf, *In eigenem Auftrag*, 253 ff; Pechmann, *Abgesang der Stasi*, 335 ff; Manfred Schell and Werner Kalinka, *Stasi und kein Ende. Die Personen und Fakten* (Bonn, 1991), 335 ff; Klemm, *Korruption und Amtsmissbrauch*, 94 ff.

28. Modrow, *Aufbruch*, 34 ff; Arnold, *Hundert Tage*, 36 ff.

29. "SED-Führungsrolle nicht mehr verfassungsmässig verankert," *LVZ*, Dec. 2, 1989; Walter Süss, "Bilanz einer Gratwanderung—Die kurze Amtszeit des Hans Modrow," *DA* 24 (1991): 596 ff.

30. Modrow, *Aufbruch*, 43 ff; Kallabis, *Ade, DDR!* 69–70.

31. Christa Luft, *Zwischen Wende und Ende* (Berlin, 1991), 64 ff; Jörg Rösler,

"Marode oder Unterlegen? Zum Kollaps der DDR-Wirtschaft," *Marxistische Blätter* (1991) 5: 33 ff.

32. Modrow, *Aufbruch*, 40 ff; and *NCDDR* 3: 75–76.

33. Thomas Falkner, "Die letzten Tage der SED," *DA* 23 (1990): 1750; *NC-DDR* 3: 34 ff; Gysi and Falkner, *Sturm aufs Grosse Haus*, 50 ff; and Bortfeld, *Von der SED*, 129 ff.

34. Texts of politburo resolution and preparatory committee papers in BA SAP, IV 2/2A, vols. 3264–65 and in *ND*, Dec. 4, 1989; Kroker interview, *ND*, Dec. 5; "Die Neugründung hat schon begonnen," *taz*, Dec. 5; Wolf, *In eigenem Auftrag*, 288 ff.

35. Eilitz, "Gregor Gysi," *Sie waren dabei*, 212 ff; Gaus, "Gregor Gysi," *Deutsche Zwischentöne*, 57 ff.

36. Gysi interview with GDR radio, Dec. 10, 1989, BPA Dok 1989, XIX: 1347; Gysi interview with *Stern*, Dec. 14; Gregor Gysi, *Einspruch. Gespräche, Briefe, Reden* (Berlin, 1992), 41 ff.

37. "Sonderparteitag vollzog den endgültigen Bruch mit der stalinistischen Vergangenheit," and speeches in *ND*, Dec. 9/10, and material in *LVZ*, Dec. 9–11, 1989; Gysi and Falkner, *Sturm*, 98 ff; *NCDDR* 3: 65 ff; and material in BPA Dok 1989, XIX: 1558 ff.

38. Wolf, *In eigenem Auftrag*, 304 ff; Bortfeld, *Von der SED*, 214 ff; Ute Reuter, *Dokumentation zum letzten Parteitag der SED* (Bonn, 1991), 3 ff; Arnold, *Die ersten hundert Tage*, 73 ff; and "SED auf der Suche nach dem dritten Weg," *taz*, Dec. 11.

39. "Wir stellen uns der Pflicht, für dieses Land Verantwortung zu tragen," and Gysi interview, *ND*, Dec. 18, 1989; Gysi interview with *Spiegel*, Dec. 18; other speeches in Reuter, *Dokumentation*, 41 ff.

40. Ottfried Suckut and Dieter Staritz, "Alte Heimat oder neue Linke?" *DA* 24 (1991): 1038 ff; Th. Ammer et al., "Vom 9. ZK-Plenum zum ausserordentlichen Parteitag der SED," *Analysen, Dokumente und Chronik zur Entwicklung der DDR*, 78 ff; Wende, *Revolutionserlebnisse*, 79–80; Kallabis, *Ade, DDR!* 79 ff; and BPA Dok 1989, XIX: 1646 ff.

41. Jens Reich, *Rückkehr nach Europa. Zur Lage der deutschen Nation* (Munich, 1991), 180 ff; *NCDDR* 3: 28, 46–47, 55, 61, 92 ff.

42. Ute Reuter and Thomas Schulte, eds., *Dokumentation zur Entwicklung der neuen Parteien und Bürgerrechtsgruppen in der DDR* (Bonn, 1990); and Bärbel Bohley in *We Were the People*, 294 ff.

43. Ingrid Köppe in *We Were the People*, 324 ff; and Thaysen, *Runder Tisch*, 55 ff. For the work of the Round Table see BA Po, DA 3, vols 1–16.

44. Protocols of the December decisions in Herles and Rose, *Vom Runden Tisch*, 27 ff; Modrow, *Aufbruch*, 69 ff.

45. Luft, *Zwischen Wende*, 139 ff; "Drittes Treffen am Runden Tisch in Berlin," *LVZ*, Dec. 23, 1989; and "Eine neue Runde am Runden Tisch," *LVZ*, Dec. 28.

46. Thaysen, *Runder Tisch*, 55 ff.

47. "Überlebensfrage für DDR: der Dritte Weg," *LVZ*, Dec. 14, 1989; Weber, *Alltag einer friedlichen Revolution*, 44 ff.

48. Photographs and lists of slogans in Schneider, *Demontagebuch*, 103 ff; Haug, *Perestroika Journal*, 181 ff.

49. Rosenlöcher, *Die verkauften Pflastersteine*, 70 ff; Weber, *Alltag einer friedlichen Revolution*, 54–55; Wende, *Revolutionserlebnisse*, 71 ff; Kallabis, *Ade DDR!* 75–76.

50. Modrow, *Aufbruch*, 91 ff; "Souveräne DDR muss ein solider Baustein für europäisches Haus sein," *ND*, Dec. 9/10, 1989. Cf. Gerhard Basler. "Die'Herbstrevolution' und die Ost-West-Beziehungen der DDR," *EA* 24 (1990), 13 ff.

51. "Hans Modrow traf USA Aussenminister," *LVZ*, Dec. 13, 1989; Mitterrand toast, Dec. 21, BPA Dok 1989, IV: 1848 ff; "Mitterrand warnt vor Grenzveränderungen," *SDZ*, Dec. 22. For GDR foreign policy see BA Po, DC 20, I/3, vol. 2883 ff.

52. *NCDDR* 3: 19, 61, 64–65, 78–79; Stefan Reiche interview, *NRZ*, Dec. 13, 1989.

53. "Dreistufenplan der nationalen Einigung," Dec. 14, *DJ* no. 11 (1989); "Neufassung der Präambel zum zweiten Entwurf des Positionspapiers," *CDU-Texte* no. 1 (1990), 22–23; and party program of DA, Dec. 17.

54. "DDR and BRD vereinbarten gemeinsamen Fonds für Reisezahlungsmittel," *ND*, Dec. 6, 1989; "Ein Stück Einheit," *MM*, Dec. 6; "Regionale Zusammenarbeit mit BRD-Bundesland erörtert," *ND*, Dec. 11; "DDR-Premier und Momper für erweiterte Zusammenarbeit," *ND*, Dec. 13. Cf. material in BPA Dok 1989, XIII.

55. "Gute Voraussetzungen, aber keine Wunder zu erwarten," *ND*, Dec. 15, 1989; Luft, *Zwischen Wende*, 119 ff; Kohl and Mitterrand interviews, Dec. 10, BPA Dok 1989: 1666 ff; "Der Gipfel bettet die deutsche Frage in die Europäische Gemeinschaft ein," *Welt*, Dec. 11; "BRD Bundespräsident warnt vor Bevormundung der DDR," *ND*, Dec. 14; and Herles, *Nationalrausch*, 114 ff.

56. "Auf dem Weg zu einer Vertragsgemeinschaft" and "Vertragsgemeinschaft—eine Idee gewinnt Gestalt," *ND*, Dec. 20, 1989; Teltschik, *329 Tage*, 87 ff.

57. "Gemeinsame Pressekonferenz in Dresden" and other material in BPA Dok 1989, XXIII: 127 ff. Cf. Modrow, *Aufbruch*, 95 ff; Arnold, *Die ersten hundert Tage*, 91–92.

58. Heinrich Seewald, ed., *Helmut Kohl: Deutschlands Zukunft in Europa. Reden und Beiträge des Bundeskanzlers* (Herford, 1990), 125ff; Teltschik, *329 Tage*, 91–92.

59. Modrow, *Aufbruch*, 99 ff; Weber, *Alltag*, 58 ff; Herles, *Nationalrausch*, 98 ff; Rosenlöcher, *Die verkauften Pflastersteine*, 80 ff. Cf. Kohl and Modrow interviews, BPA Dok 1989, XXIII: 107 ff.

60. Brandt, . . . *was zusammengehört*, 55 ff, 63 ff; "Die Stunde der grossen Emotionen," *SDZ*, Dec. 19; "Lafontaine begeistert den SPD-Parteitag," *FR*, Dec. 20.

61. "Die Deutschen in Europa. Berliner Erklärung der SPD," Dec. 11; Vogel interview, Dec. 12, BPA Dok 1989, XXIV: 673 ff; "Deutsche Träume, deutsche Sorgen," *ZEIT*, Dec. 22. Cf. *NCDDR* 3: 105 ff; and Herles, *Nationalrausch*, 104 ff.

62. Gorbachev interview with GDR students, Nov. 15, 1989, and Gorbachev statement at Kiev press conference, Dec. 7, *BPA-Ostinformationen*; Beschloss and Talbott, *Highest Levels*, 157 ff; Hans-Peter Riese, "Die Geschichte hat sich ans Werk gemacht. Der Wandel der sowjetischen Position zur Deutschen Frage," *EA* (1990): 4: 117 ff.

63. Eduard Shevardnadze CBS interview, *Mannheimer Morgen*, Dec. 12; Vyacheslav Dashichev interview, *taz*, Dec. 13; Nikolai Portugalov interview, Dec. 15; and excerpts of Shevardnadze speech, Dec. 19, BPA Dok 1989, III: 1397–97; Eduard Shevardnadze, *Die Zukunft gehört der Freiheit* (Hamburg 1991), 240 ff; and Teltschik, *329 Tage*, 92–93.

64. Texts of the speeches and Kohl interview, Dec. 22, 1989, in BPA Dok XV: 751 ff; "Modrow wünscht sich von den Deutschen Besonnenheit," *FR*, Dec.

23; "Ein Schritt der Begegnungen der Menschen fördert," *ND*, Dec. 23; and Momper, *Grenzfall*, 236 ff.

65. Figures from Spittmann, *Chronik*, 45. For the New Year celebration see the Defa documentary, "Die Mauer."

66. Modrow, *Aufbruch*, 99 ff; Werner Bramke, "Warnende Stimmen des Auslands ernst nehmen," *LVA*, Dec. 24, 1989; Andre Brie in *We Were the People*, 275 ff; and Kallabis, *Ade,* '*DDR!* 87 ff.

67. "Neonazis schändeten das Treptower Ehrenmal," *LVZ*, Dec. 29, 1989; "Betroffenheit bei der Regierung der DDR über Sudeleien in Treptow," *LVZ*, Dec. 30/31; "Einheitsfront gegen die Gefahr von Rechts," *LVZ*, Jan. 4, 1990; Kallabis, *Ade, DDR!* 103–104.

68. Walter Friedrich of the Leipzig Institute for Youth Research in *ND*, Dec. 7 (48% for unity); ADN release of Neubrandenburg survey, Dec. 11 (39% for unity); DPA release of ZdF and *Spiegel* survey, Dec. 16 (27% for unity); "Hoffnungen für das Jahr 1990 im Spiegel der Meinungen," *LVZ*, Dec. 30/31 (23.5% for unity).

69. Essays of Friedrich Schorlemmer and Gregor Gysi in Frank Blohm et al., eds., *"Nichts wird mehr so sein, wie es war." Die Zukunft der beiden deutschen Republiken* (Frankfurt, 1990).

70. Ibid.; Haug, *Perestroika Journal*, 208 ff, 214 ff.

71. Wilfried Korngiebel et al., "Von einstürzenden Mauern, europäischen Zügen und deutschen Autos," *Mauer-Show*, 31 ff; Haug, *Perestroika Journal*, 179 ff.

72. Herles, *Nationalrausch*, 116 ff; Martina Krone, "Keine Chance mehr für uns?" and Klaus Hartung, "Der Grosse Radwechsel oder die Revolution ohne Utopie," *Nichts wird mehr so sein*, 57 ff, 164 ff.

73. Hans-Ulrich Wehler, "Deutsche Frage und europäische Antwort," *FR*, Oct. 14, 1989; Günter Grass, *Deutscher Lastenausgleich. Wider das dumpfe Einheitsgebot* (Frankfurt, 1990), 7 ff. See also Frank Wössner, ed., *Reden über das eigene Land* (Munich, 1989), vol. 7.

74. Appeal in *FR*, Dec. 9, 1989; Peter Schneider, *Extreme Mittellage. Eine Reise durch das deutsche Nationalgefühl* (Hamburg, 1990), 9 ff; and Martin Walser, *Über Deutschland reden* (Frankfurt, 1989), 101 ff.

75. "George Bush: Die Deutsche Frage ist in erster Linie eine Sache der Deutschen," *HB*, Nov. 23, 1989; CNN interview with James Baker, Dec. 6, and Baker speech before the Berlin press club, Dec. 13, *Amerikadienst: Dokumentation*; Beschloss and Talbott, *Highest Levels*, 138–139. See interviews by Gordon Craig, Vernon Walters, Henry Kissinger, and Lawrence Eagleburger in BPA Dok 1989, III: 1217 ff; and Michael H. Haltzel, "Amerikanische Einstellungen zur deutschen Wiedervereinigung," *EA* 4 (1990): 127 ff.

76. Genscher TV interview about the Malta summit, Dec. 4, 1989, BPA Dok 1989, IV: 1939–40; "Dem Weissen Haus und dem Kreml geht alles viel zu schnell," *StZ*, Dec. 7; Josef Joffe, "Das Vierer-Signal von Berlin," *SDZ*, Dec. 12.

Chapter 5

1. Reich, *Rückkehr nach Europa*, 204–205; Kallabis, *Ade, DDR!* 99 ff; Wende, *Revolutionserlebnisse*, 81 ff.

2. Hans Gerlach, Hans Modrow, and Günter Maleuda, "Zum Neuen Jahr,"

LVZ, Dec. 30/31, 1989; "Die Phase der schönen Revolution ist vorbei," *taz*, Jan. 10.

3. "Runder Tisch beendete vorzeitig die 6. Tagung," *ND*, Jan. 9; Modrow, *Aufbruch*, 71–72; Gill and Schröter, *MfS*, 177 ff; Fricke, *Mfs intern*, 73–74.

4. Pflugbeil interview, *BR*, Jan. 11, 1990; Reich interview, Jan. 11, and Modrow interview, Jan. 12, BPA Dok 1990, V: 11 ff; *NCDDR* 4/5: 22 ff; Herles-Rose, *Vom Runden Tisch*, 44, 48 ff; Thaysen, *Runder Tisch*, 57 ff.

5. "Gebäude der Ex-Stasi in Berlin gestürmt," *LVZ*, Jan. 16, 1990; interview with Konrad Weiss, *BZ*, Jan. 16.

6. "Das Gespenst von Mielkeville," *Die Andere*, no. 1 (Jan. 1990); "Überall Papierschnitzel," *taz*, Jan. 17; Gill and Schröter, *MfS*, 184–185; Fricke, *MfS intern*, 73.

7. Herles-Rose, *Vom Runden Tisch*, 59 ff; Arnold, *Die ersten hundert*, 70 ff; Thaysen, *Runder Tisch*, 64 ff.

8. "Der sozialistische Sonnenstaat," *taz*, Feb. 7; and Gill and Schröter, *MfS*, 186–187; Schell and Kalinka, *Stasi*, 351 ff.

9. "DDR Premier Hans Modrow gab Regierungserklärung," *LVZ*, Jan. 11, 1990; "Zur Lage der Volkswirtschaft in der DDR," *ND*, Jan. 11.

10. Gerlinde and Hans-Werner Sinn, *Kaltstart. Volkswirtschaftliche Aspekte der deutschen Vereinigung*, 2d ed. (Tübingen, 1992), 34 ff; Hansjörg F. Buck, "Lieber bankrott als ehrlich," *RM*, June 7, 1991.

11. Literature in Hannsjörg Buck and Hans Georg Bauer, eds., *Transformation der Wirtschaftsordnung der ehemaligen DDR*, 2d ed. (Bonn, 1991).

12. Jörg Rösler, "The Rise and Fall of the Planned Economy in the GDR, 1945–1989," *German History* 9 (1991): 46–61; and Charles Maier, "Gibt es einen Sieger der Geschichte?" in *Zwischen Parteilichkeit*, 197 ff.

13. Lutz Marz, "Der prämoderne Übergangsmanager," in *Demokratischer Umbruch in Osteuropa*, ed. Rainer Deppe et al. (Frankfurt, 1991), 104 ff.

14. Lutz Marz, "Geständnisse und Erkenntnisse," (MS, Berlin, 1991); and worker and union interviews in Philipsen, *We Were the People*, 281 ff.

15. "Besen und Badematten—selten wie eine Sonnenfinsternis," *SDZ*, July 15, 1989.

16. Dieter Golombek and Dietrich Ratzke, eds., *Dagewesen und aufgeschrieben. Reportagen über eine deutsche Revolution* (Frankfurt, 1990), 53 ff.

17. Günter Mittag, *Um jeden Preis. Im Spannungsfeld zweier Systeme* (Berlin, 1991), 245 ff; and Carl-Heinz Janson, *Totengräber der DDR. Wie Günter Mittag den SED-Staat ruinierte* (Düsseldorf, 1991), 30 ff.

18. "Allein die Statistik im Griff," *Spiegel*, Sept. 9, 1991; Honecker, *Sturz*, 281 ff; and Schabowski, *Politbüro*, 37 ff. Cf. also Herbert Wolf, *Hatte die DDR je eine Chance?* (Hamburg, 1991).

19. Janson, *Totengräber*, 63 ff. Mittag interview with *Spiegel*, Sept. 9, 1991, and *Um jeden Preis*, 245 ff.

20. Rösler, "Planned Economy," 58 ff; and Doris Cornelsen interview with *MP*, Oct. 29 and 31, 1989. See the disclosures at the Nov. 10, 1989 ZK session, BA SAP, IV 2/1, vol. 709.

21. Mittag interview with *Spiegel*, Sept. 5, 1991; and Mittag, *Um jeden Preis*, 273 ff; "Zum ökonomischen Vorfeld der Herbstereignisse 1989 in der DDR," *DSt* 28 (1990): 386 ff.

22. "Hoffnung auf den Nach-Mittag," *ZEIT*, Oct. 27, 1989; Helmut Haussmann interview with *Express*, Nov. 15; Hans-Herrmann Hertle, "Der Weg in den Bankrott der DDR-Wirtschaft," *DA* 25 (1992): 127 ff.

23. Christa Luft et al., "Für aussenwirtschatfliche Öffnung und internationale Arbeitsteilung," *ND*, Nov. 17, 1989; Luft interview, Nov. 24 in BPA Dok 1989, VII: 815 ff; Friedrich Workuta interview with *Spiegel*, Nov. 27; Heinz Warzecha interview with *ZEIT*, Dec. 1. Cf. Luft, *Zwischen Wende*, 85 ff.

24. "Neues Forum legt Programm für Wirtschafts-Reformen vor," *Welt*, Nov. 27; and Neues Forum, *Wirtschaftsreform der DDR. Internationale Wirtschaftskonferenz* (Berlin, 1990), 9 ff.

25. "Das planwirtschaftliche System ist am Ende," *HB*, Nov. 9, 1989; Wolf von Amerongen interview in BPA Dok 1989, VII: 993ff; Hans-Peter Stihl interview with *Morgenpost* (Hamburg), Nov. 18; and Alfred Herrhausen interview with *Spiegel*, Nov. 20.

26. "DDR: Keine Krise, aber 'Schlamassel'," *taz*, Nov. 23, 1989; Wolfgang Roth interview, *Sbl*, Nov. 24; SPD press release, Nov. 21 and material in BPA Dok 1989, VII: 1038–39.

27. Janson, *Totengräber*, 17–18; Mittag, *Um jeden Preis*, 212 ff, 288 ff.

28. "Gespräch mit Gerhard Schürer," *DA* 25 (1992): 132 ff; Teltschik, *329 Tage*, 107, 121; Luft, *Zwischen Wende*, 78 ff.

29. "Opposition droht mit Warnstreik," *HAbl*, Jan. 8, 1990; "Rühe: Ost-CDU soll Koalition verlassen," *Welt*, Jan. 9; de Maizière interview, Jan. 14, BPA Dok 1990, V: 39 ff.

30. Modrow, *Aufbruch*, 70–71; *NCDDR* 3: 15–16, 44–45, 52–53; Arnold, *Die ersten*, 53; Luft, *Zwischen Wende*, 100ff; Weber, *Alltag*, 96; and Kallabis, *Ade, DDR!* 111ff.

31. "Endlich Kompetenzen nach tiefen Kratzern," *LVZ*, Jan. 16, 1990; "Rollentausch oder wie der Hase zum Igel wurde," *FR*, Jan. 17; Stephan Finger interview, Jan. 16 and Martin Kirchner interview, Jan. 17, BPA Dok 1990, V: 47 ff. For Modrow's reversal see BA Po, DC 20, I/3, vol. 2837 ff.

32. Herles-Rose, *Vom Runden Tisch*, 54 ff; Modrow, *Aufbruch*, 73 ff; Thaysen, *Runder Tisch*, 76 ff.

33. "Modrow vor dem Kollaps?" *Spiegel*, Jan. 22; Gysi and Falkner, *Sturm aufs grosse Haus*, 112 ff; Bortfeld, *Von der SED*, 157 ff.

34. Berghofer declaration, "Sozialdemokratisch," *taz*, Jan. 23, 1990; Modrow interview with *Express*, Jan. 23; Kallabis, *Ade, DDR!* 121–122; Thomas Falkner, "Von der SED zur PDS," *DA* 24 (1991): 30 ff.

35. "Loyalität zur Regierung erklärt, damit sie weiter arbeitsfähig bleibt," *ND*, Jan. 19, 1990; Herles and Rose, *Vom Runden Tisch*, 62 ff; Thaysen, *Runder Tisch*, 78–79; Kallabis, *Ade, DDR!* 119–20.

36. "Die Furcht in der Regierung verheizt zu werden," *Welt*, Jan. 23, 1990; Reinhardt Schult, "Die Ecken des Runden Tisches," *Die Andere*, Jan. 25; Herles and Rose, *Vom Runden Tisch*, 77–78; Modrow, *Aufbruch*, 74 ff; Thaysen, *Runder Tisch*, 89 ff; Kallabis, *Ade, DDR!* 125–25.

37. Böhme interview, *ND*, Jan. 23, 1990; de Maiziére interview, *Welt*, Jan. 25, BPA Dok 1990, V: 60 ff.

38. "Kabinett Modrow kann in Amt bleiben," *SDZ*, Jan. 27, 1990; "Opposition für unabhängige DDR-Regierung," *LVZ*, Jan. 27–28; Thaysen, *Runder Tisch*, 82 ff; Modrow, *Aufbruch*, 79; Kallabis, *Ade, DDR!* 127–28.

39. "DDR-Opposition geht in Regierung," *AAZ*, Jan. 27, 1990; Modrow, "Um wieder Vertrauen in die Zukunft zu gewinnen," *ND*, Jan. 30; "Regiert bis März Vernunft?" *LVZ*, Jan. 30.

40. "DDR vor dem Konkurs," *BR*, Jan. 30, 1990; Modrow, *Aufbruch*, 80 ff; Arnold, *Die ersten hundert*, 76–77; Thaysen, *Runder Tisch*, 90–91.

41. "Klares Votum für Demokratie und Rechtsstaatlichkeit," *ND*, Jan. 30, 1990; "Wo alles ins Schwanken gerät," *ZEIT*, Feb. 2.

42. Herles and Rose, *Vom Runden Tisch*, 91 ff; and Thaysen, *Runder Tisch*, 98 ff. Cf. Greens, eds., *Umweltreport DDR. Bilanz der Zerstörung, Kosten der Sanierung, Strategien für einen Umbau* (Frankfurt, 1990).

43. "Eine schwere 'Geburt'," *LVZ*, Feb. 2, 1990; Kallabis, *Ade, DDR!*, 134 ff; Theo Pirker et al., *FDGB—Wende zum Ende. Auf dem Weg zu unabhängigen Gewerkschaften?* (Cologne, 1990), 9–10, 121 ff.

44. Modrow speech, Feb. 6, 1990, BPA Dok 1990; Eppelmann, *Wendewege*, 17–18. Since the BPA was still compiling its documentation during the writing, volume and page numbers could not be cited for the 1990 set.

45. "Kabinett der nationalen Verantwortung gebildet," *ND*, Feb. 6, 1990; "'Staatsfeinde' sitzen jetzt auf der Regierungsbank," *RP*, Feb. 6; Modrow, *Aufbruch*, 82 ff; Luft, *Zwischen Wende*, 151 ff.

46. Wolfgang Ullmann, *Verfassung und Parlament* (Berlin, 1992), 41 ff; Wolfram Bürger and Michael Weichenhahn, eds., *Wolfgang Ullmann. Demokratie—jetzt oder nie!* (Munich, 1990), 147 ff; "Wolfgang Ullmann," *Sie waren dabei*, 150 ff.

47. "Produktion 1990 sackt auf das 85er Niveau ab," *LVZ*, Feb. 6, 1990; "Die Mehrheit will sofort die Währungsunion," *BR*, Feb. 6; Arnold, *Die ersten hundert*, 48 ff; Luft, *Zwischen Wende*, 100 ff; Herles and Rose, *Vom Runden Tisch*, 107 ff.

48. "Vor allem eine Krise der Legitimität," *TS*, Jan. 28, 1990; Wende, *Revolutionserlebnisse*, 85 ff; Tetzner, *Leipziger Ring*, 82 ff; and Hans Kromer, ed., *Dresden. Die friedliche Revolution* (Böblingen, 1990), articles of the paper *Union*.

49. Zentralinstitut für Jugendforschung Leipzig, survey of Feb. 12, 1990; "Ergebnisse aus der DDR-repräsentativen Meinungsumfrage M5," July 1990; "Wille zur Wiedervereinigung wächst hüben und drüben," *MM*, Jan. 15; Tetzner, *Leipziger Ring*, 94; Förster-Ranki, *Wende und Wahl*, 53f.

50. Haug, *Perestroika Journal*, 276 ff; Bortfeld, *Von der PDS*, 166 ff.

51. "Ruf nach Vereinigung wird immer lauter," *StZ*, Feb. 7, 1990; *NCDDR* 4/5: 94–95; Tetzner, *Leipziger Ring*, 86; Kromer, *Dresden*, Jan. 23 and 31; Weber, *Alltag*, 103–104.

52. *Chronik*, 47; "Modrow: Innenpolitik ist immer bestimmend," *LVZ*, Jan. 6/7, 1990; Modrow, *Aufbruch*, 119-20; Luft, *Zwischen Wende*, 76–79.

53. "Frankreich findet sich ab," *SDZ*, Jan. 26, 1990; Antje Vollmer, "Die Träume der alten Männer," *taz*, Jan. 6; Herles, *Nationalrausch*, 125ff; Teltschik, *329 Tage*, 97 ff.

54. Compare Kohl's speech on Jan. 12 in Duisburg with his remarks to the *Washington Post* on Jan. 18 and his talk in Bremen on Jan. 20; and other interviews in BPA Dok 1990.

55. Modrow, *Aufbruch*, 118 ff, 170 ff; Teltschik, *329 Tage*, 100–101, 103–104, 107 ff, 115.

56. "Deutschlandpolitik der UdSSR ändert sich doch," *Welt*, Jan. 15, 1990; Portugalov interview, *BILD*, Jan. 24; Eduard Shevardnadze, *Die Zukunft gehört der Freiheit*, 233 ff; Beschloss and Talbott, *Highest Levels*, 183 ff; Seiffert, *Die Deutschen und Gorbatschow*, 204 ff; and Jurii P. Davidov, "Die Haltung der Sowjetunion gegenüber der deutschen Frage," *EA* 8 (1990): 257 ff.

57. Modrow and Genscher interviews, Jan. 30, 1990, and Kohl press release, Jan. 31, BPA Dok 1990; Modrow, *Aufbruch*, 199 ff; Arnold, *Die ersten hundert*, 96 ff; Teltschik, *329 Tage*, 120–121; Herles, *Nationalrausch*, 160 ff; Hans Adomeit, "Gorbachev and German Unification," *Problems of Communism*, July–August 1990, 1–23. For Modrow's talks with Gorbachev see BA Po, DC 20, I/3, vol. 2904.

58. Modrow, *Aufbruch*, 119 ff, 184 ff; Modrow interview, Feb. 3, BPA Dok 1990. "Kurs auf einig Vaterland der Bürger deutscher Nation," *LVZ*, Feb. 2, 1990.

59. Kohl, Genscher, and Vogel statements, Feb. 1, 1990, BPA Dok 1990; "Modrow's Kapitulation," *taz*, Feb. 2; Brandt interview, *Spiegel*, Feb. 5; and Herles, *Nationalrausch*, 161–62.

60. "Bundesbank entwickelt Plan für deutsch-deutsche Währungsunion," *Welt*, Jan. 8, 1990; Ingrid Matthäus-Maier, "Signal zum Bleiben," *ZEIT*, Jan. 19. Cf. Kohl interview, Feb. 3, BPA Dok 1990; Teltschik, *329 Tage*, 126–27; and Modrow, *Aufbruch*, 128 ff.

61. Matthäus-Maier and Wolfgang Roth release on "D-Mark als gemeinsame Währung," Feb. 2, 1990; Kohl, Pöhl, and Waigel interviews, Feb. 6 and 7, BPA Dok 1990; "Der Bundeskanzler will mit Ost-Berlin sofort über Währungsunion verhandeln," *HB*, Feb. 7; Teltschik, *329 Tage*, 128–29; Modrow, *Aufbruch*, 130; and Herles, *Nationalrausch*, 163.

62. Dashichev interview, *FR*, Feb. 8, 1990; Falin interview, *ND*, Feb. 9; Kohl statement, Feb. 10, and interviews, Feb. 10 and 11, Vogel comment, Feb. 11, BPA Dok 1990; Beschloss and Talbott, *Highest Levels*, 187 ff.

63. "Schlüsselübergabe in Moskau," *SDZ*, Feb. 12, 1990; "Sekt und Rührung im Kanzler-Jet," *BR*, Feb. 12; Teltschik, *329 Tage*, 133, 135 ff; Herles, *Nationalrausch*, 170 ff.

64. "Teltschik: DDR schafft's nicht mehr bis zur Wahl," *Express*, Feb. 10, 1990; Herles, *Nationalrausch*, 170–71; "Wenn die DM den Osten überrollt," *taz*, Feb. 7, 1990; Herles and Rose, *Vom Runden Tisch*, 115 ff; Thaysen, *Runder Tisch*, 138 ff.

65. Teltschik, *329 Tage*, 144 ff; Modrow, *Aufbruch*, 131 ff; Luft, *Zwischen Wende*, 160 ff. For a transcript of the Modrow-Kohl talks see BA Po, DC 20, I/3, vol. 2912.

66. Declarations of Kohl and Modrow, *BPA-Bulletin*, Feb. 15, 1990; Kohl, Modrow, and Brandt interviews, Feb. 13, BPA Dok 1990; "Experten sollen Währungs- und Wirtschaftsgemeinschaft erörtern," *LVZ*, Feb. 14; Ullmann interview, *Spiegel*, Feb. 19; Herles, *Nationalrausch*, 180 ff.

67. "Der Katastrophe entgegen," *FAZ*, Feb. 14, 1990; "Eher eine kühle Annäherung," *TS*, Feb. 14; Antje Vollmer interview, *taz*, Feb. 15; and the appeal, "Revolutionäre Geduld," *taz*, Feb. 14; "Zur Einheit per Diktat?" *ZEIT*, Feb. 16; Herles, *Nationalrausch*, 180 ff.

68. ADN release on reactions, Feb. 14, 1990, *Deutsche Vereinigung*, 131 ff; "DDR-Regierung vom Gipfel tief enttäuscht," *AAZ*, Feb. 15; Pflugbeil interview, Feb. 15, BPA Dok 1990; Ullmann interview, *SDZ*, Feb. 17; "Modrow: Ich werde nicht auf den Knien bitten," *ND*, Feb. 20; Herles and Rose, *Vom Runden Tisch*, 162 ff.

69. Thomas Friedman, "Steps to German Unity: Bonn as a Power," *NYT*, Feb. 16, 1990; Kaiser, *Deutschlands Vereininigung*, 49 ff; and Beschloss and Talbott, *Highest Levels*, 184 ff. Incorrect in Ulrich Albrecht, *Die Abwicklung der DDR* (Opladen, 1992), 22–23.

70. Genscher interviews, Feb. 4, 7, 11, BPA Dok 1990; Teltschik, *329 Tage*, 105, 128–29, 137–38, 141; and Beschloss and Talbott, *Highest Levels*, 187 ff. See also Stephen Szabo, *The Diplomacy of German Unification* (New York, 1992), 53 ff.

71. Genscher statement, Feb. 13, 1990; and George Bush interview, Feb. 12, BPA Dok 1990; and Gorbachev interview, *Pravda*, Feb. 20.

72. "How German Unity Advanced," *NYT*, Feb. 16; Teltschik, *329 Tage*, 147

ff; Shevardnadze, *Die Zukunft gehört*, 236 ff; Beschloss and Talbott, *Highest Levels*, 189 ff.

73. Kohl, Genscher, and Vogel speeches Feb. 15, 1990, BPA Dok 1990. "Kohl würdigte grosse Finanzkraft der BRD," *LVZ*, Feb. 16; Teltschik, *329 Tage*, 149–50.

74. Green resolution, Feb. 15, 1990, BPA Dok 1990; "Weizsäcker entsetzt über den Bundestag," *NRZ*, Feb. 16; "Die Bundesdeutschen auf der Siegerstrasse," *taz*, Feb. 15.

75. Dieter Grosser et al., *Die sieben Mythen der Wiedervereinigung* (Munich, 1991), 67 ff; Haug, *Perestroika Journal*, 288 ff.

76. Kallabis, *Ade, DDR!* 132 ff, 136; Monika Maron, "Das neue Elend der Intellektuellen," *taz*, Feb. 6, 1990, and replies on Feb. 9 ff.

77. "Das einzige, was in der DDR noch funktioniert sind die Verkehrsregeln," *WR*, Feb. 8, 1990; Teltschik, *329 Tage*, 135–36; Dumas interview, *Welt*, Feb. 9; "Managing the Inevitable," *NYT*, Feb. 16.

78. Augstein, "Elektrische, furchtbare Schnelle," *Spiegel*, Jan. 22, 1990; "Die Einheit: Eher in Monaten als in Jahren rechnen," *Welt*, Feb. 2; Kallabis, *Ade, DDR!* 137–38; Herles, *Nationalrausch*, 186 ff; Grass, "Der Zug is abgefahren, aber wohin?" *taz*, Feb. 23.

79. Karl-Heinz Bohrer, "Warum wir keine Nation sind," *FAZ*, Jan. 13, 1990; Peter Glotz, "Warum wir eine Nation sind," *FAZ*, Feb. 9; Peter Glotz, *Der Irrweg des Nationalstaats* (Stuttgart, 1990); Rudolf Augstein and Günter Grass, *Deutschland, einig Vaterland?* (Göttingen, 1990), 49–50.

80. "Hohle Sprüche im hohlen Zahn der Karl-Marx Universität," *FAZ*, Feb. 20, 1990; *BILD* survey of 69 popular stars; *Quick* survey of 22 prominent East and West Germans, Jan. 4; "ZdF-Politbarometer," Jan. 22 and Feb. 19, BPA Dok 1990; Kallabis, *Ade, DDR!* 141–42.

81. Wolfgang Bergsdorf, "Wer will die deutsche Einheit?" *Politische Meinung* (1990) 248: 13 ff; "Umfrage, Zustimmung zur Einheit in Italien am grössten," *RP*, Feb. 20, 1990; "CSSR: Ja zur Einheit," *NP*, Feb. 22; "Mehrheit in Holland für Wiedervereinigung," *FAZ*, Feb. 26; "Dänen fürchten deutsche Wiedervereinigung," *NP*, Feb. 2.

82. Abraham M. Rosenthal, "Hidden Words," *NYT*, Feb. 4, 1990; Alfred Grosser, "Vor einer Bevormundung bewahren," *HB*, Jan. 16; "Einheit nicht künstlich beschleunigen," *Welt*, Jan. 25.

83. "Deutschland—ein Trauma," *ZEIT*, Feb. 9, 1990; Elie Wiesel interview, *Spiegel*, Jan. 1; interview with Simon Wiesenthal, Feb. 15, BPA Dok 1990; Amnon Neustadt, "Israelische Reaktionen auf die Entwicklung in Deutschland," *EA* 11 (1990): 351 ff.

84. Henry Kissinger, "Der Westen läuft Gefahr zum Komplizen der Sowjets zu werden," *WamS*, Jan. 14, 1990; Michel Tournier interview, *Spiegel*, Jan. 22; "Plädoyer für Deutschlands Einheit," *MP*, Jan. 20.

Chapter 6

1. Survey of prominent personalities, "Wer waren wir—wer sind wir?" *Sonntag* 17 (1990): 3–4.

2. "Was die Wahlen hüben und drüben verbindet und was sie trennt," *Horizont* no. 3 (1990).

3. "Eine Wahl der Unwägbarkeiten," *FAZ*, Feb. 3, 1990; and "Der Osten war nicht immer rot," *FR*, Mar. 16. See Helmut Jung, "Von sozialistischem Methodenpluralismus zu markwirtschaftlichem Einheitsbrei?" (MS, Frankfurt, 1991).

4. "Meinungsumfragen von minderem Wert," *taz*, Feb. 8, 1990; *Stern* poll, March 1; "DDR-Barometer sieht SPD als stärkste Partei," *FAZ*, Mar. 13; "SPD liegt bei DDR-Wahlen vorn," *Kieler Nachrichten*, Mar. 15; Kallabis, *Ade, DDR!* 180.

5. Infas surveys on Feb. 9, 16, Mar. 2, 9, 1990, BPA Dok 1990, V: 240 ff; and EMNID, FGW, and USUMA, "Vorwahluntersuchung zur Volkskammerwahl am 18. März 1990 in der DDR" (MS, Bielefeld, 1990); "Die Allianz ist auf dem Vormarsch, *SDZ*, Mar. 10, 1990; and "Das Stimmungsbild schwankt von Tag zu Tag," *Rheinpfalz*, Mar. 15.

6. Interview Sabine Zimmerling, July 1990; TV discussion, Mar. 18, 1990, BPA Dok 1990, VI: 1238 ff; Matthias Jung, "Parteiensystem und Wahlen in der DDR," *APZG* B27 (1990): 3 ff.

7. "In der Baracke begann die Suche nach Strohhalmen," *Welt*, March 19, 1990; "Der Sieger betont die Verantwortung," *BR*, Mar. 19; Teltschik, *329 Tage*, 176–77.

8. Kohl, de Maizière, and Lambsdorff analyses, Mar. 18, BPA Dok 1990, VI: 1249 ff, 1263 ff, 1273 ff; Wolfgang Gibowski, "Demokratischer (Neu)-Beginn in der DDR," *ZfP* 1 (1990): 1 ff.

9. Lafontaine and Reiche statements, as well as TV debates in Bonn and Berlin, Mar. 18, BPA Dok 1990, VI: 1244–45, 1260 ff, 1275.

10. Weber, *DDR: Grundriss der Geschichte*, 21 ff; and Peter Joachim Lapp, *Die Blockpartein im politischen System der DDR* (Melle, 1988).

11. Egon Krenz, "Kommunalwahlen 1989," *ND*, Feb. 3, 1989; "98.85 Prozent stimmten für die Kandidaten der Nationalen Front," *ND*, May 8.

12. Manfred Gerlach in *Morgen*, Sept. 20, 1989; and interviews, *Morgen*, Nov. 1, *Spiegel*, no. 45, and *TS*, Nov. 10; "Leitsätze liberal-demokratischer Politik heute," *Morgen*, Nov. 16; Katarina Belwe and Ute Reuter, eds., *Dokumentation zur Entwicklung der Blockparteien der DDR von Ende September bis Anfang Dezember 1989* (Bonn, 1989), 6 ff.

13. "Brief aus Weimar," *NZ*, Oct. 26, 1989; "Schnelles Reagieren und langer Atem," *NZ*, Oct. 27, "Was wir wollen und brauchen," *NZ*, Oct. 28; and "CDU für baldige Neuwahlen," *NZ*, Nov. 9; *Dokumentation zur Entwicklung*, 75–76. For the Eisenach Synod, see BA SAP, IV B2/14, vol. 95.

14. Interview with Lothar de Maizière; interviews with *NZ*, Nov. 6, Dec. 2, 1989; de Maizière party circular, and "Gleichberechtigte Partnerschaft bei Gestaltung der Gesellschaft," *NZ*, Nov. 18.

15. Eilitz, "Der traurige Hugenotte," *Sie waren*, 183 ff; and Gaus, *Deutsche Zwischentöne*, 35 ff.

16. Angelika Barbe interview, *GMH* no. 12 (1989): 779 ff; "Die Sozialdemokraten in der DDR wollen sich wieder SPD nennen," *Welt*, Jan. 12, 1990; Peter Weilemann et al., *Parteien im Aufbruch* (Melle, 1990), 75.

17. "Es geht um die Macht in diesem Land," *ND*, Jan. 15, 1990; Ibrahim Böhme interview, *ND*, Jan. 23; "Grundaussagen des Programms der SPD," *Dokumentation zur Entwicklung*, Jan. 10, 80 ff; *NCDDR* 4/5: 54 ff.

18. Jens Reich, "Neues Forum, 10. Partei oder Bürgerbewegung," *BZ*, Dec. 30/31, 1989; Bärbel Bohley et al., flyer, "Gegen eine Spaltung des Neuen Forum," Jan. 3, 1990; "Programm und Statut des Neuen Forum," *Dokumentation zur Entwicklung*, 42 ff.

19. "Das Neue Forum bleibt in Bewegung," *taz*, Jan. 8, 1990; "Neues Forum überstand innere Zerreissprobe," *BZ*, Jan. 29; and Marianne Schulz, "Neues Forum," *Von der Illegalität*, 36 ff.

20. Interviews by Rainer Eppelmann, *JW*, Dec. 9, 1989 and Erhard Neubert, *GMH* no. 12 (1989): 762 ff; *Programm des Demokratischen Aufbruch* (Berlin, 1989); Richter, *Erlangte Einheit*, 39 ff; Eppelmann, *Wendewege*, 12 ff; Schorlemmer, *Träume*, 155 ff.

21. *NCDDR* 4/5: 94–95; Wolfgang Schäuble, *Der Vertrag* (Stuttgart, 1991), 46 ff.

22. Carsten Tessmer, "Innerdeutsche Parteibeziehungen vor und nach dem Umbruch in der DDR," *DSt* 29 (1991): 191 ff.

23. "Wer ist wessen Schwester?" *FAZ*, Jan. 18, 1990; "Vorsprung für die Sozialdemokraten," *TS*, Jan. 18; "Die Opposition sammelt sich noch," *RP*, Jan. 25; "Die CDU empfiehlt den möglichen Partnern eine 'Deutsche Allianz,'" *BR*, Jan. 25; Schäuble, *Vertrag*, 38 ff.

24. Statements by Kohl, Rühe, and de Maizière, Feb. 5 and 6, 1990, and "Aus nationaler Verantwortung, eine Allianz für Deutschland," Feb. 6, BPA Dok 1990, VI: 321–22; Schäuble, *Vertrag*, 44–45; and Teltschik, *329 Tage*, 124, 129.

25. "Auch die Liberalen in der DDR streben ein Wahlbündnis an," *FAZ*, Feb. 7, 1990; "Bund Freier Demokraten," BPA Dok 1990, VI: 400 ff; "DDR-Liberale einigen sich über Wahlbündnis," *Welt*, Feb. 12.

26. "Wider die ständige Einmischung," Jan. 19, 1990, BPA Dok 1990, VI: 233; Stephan Bickardt interview, *taz* Jan. 15; "Das Bündnis 90 versucht es ohne Parteien-Partner aus dem Westen," *FAZ*, Feb. 8; "Grüne gründen Bündnis mit dem Frauenverband," *FAZ*, Feb. 16. Cf. Schulz, "Neues Forum," 59 ff.

27. "Ein Wahlrecht fast als Sturzgeburt," *SDZ*, Jan. 31, 1990; "Ein Wahlgesetz mit vierundvierzig Paragraphen nur für einen Tag," *FR*, Feb. 23.

28. Herles and Rose, *Vom Runden Tisch*, 58–59, 70, 103, 106–107, 146 ff and Ulrich Thaysen, "Die rechtliche Basis politischer Pluralität," *ZfP* 21 (1990): 38 ff.

29. "Für freie Wahlen fehlen Voraussetzungen," *FAZ*, Jan. 4, 1990; Konrad Weiss interview, Jan. 5, and Hans Klein release, Jan. 8, BPA Dok 1990, VI: 2 ff; Herles and Rose, *Vom Runden Tisch*, 37–38, 62–63, 103–104.

30. Gregor Gysi interview, Jan. 5, 1990; and Jan. 11, BPA Dok 1990, VI: 2 ff, 230; "Hier spricht die Opposition," *LVZ*, Dec. 9/10; *Die Andere*, no. 1 (Jan. 1990); and Thaysen, *Runder Tisch*, 134–35.

31. Bärbel Bohley interview, Feb. 10, 1990, BPA Dok 1990, VI: 15; "Ko(h)lonie der BRD?" *ND*, March 14.

32. Volker Rühe and Anke Fuchs interview, Feb. 5, 1990, BPA Dok 1990, VI: 1170 ff; "Bonn kritisiert DDR-Wahlkampfverbot," *Welt*, Feb. 6; Herles and Rose, *Vom Runden Tisch*, 106–107, 146–47; Thaysen, *Runder Tisch*, 137. For the Round Table resolution see BA Po, DA3, vol. 11.

33. "Betäubt vom Tempo der Profis," *ZEIT*, Feb. 6, 1990; Jan Bielicki's series of five campaign reports in *SB*, Feb. 9 ff; Kontakttelefon Berlin, *Wahlkampfbeobachter*, Mar. 13, Hoover Institution.

34. "Hart geführter Wahlkampf in der DDR," *NZZ*, Mar. 1, 1990; Wende,

Revolutionserlebnisse, 92–93; Herles, *Nationalrausch*, 199–200; Helmut Müller-Enbergs, *Volkskammerwahlen in der DDR 1990. Synopse von (Wahl-)Programmen 15 kandidierender Parteien* (Berlin, 1990).

35. "Wahlprogramm der PDS," *ND*, Feb. 27, 1990; flyers, "Alles vergessen?" and "Was wir wollen," Mar.; Gregor Gysi interview, Mar. 8, BPA Dok 1990, VI: 939–40; Hans Modrow interview, *ND*, Mar. 14; Bortfeld, *Von der SED*, 177 ff.

36. "Für die Schwachen eine starke Opposition" and other material in Hoover Institution; brochures on NATO, SED founding, and local government, *PDS Diskussionsangebot*, Feb.–Mar., 1990; Gysi and Falkner, *Sturm*, 131 ff; and Modrow, *Aufbruch*, 141–42.

37. *nez*, Dec. 22, 1989 and other sheets from Greifswald, Potsdam, Rostock, etc.; "Wir haben die richtigen Leute" and other leaflets; Ingrid Köppe and Jens Reich interviews, Feb. 20, Mar. 3, BPA Dok 1990, VI: 883 ff.

38. "Nach dem Höhenflug der Fall ins Leere," *SDZ*, Mar. 9; "Bürgerbewegung stellt sich auf Oppositionsrolle ein," *StZ*, Mar. 15; and Reich, *Rückkehr nach Europa*, 213 ff.

39. Handbills "SPD", "8 gute Gründe SPD zu wählen", "Wir sind das Volk," Mar. 1990; SPD, *Extrablatt: Zeitung für die Bürger der DDR*, issues for Feb. and Mar.; SPD, *Berliner StattBlatt*, Feb. 24; "Wahlprogramm der SPD," Mar. 1; and other material, Hoover Institution.

40. Interviews with Ibrahim Böhme, *WW*, Feb. 2, 1990; *Stern*, Feb. 8; *Vorwärts*, Mar. 1; "Mitten hinein ins alte Deutschland," *SDZ*, Mar. 6; "DDR-SPD will die Regierung bilden," *FAZ*, Mar. 15; and Brandt speeches, ". . . was zusammengehört," 81 ff.

41. Handbills and posters from pamphlet collection of East Berlin CDU archives; *Zeitung zur Wahl. Informationen zur Allianz für Deutschland* and *CDU Extra*, spring 1990; "Umkehr in die Zukunft—das Wahlkampfthema unserer Partei," *Union teilt mit* no. 2 (1990).

42. *Einheit Bald* and other material, Hoover Institution; de Maizière interviews, Feb. 2 and 25, 1990, and "Wahlaufruf und Sofortprogramm der Allianz für Deutschland zur Volkskammerwahl in der DDR," BPA Dok 1990, VI: 468 ff, 500 ff, 510 ff.

43. "Die verlorenen Söhne als willkommene Wahlhelfer," *HA*, Feb. 19, 1990; and material in PBA Dok 1990, VI: 853 ff.

44. "Zum Jahresbeginn Streitereien in Bonn um die polnische Westgrenze," *FAZ*, Jan. 2, 1990; Herbert Hupka letter, *FAZ*, Jan. 19; "Koalition streitet nach Kohl-Besuch bei Bush über die polnische Westgrenze," *Welt*, Feb. 27; Kaiser, *Deutschlands Vereinigung*, 89 ff.

45. Kohl statements, Mar. 5 and 6, 1990; Kohl and Genscher Bundestag speeches, Mar. 8, BPA Dok 1990; "Ende der Irritationen," *Welt*, Mar. 7. See Teltschik, *329 Tage*, 97, 104, 111–12, 132, 151, 160, 163 ff, 167 ff; and Schäuble, *Vertrag*, 58 ff.

46. "Deutschland unser Vaterland und Europa unsere Zukunft," *FAZ*, Feb. 22, 1990; "Die Allianz macht Jagd auf die SPD," *HA*, Mar. 8; "Stunden, die nicht wieder kommen," *SDZ*, Mar. 12; "Helmut, Helmut," *BILD*, Mar. 15; SPD list of CDU promises, Hoover Institution.

47. Selections from Kohl speeches, Feb. 20, Mar. 1, 9, 1990, BPA Dok 1990, VI: 654 ff; and Teltschik, *329 Tage*, 153–54, 165, 168, 172 ff.

48. Kallabis, *Ade, DDR!* 165, 169; Wende, *Revoutionserlebnisse*, 101 ff; Rosenlöcher, *Verkaufte Pflastersteine*, 100 ff.

49. Herles and Rose, *Vom Runden Tisch*, 189 ff, 238 ff, 294 ff; "Berliner Aufruf: Für eine unabhängige DDR," Hoover Institution; Gransow and Jarausch, *Deutsche Vereinigung*, 145 ff; "Warten auf die Zukunft," *KSA*, Mar. 1, 1990; Teltschik, *329 Tage*, 173; Modrow, *Aufbruch*, 138. For government and Round Table efforts see BA Po, DC 20, I/3, vols. 2921ff.

50. "Amtliches Endergebnis der Wahlen zur Volkskammer am 18. März 1990," *ND*, Mar. 24, 1990; "Wahlergebnisse in den ehemaligen Ländern der DDR," *ZEIT*, Mar. 23.

51. Survey analysis, *FAZ*, Mar. 23, 1990; "Wo die Parteien die besten Ergebnisse erzielten," *TS*, Mar. 25; Jung, "Parteiensystem und Wahlen," 8 ff; and Gibowski, "Demokratischer (Neu-)Beginn," 9 ff.

52. "Wahlsieger," *HA*, Mar. 19, 1990; TV discussion, Mar. 18, BPA Dok 1990, VI: 1373 ff; "Kohls Sieg," *FR*, Mar. 19; "Gedanken nach der Wahl," *ND*, Mar. 20; "Kohl gewinnt an Gewicht," *SDZ*, Mar. 20; "Wurde mit der CDU die schnelle DM gewählt?" *LVZ*, Mar. 20.

53. "Grosser Triumph," *Welt*, Mar. 19, 1990; Schäuble, *Vertrag*, 51; "Votum für die Einheit in der DDR," *NZZ*, Mar. 20; interviews with foreign experts, Mar. 19, BPA Dok 1990, VI: 1671 ff. "Washington begrüsst den Sieg der Konservativen," *HB*, Mar. 20.

54. Infratest survey, "Vor der Volkskammerwahl," Mar. 15, 1990; EMNID, FGW, and USUMA survey, Mar. 18; Donald Abenheim, "Volkskammer Elections, GDR," Hoover Institution; and Maaz, *Gefühlsstau*, 157.

55. Wende, *Revolutionserlebnisse*, 105 ff; Rosenlöcher, *Verkaufte Pflastersteine*, 112–13; Weber, *Alltag*, 117 ff; Kallabis, *Ade, DDR!* 182 ff; and Horst D. Schlosser, "Ein nur scheinbar bundesdeutscher Wahlkampf," *DA* 23 (1990): 520 ff.

56. "Ich weiss nicht, ob ich es machen soll," *BILD*, Mar. 20, 1990; "Erklärung der Allianz für Deutschland im Wortlaut," Mar. 20, BPA Dok 1990, V: 1312 ff.

57. De Maizière and Kohl interviews, Mar. 19, 1990; Helmut Kohl victory statement, Mar. 19, BPA Dok 1990, VI: 1301 ff; "Einheit? Ja, aber bitte billig!" *ZEIT*, Mar. 9; Teltschik, *329 Tage*, 177–78; and Schäuble, *Vertrag*, 74 ff.

58. Interviews with Ibrahim Böhme, Markus Meckel, Mar. 19, 1990, Angela Barbe, Mar. 20, and Otto Lambsdorff, Mar. 23, BPA Dok 1990, VI: 1300 ff; "Konservative Allianz für möglichst grosse Koalition," *SDZ*, Mar. 20.

59. "De Maizière sucht Rat beim Kanzler," *Welt*, Mar. 22, 1990; "De Maizière will DDR-Ministerpräsident werden," *SDZ*, Mar. 24.

60. Anke Fuchs interview, Mar. 19, 1990, BPA Dok 1990, VI: 1296; "In der Koalitionsfrage ist die DDR-SPD noch uneins," *Welt*, Mar. 22.

61. "Die Angst vom ungeliebten Partner umarmt zu werden," *StZ*, Mar. 23, 1990; de Maizière *WaMS* interview, Mar. 25; and Hermann Rappe interview, Mar. 26, BPA Dok 1990, VI: 1838–39. Cf. Richard Schröder, *Deutschland schwierig Vaterland* (Freiburg, 1993), 51 ff.

62. Interviews by de Maizière, Mar. 28, 1990; Richard Schröder, Mar. 30 and Apr. 3, BPA Dok 1990, VI: 1842 ff; "Die SPD in der DDR ist zu Verhandlungen mit der CDU bereit," *FAZ*, Mar. 28, 1990.

63. Interviews with Meckel, Apr. 2, 4, and 7, 1990; and Schorlemmer, Apr. 11; "Erklärung der SPD zur Aufnahme von Koalitionsgesprächen," Apr. 4, in BPA Dok 1990, VI: 1842 ff.

64. "Es muss alles raus," *Spiegel*, Mar. 26, 1990; and Reiner Kunze, *Deckname 'Lyrik'* (Frankfurt, 1990), 113 ff.

65. Interview with Markus Meckel; Eilitz, "Der vergessene Medienstar," and

"Philosoph im Aussenamt," *Die waren dabei*, 61 ff, 101 ff; and Albrecht, *Abwicklung*, 16 ff.

66. "Koalition in der DDR so gut wie perfekt," *SDZ*, Apr. 9, 1990; "Grosse Koalition steht," *Welt*, Apr. 10; Kallabis, *Ade, DDR!* 214.

67. "Grundsätze der Koalitionsvereinbarung," Apr. 12, 1990 in *Dokumentation zur politischen Entwicklung in der DDR und zu den innerdeutschen Beziehungen April 1990*, ed. Ute Reuter (Bonn, 1990), 6 ff.

68. "Eine Regierung für die DDR," *GA*, Apr. 10, 1990; "Standpunkte und Meinungen von sieben Ministern," *ND*, Apr. 14; Herles and Rose, *Vom Runden Tisch*, 379 ff; Hans-Dieter Schütt, *Regine Hildebrandt* (Berlin, 1992), 163 ff; Eppelmann, *Wendewege*, 18–19. For the new cabinet see BA Po, DC 20, I/3, vol. 2943.

69. De Maizière interviews, Apr. 12 and 14, 1990, BPA Dok 1990, VI: 1891 ff; "Ein historischer Tag, nicht frei von Peinlichkeiten," *FR*, Apr. 14; Kallabis, *Ade, DDR!* 215; and Erich Fischer, "Waren Sie das Volk?" *DA* 24 (1991): 279 ff.

70. Hans Modrow, "Bilanz nach 150 Tagen," *ZEIT*, Apr. 20, 27, and May 4, 1990; Modrow, *Aufbruch*, 143 ff.

71. Verfassungsausschuss des Runden Tisches, "Verfassung der DDR. Entwurf," *Dokumentation zur politischen Entwicklung*, 58 ff; Herles and Rose, *Vom Runden Tisch*, 301; Thaysen, *Runder Tisch*, 143 ff.

72. Lothar de Maizière, "Politik für unser Volk," Apr. 19, 1990, in BPA Dok 1990, VI: 2261 ff.

73. Ibid.; Teltschik, *329 Tage*, 202. See also *Protokolle der Volkskammer* 10. Wahlperiode, vol. 27.

74. De Maizière interview, Apr. 19, 1990, BPA Dok 1990, VI: 2283 ff; "Regierungserklärung beraten," *LVZ*, Apr. 21/22, 1990; Kallabis, *Ade, DDR!* 223–24 ; Reich, *Rückkehr*, 217 ff; Schütt, *Hildebrandt*, 172.

75. Karl-Heinz Hornhues, Oskar Lafontaine, and Jürgen Reents statements, Apr. 19, 1990; Rudolf Seiters interview, Apr. 19, BPA Dok 1990, VI: 2283 ff; "Glaubwürdigkeit und Würde," *GA*, Apr. 20; "Das Programm," *WamS*, Apr. 22; and Herles, *Nationalrausch*, 219–20.

76. Schevardnadze interviews, Feb. 20 and Mar. 8, 1990, Mitterrand interview, Mar. 25, PBA Dok 1990; "Bush und Kohl sind sich einig," *StZ*, Feb. 26; Beschloss and Talbott, *Highest Levels*, 190 ff.

77. Kohl speech at Cambridge, Mar. 29, 1990, and interview in *Izvestiia*, Apr. 6, BPA Dok 1990; "Frau Thatcher und Kohl," *FAZ*, Mar. 31; Teltschik, *329 Tage*, 157–203; Beschloss and Talbott, *Highest Levels*, 198.

78. Klaus Hartung, *Neunzehnhundertneunundachtzig. Ortsbesichtigungen nach einer Epochenwende* (Frankfurt, 1990), 81 ff; Haug, *Perestroika Journal*, 348, 353, 359, 415 ff.

79. Kallabis, *Ade, DDR!* 216–17; and Ash, *Magic Lantern*, 131 ff.

80. Papers by Christoph Klessmann, Jürgen John, and Konrad H. Jarausch on "Communist Collapse or Civic Revolution?" at the 1991 AHA meeting in Chicago.

81. Philippe Schmitter, "The Consolidation of Democracy and the Choice of Institutions" (MS, Stanford, 1992).

82. "Essener Aufruf zur Politik der Annäherung von BRD und DDR," *FR*, Mar. 24, 1990; Michael Schneider, *Die abgetriebene Revolution* (Berlin, 1990); Thomas Schmid, *Staatsbegräbnis. Von ziviler Gesellschaft* (Berlin, 1990); Peter Decker and Karl Held, *Der Anschluss* (Munich, 1990).

83. Peter Schneider, *Extreme Mittellage. Reise durch das deutsche Nationalgefühl* (Hamburg, 1990) and "Den Völkern Gespött oder Furcht," *ZEIT*, Apr. 6, 1990.

84. Party answers on socialism and unification in *Stern extra zur Wahl* (Hamburg, 1990). See also Zwahr, *Ende einer Selbstzerstörung*, 136 ff.

85. Abenheim, "Volkskammer Elections," Hoover Institution; Wolfgang Bergsdorf, "Von der Vorhut zur Nachhut," *DA* 24 (1992): 133 ff.

Chapter 7

1. Diestel, Gysi, Ullman, Platzeck, and Thierse interview in *taz*, June 30, 1990; "Der Weg zur Währungsunion," *NZ*, June 30; Deutsche Bank, *DDR Perspektiven* (Frankfurt, 1990), 7–8.

2. De Maizière interview, *NZ*, July 2, 1990; Lothar de Maizière and Lutz Wicke, *Öko-Soziale Marktwirtschaft für Ost und West* (Munich, 1990), 171–72; Deutsche Bank, *DDR Themen*, Feb. 7.

3. "Wie der Kontentausch praktisch vonstatten geht," *BZ*, May 26, 1990; "Von jetzt an gilt: 'Ich könnte mir sogar den Schatten kaufen!'" *NZ*, June 30; "Was tun mit der ersten 'harten' Mark?" *Morgen*, June 27; "Tausend Ängste, tausend Hoffnungen," *RM*, June 29.

4. "Ost-Berliner im Konsumfieber?" *Morgen*, June 23, 1990; drawings for "Der kluge Ludwig," Hoover Institution; Deutsche Bank, *German Economic and Monetary Union* (Frankfurt, 1990).

5. "Das neue Geld kommt über Nacht," *NZ*, June 30, 1990; "Die ganze Welt blickt auf uns, ob denn das geht," *Berliner Allgemeine*, June 30; "Ohne Härte keine D-Mark," *JW*, July 2.

6. "Aufs harte Geld geduldig gewartet," *LVZ*, July 2, 1990; Peter Christ and Ralf Neubauer, *Kolonie im eigenen Land* (Berlin, 1991), 93 ff.

7. Hans Klein releases, June 28 and 29, 1990, BPA Dok 1990; "Alu-Chips im feurigen Schlund," *RM*, June 29; "Das Währungsabenteuer," *FR*, June 30.

8. Helmut Kohl speech, June 28, 1990, Hans-Jochen Vogel release and Otto Lambsdorff interview, June 30, BPA Dok 1990; "Ein schneller Aufbruch mit sozialen Härten," *ND*, June 30; "Kohl macht allen Deutschen Mut," *WAZ*, June 30.

9. SMAD order no. 111, June 23, 1948, in *DDR: Dokumente zur Geschichte der DDR 1945–1985*, ed. Hermann Weber (Munich, 1986), 113 ff.

10. Weber, *DDR 1945–1985*, 113 ff; "Der Weg in die Währungsunion," *NZ*, June 30, 1990.

11. Werner Abelshauser, *Wirtschaftsgeschichte der Bundesrepublik Deutschland 1945–1980* (Frankfurt, 1983).

12. Anthony J. Nicholls, "Ludwig Erhard," in *In Search of a Liberal Germany*, ed. Konrad Jarausch and Larry Jones (New York, 1990), 389 ff; and Christ and Neubauer, *Kolonie*, 18 ff.

13. Theo Mönch-Tegeder, "Die demaskierte Ost-Mark," *RM*, Nov. 17, 1989; Klaus von Dohnanyi, *Das deutsche Wagnis* (Munich, 1990), 60 ff.

14. Klaus Müller, "Welcher Währungskurs ist richtig?" *Horizont* no. 2 (1990); Sinn, *Kaltstart*, 60 ff.

15. "Angenommen die D-Mark käme," *Horizont* no. 3 (1990).

16. Matthias Wissmann release, Jan. 21, 1990, BPA Dok 1990; Hartung, *Neunzehnhundertneunundachtzig*, 97 ff.

17. "Wohin geht das Geld," *Morgen*, Apr. 21, 1990; "Verwendung des verfügbaren Monatseinkommens," *Morgen*, July 3.

18. Gunnar Winkler, ed., *Sozialreport DDR 1990* (Bonn, 1990), 123 ff, 157–58; and Günter Fischbar, ed., *DDR Almanach '90* (Bonn, 1990), 29–30.

19. Walter Friedrich, "Mentalitätswandlungen der Jugend in der DDR," *APZG* B 16/17 (1990): 25 ff.

20. Maaz, *Gefühlsstau*, 64 ff; John Borneman, *After the Wall* (New York, 1991), 179 ff.

21. Lemke, *Die Ursachen des Umbruchs*, 187 ff.

22. Antonia Grunenberg, *Aufbruch der inneren Mauer* (Bremen, 1990), 235 ff.

23. Friedrich Schorlemmer interview, *taz*, Nov. 14, 1989; Klaus Humann, *Wir sind das Geld* (Reinbeck, 1990), 16 ff; Maaz, *Gefühlsstau*, 152 ff.

24. "Einbruch beim Zuwachs und Erdrutsch beim Bau," *BZ*, Jan. 22, 1990; Luft interview, *ND*, Feb. 3/4; "Warenproduktion Februar sank auf 87er Volumen," *ND*, Mar. 13; "Soziale Marktwirtschaft," *BZ*, Mar. 22.

25. ZdF-Politbarometer of Jan. 22, Feb. 19, and Mar. 18, 1990, BPA Dok 1990; "Bürger wollen die Einheit zum Nulltarif," *StZ*, Mar. 31; "Deutschstunde," *Capital* no 3 (1990): 127; "Umfrage: Einheit ja, aber ohne Überstürzung," *MP* Mar. 11.

26. "Keiner hat Nachteile zu befürchten," *MP*, Mar. 4, 1990; Genscher, "Die nationale Einheit ist nicht zum Nulltarif zu bekommen," *SDZ*, Feb. 2; de Maizière, "Politik für unser Volk," Apr. 19, BPA Dok 1990, VI: 2261 ff; Jürgen Habermas, "Der DM-Nationalismus," *ZEIT*, Mar. 30, 1990; Teltschik, *329 Tage*, 125–26, 130 ff, 144, 152.

27. "Necker schlägt eine Wirtschafts- und Währungsunion mit der DDR bis 1992 vor," *HB*, Jan. 24, 1990; "Bindung der Ostmark an die DM denkbar," *FAZ*, Feb. 1; Haussmann interview, Feb. 8, BPA Dok 1990; "Schnelle Verwirklichung der Währungsunion kann Strukturprobleme der DDR nicht lösen," *HB*, Feb. 8.

28. Sachverständigenrat, "Sondergutachten," Jan. 20, 1990, Hoover Institution; Green press release, Feb. 7; Rainer Schult interview, Feb. 12, BPA Dok 1990; "Währungsunion jetzt," *ND*, Feb. 9; Jörg Rösler, "Die verschwundene Alternative, *Utopie kreativ* (1991), 7: 48–49.

29. "Frau Matthäus-Maier schlägt eine Währungsunion mit der DDR vor," *FAZ*, Jan. 18, 1990; Matthäus-Maier and Wolfgang Roth release, Feb. 2; Kohl and Waigel interview, BPA Dok 1990; "Der Bundeskanzler will mit Ost-Berlin sofort über Währungsunion verhandeln," *HB*, Feb. 7.

30. Hans Willgerodt, "Kein Platz für Pessimisten," *RM*, Feb. 16, 1990; "Ungeheurer Zielkonflikt," *WW*, Feb. 16; Pöhl interview with *Spiegel*, Feb. 26; and Dohnanyi, *Deutsches Wagnis*, 144 ff.

31. Matthäus-Maier release, Mar. 5, 1990; Pöhl interview, Apr. 1, and Kohl statement Apr. 2 in BPA Dok 1990; "Die Kaufkraft der D-Mark wird im Ostteil deutlich höher sein," *Welt*, Mar. 6.

32. "Bei einem Umtauschkurs von 1:1 sind DDR-Betriebe nicht wettbewerbsfähig," *HB*, March 27, 1990; "CDU Sozialausschüsse bestehen auf Umstellungskurs von 1:1," *OZ*, Mar. 31; Sinn, *Kaltstart*, 52 ff.

33. Theo Waigel interview, Feb. 2, 1990, BPA Dok 1990; "Solidarität und Verantwortung," *Bayernkurier*, Feb. 17; interview, *AAZ*, Mar. 17; Schäuble, *Vertrag*, 100.

34. Romberg interviews: *Welt*, Apr. 14, 1990, *Bremer Nachrichten*, Apr. 21, and *Weserkurier*, Apr. 23; Luft, *Zwischen Wende*, 157.

35. Hans Tietmeyer and Norbert Blüm interviews, and Lafontaine release Apr. 2, 1990, BPA Dok 1990; "Demonstranten in der DDR," *ND*, Apr. 6; and Helmut Schlesinger interview, *SDZ*, Apr. 14.

36. Kohl and Rühe statements, Apr. 23, 1990; "Angebot der Bundesregierung für den Staatsvertrag mit der DDR," Apr. 23; Lafontaine, Romberg and Lutz Hoffmann interviews, Apr. 24, BPA Dok 1990; "Noch gibt es etliche Ungereimtheiten," *ND*, Apr. 26; Deutsche Bank, "Deutsche Währungsunion," Apr. 27; Schäuble, *Vertrag*, 97 ff.

37. "Experts Fear a German Inflation Rise," *NYT*, Apr. 25, 1990; A. M. Rosenthal, "The German Question Remains Open," *NYT*, Apr. 26; EC report, Apr. 28, *BfdiP* (1990) 8: 759 ff; Albrecht, *Abwicklung*, 36–37.

38. Teltschik, *329 Tage*, 207 ff, 211 ff; Schäuble, *Vertrag*, 103 ff.

39. Waigel interview, *WamS*, Apr. 29, 1990; Minister Seiters announcement, May 2, Krause interview, May 2, BPA Dok 1990; "Angebot der Bundesregierung bedarf noch der Modifizierung," *FAZ*, Apr. 26.

40. Hildebrandt, Meckel, Rudi Walter and Romberg interviews, May 3, 1990, BPA Dok 1990; "Mehr war nicht drin, lautete der Kommentar," *RP*, May 5; "Das deutsche Experiment," *SDZ*, May 5; Teltschik, *329 Tage*, 213.

41. Gysi interview, *ND*, May 4, 1990; "Wir werden wieder demonstrieren," *taz*, May 5; Lehmann-Grube interview, *LVZ*, Apr. 24; Jung, "Parteiensystem," 14–15.

42. "Die SPD hat Leipzig erobert," *Wir in Leipzig*, May 7, 1990; "So stimmten die Wähler am Sonntag," *ND*, May 8; Teltschik, *329 Tage*, 224; Jan Wielgohs, "Die Vereinigungen der Ökologie- und Bürgerbewegungen der DDR im Lichte der Kommunalwahlen" (MS Berlin, 1990).

43. Hildebrandt interview, May 8, 1990; de Maizière interview, May 10; Kohl statement, May 14; Johannes Rau interview, May 16; Kurt Biedenkopf interview, May 17, BPA Dok 1990; Waigel interview, *AAZ*, May 7; "Landesweite Warnstreiks in der DDR," *Welt*, May 11; "Blüm: Niemand in der DDR braucht Angst zu haben," *BILD*, May 12; "Staatsvertrag im Entwurf fertig," *ND*, May 14. For results of Eastern pressure see BA Po, DC 20, I/3, vol. 2955.

44. Kohl and de Maizière statements as well as interviews, May 18, 1990; Günter Krause, Hildebrandt, Schroeder and Vogel interviews, May 18; Dregger statement, May 18, BPA Dok 1990; Andre Brie, "Selbstbewusstsein kontra Auslöschung," *ND*, May 19. Cf. Herles, *Nationalrausch*, 236–37; and Teltschik, *329 Tage*, 239 ff.

45. "Vertrag über die Schaffung einer Währungs-, Wirtschafts- und Sozialunion zwischen der BRD und der DDR," May 18, 1990, *BPA-Bulletin* (1990) 63: 517–21.

46. Ingo von Münch, ed., *Die Verträge zur Einheit Deutschlands* (Munich 1991), xv ff, 1 ff; and Dietrich Rauschning, "Der deutsch-deutsche Staatsvertrag als Schritt zur Einheit Deutschlands," *APZG* B33 (1990): 3 ff.

47. SPD press releases, May 16, 21, June 11, 14, 1990; Vogel interviews, May 22, 25, 30; Kohl and Vogel interviews, May 23, June 12; Dregger, "Chronologie einer Niederlage," June 12, and Bundesrat release, June 22, BPA Dok 1990. Herles, *Nationalrausch*, 235–36.

48. "Die Volkskammer war nicht in der Stimmung zum Feiern," *RP*, June 22, 1990; Bundestag, *Stenographische Berichte*, June 21, col. 17141; "Auch der Bundesrat

billigt den Staatsvertrag," *FAZ*, June 23; Eveline Kolloch, "Grösstes Experiment der Finanzgeschichte?" *Horizont* 15 (1990): 6 ff; Bündnis 90 and Greens, *Gemeinsame Erklärung zum Staatsvertrag* (Bonn, 1990). For the committee discussion see BA Po, DA 1, vol. 4580.

49. "DDR-Bürger stürmen jetzt die Kaufhallen," *BR*, May 29, 1990; "Für viele bliebt die neue DM 'erst mal auf der Bank'," *TS*, June 1. See Jutta Chalupsky and Renate Rothmann, *Freier Markt auf nackter Haut* (Berlin, 1991).

50. De Maizière interview, *NRZ*, June 25, 1990; "Die DDR hat bessere Chancen als jedes andere osteuropäische Land," *SDZ*, June 23; "Wirtschafts-, Währungs- und Sozialunion," *CDU-Dokumentation* 18 (1990).

51. Klaus Wolfram, "Die Enteignung der Revolution?" *BZ*, June 20, 1990; Helmut Kohl, "Wohlstand und Sicherheit für alle," *FAZ*, May 28; Kohl and Romberg interviews, May 21, BPA Dok 1990; Theo Waigel, "Der Weg nach Deutschland," *Bayernkurier*, May 26.

52. Karl Otto Pöhl, "Kräftige Starthilfe," *WW*, June 22, 1990; "Ein Vertrag für die Einheit," *FAZ*, May 19; "Übernahme der DDR in die BRD—Ende oder Anfang?" *ND*, June 22.

53. "Start in den Markt," special issue of *WW*, summer 1990; "Viel Neugier, aber noch kein Kaufrausch," *LVZ*, July 3, 1990.

54. "Schwimmen im kalten Wasser," *LVZ*, July 3, 1990; "Money, Money, Money? Kaufrausch blieb aus," *JW*, July 3.

55. "Kauft nicht bei Wucherern," *Spiegel*, July 16, 1990; "Erregte Debatte über unzureichende Versorgungslage," *TS*, July 7; "Mit ALDI-Märkten gegen Willkür des DDR-Handels," *LVZ*, July 6.

56. "Käufergroll und Reaktionen," *LVZ*, July 13, 1990; "Mit Krediten und Export gegen drohenden Kollaps," *LVZ*, July 19.

57. "Das gleicht Kapitulation nach verlorenem Krieg," *ND*, May 18, 1990; "Haben wir umsonst gespart?" *Berliner Allgemeine*, Mar. 9; "Der Sparer bezahlt die Währungsunion mit 3,500 Mk," *Berliner Allgemeine*, May 10.

58. "Warenkorb für einen 4-Personen Arbeiter- und Angestelltenhaushalt in der DDR mit mittlerem Einkommen," *ND*, May 21, 1990. "Was wollen die Verbraucher?" *JW*, July 4; and *NCDDR* 7/8: 149.

59. Jonas Maron and Rainer Schedlinski, *Innenansichten DDR. Letzte Bilder* (Hamburg, 1990); Chapulsky, *Freier Markt*, 68 ff.

60. "Ein Riecher für die eigenen Füsse," *JW*, July 12; "Total abgefahren," *ZEIT*, Aug. 3; and Humann, *Wir sind das Geld*, 61 ff.

61. "Wechselbad der Gefühle," *ZEIT*, July 13, 1990; "Erheblicher Produktionsrückgang," *LVZ*, July 20; Waigel interview, *LVZ*, July 26.

62. Lutz Marz, "Der prämoderne Übergangsmanager," in *Demokratischer Umbruch*, 104 ff; "Der fatale Konsens," *Zeitschrift für sozialistische Politik und Wirtschaft* (1991), 58: 17 ff; Dohnanyi, *Deutsches Wagnis*, 160 ff.

63. Wolfram Krause statements Mar. 1 and 14, 1990, BPA Dok 1990; "Millionen Werktätige arbeiten künftig in GmbH oder in AG," *ND*, Mar. 5, 1990; Gero Neugebauer, "Privatisierung in der ehemaligen DDR. Materialien zur Arbeit der THA," *Berliner Arbeitshefte* no. 58 (1992): 7–8; Herles and Rose, *Vom Runden Tisch*, 222 ff; Modrow, *Aufbruch*, 88 ff. For Ullmann's suggestion see BA Po, DA 3, vol. 2979.

64. "DDR-Gesetzgeber will jetzt wenigstens die Privatisierung," *HB*, June 12, 1990; "Volkseigenes Vermögen wechselt in Privathand," *FR*, June 19; text of

"Treuhandgesetz," *ND*, June 29; Neugebauer, "Privatisierung," 9 ff. For the revised law see BA Po, DC 20, I/3, vol. 2979.

65. "Von der Last erdrückt," *Spiegel*, Aug. 27, 1990; "Die Herrschaft der alten Kader," *FAZ*, Oct. 5; Rohwedder interview, *FAZ*, Oct. 29.

66. Christ-Neubauer, *Kolonie*, 116 ff; Heinz Suhr, *Der Treuhand Skandal* (Frankfurt, 1991), 84–85; Priewe-Hickel, *Preis der Einheit*, 164–65.

67. Rohwedder interview, *WW*, Nov. 23, 1990; Fritz Homann, "Treuhandanstalt: Zwischenbilanz, Perspektiven," *DA* 24 (1991): 1277 ff.

68. Priewe and Hickel, *Preis der Einheit*, 169 ff; Robert Kurz, *Honeckers Rache* (Berlin, 1991), 111 ff.

69. "Treuhand schliesst die Blende der 'Praktika'," *Welt*, Oct. 5, 1990; "Die Herkules-Aufgabe der deutschen Treuhandanstalt," *NZZ*, Nov. 2.

70. Christ-Neubauer, *Kolonie*, 155 ff; Suhr, *Treuhandskandal*, 149 ff; Priewe and Hickel, *Preis der Einheit*, 174 ff.

71. "Brotkorb für Exporte in RWG-Länder hoch gehängt," *HB* Nov. 29, 1990; Christ and Neubauer, *Kolonie*, 192 ff; Sinn, *Kaltstart*, 38 ff.

72. EC Commission memorandum on "Die Gemeinschaft und die deutsche Einigung," Aug. 21, 1990, Hoover Institution; Suhr, *Treuhandskandal*, 182–83; Dohnanyi, *Deutsches Wagnis*, 179 ff. For the cabinet's emergency responses see BA Po, DC 20, I/3, vol. 3025.

73. Katarina Belwe, "Zur Beschäftigungssituation in den neuen Bundesländern," *APZG* 29 (1991): 28 ff; "Frauenpolitische Aspekte der Arbeitsmarktentwicklung in Ost- und Westdeutschland," *DIW Wochenbericht* 31 (1991): 421 ff.

74. Hildebrandt interview, *NZ*, July 23, 1990; Haussmann interview, *NZ*, Aug., 14; Priewe and Hickel, *Preis der Einheit*, 23 ff.

75. Joseph Schumpeter, *Capitalism, Socialism and Democracy* (New York, 1942), 81 ff; Franz Steinkühler, "Treuhand wird den in sie gesetzten Erwartungen bisher nicht gerecht," *HB*, Oct. 19, 1990.

76. "Von der Stalinisten-Diktatur zum Manchester Kapitalismus," *BZ*, July 25, 1990; *DIW Wochenbericht* 42/43 (1991): 589 ff; Priewe and Hickel, *Preis der Einheit*, 174 ff.

77. Ludwig Erhard, "Zur Wiedervereinigung," *WW*, Feb. 9, 1990; material on "Kampagne," June 29, BPA Dok 1990; "Wirtschafts-, Währungs- und Sozialunion," *CDU-Dokumentation* no. 18 (1990).

78. Leaflet, "Was sagt die CDU zum Thema Staatsvertrag mit der DDR" (Bonn, 1990); "Mit dem Staatsvertrag zur deutschen Einheit," *Union in Deutschland* no. 21 (1990); "Der Vereinigungsboom findet nur im Westen statt," *BZ*, No. 1; Dohnanyi, *Deutsches Wagnis*, 157–58.

79. "Weder Kommandowirtschaft noch Marktromantizismus," *ND*, Sept. 15/16, 1990; Herbert Ehrenberg, *Damit keiner unter die Räder kommt* (Cologne, 1990); Gerd Grözinger, *Teures Deutschland* (Berlin, 1990); and Maaz, *Gefühlsstau*, 179 ff.

80. *Spiegel* cover, "Schieber, Schwindler, Spekulanten," Oct. 29, 1990; and "Der Schalck-Skandal," May 6, 1991; Christ and Neubauer, *Kolonie*, 206–207; Suhr, *Treuhandskandal*, 174 ff.

81. Compare Berthold Busch et al., *DDR. Schritte aus der Krise* (Bonn, 1990), with Priewe and Hickel, *Preis der Einheit*, 23 ff. Figures from *DIW. Wochenbericht* (1991) 42/3: 595 ff.

82. Theo Mönch-Tegeder, "Noch stottert der Wundermotor," *RM*, Sept. 28, 1990; Chalupsky, *Freier Markt*, 42 ff.

83. "Höchste Zeit," *Horizont* (1990), 15: 5; Sinn, *Kaltstart*, 104 ff.

84. Maier, "Gibt es einen Sieger der Geschichte?" 197 ff; Karl Otto Pöhl, "Aspekte der deutschen und eropäischen Währungsunion," in Hilmar Hoffmann and Dieter Krause, eds., *Der Umbau Europas* (Frankfurt, 1991), 30 ff.

Chapter 8

1. "Allianz der Ängste," *FAZ*, June 7, 1990; "Abschied vom Gestern," *SDZ*, June 16; Stolpe speech in *BfdiP* 7 (1990): 858 ff.

2. "Hals-über Kopf-Anschluss der DDR an die BRD vom Premier gebremst," *LVZ*, June 18, 1990; and de Maizière interview, *GA*, June 23.

3. Teltschik, *329 Tage*, 319 ff.

4. Hans Klein, *Es begann im Kaukasus. Der entscheidende Schritt in die Einheit Deutschlands* (Frankfurt, 1991), 64 ff.

5. Teltschik, *329 Tage*, 333–34; and Klein, *Kaukasus*, 253–54.

6. Klein, *Kaukasus*, 253–54; and Jochen Franzke, "Kurswechsel Moskaus in der deutschen Frage," *DA* 23 (1991): 1371 ff.

7. Press conference in Shelesnovodsk, July 16 and in Bonn, July 17, 1990, BPA Dok 1990; "Kohl und Gorbatschow einig," *LVZ*, July 17; "Das Tor ist offen," *TS*, July 17; "Kohls grosser Coup," *Spiegel*, July 23; and Klein, *Kaukasus*, 269 ff.

8. Teltschik, *329 Tage*, 339 ff; Shevardnadze, *Zukunft*, 251 ff; and Albrecht, *Abwicklung*, 84 ff.

9. Günter Fischbach, *DDR-Almanach '90* (Bonn, 1990), 36–37; and Fischer Weltalmanach, *Sonderband DDR* (Frankfurt, 1990), 171–72.

10. Jörg Bremer, "Spaziergänge im alten Sperrgebiet," *FAZ*, Feb. 24, 1990.

11. David Marsh, *The Germans: A People at the Cross-Roads* (New York, 1989), 226 ff; Krisch, *GDR*, 43 ff.

12. John Gimbel, *The American Occupation of Germany* (Stanford, 1968).

13. Wolfram F. Hanrieder, *Germany, America, Europe: Forty Years of German Foreign Policy* (New Haven, 1989).

14. Christian Hacke, *Weltmacht wider Willen* (Stuttgart, 1988).

15. Christoph Klessmann, *Die doppelte Staatsgründung* (Göttingen, 1982), 296 ff.

16. Wolfgang Ribbe, "Kritische Anmerkungen zur historischen Berlin-Forschung der DDR," and Peter Jelavich, "Kulturgeschichtliche Bemerkungen zur Berlin-Historiographie" in *Parteilichkeit*, 91–92, 107–108.

17. Sylvia Greiffenhagen, "Die Politische Kultur der Bundesrepublik Deutschland," in *Die Deutschen in ihrer Welt*, ed. Paul Mog (Berlin, 1992), 213 ff; Ralf Rytlewski, "Ein neues Deutschland?" in *Politische Kultur in der DDR*, ed. Hans-Georg Wehling (Stuttgart, 1989), 11 ff.

18. Ursula Feist, "Zur politischen Akkulturation der vereinten Deutschen," *APZG* B11/12 (1991): 21 ff.

19. Menge, *Ohne uns*, 12 ff; Golombeck, *Dagewesen*, 13 ff.

20. Essays in Werner Weidenfeld and Hartmut Zimmermann, eds., *Deutschland-Handbuch. Eine doppelte Bilanz 1949–1989* (Bonn, 1989).

21. Wolf Oschlies, *"Vierzig zu Null im Klassenkampf?" Sprachliche Bilanz von vier*

Jahrzehnten DDR (Melle, 1990); Rheinischer Merkur, ed., *Zurück nach Deutschland* (Bonn, 1990), 28 ff.

22. Thomas Koch, "Deutsch-deutsche Einigung als Kulturproblem," *DA* (1991) 24: 16 ff; Dirk Verheyen, *The German Question* (Boulder, 1991), 82 ff.

23. Categories from Hans-Joachim Althaus and Paul Mog on "Grundmuster Deutscher Mentalität," *Die Deutschen*, 43 ff; Maaz, *Gefühlsstau*, 9 ff; Lothar Baier, *Volk ohne Zeit* (Berlin, 1990), 103 ff.

24. Marcuse, *A German Way of Revolution*, 25 ff.

25. Hartmut Jäckel, "Unser schiefes DDR-Bild," *DA* 23 (1990): 1557; Gerd Meyer, "Die westdeutsche DDR- und Deutschlandforschung im Umbruch," *DA* 25 (1992): 273 ff.

26. Manfred Stolpe, "Die Erinnerung hat zum Ziel geführt," in his *Den Menschen Hoffnung geben* (Berlin, 1991), 258–59. See Günter Gaus, *Wo Deutschland liegt. Eine Ortsbeschreibung* (Hamburg, 1983).

27. Rotfeld and Stützle, *Germany*, 76 ff; Kaiser, *Vereinigung*, 94–95.

28. "Ist Deutschenhass nur ein zynischer Trick?" *Welt*, May 5, 1990; Shevardnadze, *Zukunft*, 238–39; Hans-Dietrich Genscher, *Zukunftsverantwortung. Reden* (Berlin, 1990), 153 ff.

29. Meckel interview, May 4, 1990; Genscher speech and interview, May 5; Baker address, BPA Dok 1990; Albrecht, *Abwicklung*, 41 ff. For Meckel's policy see BA Po, DC 20, I/3, vol., 3009. Cf. Kvitsinskii, *Sturm*, 11 ff; and Szabo, *Diplomacy*, 79 ff.

30. Teltschik interview, May 4, 1990, Kohl declaration, May 6, and Shevardnadze interview, May 7, in BPA Dok 1990; "Fortschritte an der Bonner Deutschlandkonferenz," *NZZ*, May 8; Teltschik, *329 Tage*, 217 ff; Shevardnadze, *Zukunft*, 244 ff; Klein, *Kaukasus*, 241 ff; and Beschloss and Talbott, *Highest Levels*, 207–8.

31. Genscher interview, June 6, 1990, BPA Dok 1990; Rupert Scholz, "Deutsche Frage und europäische Sicherheit," *EA* (1990) 7: 239 ff; Shevardnadze, *Zukunft*, 237 ff; Albrecht, *Abwicklung*, 45 ff.

32. De Maizière speech, May 18, 1990; Nikolai Portugalov article, *Welt*, May 21, 1990; Valentin Falin interview, *ND*, May 21 in BPA Dok 1990; Teltschik, *329 Tage*, 192–193, 205 ff, 226 ff, 230 ff, 243 ff, 259 ff.

33. Roland Dumas interview, May 19, 1990 and Genscher speeches May 26 and 29, and interview, June 9, BPA Dok 1990; Teltschik, *329 Tage*, 207 ff, 241–42, 244–45, 247–48; Shevardnadze, *329 Tage*, 246–47.

34. "Der überzeugendste Verbündete," *FAZ*, May 16, 1990; Teltschik, *329 Tage*, 237 ff; Pond, *After the Wall*, 67 ff.

35. Geissler interview, June 16, 1990, BPA Dok 1990; Kaiser, *Vereinigung*, 89 ff, 226 ff.

36. Genscher to Skubiszewski, June 21, 1990; Klein press release, June 22; Herbert Czaja interview, June 22; Alfred Dregger interview, June 24, BPA Dok 1990; Teltschik, *329 Tage*, 249–50, 253 ff, 261.

37. Genscher interviews and Meckel interview, June 22, 1990, BPA Dok 1990; Shevardnadze, *Zukunft*, 249–49; Albrecht, *Abwicklung*, 73 ff. See also Kvitsinskii, *Sturm*, 40 ff.

38. "Kein Durchbruch aber doch passable Ausblicke," *ND*, June 25, 1990; "Westmächte wollen Singularisierung Deutschlands nicht akzeptieren," *Welt*, June 26; James Baker interview, *Amerika-Dienst*, June 27; Teltschik, *329 Tage*, 284–85; and Bechloss and Talbott, *Highest Levels*, 232–33.

39. Genscher interview, July 5, 1990, and Wörner interview, July 4, BPA Dok 1990; Teltschik, *329 Tage*, 262, 281–82, 288, 291–92; Albrecht *Abwicklung*, 89 ff.

40. Kohl statement and interviews, July 5, 1990; Wörner interview, July 5; London Declaration, July 6, in BPA Dok 1990; "NATO will weg von Konfrontation," *LVZ*, July 7/8; "Wirtschaftsgipfel in Houston begrüsst deutsche Einigung," *TS*, July 11; Teltschik, *329 Tage*, 298–310; Shevardnadze, *Zukunft*, 251; Beschloss and Talbott, *Highest Levels*, 234 ff.

41. "Eher geteiltes Deutschland eine Gefahr," *BR*, May 10, 1990; Dashichev interview, June 5; Albrecht, *Abwicklung*, 54 ff.

42. Gorbachev interview, June 13; "Lange wurde in Moskau die Existenz einer deutschen Frage geleugnet," *FAZ*, May 28; Shevardnadze, *Zukunft*, 250–51; and Teltschik, *329 Tage*, 297–98, 304–305, 311.

43. Transcript of joint press conference, July 16, 1990, Kohl and Gorbachev interviews of the same day, and other documents in BPA Dok 1990. See also Kvitsinskii, *Sturm*, 47ff.

44. Teltschik, *329 Tage*, 340; Shevardnadze, *Zukunft*, 252 ff; Klein, *Kaukasus*, 274 ff; Albrecht, *Abwicklung*, 86–87.

45. Gorbachev and Kohl interviews, July 17, 1990, BPA Dok 1990; "Der zweite Durchbruch," *FAZ*, July 17; "Der Geist von Schelesnowodsk," *SDZ*, July 18; Beschloss and Talbott, *Highest Levels*, 238 ff.

46. "Zwei, die sich näher kommen," *RM*, July 20; Beschloss and Talbott, *Highest Levels*, 240. During the talks the Soviet government promised to find a solution for the two million Volga Germans, dispersed by Stalin.

47. Kohl press conference and interview, July 17, 1990; Lambsdorff, Ehmke, Vollmer, de Maizière, and Meckel interviews, July 17; Weizsäcker interview, July 19, BPA Dok 1990; "Am Ende ein Gefühl als könne man Berge versetzen," *KSA*, July 18; "In der Stunde des Sieges blieb der Kanzler gelassen," *NRZ*, July 18; Klein, *Kaukasus*, 324 ff.

48. Survey of TV comments, July 16, 1990, BPA Dok 1990; "Gorbi gibt ganz Deutschland frei," *BILD*, July 17; "Kohl im Glück," *WAZ*, July 17; "Einheit auf Kredit," *SB*, July 20; "Eine neue Epoche," *Welt*, July 18; "Bundeskanzler Kohl hat sein politisches Lebensziel erreicht," *BR*, July 18; "Die Welt staunt über Kohl," *BILD*, July 18.

49. "Kohl beruhigt die Verbündeten," *FAZ*, July 18; "Die Prawda zu Kohl in Moskau," *FAZ*, July 21; "Ein souveränes Deutschland in Europa," *NZZ*, July 22; Teltschik, *329 Tage*, 343–44; Albrecht, *Abwicklung*, 108 ff.

50. Kohl interview, July 17, 1990; Shevardnadze and Baker statements, and Herbert Hupka interview, July 18, BPA Dok 1990; "Zwei-plus-vier-Gespräche in Paris erfolgreich abgeschlossen," *FAZ*, July 18; Shevardnadze, *Zukunft*, 258–59; Teltschik, *329 Tage*, 344–45.

51. ZdF-Politbarometer, June 17, 1990; Infas Meinungsreport, June 26, BPA Dok 1990; *Spiegel* surveys, July 30 and Aug. 27.

52. Zentralinstitut für Jugendforschung, "Ergebnisse der DDR-repräsentativen Meinungsumfrage M 8" (MS, Leipzig, 1990); and "Trend zur Befürwortung der Einheit hat sich stabilisiert," *TS*, Aug. 16, 1990; Albrecht, *Abwicklung*, 54 ff.

53. Wolfgang Schäuble, "Der Einigungsvertrag in seiner praktischen Bedeutung," *DA* 25 (1992): 233 ff.

54. "Schäuble," *Welt*, June 27, 1990; Herta Däubler-Gmelin interview and SPD release, June 27, BPA Dok 1990; Schäuble, *Vertrag*, 14 ff.

55. "Dann bin ich fällig," *Spiegel*, Oct. 15, 1990; Schäuble, *Vertrag*, 13 ff.

56. Eilitz, "Günter Krause," *Sie waren dabei*, 162 ff.

57. Schäuble interview, July 2, 1990 and Lafontaine interview, July 5, BPA Dok 1990; "Bonn will die Einheit nun schnell," *FR*, July 3; Schäuble, *Vertrag*, 53–54, 107–122; Teltschik, *329 Tage*, 199.

58. "Überleitung," *ND*, June 27, 1990; "De Maizière will den Beitritt 'so schnell wie möglich und so geordnet wie nötig,'" *FAZ*, July 21; Albrecht, *Abwicklung*, 117 ff. For East German preparations see BA Po, DA 1, vol. 4581 and DC 20, I/3, vol. 3024.

59. SPD, "Wesentliche Positionen," July 6, 1990, Hoover Institution; "Ziel ist eine abschliessende völkerrechtliche Regelung," *GA*, July 7; "Erste Verhandlungsrunde in Ostberlin," *NZZ*, July 8.

60. "Offene Linie," *Spiegel*, July 9, 1990; Schäuble, *Vertrag*, 123–39.

61. "Für DDR-Bürger noch viele Fragen offen," *ND*, July 25, 1990; "DDR-Entwurf für den Vertrag über die Einheit," *MP*, Aug. 2; "Ein guter Tag für Deutschland," *FAZ*, Aug. 3.

62. Richard Schröder interview, Aug. 2, 1990, BPA Dok 1990; "Aus Rohskizze wurde Entwurf," *FR*, Aug. 6; Schäuble, *Vertrag*, 150–184.

63. De Maizière, Lambsdorff and Schäuble interviews, July 24, 1990, BPA Dok 1990; "Lambsdorff verteidigt die DDR-Liberalen," *FAZ*, July 25; "Standhaft steht Lothar de Maizière im Strudel," *StZ*, July 26; "Eine Schar von Laienspielern?" *FR*, Aug. 16; Schäuble, *Vertrag*, 140–41.

64. De Maizière, Romberg, Thierse interviews, Aug. 15, 16, 19, 1990; Manfred Becker, Rühe interviews, Aug. 17, BPA Dok 1990; "Ost-SPD überstimmte Franktionschef und Minister," *MP*, Aug. 21; Richard Schröder interview, *taz*, Aug. 23; Schäuble, *Vertrag*, 185–86. For the cabinet flap see BA Po, DC 20, I/3, vol. 3038.

65. De Maizière interview, Aug. 19, 1990; Krause and Lafontaine interviews, Aug. 20, BPA Dok 1990; "Der Einigungsvertrag droht zu scheitern," *FR*, Aug. 18; "De Maizière warnt die Sozialdemokraten," *FAZ*, Aug. 20; Schäuble, *Vertrag*, 188 ff.

66. Lafontaine interview, Aug. 20, 1990, PBA Dok 1990; "SPD Länder nennen Bedingungen für Zustimmung zum Einigungsvertrag," *TS*, Aug. 21; "Einigungsvertrag regelt Neugestaltung des DDR-Rundfunks," *TS*, Aug. 27; Schäuble, *Vertrag*, 192–208.

67. Krause interviews, Aug. 24 and 25, 1990; Lafontaine and Schäuble interviews, Aug. 27; SPD release, Aug. 27, BPA Dok 1990; "Kohl gibt dem Verlangen von SPD und FDP nach," *SDZ*, Aug. 25; "Kohl berät mit Parteivorsitzenden über den Einigungsvertrag," *FAZ*, Aug. 27.

68. Bundesrat press release, Aug. 30, 1990, BPA Dok 1990; Schäuble, *Vertrag*, 209–28.

69. Adam-Schwätzer interview, Aug. 16, 1990; Boetsch interview, Aug. 23, BPA Dok 1990; "Abtreibung muss strafbar bleiben," *Welt*, July 23; "Kein Entscheid ohne uns," *FR*, Aug. 14; "Abtreibung im einigen Deutschland," *FAZ*, Aug. 23.

70. Lambsdorff interview, Aug. 27, 1990; Schäuble and Däubler-Gmelin interviews, Aug. 30, BPA Dok 1990; "FDP stellt sich beim Streit über Abtreibungsrecht auf die Seite der SPD," *SDZ*, Aug. 28; "Die SPD bezeichnet den Kompromiss zum Paragraphen 218 als Durchbruch," *FAZ*, Sept. 2; Schäuble, *Vertrag*, 229–50.

71. Lafontaine interview, *Abendzeitung*, Aug. 26; Schäuble interview, Aug. 27, BPA Dok 1990; Schäuble, *Vertrag*, 254 ff.

72. "Die wichtigsten Hindernisse sind beseitigt," *SDZ*, Aug. 29; "Es wäre einfacher gegangen," *Welt*, Aug. 31; Sinn, *Kaltstart*, 91 ff.

73. "Gespenstische Aussicht auf noch perfektere Bespitzelung," *ND*, Aug. 2, 1990; "Gesetz über Stasi-Akten bekräftigt," *LVZ*, Aug. 31; "Vernichtung erforderlich," *Spiegel*, Sept. 3.

74. Joachim Gauck, *Die Stasi-Akten. Das unheimliche Erbe der DDR* (Reinbeck, 1991), 101 ff; and Schäuble, *Vertrag*, 265–77. For the final compromises see BA Po, DC 20, I/3, vols. 3052 and 3055.

75. De Maizière and Schäuble speeches, Krause interview, Dieter Vogel release, Aug. 31, 1990, BPA Dok 1990; "Eines der bedeutendsten Vertragswerke," *TS*, Sept. 1; "Um 13.42 hatte die Spalterflagge endgültig ausgedient," *FR*, Sept. 1; Schäuble, *Vertrag*, 251–54.

76. Statements by Rühe, Thierse, SPD press service, and Vollmer, Aug. 31, 1990; Lafontaine and Vogel interviews, Aug. 31, BPA Dok 1990; "Ein historischer Tag für Deutschland," *Welt*, Aug. 31; "Endlich einig," *OZ*, Sept. 1; and "Eine Beamtenleistung," *FAZ*, Sept. 1.

77. Schäuble, "Heute ist ein Tag der Freude und Zuversicht für die Deutschen," *HA*, Sept. 1, 1990; Münch, *Verträge zur Einheit*, 43–569.

78. Klaus Stern, "Der verfassungsändernde Charakter des Einigungsvertrages," and Johannes Wasmuth, "Das Regelwerk des Einigungsvertrages," *Deutsch-Deutsche Rechts-Zeitschrift* 1 (1990): 289 ff.

79. De Maizière interviews and TV comment, Aug. 31, Sept. 1 and 2, 1990, BPA Dok 1990; "Die Einheit der Deutschen leuchtet schwarz-rot-gold," *NRZ*, Sept. 1; "Historisch," *ND*, Sept. 1; Schäuble, *Vertrag*, 284 ff.

80. Albrecht, *Abwicklung*, 117–18; Schäuble, "Einigungsvertrag," 241–42.

81. Kohl interview, *Welt*, March 30, 1990; De Maizière interviews, *Quick*, Aug. 23 and *ND*, Sept. 7; Falin interview, *ZEIT*, March 29; Kohl speech to refugees, Aug. 17, BPA Dok 1990.

82. Schäuble, *Der Vertrag*, 284 ff; Albrecht, *Abwicklung*, 123–24.

83. Genscher interviews, Aug. 8, 20, 1990, BPA Dok 1990; "Nur vier Prozent der Bürger sind gegen die deutsche Einheit," *SDZ*, Aug. 18; Schneider, *Abgetriebene Revolution*, 138–39.

84. Teltschik, *329 Tage*, 223, 237, 321, 348; Hartung, *Neunzehnhundertneunundachtzig*, 112 ff; Baier, *Volk ohne Zeit*, 99 ff.

85. Renate Fritsch-Bournazel, "German Unification," *GSR* 14 (1991): 575 ff; Wilhelm Bruns, "Die Regelung der äusseren Aspekte der deutsche Einigung," *DA* 23 (1990), 1726 ff.

86. Waigel interview July 18, 1990; Weizsäcker interview, July 22, BPA Dok 1990; Falin and Bahr interviews, *ZEIT*, March 29, 1990.

87. "Christa Wolf ruft nach mehr Selbstbewusstsein," *StZ*, July 9, 1990; Günter Grass interview, *FR*, July 27; Reich, *Rückkehr nach Europa*, 220 ff, 242 ff.

88. Schäuble, "Einigungsvertrag," 234–35; Dohnanyi, *Deutsches Wagnis*, 306 ff.

Chapter 9

1. "Am Ende Schwüre, Anarchie und etwas Wehmut," *SDZ*, Oct. 2, 1990; "Wir können uns selbst einen Nachruf halten," *BR*, Oct. 3.

2. "Springt der Götterfunke der neunten Sinfonie über in eine neue Zeit?" *Welt*, Oct. 3, 1990; "Die Deutschen wissen zu wenig von einander," *NZ*, Oct. 3; "20 Fragen, die für alle Deutschen wichtig sind," *Quick*, Oct. 4.

3. De Maizière speech, Oct. 2, *Dokumentation zum 3. Oktober* (Bonn, 1990); "Die einzigartige Nacht der Einheit," *TS*, Oct. 4, 1990; "Heute Nacht freuen wir uns vor allem von innen," *FR*, Oct. 4.

4. Weizsäcker, "Dem Frieden der Welt dienen," *BZ*, Oct. 3, 1990; "Plötzlich war die Einheit da," *KSA*, Oct. 4; "Gegen das deutsche Einerlei," *taz*, Oct. 4; "Strassenfeste und Feiern in vielen deutschen Städten," *TS*, Oct. 4.

5. Weizsäcker speech, Oct. 3, 1990, *Dokumentation*, 39 ff; "Staatsakt zum 3. Oktober in der Berliner Philharmonie," *TS*, Oct. 4; "Feiern zur Einheit in würdigem Rahmen und mit richtigen Tönen," *RP*, Oct. 4.

6. "Die Freudentränen waren längst geweint," *BZ*, Oct. 4, 1990; "Halt's Maul Deutschland," *taz*, Oct. 4; "Rufe nach dem Arbeitslager," *FR*, Oct. 5; "Ein harmonisches Fest," *FAZ*, Oct. 4.

7. CDU release, "Wir feiern den Tag der deutschen Einheit," BPA Dok 1990; "Ein Volksfest," *KSA*, Oct. 4, 1990. Cf. George L. Mosse, *The Nationalization of the Masses* (New York, 1975).

8. "Eine Nacht der Würde," *BR*, Oct. 4, 1990; "Freude, Nachdenklichkeit," *Welt*, Oct. 4; "Gedämpft beschwingt," *FR*, Oct. 4; "Freude," *ND*, Oct. 4.

9. Werner Weidenfeld, ed., *Geschichtsbewusstsein der Deutschen* (Cologne, 1987); and Antonia Grunenberg, ed., *Welche Geschichte wählen wir?* (Hamburg, 1992).

10. Charles S. Maier, *The Unmasterable Past* (Cambridge, Mass., 1988); Konrad H. Jarausch, "Removing the Nazi Stain?" *GSR* 11 (1988): 285–86.

11. See Hans-Ulrich Wehler, *The German Empire, 1871–1918* (Leamington Spa, 1985) versus *The Other Germany: A Reconsideration of the Imperial Era*, ed. Joachim Remak et al. (Boulder, 1988).

12. Peter Glotz, *Der Irrweg des Nationalstaats* (Stuttgart, 1990); Ralf Dahrendorf, "Angst vor der Nation," *Liberal* 32 (1990): 85 ff; Roland Hahn, "Die Idee der Nation und die Lösung der deutschen Frage," *APZG* B29 (1990): 3–12.

13. Lutz Niethammer, *Lebensgeschichte und Sozialkultur im Ruhrgebiet 1930 bis 1960* (Berlin, 1983); Michael Marrus, *The Holocaust in History* (Hanover, 1987).

14. Grass, "Kleine Nestbeschmutzerrede," *taz*, Sept. 28, 1990; Michael Lerner, "No to German Reunification," *Tikkun*, Mar./Apr. 1990; Kohl, "Verantwortung des vereinigten Deutschland gegenüber dem jüdischen Volk," *Allgemeine jüdische Wochenzeitung*, Sept. 20.

15. Wilfried Schubarth et al., "Verordneter Antifaschismus und die Folgen," *APZG* B9 (1991): 3 ff; and Konrad H. Jarausch, "The Failure of East German Anti-Fascism," *GSR* 14 (1991): 85 ff.

16. Rolf Reissig interview, *KSA*, Aug. 18, 1990; Stephan Heym interview, *Weserkurier*, Nov. 9; Hans Mayer, *Der Turm von Babel* (Frankfurt, 1991).

17. Christian Meier, *Deutsche Einheit als Herausforderung* (Munich, 1990), 58 ff.

18. Niklas Luhmann, "Dabeisein und Dagegensein," *FAZ*, Aug. 22, 1990; Ernst Nolte, "Untergang der Bundesrepublik," *FAZ*, Sept. 5.

19. "Das Chequers-Protokoll," *BfdiP* (1990) 8: 1021 ff; Timothy G. Ash, "Wie es eigentlich war," *FAZ*, July 18, 1990; Fritz Stern, "Die zweite Chance," *FAZ*, July 26; Fritsch-Bournazel, *Europa*, 231 ff.

20. "Saying the Unsayable about the Germans," *Spectator*, July 14, 1990; "Angst vor einem vereinten Deutschland?" *Rheinpfalz*, July 31; "Vertrauensvorschuss für das neue Deutschland," *TS*, Oct. 6; Wickert, *Angst*, 141–42.

21. Wolfgang Kil on "the spiritual colonization of the GDR," *taz*, June 29, 1990; Glotz, *Der Irrweg*, 17 ff; Thomas Nipperdey, "Die Deutschen wollen und dürfen eine Nation sein," *FAZ*, July 13, 1990.

22. Hans-Peter Schwarz, "Das Ende der Identitätsneurose," *RM*, Sept. 7, 1990; and Klaus von Dohnanyi, *Deutsches Wagnis*, 323–24.

23. Helmut Berchin, "Quo vadis, Wiedervereinigung? Wege eines Wortes," *DA* 23 (1990): 1266 ff; Meier, *Deutsche Einheit*, 46 ff.

24. Stefan Heym, "Ungleicher Bund," *FR* Oct. 2, 1990; Chapulsky, *Freier Markt*, 138 ff.

25. Lutz Rathenow, "Mit Befürchtungen, aber ohne Angst," *GA*, Sept. 29; "Was wird bleiben von der DDR?—Wir!" *ND*, Oct. 1; Eppelmann, *Wendewege*, 168 ff; Weizsäcker interview, *BUNTE*, Sept. 27, and Luhmann, "Dabeisein und Dagegensein," *FAZ*, Aug. 22.

26. "Nicht im Handstreich," *TS*, June 19, 1990; *NCDDR* 7/8: 86 ff, 92.

27. Ullmann interview, *taz*, June 19, 1990; "Die 'klugen' 23er aus Ost-Berlin," *FR*, June 19; Schäuble, *Vertrag*, 79–80, 107 ff. See also *Volkskammer Protokolle*, 10. Wahlperiode, vol. 28.

28. Seiters interview, *WamS*, Aug. 5, 1990; Schäuble interview, *GA*, Aug. 8; Richard Schröder, "Erblast der Gespensterfurcht," *FAZ*, Sept. 29; *NCDDR* 7/8: 158, 161; Schäuble, *Vertrag*, 158–59.

29. Lafontaine interview, Aug. 21, 1990; Thierse interview, Aug. 22; Seiters interview, Aug. 23; Kohl statement, Aug. 24, BPA Dok 1990; "De Maizière: Beitrittserklärung mit einem gewissen Mass an Würde abgeben," *TS*, Aug. 22; "Der Weg ist frei," *GA*, Aug. 24; *Volkskammer Protokolle*, vol. 29.

30. Genscher interview, Sept. 11, 1990, BPA Dok 1990; "Genugtuung Bonns über den Moskauer Vertrag," *NZZ*, Sept. 14; Albrecht, *Abwicklung*, 142 ff.

31. "Ein Ereignis mit Stimmungselementen," *SDZ*, Sept. 15, 1990; Teltschik, *329 Tage*, 359 ff; Rotfeld, *Germany and Europe*, 191 ff; Kvitsinskii, *Sturm*, 53 ff.

32. Genscher interviews, Sept. 12 and 13, 1990; Schevardnadze interview, Sept. 13, BPA Dok 1990; "Nachts klingelte Genscher den Kollegen Baker aus dem Bett," *GA*, Sept. 14; Albrecht, *Abwicklung*, 135 ff.

33. Genscher declaration, Sept. 12, 1990, and interview, Sept. 14; Ehmke statement and de Maizière interview, Sept. 12; media summary, Sept. 12, BPA Dok 1990; Shevardnadze, *Zukunft*, 259 ff.

34. "Mit einem Briefwechsel soll das brisante Kapitel Stasi-Akten ad acta gelegt werden," *HB*, Sept. 12, 1990; "Stasi und noch kein Ende," *LVZ*, Sept. 29/30.

35. Gauck, *Stasi-Akten*, 102 ff; Schäuble, *Vertrag*, 277 ff; *NCDDR* 7/8: 222, 226, 241. For the final East German demands see BA Po, DA 1, vol. 4582.

36. Schäuble speeches, Sept. 5, 7, 1990; Däubler-Gmelin, Lambsdorff, and Bötsch speeches, Sept. 5, BPA Dok 1990; "Kohl liess seinem Innenminister den Vortritt," *GA*, Sept. 6.

37. De Maizière speech, Sept. 6, 1990, *Regierungspressedienst DDR*, no. 36; "DDR kann erhobenen Hauptes beitreten," *FAZ*, Sept. 14; "Mehrheit im DDR-Parlament für den Einigungsvertrag gesichert," *TS*, Sept. 14.

38. Genscher, Lafontaine, Schäuble and Czaja speeches, Sept. 20, 1990, Bundestag, *Stenographische Berichte*, 226. Sitzung, cols. 17803 ff; "Schlussdebatten," *GA*, Sept. 21; "Ausdauer für die Einheit," *FR*, Sept. 21.

39. *Für ein liberales Deutschland* (Aug. 11/12, 1990); *Manifest zur Wieder-*

herstellung der Einheit der SPD (Sept. 27); "Zum Abschied kam Brandt als Tröster," *HA*, Sept. 27.

40. CDU unification manifesto, *CDU Dokumentation* no. 31 (1990); De Maizière interviews, *AAZ*, Sept. 26, *Stuttgarter Nachrichten*, Sept. 27, 1990; "CDU nach 45-jähriger Trennung wieder vereint," *LVZ*, Oct. 2.

41. "Die 144 neuen Abgeordneten des deutschen Parlaments," *FAZ*, Oct. 5, 1990.

42. "Erwacht der Reichstag zu einem neuen, langen Leben?" *FAZ*, Oct. 5, 1990; Kohl speech, Oct. 4, *CDU Dokumentation* no. 32 (1990).

43. Kohl, "Der Tag der Wiedervereinigung ist ein Tag der Freude," *BUNTE*, Sept. 27, 1990; contribution to *FAZ*, Oct. 2, and interview with *Pravda*, Oct. 3; de Maizière, "Wir werden nicht vergessen, woher wir kommen," *NZ*, Oct. 2.

44. Genscher letter to Halle, Sept. 28, 1990; and article in *Morgen*, Oct. 3; SPD, "Aufruf zum 3. Oktober 1990," BPA Dok 1990; "In Freiheit zur Einheit," *NZ*, Oct. 3.

45. Leonhard interview, *taz*, Oct. 2, 1990; "Grass: Einheit löst unsere Probleme nicht," *Express*, Oct. 4.

46. Hans Modrow, "Eine lebenswerte Welt übergeben," *Morgen*, Oct. 3, 1990; Lafontaine, "Die Mühen der Ebene," *Passauer Neue Presse*, Oct. 3; Joschka Fischer, "Hurra, Deutschland," *Spiegel*, Oct. 1.

47. "Sympathie und Gelassenheit überwiegen schlechte Erinnerungen," *FAZ*, Oct. 1, 1990; Albrecht, *Abwicklung*, 139; Harold James, ed., *When the Wall Came Down: Reactions to German Unification* (New York, 1992).

48. "Stimmen aus dem Ausland," *RM*, Sept. 28, 1990; "USA: Den kalten Krieg am Ende doch gewonnen," *Weserkurier*, Oct. 3; "Kein Grund sich mit den Deutschen zu freuen," *Welt*, Oct. 3.

49. Back cover of *Telegraph*, Feb. 6, 1990; mainstream caricature, summer 1990; Wolfgang Marienfeld, *Die Geschichte des Deutschlandproblems im Spiegel der politischen Karikatur* (Hameln, 1990), 249–50.

50. Bensch in *HB*, May 17, 1990; Lurie cartoon, reprinted in *Spiegel*, Oct. 8; Egon Bahr, "Spätere Liebe nicht ausgeschlossen," *ZEIT*, Dec. 14.

51. "Chancen eines neuen Deutschlands," *taz*, Oct. 4, 1990; Hartung, *Neunzenhundertneunundachtzig*, 178 ff.

52. "Frappierende Übereinstimmung," *BR*, Oct. 2, 1990; Schäuble, *Vertrag*, 286–87.

53. "Länder oder Bezirke?" *Sonntag* no. 5 (1990): 10; "Fünf sind besser als eins—aber sind sie optimal?" *ND*, June 21; Karlheinz Blaschke, "Alte Länder—Neue Länder," *APZG* B27 (1990): 39 ff. For the restoration of the States see BA Po, DC 20, I/3, vol. 2947.

54. "Fünf Länder nun perfekt—Berlin mit Länderbefugnis," *LVZ*, July 23, 1990; Deutsche Bank, *The New German Federal States* (Frankfurt, 1990).

55. "Profis gefragt," *HA*, Aug. 29, 1990; "Wer nach den Kosten fragt ist eine Krämerseele," *RP*, Sept. 27; "Es ist Wahlkampf—und keiner geht hin," *SDZ*, Oct. 2.

56. "Lafontaine schlägt in der DDR Unlust an der Politik entgegen," *WR*, Sept. 20, 1990; "Die Bundesratsmehrheit der SPD in der Schwebe," *NZZ*, Oct. 11.

57. "Wahlergebnisse nach Ländern," *Welt*, Oct. 16, 1990; "Geringe Wahlbeteiligung und landspezifische Abstimmungen," *HA*, Oct. 16; "Vier der fünf ostdeutschen Länder an die CDU," *NZZ*, Oct. 17.

58. Allensbach surveys Oct. 9 and 16, 1990, BPA Dok 1990; Rühe and Thierse interviews, Oct. 14; Berlin discussion, Oct. 14; Bonn debate, Oct. 14, in BPA Dok 1990; "Triumph des Kanzlers," *HB*, Oct. 15; and "Eine Banane reicht zur Erklärung nicht aus," *StZ*, Nov. 5.

59. Interviews of Biedenkopf, Duchac, Gies, Gomolka, Stolpe, and others, Oct. 14 and 15, BPA Dok 1990; "Biedenkopf, Gies und Gomolka zu Ministerpräsidenten gewählt," *FAZ*, Oct. 29; "Stolpe zum Ministerpräsidenten von Brandenburg gewählt," *FAZ*, Nov. 2.

60. "Die Zeit des Leidens wird noch kommen," *FR*, Oct. 15, 1990; "Schwieriger Aufbau der Länderstrukturen im Gebiet der ehemaligen DDR," *NZZ*, Nov. 28; Chapulsky, *Freier Markt*, 41 ff.

61. Stolpe interviews, Aug. 30, and Oct. 14, 24, 26, 1990, BPA Dok 1990; interviews in *MP*, Oct. 16 and *WR*, Oct. 31; "Ampel auf Demokratie," *taz*, Oct. 26; "Manfred Stolpe," *Sie waren dabei*, 127 ff.

62. Biedenkopf interviews, Aug. 28, and Oct. 14, 21, 27, 1990, BPA Dok 1990; "Der Wille suchte sich die Pflicht," *RM*, Aug. 31; "Nach sieben Stunden kann Biedenkopf strahlen," *HA*, Oct. 29; "Den sozialen Rechtstaat durch ökologische Dimensionen ergänzen," *FR*, Nov. 22.

63. "Ostberliner Koalition wegen Streit um Wahlrecht weiter in der Zerreissprobe," *TS*, July 23, 1990; Schäuble, *Vertrag*, 82–97.

64. "Die erforderliche Mehrheit stimmte für den Wahlvertrag," *LVZ*, Aug. 23, 1990; text of Bundesverfassungsgericht judgment, Sept. 29, Hoover Institution; election treaty in Münch, *Verträge*, 25 ff.

65. "Kanzler-Wahl," *WamS*, Oct. 21, 1990; "Ein Jäger läuft ins Leere," *Sbl*, Nov. 30; and Dirk Honholz, "Die Wahl zum 12. Deutschen Bundestag am 2. Dezember, 1990" (MS, 1990), 17 ff.

66. "Die Furcht vor zuviel Zuversicht," *Sbl*, Nov. 2, 1990; "Völlig lustlos zum vierten Urnengang," *BR*, Nov. 26; "Die Verlierer stehen schon fest," *BILD*, Dec. 2.

67. "Jeder vierte SPD-Wähler will Kohl wählen," *NP*, Sept. 24, 1990; Infas report, Sept. 25, BPA Dok 1990; Lafontaine, "Lasst uns kämpfen!" *Vorwärts*, Sept. 1; "Deutschland: Ökologisch, sozial und wirtschaftlich stark," *Vorwärts*, Nov. 1; "SPD kann gewinnen," *KSA*, Sept. 27.

68. Posters, "Der neue Weg," Hoover Institution; "Ein Oskar für die Umwelt," flyer; "Mit uns gelingt's," *TS*, Nov., 3, 10, 1990; "Frauen für Oskar Lafontaine," *taz*, Nov. 14; Lafontaine interviews, *NRZ*, Nov. 7, TV, Nov. 12, *NP*, Nov. 20, and TV, Nov. 25; "Die SPD im Kampf gegen das Stimmungstief," *FR*, Nov. 28.

69. "Im Wahlkampf setzt CDU ganz auf Kohl," *KSA*, Sept. 8, 1990; "Der Kanzler als Programm," *GA*, Oct. 25; "'King Kohl' als Staatsmann," *NRZ*, Nov. 15; "Staatsmann statt Wahlkämpfer," *MP*, Nov. 25; CDU program, *Ja zu Deutschland—Ja zur Zukunft* (Bonn, 1990).

70. Kohl circular, Nov. 1990, Hoover Institution; Kohl interviews, *Deutschland Magazin*, Nov. 1, 1990 and elsewhere Oct. 23, Nov. 14, and 25, BPA Dok 1990; "Drei gute Gründe CDU zu wählen," *Express*, Nov. 19; Peter Radunski, "Vor der Deutschlandwahl," *Politische Meinung*, Nov. 1990.

71. "Wahlprognose: Keine Verschiebungen," *FAZ*, Dec. 1, 1990; "Das vorläufige amtliche Endergebnis," and articles on state results, *FAZ*, Dec. 4; FDP election program and posters, Hoover Institution.

72. "Wahlnachlese," *ND*, Dec. 24, 1990; election program of the Greens, Hoover Institution; Kohl interviews, Dec. 2, BPA Dok 1990.

73. Surveys by Infas, Nov. 16, 1990; Forschungsgruppe Wahlen, Nov. 18; and ZdF, Dec. 2, BPA Dok 1990; "Triumph und Erdrutsch," *taz*, Dec. 4, 1990; Wolfgang Gibowski and Max Kaase, "Auf dem Weg zum politischen Alltag," *APZG* B11/12 (1991): 3 ff.

74. Allensbach survey, Nov. 27, 1990, BPA Dok 1990; Infas analysis, *TS*, Dec. 4; "Die deutsche Frage im Westen kein Thema," *SDZ*, Dec. 8; "Andere Generation, anderer Wahltrend," *FR*, Dec. 15; "Lohn der Einheit," *BILD*, Dec. 3; Franz U. Pappi's analysis in *APZG* B44 (1992): 18 ff.

75. Bonn party leader debate, Dec. 2, 1990; Geissler, Ehmke, Thierse, Rühe, and Fuchs statements, Dec. 2; Fischer interview, Dec. 3, BPA Dok 1990; "Trotz Schlappe gibt Lafontaine den Ton an," *KSA*, Dec. 3; "Bestätigung für Kohls Deutschlandpolitik," *NZZ*, Dec. 4.

76. TV editorials, Dec. 2, 1990, BPA Dok 1990; "Verdienter Sieg," *Welt*, Dec. 3, 1990; "Kanzler für Deutschland," *FAZ*, Dec. 3; "Kein Kanzler-Triumph," *HB*, Dec. 3; "Kohl, aber. . . ," *StZ*, Dec. 3.

77. Claus Offe's and Karl-Ulrich Mayer's essays in *Experiment Vereinigung* ed. Bernd Giesen and Claus Leggewie (Berlin, 1991), 77 ff, 87 ff.

78. Hans-Ulrich Wehler, *Deutsche Gesellschaftsgeschichte, 1700–1815* (Munich, 1987), 57–58.

79. Christoph F. Buechtermann and Juergen Schupp, "Repercussions of Reunification," *DIW Discussion Paper* no. 4 (Berlin, 1992); Rolf Habich et al., "Ein unbekanntes Land," *APZG* B32 (1991): 13 ff.

80. Marlies Menge's articles on "Die unsichtbare Grenze," *ZEIT*, Nov. 16 ff, 1990; Lutz Marz, "Dispositionskosten des Transformationsprozesses," *APZG* B24 (1992): 3 ff.

81. Buechtermann-Schupp, "Repercussions of Reunification," 20 ff; Artur Maier, "Abschied von der sozialistischen Ständegesellschaft," *APZG* B16/17 (1990): 3 ff.

82. Peter A. Berger, "Was früher starr war, ist nun in Bewegung," in *Abbruch und Aufbruch*, ed. Michael Thomas (Berlin, 1992).

83. Thomas Koch, "Hier ändert sich nie was!" *Abbruch und Aufbruch*, 319 ff.

84. Frank Adler, "Soziale Umbrüche," in Glaessner and Reissig, *Das Ende eines Experiments*, 201 ff.

Conclusion

1. Mohr cartoon in *FAZ*, Oct. 2, 1990; Gransow-Jarausch, *Deutsche Vereinigung*, 11 ff.

2. Lewis H. Gann and Peter Duignan, *Germany: Key to a Continent* (Stanford, 1992).

3. "Several Germanys Since 1871, but Today's Is 'Very Different,'" *NYT*, Oct. 3, 1990; BPA, *Cities, Towns and Countryside in Germany '92* (Bonn, 1991).

4. "One Germany," *NYT*, Oct. 3, 1990; Kohl interview, Aug. 13, 1992, *Statements and Speeches* 15, no. 12 (1992).

5. Peter Hoff, "Armenbegräbnis für eine teuere Verblichene," and Michael

E. Geisler, "Mehrfach gebrochene Mauerschau," in Bohn, *Mauer-Show*, 175 ff, 257 ff.

6. Karin and Karlheinz Lau, *Deutschland auf dem Weg zur Einheit* (Braunschweig, 1990) versus Michael Schneider, *Die abgetriebene Revolution* (Berlin, 1990).

7. Ash, *Magic Lantern*, 61 ff; Darnton, *Berlin Journal*, 72 ff, and Hagen Schulze, "German Unification in the Context of European History," *GSR* special issue, (Winter, 1992): 7 ff.

8. Eppelmann, *Wendewege*, 178 ff. Cf. Otto Pflanze, *Bismarck and the Development of Germany*, vol. 1 (Princeton, 1990).

9. Compare the dissident *Umweltblätter* and *Telegraph* (editorial, May 31, 1990) with the Marxist journal *Weltbühne* (article by Joachim Garstecki, July 19, 1990).

10. Erich Kuby, *Der Preis der Einheit* (Hamburg, 1990); Reich, *Anschied von Lebenslügen*, 7 ff; and Gysi, *Einspruch*, 191 ff.

11. Hanns W. Maull and Achim von Heynitz, "Osteuropa: Durchbruch in die Postmoderne?" *EA* 15 (1990): 441 ff; and Gale Stokes' forthcoming book on this topic.

12. Bernard Gwertzman and Michael T. Kaufman, eds., *The Collapse of Communism* (New York, 1990); and Robert Weiss, *Chronik eines Zusammenbruchs* (Berlin, 1990), 121 ff.

13. Fred Klinger, "Das Scheitern des real-existierenden Sozialismus in der DDR," *DSt* 28 (1990), 3 ff; term from Gransow and Jarausch, *Deutsche Vereinigung*, 16–17.

14. Gero Neugebauer, "Von der Wende zur Wahl. Der Zusammenbruch des politischen Systems der DDR" (MS, Berlin, 1990); and Glaessner, *Der schwierige Weg*, 203 ff.

15. John Breuilly, "Nationalism and German Reunification," in his *The State of Germany* (London, 1992), 225 ff.

16. Thomas Gensicke, "Sind die Ostdeutschen konservativer als die Westdeutschen?" *Das Ende eines Experiments*, 287 ff; Russell J. Dalton, "Politics in the New Germany," (MS, Irvine, Calif., 1991).

17. Albrecht, *Abwicklung*, 153 ff; Kaiser, *Vereinigung*, 33 ff.

18. Beate Kohler-Koch, "Deutsche Einigung im Spannungsfeld internationaler Umbrüche," *Politische Vierteljahrsschrift* 32 (1991): 605–20.

19. Baier, *Volk ohne Zeit*, 99–100; Schneider, *Revolution*, 138–139.

20. Hartung, *Neunzehnhundertneunundachtzig*, 185 ff.

21. Gunter Hofmann and Werner A. Perger, *Richard von Weizsäcker im Gespräch* (Frankfurt, 1992), 31-32.

22. Wolfgang Bergsdorf, "West Germany's Political System under Stress: Decision-Making Process in Bonn 1990" (MS, Bonn, 1991).

23. Kocka, "Revolution und Nation," *Tel Aviver Jahrbuch für deutsche Geschichte*, 679 ff.

24. Charles S. Maier, "The DDR Upheaval of November 1989 and the Issue of German Revolution," in *Nach dem Erdbeben: (Re-)konstruktionen ostdeutscher Geschichte und Geschichtswissenschaft*, ed. Konrad H. Jarausch and Matthias Middell (Leipzig, 1993).

25. Heinrich Best, "Nationale Verbundenheit und Entfremdung im zweistaatlichen Deutschland," *KZSS* 42 (1990): 1 ff.

26. Winkler, "Nationalismus, Nationalstaat und nationale Frage," *APZG* B40 (1991): 22 ff; Breuilly, *The State of Germany*, 231 ff.

27. Wolfgang Herles, *Geteilte Freude. Das erste Jahr der dritten Republik* (Munich,

1992); and Thomas Koch, "Deutsch-Deutsche Einigung als Kulturproblem," *DA* (1991), 17 ff.

28. Kurt Biedenkopf, "Die geeinte Nation im Stimmungstief," *ZEIT*, Oct. 9, 1992; "United Germany at Two," *The Week in Germany*, Oct. 9.

29. Irwin L. Collier, "On the First Year of German Monetary, Economic and Social Union," *Journal of Economic Perspectives* 5 (1991), 1 ff; Harald Becker, "Wirtschaft in den neuen Bundesländern," *DA* 25 (1992): 461 ff.

30. Sinn, *Kaltstart*, 208 ff; Hofmann, *Weizsäcker*, 32 ff; Richard Smyser, *The Economy of United Germany* (New York, 1992).

31. Johannes M. Becker, *Ein Land geht in den Westen* (Bonn, 1991); Konrad H. Jarausch, ed., *Zwischen Parteilichkeit und Professionalität. Bilanz der Geschichtswissenschaft der DDR* (Berlin, 1991).

32. Wolfgang Küttler, "Neubeginn in der ostdeutschen Geschichtswissenschaft," *APZG* B17/18 (1992): 3 ff; Rainer Eckert et al., eds., *Krise, Umbruch, Neubeginn* (Stuttgart, 1992); and Jürgen Kocka, "Die deutsche Einheit und die Sozialwissenschaften," *TS*, Sept. 16, 1992.

33. Hans-Joachim Maaz, *Das gestürzte Volk* (Berlin, 1991), 10 ff; and Albrecht Schönherr, ed., *Ein Volk am Pranger?* (Berlin, 1992).

34. Antonia Grunenberg, "Das Ende der Macht ist der Anfang der Literatur," *APZG* B44 (1990): 17 ff; Karl Deiritz and Hannes Krauss, eds., *Der deutsch-deutsche Literaturstreit* (Hamburg, 1991); and the forthcoming volume on "The Responsibility of the Intellectuals" edited by Michael Geyer and Robert von Hallberg.

35. Alexander Osang, *Das Jahr Eins. Berichte aus der neuen Welt der Deutschen* (Berlin, 1992), 62 ff; articles on abortion in "Germany and Gender," special issue of *GPS* (1991–1992) 24/25: 111 ff.

36. Hajo Funke, '*Jetzt sind wir dran.' Nationalismus im geeinten Deutschland* (Berlin, 1991).

37. Arnulf Baring, *Deutschland, was nun?* (Berlin, 1991); Hofmann, *Weizsäcker*, 87 ff, 111 ff; Andrei S. Markovits and Simon Reich, "Should Europe Fear the Germans?" *GPS* 23 (1991): 1 ff.

38. Ronald D. Asmus, "Deutschland im Übergang. Nationales Selbstvertrauen und internationale Zurückhaltung," *EA* 8 (1992): 199 ff; and Burkhard Koch, *Germany's New Assertiveness in International Relations* (Stanford, 1992).

39. Genscher interview and Hans-Magnus Enzensberger, "Hitlers Wiedergänger," *Spiegel*, Feb. 4, 1991.

40. Peter Glotz, "Der ungerechte Krieg," *Spiegel*, Feb. 25; and Herles, *Geteilte Freude*, 179 ff.

41. Istvan Deak, "German Unification: Perceptions and Politics in East Central Europe," *GPS* 20 (1990): 22 ff; Wickert, *Angst vor Deutschland*, 231 ff.

42. Baring, *Deutschland*, 83 ff; and Herles, *Geteilte Freude*, 193 ff.

43. "Deutschland wird deutscher," *ZEIT*, Mar. 3, 1992; Hoffmann-Kramer, *Der Umbau Europas*, 13 ff and the forthcoming volume on European integration, edited by Phillippe Schmitter.

44. Otto Schmuck, "Der Maastrichter Vertrag zur Europäischen Union," *EA* 4 (1992): 97 ff; Herles, *Geteilte Freude*, 199 ff; Baring, *Deutschland*, 153 ff.

45. Leslie H. Gelb, "To Be Father and Bride," *NYT*, May 11, 1992; William E. Odom, "Germany, America and the Strategic Reconfiguration of Europe," in *The Future of Germany*, ed. Gary Geipel (Indianapolis, 1990), 190 ff.

46. Asmus, "Deutschland im Übergang," 199 ff; Gregor Schöllgen,

"Deutschlands neue Lage," *EA* 5 (1992): 125 ff; Baring, *Deutschland*, 145 ff; Werner Dähnhardt and Paul Lersch, "Die United Übermacht," *Spiegel*, Mar. 22, 1993.

47. Biedenkopf interview, *Spiegel*, Oct. 5, 1992; Christian Meier, *Die Nation die keine sein will* (Munich, 1991), 10 ff; Matthias Jung and Dieter Roth, "Politische Einstellungen in Ost- und Westdeutschland seit der Bundestagswahl 1990," *APZG* B19 (1992): 3 ff.

48. Peter Longerich, *"Was ist des Deutschen Vaterland?"* (Munich, 1990); Michael Stürmer, *Die Grenzen der Macht. Begegnung der Deutschen mit der Geschichte* (Berlin, 1992); Baring, *Deutschland*, 163–64; and Harold James, "Reflections on German Identity," *GSR*, special issue (Winter, 1992): 1 ff.

49. Herles, *Geteilte Freude*, 239 ff; Brigitte Seebacher-Brandt, *Die Linke und die Einheit* (Berlin, 1991); Elke Mocker and Birgit Sauer, "Politische Kultur und Geschlechterverhältnis in den neuen Bundesländern," *DA* 24 (1991): 1313 ff; and Jürgen Habermas, "Die zweite Lebenslüge der Bundesrepublik," *ZEIT*, Dec. 18, 1992.

50. Bundestag, *Stenographische Berichte. 12 Wahlperiode, 34. Sitzung* (Bonn, 1991), 2845 ff; and the arguments of Hans Daniel for Bonn and Walter Momper for Berlin, *ZEIT*, Nov. 16, 1990.

51. "Berlin wird Parlaments- und Regierungssitz," *GA*, June 21, 1991; and Irma Hanke, "Experiment Deutschland oder ein neues deutsches Nationalgefühl?" *DA* 24 (1991): 154 ff.

52. Wolfgang Mauersberg, "The Radical Right Gains in Two Land Elections," *German Tribune*, Apr. 10, 1992; "Ein einig Volk von Blutsbrüdern," *Spiegel* 47, no. 11 (1993): Hermann Kurthen, "Immigration and Immigration Policy in Germany," (MS, Chapel Hill, N.C., January 1993).

53. John Eisenhammer on the explosion of racism in Rostock, *Toronto Star*, Aug. 30, 1992; Craig Whitney, "East Europe's Frustration Finds Target: Immigrants," *NYT*, Nov. 13; German Information Center, . . . *Rightwing Radicalism in Germany* (New York, 1993).

54. Stephen Kinzer, "Germany Ablaze: It's Candlelight, Not Firebombs," *NYT*, Jan. 13, 1993; Richard von Weizsäcker, "The Dignity of Man is Inviolable," *Statements and Speeches* 15, no. 17 (1992); "Coalition Parties and SPD Debate Proposed Asylum Legislation in First Reading," *The Week in Germany*, Jan. 22, 1993.

55. Diethelm Prowe, "Prospects for the New Germany," *Historian* 53 (1991): 1 ff; Wilhelm von Sternburg, ed., *Geteilte Ansichten über eine vereinte Nation* (Bergisch Gladbach, 1992), 335 ff; and Harold James, *A German Identity, 1770–1990* (New York, 1989), 210 ff.

56. Richter, *Erlangte Einheit*, 203 ff; Winfried Thaa, "Mehr Adaptation und Regression," *DA* 24 (1991): 831 ff; Richard Schröder, *Deutschland schwierig Vaterland* (Freiburg, 1993); and Helmut Schmidt, "Wir sind noch kein normales Volk," *ZEIT*, Apr. 9, 1993.

Selected Bibliography

Archives and Collections

Bundesarchiv (Potsdam), Files of the GDR Government.
Bundespresseamt (Bonn), Speeches and Interviews on Unification.
CDU Archive (East Berlin), Material on Party and Elections.
DDR Institut Archive (FU Berlin), Material on Civic Movement.
Demokratie Jetzt (Berlin), Material on Civic Movement.
Gesamtdeutsches Institut (Bonn), Unification Analyses.
Hoover Institution (Stanford University), German Unification Collection.
Leipziger Volkszeitung Archive (Leipzig), Press Clipping File.
Neues Forum (Berlin), Material on Civic Movement.
Rush Collection (Leipzig), Material on Leipzig Demonstrations.
Stadtbibliothek (East Berlin), Press Clipping File.
Stiftung Archiv der Parteien (Berlin), Records of the SED
Umweltbibliothek (East Berlin), Material on Civic Movement.
Zentralinstitut für Jugendforschung (Leipzig), Survey Material.
Zimmerling Collection (East Berlin), Material on Unification.

Documents and Memoirs

Aischmann, Bernd, et al., eds. *"Menschen wichtiger als Macht. . . ." Briefe an Hans Modrow.* Berlin, 1990.
Aktiv Staatssicherheit . . . des Bezirkstages Suhl, *Genossen! Glaubt's mich doch!* Suhl, 1990.
Albrecht, Ulrich. *Die Abwicklung der DDR.* Opladen, 1992.
Andert, Reinhold, and Wolfgang Herzberg. *Der Sturz. Erich Honecker im Kreuzverhör.* Berlin, 1990.
Auswärtiges Amt., ed. *Deutsche Aussenpolitik 1990/1. Eine Dokumentation.* Munich, 1991.
Bahr, Eckard. *Sieben Tage im Oktober. Aufbruch in Dresden.* Leipzig, 1990.
Becker, Johannes M. *Ein Land geht in den Westen.* Bonn, 1991.
Beier, Brigitte, el al. *9. November 1989. Der Tag der Deutschen.* Hamburg, 1989.

Belwe, Katarina, and Ute Reuter, eds. *Dokumentation zur Entwicklung der Blockparteien der DDR von Ende September bis Anfang Dezember 1989.* Bonn, 1989.

Besier, Gerhard, and Stephan Wolf, eds. *"Pfarrer, Christen und Katholiken." Das MfS der ehemaligen DDR und die Kirchen.* 2d. ed. Neukirchen, 1992.

Bickardt, Stefan, ed. *Recht ströme wie Wasser. Christen in der DDR für Absage an Praxis und Prinzip der Ausgrenzung.* Berlin, 1988.

Bohley, Bärbel, et al., eds. *40 Jahre DDR . . . und die Bürger melden sich zu Wort.* Berlin, 1989.

Brandt, Willy, *". . . was zusammengehört." Reden zu Deutschland.* Bonn, 1990.

Bresch, Ulrike, et al., eds. *Oktober 1989. Wider den Schlaf der Vernunft.* Berlin, 1990.

Bundespresse- und Informationsamt. *Deutschland 1989.* 25 vols. Bonn, 1991.

———. *Deutschland 1990.* (in preparation).

Bürger, Wolfram, and Michael Weichenhahn, eds. *Wolfgang Ullmann.* Munich, 1990.

Bürgerkommittee Leipzig. *Stasi intern. Macht und Banalität.* Leipzig, 1991.

Dahn, Daniela, and Fritz-Jochen Kopka. *Und diese verdammte Ohnmacht. Report der unabhängigen Untersuchungskommission.* Berlin, 1991.

Darnton, Robert. *Berlin Journal, 1989–1990.* New York, 1991.

Deiritz, Karl, and Hannes Krauss, eds. *Der deutsch-deutsche Literaturstreit.* Hamburg, 1991.

DGB-Bundesvorstand, ed. *Das Neue Forum. Selbstporträt einer Bürgerbewegung.* Bonn, 1990.

Dieckmann, Friedrich. *Glockenläuten und offene Fragen.* Frankfurt, 1991.

Ebert, Andreas, et al., eds. *Räumt die Steine hinweg.* Munich, 1989.

Eppelmann, Rainer. *Wendewege. Briefe an die Familie.* Bonn, 1992.

Evangelischer Pressedienst. *Problem Ausreissewelle.* Frankfurt, 1989.

Gauck, Joachim. *Die Stasi-Akten. Das unheimliche Erbe der DDR.* Reinbeck, 1991.

Genscher, Hans-Dietrich. *Zukunftsverantwortung. Reden.* Berlin, 1990.

Greens, eds. *Umweltreport DDR. Bilanz der Zerstörung, Kosten der Sanierung, Strategien für einen Umbau.* Frankfurt, 1990.

Gwertzman, Bernard, and Michael T. Kaufmann, eds. *The Collapse of Communism.* New York, 1990.

Gysi, Gregor. *Einspruch. Gespräche, Briefe, Reden.* Berlin, 1992.

———, ed. *Wir brauchen einen dritten Weg.* Hamburg, 1990.

Gysi, Gregor, and Thomas Falkner. *Sturm aufs grosse Haus.* Berlin, 1990.

Hahn, Annegret, et al., eds. *4. November '89.* Frankfurt, 1990.

Haug, Fritz. *Versuch beim täglichen Verlieren des Bodens unter den Füssen neuen Grund zu gewinnen. Perestroika Journal.* Hamburg, 1990.

Henrich, Rolf. *Der vormundschaftliche Staat. Vom Versagen des real existierenden Sozialismus.* Reinbeck, 1989.

Herles, Helmut, and Ewald Rose, eds. *Vom Runden Tisch zum Parlament.* Bonn, 1990.

———. *Parlaments-Szenen einer deutschen Revolution.* Bonn, 1990.

Heym, Stefan, and Werner Heiduczek, eds. *Die sanfte Revolution.* Leipzig, 1990.

Hofmann, Gunter, and Werner A. Perger. *Richard von Weizsäcker im Gespräch.* Frankfurt, 1992.

Honecker, Erich. *Zu den dramatischen Ereignissen.* Hamburg, 1992.

Horn, Guyla. *Freiheit, die ich meine.* Hamburg, 1991.

Initiativgruppe 4. 11. 89, ed. *TschüssSED. 4. 11. 89.* Bonn, 1989.

Janson, Carl-Heinz. *Totengräber der DDR. Wie Günter Mittag den SED-Staat ruinierte.* Düsseldorf, 1991.

Kahlau, Cordula, ed. *Aufbruch—Frauenbewegung in der DDR.* Berlin, 1990.

Kallabis, Heinz. *Ade, DDR! Tagebuchblätter, 7. Okt. 1989–8. Mai 1990.* Treptow, 1990.

Klein, Hans. *Es begann im Kaukasus. Der entscheidende Schritt in die Einheit Deutschlands.* Frankfurt, 1991.

Knabe, Hubertus, ed. *Aufbruch in eine andere DDR.* Hamburg, 1989.

Kohl, Helmut. *Deutschlands Zukunft in Europa.* Herford, 1990.

Königsdorf, Helga. *Adieu DDR. Protokolle eines Abschieds.* Reinbeck, 1990.

Krenz, Egon. *Wenn Mauern fallen. Die friedliche Revolution.* Vienna, 1990.

Kromer, Hans, ed. *Dresden. Die friedliche Revolution.* Böblingen, 1990.

Kuczynski, Jürgen. *Schwierige Jahre—mit einem besseren Ende? Tagebuchblätter 1986–1989.* Berlin, 1990.

Kunze, Reiner. *Deckname "Lyrik."* Frankfurt, 1990.

Kvitsinskii, Julii. *Vor dem Sturm. Erinnerungen eines Diplomaten.* Berlin, 1993.

Lafontaine, Oskar. *Deutsche Wahrheiten. Die nationale und die soziale Frage.* Hamburg, 1990.

Land, Rainer, ed. *Das Umbaupapier. Argumente gegen die Wiedervereinigung.* Berlin, 1990.

Lang, Ewald, ed. *Wendehals und Stasi-Laus. Demo-Sprüche aus der DDR.* Munich, 1990.

Lau, Karin, and Karlheinz Lau, eds. *Deutschland auf dem Weg zur Einheit. Dokumente einer Revolution.* Braunschweig, 1990.

Liebisch, Heike. *Dresdener Stundenbuch. Protokoll einer Beteiligten im Herbst 1989.* Wuppertal, 1989.

Liedtke, Klaus, ed. *Vier Tage im November.* Hamburg, 1989.

Loest, Erich. *Die Stasi war mein Eckermann.* Göttingen, 1991.

Longerich, Peter, ed. *"Was ist des Deutschen Vaterland?" Dokumente zur Frage der Deutschen Einheit 1800 bis 1990.* Munich, 1990.

Luft, Christa. *Zwischen Wende und Ende.* Berlin, 1991.

Marcuse, Peter. *A German Way of Revolution.* Berlin, 1990.

Matussek, Matthias. *Palasthotel Zimmer 6101. Reporter im rasenden Deutschland.* Hamburg, 1991.

Mayer, Hans. *Der Turm von Babel.* Frankfurt, 1991.

Meinel, Reinhard, and Thomas Wernicke, eds. *Mit Tschekistischem Gruss.* Potsdam, 1990.

Mittag, Günter. *Um jeden Preis. Im Spannungsfeld zweier Systeme.* Berlin, 1991.

Mitteldeutscher Verlag. *mdv transparent: Wir sind das Volk.* 3 vols. Halle, 1990.

Mitter, Armin, and Stefan Wolle, eds. *"Ich liebe Euch doch alle." Lageberichte des MfS.* Berlin, 1990.

Modrow, Hans. *Aufbruch und Ende.* Hamburg, 1991.

Momper, Walter. *Grenzfall. Berlin im Brennpunkt deutscher Geschichte.* Munich, 1991.

Münch, Ingo von, ed. *Die Verträge zur Einheit Deutschlands.* Munich, 1991.

Naumann, Michael, ed. *Die Geschichte ist offen . . . Schriftsteller aus der DDR über die Zukunftschancen ihres Landes.* Hamburg, 1990.

Nawrocki, Joachim. *Die Beziehungen zwischen den beiden Staaten in Deutschland.* Berlin, 1986.

Neubert, Ehrhard. *Gesellschaftliche Kommunikation im sozialen Wandel.* Berlin, 1989.

Neues Forum Leipzig. *Jetzt oder nie—Demokratie*. Leipzig, 1989.

Neumann, Peter, ed. *Träumen verboten. Aktuelle Stellungnahmen aus der DDR*. Göttingen, 1990.

Noteboom, Cees. *Berliner Notizen*. Frankfurt, 1991.

Ott, Matthias. *Deutschland—Ein Ausreisemärchen*. Koblenz, 1989.

Pechmann, Roland, and Jürgen Vogel, eds. *Abgesang der Stasi. Das Jahr 1989 in Presseartikeln und Stasi-Dokumenten*. Braunschweig, 1991.

Philipsen, Dirk, ed. *"We Were the People": Voices from East Germany's Revolutionary Autumn of 1989*. Durham, 1992.

Przybylski, Peter, ed. *Tatort Politbüro. Die Akte Honecker*. Berlin, 1991.

Rein, Gerhard, ed. *Die Opposition in der DDR*. Berlin, 1989.

———. *Die protestantische Revolution, 1987–1990. Ein deutsches Lesebuch*. Berlin, 1990.

Reuter, Ute, ed. *Dokumentation zum letzten Parteitag der SED*. Bonn, 1990.

———, ed. *Dokumentation zur politischen Entwicklung in der DDR und zu den innerdeutschen Beziehungen April 1990*. Bonn, 1990.

Reuter, Ute, and Thomas Schulte, eds., *Dokumentation zur Entwicklung der neuen Parteien und Bürgerrechtsgruppen in der DDR*. Bonn, 1990.

Richter, Edelbert. *Erlangte Einheit, verfehlte Identität*. Berlin, 1991.

Riecker, Ariane, et al., *Stasi intim. Gespräche mit ehemaligen MfS-Mitarbeitern*. Leipzig, 1990.

Rosenlöcher, Thomas. *Die verkauften Pflastersteine. Dresdener Tagebuch*. Frankfurt, 1990.

Rotfeld, Adam D., and Walter Stützle, eds. *Germany and Europe in Transition*. Oxford, 1991.

Runge, Irene, and Uwe Stelbrink. *Gregor Gysi: "Ich bin Opposition."* Berlin, 1990.

Schabowski, Günter. *Das Politbüro. Ende eines Mythos*. Hamburg, 1990.

———. *Der Absturz*. Berlin, 1991.

Schäuble, Wolfgang. *Der Vertrag. Wie ich über die deutsche Einheit verhandelte*. Stuttgart, 1991.

Schnauze! Gedächtnisprotokolle 7. und 8. Oktober 1989. Berlin, 1990.

Schneider, Rolf. *Frühling im Herbst. Notizen vom Untergang der DDR*. Göttingen, 1991.

Schneider, Wolfgang, ed. *Leipziger Demontagebuch*. Leipzig, 1990.

Schönherr, Albrecht, ed. *Ein Volk am Pranger?* Berlin, 1992.

Schorlemmer, Friedrich. *Bis alle Mauern fallen*. Berlin, 1991.

———. *Worte öffnen Fäuste. Rückkehr in ein schwieriges Vaterland*. Munich, 1992.

Schreiter, Helfried, ed. *Die letzten Tage der DDR*. Berlin, 1990.

Schröder, Richard. *Deutschland schwierig Vaterland*. Freiburg, 1993.

Schüddekopf, Charles, ed. *Wir sind das Volk! Flugschriften, Aufrufe und Texte aus einer deutschen Revolution*. Reinbeck, 1990.

Schütt, Hans-Dieter. *Regine Hildebrandt: "Bloss nicht aufgeben!"* Berlin, 1992.

Schützsack, Axel. *Exodus in die Einheit. Die Massenflucht aus der DDR 1989*. Melle, 1990.

Shevardnadze, Eduard. *Die Zukunft gehört der Freiheit*. Hamburg, 1991.

Sievers, Hans-Jürgen, ed. *Stundenbuch einer deutschen Revolution*. Zollikon, 1990.

Simon, Günter. *Tisch-Zeiten*. Berlin, 1990.

Stolpe, Manfred. *Den Menschen Hoffnung geben*. Berlin, 1991.

———. *Schwieriger Aufbruch*. Berlin, 1992.

Süssmuth, Hans, ed. *Wie geht es weiter mit Deutschland?* Baden-Baden, 1990.

Swoboda, Jörg, ed. *Die Revolution der Kerzen*. Opladen, 1990.

taz, ed. *DDR Journal*. 2 vols. Berlin, 1989.

Teltschik, Horst. *329 Tage*. Berlin, 1991.

Tetzner, Rainer. *Leipziger Ring. Aufzeichnungen eines Montagsdemonstranten*. Frankfurt, 1990.

Thierse, Wolfgang. *Mit eigener Stimme sprechen*. Munich, 1992.

Ullmann, Wolfgang. *Verfassung und Parlament*. Berlin, 1992.

Ullrich, Renate. *Mein Kapital bin ich selber. Gespräche mit Theaterfrauen in Berlin-O 1990/91*. Berlin, 1991.

Weber, Christian. *Alltag einer friedlichen Revolution. Notizen aus der DDR*. Stuttgart, 1990.

Weber, Hermann, ed. *DDR: Dokumente zur Geschichte der DDR 1945–1985*. Munich, 1986.

Weizsäcker, Richard von. *Speeches for Our Time*. Washington, D.C., 1992.

Die Weltbühne im Wirbel der Wende. Eine Zeitschrift im Umbruch. Berlin, 1992.

Wende, Franziska. *Die Zeit ist reif. Revolutionserlebnisse einer Leipziger Postbotin*. Amberg, 1990.

Wicke, Lutz, et al. *Öko-Soziale Marktwirtschaft für Ost und West*. Munich, 1990.

Wickert, Ulrich, ed. *Angst vor Deutschland*. Hamburg, 1990.

Wolf, Christa. *Was bleibt*. Frankfurt, 1990.

Wolf, Markus. *In eigenem Auftrag*. Munich, 1991.

Wroblewsky, Clement von, ed. *"Da wachste eines Morgens uff und hast 'nen Bundeskanzler."* Hamburg, 1990.

Zimmerling, Zeno, and Sabine, Zimmerling, eds. *Neue Chronik DDR*. 8 vols. Berlin, 1990.

Refections and Analyses

Appel, Reinhard, ed. *Helmut Kohl im Spiegel seiner Macht*. Bonn, 1990.

Arnold, Heinz. *Die ersten hundert Tage des Hans Modrow*. Berlin, 1990.

Ash, Timothy Garton. *The Magic Lantern*. New York, 1990.

Augstein, Rudolf, and Günter Grass. *Deutschland, einig Vaterland?* Göttingen, 1990.

Bahrmann, Hannes, and Peter-Michael Fritsch. *Sumpf. Privilegien, Amtsmissbrauch, Schiebergeschäfte*. Berlin, 1990.

Baier, Lothar. *Volk ohne Zeit*. Berlin, 1990.

Baring, Arnulf. *Deutschland, was nun?* Berlin, 1991.

Bark, Dennis L., and David R. Gress. *A History of West Germany*. 2 vols. Oxford, 1989.

Barthèlemy, Françoise, and Lutz Winkler, eds. *Mein Deutschland findet sich in keinem Atlas*. Frankfurt, 1990.

Belwe, Katharina. *Psycho-Soziale Befindlichkeit der Menschen in den neuen Bundesländern nach der Wende im Herbst 1989*. Bonn, 1991.

Beschloss, Michael, and Strobe Talbott. *At the Highest Levels: The Inside Story of the End of the Cold War*. Boston, 1993.

Bittermann, Klaus, ed. *Gemeinsam sind wir unausstehlich. Die Wiedervereinigung und ihre Folgen*. Berlin, 1990.

Blanke, Thomas, and Rainer Erd, eds. *DDR—Ein Staat vergeht*. Frankfurt, 1990.

Blohm, Frank, and Wolfgang Herzberg, eds. *"Nichts wird mehr so sein, wie es war."* *Die Zukunft der beiden deutschen Republiken.* Frankfurt, 1990.

Bohn, Rainer, et al. *Mauer Show. Das Ende der DDR, die deutsche Einheit und die Medien.* Berlin, 1992.

Borneman, John. *After the Wall: East Meets West in the New Berlin.* New York, 1991.

Bortfeld, Heinrich. *Von der SED zur PDS. Wandlung zur Demokratie?* Bonn, 1992.

Breuilly, John, ed. *The State of Germany.* London, 1992.

Brüsewitz-Zentrum, ed. *Fachtagung zur psychischen Situation von DDR-Übersiedlern.* 1985.

Buck, Hannsjörg, and Hans Georg Bauer, eds. *Transformation der Wirtschaftsordnung der ehemaligen DDR.* Bonn, 1991.

Chalupsky, Jutta, and Renate Rothmann. *Freier Markt auf Nackter Haut. Wessi-Report aus Leipzig.* Berlin, 1991.

Christ, Peter, and Ralf Neubauer. *Kolonie im eigenen Land.* Berlin, 1991.

Conradt, David. *United Germany at the Polls.* Washington, 1990.

Dahrendorf, Ralf. *Reflections on the Revolution in Europe.* New York, 1990.

Decker, Peter, and Karl Held. *Der Anschluss.* Munich, 1990.

Deppe, Rainer, et al., eds. *Demokratischer Umbruch in Osteuropa.* Frankfurt, 1991.

Dohnanyi, Klaus von. *Das deutsche Wagnis.* Munich, 1990.

Dowe, Dieter, ed. *Sozialdemokratie und Nation in Geschichte und Gegenwart.* Bonn, 1990.

———. *Von der Bürgerbewegung zur Partei. Die Gründung der Sozialdemokratie in der DDR.* Bonn, 1993.

Eckert, Rainer, et al., eds. *Krise, Umbruch, Neubeginn.* Stuttgart, 1992.

———. *Wendezeiten—Zeitenwende.* Cologne, 1991.

Ehrenberg, Herbert. *Damit keiner unter die Räder kommt.* Cologne, 1990.

Eilitz, Ernst. *Sie waren dabei. Ostdeutsche Profile.* Stuttgart, 1991.

Fischbar, Günter, ed. *DDR Almanach '90.* Bonn, 1990.

Fischer, Erika, and Petra Lux. *Ohne uns ist kein Staat zu machen.* Cologne, 1990.

Fischer Weltalmanach. *Sonderband DDR.* Frankfurt, 1990.

Förster, Peter, and Günter Roski. *DDR zwischen Wende und Wahl. Meinungsforscher analysieren den Umbruch.* Berlin, 1990.

Forum Verlag Leipzig. *Von Leipzig nach Deutschland.* Leipzig, 1991.

Fricke, Karl Wilhelm. *MfS intern. Macht, Strukturen, Auflösung der DDR-Staatsicherheit.* Cologne, 1991.

Friedrich, Walter, and Hartmut Griese, eds. *Jugend und Jugendforschung in der DDR.* Opladen, 1991.

Friedrich, Wolfgang-Uwe, ed. *Die USA und die deutsche Frage, 1945–1990.* Frankfurt, 1991.

Fritsch-Bournazel, Renata. *Europa und die deutsche Einheit.* Munich, 1990.

Funke, Hajo. *"Jetzt sind wir dran."* *Nationalismus im geeinten Deutschland.* Berlin, 1991.

Gaus, Günter. *Deutsche Zwischentöne.* Hamburg, 1990.

Geipel, Gary, ed. *The Future of Germany.* Indianapolis, 1990.

Gesamtdeutsches Institut. *Analysen, Dokumentationen und Chronik zur Entwicklung der DDR.* Bonn, 1990.

Gewerkschaftliche Monatshefte, ed. *Auf dem Weg zur Einheit.* Cologne, 1990.

Geyer, Michael, and Robert von Hallberg, eds. *The Responsibility of the Intellectuals: State Security Services and Intellectual Life in the Former GDR.* Chicago, 1994.

Giesen, Bernd, and Claus Leggewie, eds. *Experiment Vereinigung. Ein sozialer Grossversuch.* Berlin, 1991.

Gill, David, and Ulrich Schröter. *Das Ministerium für Staatssicherheit. Anatomie des Mielke-Imperiums.* Berlin, 1991.

Glaessner, Gert. *Der schwierige Weg zur Demokratie. Vom Ende der DDR zur deutschen Einheit.* Opladen, 1992.

————. *Die DDR in der Ära Honecker. Politik, Kultur, Gesellschaft.* Opladen, 1989.

Glaessner, Gert, and Rolf Reissig, eds. *Das Ende eines Experiments.* Berlin, 1991.

Glotz, Peter. *Der Irrweg des Nationalstaats.* Stuttgart, 1990.

Golombek, Dieter, and Dietrich Ratzke, eds. *Dagewesen und aufgeschrieben. Reportagen über eine deutsche Revolution.* Frankfurt, 1990.

Gransow, Volker, and Konrad H. Jarausch, eds. *Die deutsche Vereinigung: Bürgerbewegung, Annäherung und Beitritt.* Cologne, 1991.

Grass, Günter. *Deutscher Lastenausgleich. Wider das dumpfe Einheitsgebot.* Berlin, 1990.

Grosser, Dieter, et al., eds. *Die sieben Mythen der Wiedervereinigung.* Munich, 1991.

Grözinger, Gerd. *Teures Deutschland.* Berlin, 1990.

Grunenberg, Antonia. *Aufbruch der inneren Mauer.* Bremen, 1990.

————, ed. *Welche Geschichte wählen wir?* Hamburg, 1992.

Habermas, Jürgen. *Die nachholende Revolution.* Frankfurt, 1990.

Hahn, Reinhardt O. *Ausgedient. Ein Stasi Major erzählt.* Halle, 1990.

Hamilton, Daniel. *After the Revolution.* Washington, 1990.

Hanrieder, Wolfram F. *Germany, America, Europe: Forty Years of German Foreign Policy.* New Haven, 1989.

Hartung, Klaus. *Neunzehnhundertneunundachtzig. Ortsbesichtigungen nach einer Epochenwende.* Frankfurt, 1990.

Heine, Michael, et al., eds. *Die Zukunft der DDR-Wirtschaft.* Reinbeck. 1990.

Heinrich, Arthur, and Klaus Naumann. *Alles Banane. Ausblicke auf das endgültige Deutschland.* Cologne, 1990.

Helweg, Gisela. *Die letzten Jahre der DDR.* Cologne, 1990.

Herles, Wolfgang. *Geteilte Freude. Das erste Jahr der dritten Republik.* Munich, 1992.

————. *Nationalrausch. Szenen aus dem gesamtdeutschen Machtkampf.* Munich, 1990.

Hettling, Manfred, ed. *Revolution in Deutschland? 1789–1989.* Göttingen, 1991.

Hoffmann, Hilmar, and Dieter Kramer, eds. *Der Umbau Europas. Deutsche Einheit und europäische Integration.* Frankfurt, 1991.

Humann, Klaus, ed. *Wir sind das Geld. Wie die Westdeutschen die DDR aufkaufen.* Reinbeck, 1990.

James, Harold, and Marla Stone, eds. *When the Wall Came Down: Reactions to German Unification.* New York, 1992.

Jarausch, Konrad H., ed. *Zwischen Parteilichkeit und Professionalität. Bilanz der DDR Geschichtswissenschaft.* Berlin, 1991.

Jarausch, Konrad, H., and Matthias Middell, eds. *Nach dem Erdbeben. (Re-)Konstruktionen ostdeutscher Geschichte und Geschichtswissenschaft.* Leipzig, 1993.

Kaiser, Karl. *Deutschlands Vereinigung. Die internationalen Aspekte.* Bergisch Gladbach, 1991.

Kirschey, Peter. *Wandlitz/Waldsiedlung—die geschlossene Gesellschaft.* Berlin, 1990.

Klein, Thomas, et al. *Keine Opposition Nirgends? Linke in Deutschland nach dem Sturz des Realsozialismus.* Berlin, 1991.

Klemm, Volker. *Korruption und Amtsmissbrauch in der DDR.* Stuttgart, 1991.

Knopp, Guido, and Ekkehard Kuhn. *Die deutsche Einheit. Traum und Wirklichkeit.* Erlangen, 1990.

Krisch, Henry. *The German Democratic Republic.* Boulder, 1985.

Kuby, Erich. *Preis der Einheit.* Hamburg, 1990.

Kurz, Robert. *Honeckers Rache. Zur politischen Ökonomie des wiedervereinigten Deutschland.* Berlin, 1991.

Lapp, Peter Joachim. *Die Blockparteien im politischen System der DDR.* Melle, 1988.

Lemke, Christiane. *Die Ursachen des Umbruchs 1989: Politische Sozialization in der ehemaligen DDR.* Opladen, 1991.

Lemke, Christiane, and Gary Marks, eds. *The Crisis of Socialism.* Durham, N.C., 1992.

Links, Christoph, and Hannes Bahrmann. *Wir sind das Volk. Die DDR im Aufbruch.* Wuppertal, 1990.

Loth, Wilfried. *Ost-West Konflikt und deutsche Frage.* Munich, 1989.

Maaz, Hans-Joachim. *Der Gefühlsstau. Ein Psychogramm der DDR.* Berlin, 1990.

———. *Das gestürzte Volk.* Berlin, 1991.

Maier, Charles. *Across the Wall: Revolution and Reunification of Germany.* Princeton, 1994.

Maier, Harry, and Siegrid Maier, *Vom innerdeutschen Handel zur deutsch-deutschen Wirtschafts- und Währungsgemeinschaft.* Cologne, 1990.

Marienfeld, Wolfgang. *Die Geschichte des Deutschlandproblems im Spiegel der politischen Karikatur.* Hameln, 1990.

Maron, Jonas, and Rainer Schedlinski. *Innenansichten DDR. Letzte Bilder.* Hamburg, 1990.

Marsh, David. *The Germans: A People at the Cross-Roads.* New York, 1989.

Meier, Christian. *Die Nation die keine sein will.* Munich, 1991.

———. *Deutsche Einheit als Herausforderung.* Munich, 1990.

Menge, Marlies. *Ohne uns geht nichts mehr. Die Revolution in der DDR.* Stuttgart, 1990.

Meuschel, Sigrid. *Legitimation und Parteiherrschaft. Zum Paradox von Stabilität und Revolution in der DDR.* Frankfurt, 1992.

Mitter, Armin, and Stefan Wolle. *Untergang auf Raten.* Munich, 1993.

Mog, Paul, ed. *Die Deutschen in ihrer Welt.* Berlin, 1992.

Müller-Enbergs, Helmut. *Volkskammerwahlen in der DDR 1990. Synopse von (Wahl-)Programmen 15 kandidierender Parteien.* Berlin, 1990.

Müller-Enbergs, Helmut, et al., eds. *Von der Illegalität ins Parlament. Werdegang und Konzept der neuen Bürgerbewegungen.* Berlin, 1991.

Niethammer, Lutz. *Die volkseigene Erfahrung. Eine Archäologie des Lebens in der Industrieprovinz der DDR.* Berlin, 1991.

Osang, Alexander. *Das Jahr Eins. Berichte aus der neuen Welt der Deutschen.* Berlin, 1992.

Oschlies, Wolf. *"Vierzig zu Null im Klassenkampf": Sprachliche Bilanz nach vier Jahrzehnten DDR.* Melle, 1990.

Pirker, Theo, et al. *FDGB—Wende zum Ende. Auf dem Weg zu unabhängigen Gewerkschaften?* Cologne, 1990.

Pond, Elizabeth. *After the Wall: American Policy Toward Germany.* New York, 1990.

Priewe, Jan, and Rudolf Hickel. *Preis der Einheit.* Frankfurt, 1991.

Reich, Jens. *Rückkehr nach Europa. Zur Lage der deutschen Nation.* Munich, 1991.

———. *Abschied von den Lebenslügen. Die Intelligenz und die Macht.* Berlin, 1992.

Rheinischer Merkur, ed. *Zurück nach Deutschland. Umsturz und demokratischer Aufbruch in der DDR.* Bonn, 1990.

Rüddenklau, Wolfgang. *Störenfried. DDR-Opposition 1986–1989.* Berlin, 1992.

Runge, Irene. *Ausland DDR. Fremdenhass.* Berlin, 1990.

Schell, Manfred, and Werner Kalinka. *Stasi und kein Ende. Die Personen und Fakten.* Frankfurt, 1991.

Schmid, Thomas. *Staatsbegräbnis. Von ziviler Gesellschaft.* Berlin, 1990.

Schneider, Michael. *Die abgetriebene Revolution.* Berlin, 1990.

Schneider, Peter. *Extreme Mittellage. Eine Reise durch das deutsche Nationalgefühl.* Hamburg, 1990.

Schumann, Frank. *100 Tage die die DDR erschütterten.* Berlin, 1990.

Seebacher-Brandt, Brigitte. *Die Linke und die Einheit.* Berlin, 1991.

Seiffert, Wolfgang. *Die Deutschen und Gorbatschow.* Erlangen, 1989.

Sinn, Gerlinde, and Hans-Werner Sinn. *Kaltstart. Volkswirtschaftliche Aspekte der deutschen Vereinigung.* Tübingen, 1991.

Smith, Gordon et al. eds. *Developments in German Politics.* Durham, 1992.

Spittmann, Ilse. *Die DDR unter Honecker.* Cologne, 1990.

Spittmann, Ilse, and Gisela Helwig, eds. *Chronik der Ereignisse in der DDR.* 3d ed. Cologne, 1990.

———. eds. *Die DDR auf dem Weg zur deutschen Einheit.* Cologne, 1990.

Sternburg, Wilhelm von, ed. *Geteilte Ansichten über eine vereinigte Nation.* Bergisch Gladbach, 1992.

Stolpe, Manfred, ed. *Die Zukunft der Deutschen in Europa.* Berlin, 1990.

Stürmer, Michael. *Die Grenzen der Macht. Begegnung der Deutschen mit der Geschichte.* Berlin, 1992.

Suhr, Heinz. *Der Treuhand Skandal.* Frankfurt, 1991.

Szabo, Stephen F. *The Diplomacy of German Unification.* New York, 1992.

Thaysen, Uwe. *Der Runde Tisch. Oder: Wo blieb das Volk?* Opladen, 1990.

Thomas, Michael, ed. *Abbruch und Aufbruch. Sozialwissenschaften im Transformationsprozess.* Berlin, 1992.

Venohr, Wolfgang, ed. *Ein Deutschland wird es sein.* Erlangen, 1990.

Walser, Martin. *Über Deutschland reden.* Frankfurt, 1989.

Warbeck, Joachim. *Die deutsche Revolution 1989/90.* Berlin, 1991.

Weber, Hermann, *DDR. Grundriss der Geschichte 1945–1990.* Hanover, 1991.

Wehling, Hans-Georg, ed. *(Wieder-)Vereinigungsprozess in Deutschland.* Stuttgart, 1990.

———. *Politische Kultur in der DDR.* Stuttgart, 1989.

Weidenfeld, Werner, ed. *Das Geschichtsbewusstsein der Deutschen.* Cologne, 1987.

Weidenfeld, Werner, and Hartmut Zimmermann, eds. *Deutschland-Handbuch. Eine doppelte Bilanz 1949–1989.* Bonn, 1989.

Weiss, Robert. *Chronik eines Zusammenbruchs.* Berlin, 1990.

Wengst, Udo, ed. *Historiker betrachten Deutschland.* Bonn, 1992.

Wewer, Gottrik, ed. *DDR. Von der friedlichen Revolution zur deutschen Vereinigung.* Opladen, 1990.

Wilkening, Christina. *Staat im Staate. Auskünfte ehemaliger Stasi-Mitarbeiter.* Berlin, 1990.

Winkler, Gunnar, ed. *Sozialreport DDR 1990.* Bonn, 1990.

Wolf, Christa. *Im Dialog. Aktuelle Texte.* Berlin, 1990.

Zwahr, Hartmut. *Ende einer Selbstzerstörung. Leipzig und die Revolution in der DDR.* Göttingen, 1993.

Index

272 *Index*

Federal Republic of Germany (*continued*)
Bundesrat, 147, 148, 185
Bundestag, 68, 147–48, 185–86, 191–94
capital controversy, 208–9
Caucasus agreement, 157–58, 166–68, 184
cooperation treaties with Czechoslovakia and Poland, 206
currency reform, 8, 139, 147–48, 154
DM credits to East Germany, 9, 100, 164
and East German protest demonstrations, 49–50, 52
and East German refugees, 25, 26–27, 142
and European Community, 8, 160, 176, 180, 201, 205, 206–7
GNP, 101, 197
immigration policy, 17, 209
interest rates, 204
international role, 205–6, 207
in NATO, 8, 92, 94, 111, 132, 160, 176, 180, 201, 205, 206–7
occupation rights suspended, 187
population size, 197
reunited with the German Democratic Republic, 187, 197–98, 203–10
Supreme Court, 30, 191
transition problems of unification, 203–8
"treaty community" with East Germany, 66–67, 68, 69, 70, 72, 88–89, 90, 92, 107–8
treaty for economic cooperation with the Soviet Union, 183–84
and the United Nations, 206, 207
and the United States, 206, 207
unification polls, 30, 66, 113–14
youth revolt of 1968, 161, 181
Federal Reserve Bank, 138
Feminist movement, 41–42, 103, 107, 208
Independent Women's Association, 42, 76, 105, 120
Fischbeck, Hans-Jürgen, 40
Fischer, Joschka, 29
Fischer, Oskar, 15, 20, 21, 63
Forck, Gottfried, 41, 75
France, 6, 11, 30, 69, 88, 92, 107, 111, 113, 114, 163, 164, 187
Franco-German Eurocorps, 207
Franco-German summit, 164
Free Democratic Party (East Germany), 119–31 *passim*, 167, 171, 183
and the GDR election, 119, 120, 125–27

and the coalition government, 128, 129, 130, 131
and the currency union, 144, 146
merged with the West German FDP, 185
Free Democratic Party (West Germany), 107, 111, 124, 185, 194
and the abortion issue, 172–73
coalition with CDU, 27–28
and the unification issue, 29, 68, 185
Free Democratic Youth (FDJ), 46, 53, 56, 57, 59, 81, 209
Free German Trade Union (FDGB), 56, 61, 76, 104–5, 144, 154
Fuchs, Anke, 189
"Fund for Germany Unity," 146

GDR. *See* German Democratic Republic
Gansel, Norbert, 29
Gauck, Joachim, 173, 205
Geissler, Heiner, 27
Genscher, Hans-Dietrich, 32, 68, 70, 120, 124, 142, 206
and the CDU/FDP coalition, 27–28
and the East German refugees, 16, 21–22
and the federal election, 193, 194
and the "two-plus-four" negotiations, 111, 112, 163, 165, 176, 184, 201
Geremek, Bronislaw, 30
Gerlach, Manfred, 61, 63, 117
German citizenship, 17, 209
German Democratic Republic (GDR)
civic revolution, 70–72, 92
COMECON trade, 152, 153
and Czech uprising of 1968, 9, 48, 131
de Maizière's coalition government, 128–32
diplomatic destabilization, 107–12, 113
dissent in, 33–52
economic planning, failure of, 82–83, 97–101, 105–6, 112, 142, 151–56, 199, 203
environmental degradation, 37, 42, 104, 203
and the European Community, 63, 68
fortieth anniversary, 34, 53
general elections, the first free, 76, 103–4, 105, 107, 115–28, 199, 200
GNP, per capital, 101, 155
government organization, 55–56
"implosion" of, 32, 71, 112–14, 180, 202
income, personal, 140–41, 144, 149–50, 156

Gorbachev, Mikhail (*continued*)
  and the German unification issue,
    29–30, 87, 90, 108, 109, 111, 133,
    201
  and the Krenz government, 59, 61, 62
  and *perestroika*, 10, 19, 30–31, 53, 58,
    59, 61, 90
  and the Soviet-German treaty for
    economic cooperation, 183–84
  and the "two-plus-four" negotiations,
    164, 165, 166
Götting, Wolfgang, 63, 118
Grass, Günter, 66, 93, 113, 180
Great Britain, 30, 69, 92, 111, 114, 163,
  181, 187, 207
Green League, 76, 105
Green party (East Germany), 42, 76, 88,
  193
  and the currency union, 143, 146, 147
  and the GDR election, 120, 123, 127
  and the political crisis, 103, 105
  and the unification treaty, 174, 176, 186
Green party (West Germany), 28, 37, 120,
  132, 167
  and the federal election, 193, 194
  and the unification issue, 29, 69, 92,
    110, 184
Grosser, Alfred, 114
Gueffroy, Chris, 19
Guest workers, 209
Gulf War, 205–6, 207
Gutzeit, Martin, 39, 85
Gysi, Gregor, 49, 64, 85, 91, 103, 122,
  146, 186, 194
  political background, 83–84

Habermas, Jürgen, 142–43
Hager, Kurt, 10, 54, 61
"Hallstein doctrine," 8
Hamburg, 194
Hartmann, Günter, 69
Haug, Fritz, 31, 93
Haussmann, Helmut, 89, 101, 143
Havel, Vaclav, 107
Havemann, Robert, 77
Hein, Christoph, 48, 49, 58
Helsinki Accords of 1975, 9, 38
Hempel, Johannes, 34
Henrich, Rolf, 40
Herger, Wolfgang, 54, 62
Hermlin, Stefan, 48
Herrhausen, Alfred, 101
Herrmann, Joachim, 54, 57
Heuer, Jens-Uwe, 58
Heym, Stefan, 49, 67, 142

Hildebrandt, Regine, 130
Hoffmann, Theodor, 63
Holding company. *See* Treuhand
Holland, 69, 114, 187
Holocaust, 12, 69, 113, 114, 131, 180, 202
Honecker, Erich, 10, 46, 57, 81, 113
  and the Berlin Wall, 3, 8, 19
  and the economy, 99, 100, 101
  fall of, 22, 53–54, 58–59, 60, 70, 72, 83,
    198, 200, 201
  and the Free Democratic Youth, 46, 57,
    59
  long illness of, 20, 31, 58
  and *perestroika*, 45, 58
  and travel and emigration laws, 17, 19,
    21–22
Höppner, Reinhard, 189
Horn, Guyla, 15–16, 20, 27
Hornhues, Karl-Heinz, 30
Howard, Michael, 4
Human rights, 9, 31, 43, 60–61
Human Rights Initiative (IFM), 37, 43, 76,
  85, 103, 105, 120
Humboldt University (Berlin), 42, 47, 79
Hungary, 114
  and East German refugees, 15–16,
    19–20, 28, 31
  reform in, 10, 19, 75, 180, 200
Hurd, Douglas, 111, 184

IFM. *See* Human Rights Initiative
IG Metall, 150
Immigration policy, 17, 209
Income-tax surcharge, 204
Independent Women's Association (UFV),
  42, 76, 105, 120
Institutional restructuring, 204
Intellectuals, 48–49, 85, 119, 161, 176
  and East German reform, 29, 58, 67
  and the GDR election, 115, 125, 127,
    128
  as grassroots activists, 37, 38, 39–40
  and the "Third Way," 77, 78, 79, 80,
    102, 198
  and the unification issue, 5, 6, 12, 66,
    67, 69, 91, 92, 93–94, 112, 113,
    133–34, 178
  after the unification treaty, 186–87, 198,
    199, 200, 205, 206
Interflug, 153
Interhotel chain, 155
Iraq, 206
Iron Curtain, 8, 10, 15, 31, 58
Israel, 94, 114, 187, 206
Italy, 114, 207